Halliday

POCKET WINE COMPANION

The 2022 guide to Australia's best value wines

Hardie Grant

BOOKS

The *Pocket Wine Companion 2022* presents the best value wines from Australia's definitive wine guide. While value can be difficult to define with wine, it's a big part of the decision when it comes to choosing a bottle. Her we've put it front and centre by only featuring the wineries and wines with special value ratings from the *Wine Companion 2022*.

This guide is divided into states, so that you can find a value drop wherever you are in Australia – whether you're looking to visit a winery, buy local, or learn which areas are able to produce which wine varieties at great-value price points. Within these states, we're also looking at zones and regions, which the map on the next page will help you navigate.

Wine zones and regions

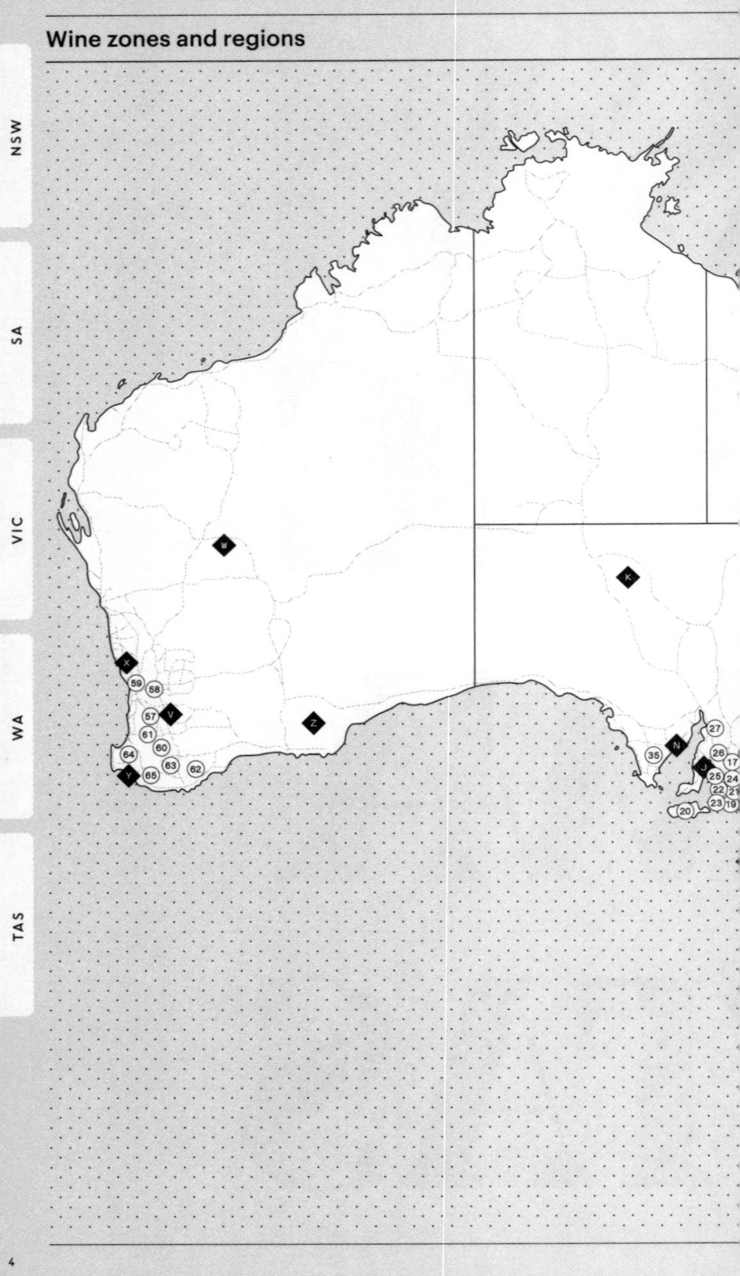

ZONE	REGION
New South Wales	
A Big Rivers	1 Murray Darling
	2 Perricoota
	3 Riverina
	4 Swan Hill
B Central Ranges	5 Cowra
	6 Mudgee
	7 Orange
C Hunter Valley	8 Hunter
D Northern Rivers	9 Hastings River
E Northern Slopes	10 New England Australia
F South Coast	11 Shoalhaven Coast
	12 Southern Highlands
G Southern New South Wales	13 Canberra District
	14 Gundagai
	15 Hilltops
	16 Tumbarumba
H Western Plains	
South Australia	
J* Barossa	17 Barossa Valley
	18 Eden Valley
Fleurieu	19 Currency Creek
	20 Kangaroo Island
	21 Langhorne Creek
	22 McLaren Vale
	23 Southern Fleurieu
Mount Lofty Ranges	24 Adelaide Hills
	25 Adelaide Plains
	26 Clare Valley
K Far North	27 Southern Flinders Ranges
L Limestone Coast	28 Coonawarra
	29 Mount Benson
	30 Mount Gambier
	31 Padthaway
	32 Robe
	33 Wrattonbully
M Lower Murray	34 Riverland
N The Peninsulas	35 Southern Eyre Peninsula
Victoria	
P Central Victoria	36 Bendigo
	37 Goulburn Valley
	38 Heathcote
	39 Strathbogie Ranges
	40 Upper Goulburn
Q Gippsland	
R North East Victoria	41 Alpine Valleys
	42 Beechworth
	43 Glenrowan
	44 King Valley
	45 Rutherglen
S North West Victoria	46 Murray Darling
	47 Swan Hill
T Port Phillip	48 Geelong
	49 Macedon Ranges
	50 Mornington Peninsula
	51 Sunbury
	52 Yarra Valley
U Western Victoria	53 Ballarat
	54 Grampians
	55 Henty
	56 Pyrenees
Western Australia	
V Central Western Australia	
W Eastern Plains, Inland and North of Western Australia	
X Greater Perth	57 Peel
	58 Perth Hills
	59 Swan District
Y South West Australia	60 Blackwood Valley
	61 Geographe
	62 Great Southern
	63 Manjimup
	64 Margaret River
	65 Pemberton
Z West Australian South East Coastal	
Tasmania	
	66 East Coast Tasmania
	67 Northern Tasmania
	68 Southern Tasmania
Queensland	
	69 Granite Belt
	70 South Burnett

* Adelaide Super Zone

2022

Tyson Stelzer

The world of Australian wine is a dynamic and rapidly changing place, and there has perhaps never been a period that more dramatically exemplified its far-flung extremes than 2020–21. From the opening days of the growing season all the way through to the sales dynamics in domestic and export markets, this has been one roller-coaster year of white-knuckle turns and loops like nobody could ever have anticipated.

The collective industry heaved a sigh of relief at the conclusion of the late and tumultuous 2021 season. Off the back of relentless years of drought and its dire repercussions in bushfires and smoke taint in early 2020, the rains of La Niña came as a welcome relief in spring, ushering in the coolest ripening season in a decade, only to later unleash a deluge on the east and west coasts that would mercilessly coincide with the 2021 harvest. Spared the extremes of the coasts, most of Victoria and all of South Australia and Tasmania flourished under mild conditions harking back to those wonderfully cool, classic seasons of decades past.

Labour-intensive viticultural and picking attempts to mitigate rain impact were doubly challenged by labour shortages in the wake of pandemic-induced border closures. Winery staff were redeployed in vineyards, and unexpected helpers heeded cries for assistance, with even grey nomads joining picking teams. Their efforts were rewarded, and 2021 delivered Australia's all-time record harvest, exceeding 2 million tonnes for the first time.

The pandemic played out dramatically in the market too. With international borders shut tight for the foreseeable future, a surplus of discretionary spending fuelled unprecedented domestic demand for premium wine both on- and off-premises. The balance of supply and demand was thrown into turmoil as domestic sales experienced an acute shift, while cellar doors and venues continued to struggle with the ongoing uncertainty of lockdowns and travel bans.

The diplomatic tussle with China, which saw Australia's biggest wine export partner and more than 40% of exports all but erased in 2020, has shown no signs of abating, and the industry continues to scramble to get its eggs out of this crumbling basket. Yet for all that this

ʋild year has thrown at them, the ptimism, adaptability and resilience or which Australian winemakers are espected the world over has again ourished in the face of adversity n every side.

n such a period of profound change cross our vast industry, it is timely o introduce a brand new era for he *Halliday* books. Stepping up as hief editor for the first time, the esponsibility of vigorously seeking ut and championing the finest wines f the year has been a tremendous oy and privilege. Fundamental to his has been elevating an expanded tasting team to new region-specific roles and a stronger voice in every detail of the process.

The finest wines to be unleashed this year rank among the greatest this country has ever witnessed – testimony that, against all odds, Australian wine has never been in a stronger place. This *Pocket Companion* represents a distilled line-up of the best value wines of this vintage. It is to the celebration of these wines and their resilient and tireless growers and makers that this edition is devoted.

How to use this book

94 **Yarra Valley Shiraz 2019** This is still in a youthful, primary phase, but that won't stop anyone drinking it today. Super-bright fruit, laced with spices, well-handled smoky/meaty reduction, more of the prosciutto variety. A grind of pepper, juniper and mint add to the savoury flavours. The palate is taut, tannins giving, and bright acidity to match. Well played. Screw cap | 13% alc. | To 2030 | $27 | JF

9

1 **Yarra Yering** Winery of the Year 2022 10 ★★★★★

5

4 Briarty Road, Coldstream, Vic 3770 **T** (03) 5964 9267 **www**.yarrayering.com **OPEN** 7 days 10-5 2
WINEMAKER Sarah Crowe **EST.** 1969 **DOZENS** 5000 **VYDS** 112ha

3 6 8 7

In September 2008, founder Bailey Carrodus died and in April '09 Yarra Yering was on the market. It was Bailey Carrodus' clear wish and expectation that any purchaser would continue to manage the vineyard and winery, and hence the wine style, in much the same way as he had done for the previous 40 years. Its acquisition in June '09 by a small group of investment bankers has fulfilled that wish. The low-yielding, unirrigated vineyards have always produced wines of extraordinary depth and intensity. Sarah Crowe was appointed winemaker after the 2013 vintage. She has made red wines of the highest imaginable quality right from her first vintage in '14 and, to the delight of many, myself (James) included, has offered all the wines with screw caps. For good measure, she introduced the '14 Light Dry Red Pinot Shiraz as a foretaste of that vintage and an affirmation of the exceptional talent recognised by her being named Winemaker of the Year in the *Wine Companion 2017*.

98 **Dry Red No. 2 2019** Shiraz, mataro, viognier. It's easy to be bowled over by this wine's beauty, from its bright colour to its heady fragrance of violets, Middle Eastern spices, fresh currants and blue fruits. Then magic happens. It is superfine, graced with perfectly formed silky tannins. The oak is seamlessly integrated, then flavour builds across the barely medium-bodied palate. While there's a lightness of touch, it's layered and complex. A complete wine full of style, elegance and substance. Screw cap | 13.5% alc. | To 2034 | $120 | JF | ♥

11

12 **Dry Red No. 1 2019** Winner of 3 awards in the *Wine Companion 2022*: Wine of the Year, Red Wine of the Year and Cabernet & Family of the Year. This is mesmerising. Do take time to bask in its fragrance – all floral and spicy with some aniseed and fresh herbs. Enjoy the poised fruit flavours of blackberries, mulberries and a hint of blueberries coated in spicy oak and tethered to the body of the wine. Pulsing acidity and beautiful tannin structure shape this and offer a promise of more to come in time. Wow – what a wine. Screw cap | 13.5% alc. | To 2039 | $120 | JF | ♥

Yeringberg ★★★★★

Maroondah Highway, Coldstream, Vic 3770 **T** (03) 9739 0240 **www**.yeringberg.com.au **OPEN** By appt
WINEMAKER Sandra de Pury **EST.** 1863 **DOZENS** 1500 **VYDS** 3.66ha

Guill de Pury and daughter Sandra, with Guill's wife Katherine in the background, make wines for the new millennium from the low-yielding vines re-established in the heart of what was one of the most famous (and infinitely larger) vineyards of the 19th century. In the riper years, the red wines have a velvety generosity of flavour rarely encountered, while never losing varietal character.

97 **Yarra Valley Cabernet Sauvignon 2019** While this has the exuberance of youth, it is also a composed and classy cabernet. A harmonious blend of mulberries and plums, cedary oak, cigar box and a touch of iodine. The palate is detailed from the ultrafine tannins, the brightness of the acidity to its impressive length. Elegance in a glass. Screw cap | 13.5% alc. | To 2042 | $95 | JF

Yeringberg 2019 This was tasted less than a month after it was bottled and while it's a very fine Yeringberg with its beauty on show, it's reserved and needs time to adjust and settle. Everything is in sync. Lovely aromas of violets, autumn leaves, mulberries and more. The medium-bodied palate is layered with fine, textural tannins, dazzled with fresh acidity and exceptional length. Screw cap | 13% alc. | To 2044 | $95 | JF

95 **Yarra Valley Viognier 2019** Few producers can match Yeringberg's viognier. Harmony is the aspiration, achieved by picking fruit over 8 days, so there's acidity, freshness and ripeness. There's also wild fermentation in barrel, no mlf and maturation in large-format, used oak. Ripe stone fruit, apricot and kernel, with ginger cream drizzled in honey. All tempered by lemon zest acidity and lime marmalade tang. There's richness here, without heaviness. A lovely viognier. Screw cap | 13.5% alc. | To 2027 | $35 | JF

Vineries

Name
he name of the producer, as it appears on the front label, is used throughout ie book.

Opening hours
hese only appear when a winery is open regularly, although many vineries may in fact be prepared to open by appointment. A telephone all will establish whether this is possible or not. For space reasons we ave simplified the open hours listed; where the hours vary each day or for olidays, we simply refer the reader to the website.

Winemakers
ı all but the smallest producers, the winemaker is simply the head of a team; iere may be many executive winemakers actually responsible for specific vines in the medium to large companies (80000 dozens and upwards).

Contact details
he contact details are usually those of the winery and cellar door, but in a ew instances may simply be a postal address; this occurs when the wine s made at another winery or wineries, and is sold only through the website nd/or retail outlets.

Website
n important reference point, normally containing material not found (for pace reasons) in this book.

Established
eep in mind that some makers consider the year in which they purchased he land to be the year of establishment, others the year in which they first lanted grapes, others the year they first made wine, and so on.

Vineyards
hows the hectares of vineyard(s) owned by the winery.

Dozens
his figure (representing the number of 9-litre/12-bottle cases produced ach year) is merely an indication of the size of the operation. Some winery ntries do not feature a production figure: this is typically because the winery egards this information as confidential.

Features
hese symbols highlight what a winery offers as part of their cellar door xperience, to help you in planning a visit.

Cellar door sales.

Food. From lunch platters to à la carte restaurants.

Accommodation. From B&B cottages to luxury vineyard apartments.

Music events. From monthly jazz in the vineyard to spectacular yearly concerts.

❿ Winery ratings

★★★★★	Outstanding winery regularly producing wines of exemplary quality and typicity. Where the winery name itself is printed in gold, it is a winery generally acknowledged to have had a long track record of excellence in the context of its region, having held a 5-star rating continuously for 10 years – truly the best of the best.
★★★★★	Outstanding winery capable of producing wines of very high quality, and did so this year.
★★★★☆	Excellent winery able to produce wines of high to very high quality, knocking on the door of a 5-star rating.
★★★★	Very good producer of wines with class and character. A solid, usually reliable, maker of good, sometimes very good, wines.
★★★☆	A solid, usually reliable, maker of good, sometimes very good, wines.
★★★	A typically good winery, but often has a few lesser wines.

⓫ Wine ratings

97–99	**Exceptional.** Wines of major trophy standard in important wine shows.
95–96	**Outstanding.** Wines of gold medal standard, usually with a great pedigree.
94	Wines on the cusp of gold medal status.
90–93	**Highly recommended.** Wines of silver medal standard, wines of great quality, style and character, and worthy of a place in any cellar.
89	**Recommended.** Wines on the cusp of silver medal standard.
86–88	Wines of bronze medal standard; well-produced, flavoursome wines, usually not requiring cellaring.
84–85	**Acceptable.** Wines of good commercial quality, free from significant fault.
80–83	**Over to you.** Everyday wines without much character and/or somewhat faulty.
75–79	**Not recommended.** Wines with one or more significant winemaking faults.

⓬ Tasting notes

The tasting note opens with the vintage of the wine tasted. This tasting note will have been written within the 12 months prior to publication. Even that is a long time, and during the life of this book the wine will almost certainly change.

Ⓐ Ⓑ Ⓒ Ⓓ Ⓔ

`Screw cap | 13% alc. | To 2026 | $50 | JF`

Ⓐ Closure

This is the closure used for this particular wine. The closures in use for the wines tasted for this year's *Wine Companion* are (in descending order): screw cap 86.8% (last year 86.2%), one-piece natural cork 6.0% (last year 6.8%), Diam 5.6% (last year 4.4%) and crown seal 0.8%. The remaining 0.8% (in order of importance) are Vino-Lok, agglomerate, Twin Top, synthetic cork, ProCork, Zork and Zork SPK.

Ⓑ Alcohol percentage

This information is in one sense self-explanatory. What is less obvious is the increasing concern of many Australian winemakers about the rise in alcohol levels, and much research and practical experimentation (for example, picking earlier or higher fermentation temperatures in open fermenters) is occurring. Reverse osmosis and yeast selection are two of the options available to decrease higher-than-desirable alcohol levels. Recent changes to domestic and export labelling mean the stated alcohol will be within a maximum of 0.5% difference to that obtained for analysis.

Ⓒ 'Drink-to' date

The optimal time to drink a wine is of course subjective; some of us love young wines and others old. This is as personal to the taster as their review and their score. We have proposed dates to when we would most love to drink this wine, and we commend these to you as a reference for managing your cellar and when to drink each bottle.

Ⓓ Price

I use the price provided by the winery. It should be regarded as a guide, particularly if purchased retail.

Ⓔ Taster

The initials EL, JF, JH, JP, NG, SC, TL and TS appearing at the end of the note signify that Erin Larkin, Jane Faulkner, James Halliday, Jeni Port, Ned Goodwin, Steven Creber, Tony Love or Tyson Stelzer tasted the wine and provided the tasting note and rating.

♥ Shortlisted for 2022 awards

Nominated by the tasting team as the best example of its variety/style in its region.

✪ Value rosette

The *Wine Companion* uses the value rosette to show wines considered to hold special value for money in the context of their rating. As the *Pocket Wine Companion* only includes wines deemed to be special value, the value rosette itself does not appear.

James Halliday

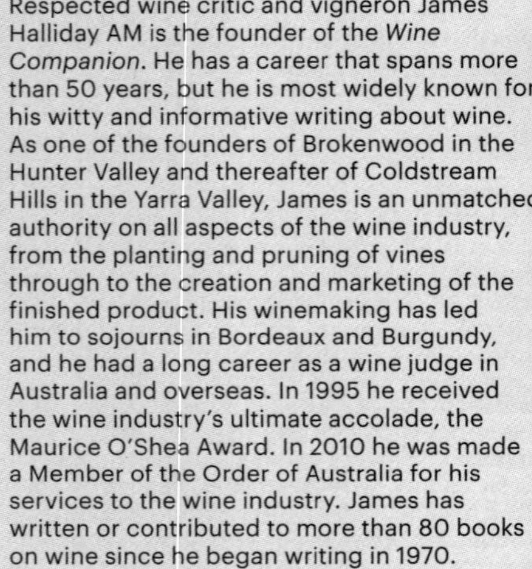

Respected wine critic and vigneron James Halliday AM is the founder of the *Wine Companion*. He has a career that spans more than 50 years, but he is most widely known for his witty and informative writing about wine. As one of the founders of Brokenwood in the Hunter Valley and thereafter of Coldstream Hills in the Yarra Valley, James is an unmatched authority on all aspects of the wine industry, from the planting and pruning of vines through to the creation and marketing of the finished product. His winemaking has led him to sojourns in Bordeaux and Burgundy, and he had a long career as a wine judge in Australia and overseas. In 1995 he received the wine industry's ultimate accolade, the Maurice O'Shea Award. In 2010 he was made a Member of the Order of Australia for his services to the wine industry. James has written or contributed to more than 80 books on wine since he began writing in 1970.

Tyson Stelzer

Tyson Stelzer is the chief editor for the *Halliday Wine Companion 2022*. He is a multi-award-winning wine writer, TV host and producer, international speaker and a regular judge and chair of wine shows throughout Australia. Tyson is the author of 17 wine books, including six editions of *The Champagne Guide*, and a contributor to Jancis Robinson's *The Oxford Companion to Wine (3rd edition)*.

Regional focus: Barossa Valley, Tasmania, Queensland

rin Larkin

Erin Larkin is a wine writer, judge and presenter. Multi-skilled when it comes to the business of wine, she is also an active consultant for retail and private clients, with a keen eye for quality and creativity in wine, marrying classic and contemporary perspectives.

Regional focus: Western Australia

ane aulkner

Jane Faulkner is a respected journalist with more than 25 years' experience. She has a special interest in Italian and alternative varieties and chairs several wine shows. Aside from her love of wine, Jane is an avid traveller and zealous environmentalist.

Regional focus: Southern New South Wales including Canberra; Coonawarra and the Limestone Coast, Clare Valley, Riverland, Southern Flinders Ranges, Southern Eyre Peninsula; Mornington Peninsula, Macedon Ranges, Sunbury, Gippsland, Yarra Valley and North West Victoria

ni Port

Jeni Port is a wine writer and judge. She was the longest-serving wine writer at *The Age* newspaper (30 years), is deputy chair of the Wine List of the Year Awards, for both Australia and China, and was a founding board member of the Australian Women in Wine Awards. Her numerous awards include the 2018 Wine Communicators of Australia Legend of the Vine.

Regional focus: Geelong, Central Victoria, North East Victoria, Western Victoria

ed oodwin MW

Ned has worn many hats, including show judge, dux of the Len Evans Tutorial, sommelier, educator, TV host, wine buyer, consultant, critic and writer. Born in London, raised in Australia and educated in France and Japan, and with continued business across Asia, his varied international experience brings a fresh perspective to the *Wine Companion* tasting team.

Regional focus: McLaren Vale; Hunter Valley and regional New South Wales

ony Love

Tony Love is a wine writer and consultant. As a career journalist and editor, he worked across newspapers, magazines and books Australia-wide, writing about food and wine, and was the national wine industry editor and writer for all of NewsCorp's Australian daily mastheads.

Regional focus: Adelaide Hills, Langhorne Creek, Kangaroo Island, Currency Creek, Southern Fleurieu

Value wineries

While great value can occur at any price point, a wine holds a special place for us all when at an everyday quaffing price. In narrowing down our top 10 Best Value Wineries of the year we prioritised not only the highest numbe of value rosettes awarded and the highest strike rate but also inclusion of at least one value wine at $20 or below. When it comes to value, Western Australia leads the country, with 8 of our 10 top contenders. But it is ultimately Lake Breeze Wines that heads up the list as this year's Best Value Winery; the remaining wineries are listed in alphabetical order.

1 Lake Breeze Wines
LANGHORNE CREEK

Vine for wine and dollar for dollar, ıe value for money represented ·y Lake Breeze is nothing short of xtraordinary. Since the 1880s, the ollett family has embodied the heart nd soul of all that we love about ustralian winemaking.

2 Castelli Estate
GREAT SOUTHERN

;astelli Estate sources fruit from all ver Western Australia's southwest, pecifically the Great Southern egion. Spanning a number of styles nd price points, they demonstrate n ability to extract eloquent egional expressions worthy of oth immediate drinking and ellaring potential.

3 Castle Rock Estate
PORONGURUP

ob Diletti has spent years building n enduring reputation for the cool-limate and exceedingly elegant vines of Porongurup. His wines – articularly, but not exclusively his ieslings – are consistently brilliant nd all priced under $40.

Deep Woods Estate
MARGARET RIVER

ulian Langworthy and his team make eriously styled, seriously structured vines from great vineyards within Aargaret River. Never underestimate heir ability to wow and please. They onsistently clean up at wine shows vith wins, including the 2019 Jimmy Natson trophy.

5 Duke's Vineyard
PORONGURUP

)uke's wines are made by Rob Diletti Castle Rock) and are famed for their ool-climate elegance, light touch nd finesse. The vineyard is planted o just shiraz, cabernet and riesling, anking among the finest in the tate, representing ridiculous bang-or-buck.

6 Harewood Estate
DENMARK

Harewood's wine offering spans a host of varieties and styles, most of which are sourced from vineyards within the Great Southern. Refreshingly priced between $20 and $30, no fewer than nine labels scored between 90 and 95 points this year.

7 Mike Press Wines
ADELAIDE HILLS

Two decades after planting, Mike Press' vines are attaining maturity and he's settling into his groove. For single-vineyard, cool-climate wines tantalisingly priced almost entirely between $12 and $15, he is in a league all of his own.

8 Stella Bella Wines
MARGARET RIVER

Nestled in the heart of 'cabernet and chardonnay country', Stella Bella is well positioned to continue its inexorable rise. The quality and definition of house style makes these great wines to purchase at any price point.

9 West Cape Howe Wines
MOUNT BARKER

This estate in Mount Barker epitomises value for money, consistently producing superb and satisfying wines that offer joy and pleasure beyond their price. Of West Cape Howe's 10 submissions this year, nine were awarded value rosettes.

10 Xanadu Wines
MARGARET RIVER

It's not possible to overstate the exceptional value for money that Xanadu Wines' offering represents. All credit to Glenn Goodall and Brendan Carr's desire to let the fruit do the talking; their sensitive winemaking has yielded astoundingly impressive wines.

34461ha | 8 zones | 16 regions

NSW

Led by Sydney and its population of more than 5 million people, New South Wales consumes more wine than any other state, but it has only half the number of wineries of Victoria or South Australia. But statistics being damned lies, NSW contributed 29% of the 2021 national crush, more than 1.7 times that of Victoria. Of its 16 regions, most are situated on the hills and foothills of the western side of the Great Dividing Range. Elevation is more important than latitude in shaping the climate of these regions.

The **Hunter Valley**, only an hour's drive north of Sydney, has truly unique, long-lived (7–20+ years) semillon and supple, medium-bodied shiraz as its foundations. Its erratic climate is hot but humid, and vintage rain a threat. It is a major tourist destination.

The Southern New South Wales zone has three regions of particular importance. The overall quality of the **Canberra District** is excellent. Its climate is strongly continental, with warm days and cold nights. Riesling and shiraz, with or without viognier, are its calling cards. **Hilltops** is adjacent, only a few kilometres from the northwestern tip of Canberra District. It is an important contract grapegrower of shiraz, cabernet sauvignon and chardonnay, plus small plantings of that most temperamental variety, nebbiolo. Finally, there is the tadpole-shaped region of **Tumbarumba**, its long western boundary the border with Victoria. Its cool elevations of 300–800m are well suited to chardonnay and pinot noir, which decorate the highest and most vertiginous slopes, with shiraz shouldering arms in the lower parts. Like Hilltops, it's a grapegrowing region with considerable potential.

The Central Ranges zone is home to **Mudgee**, at an elevation of 450m. Sturdy shiraz and cabernet sauvignon cover much of its vineyard area. The zone's other important region is **Orange**, spanning lofty altitudes between 800m and 1100m. Elevation and aspect result in an unexpectedly wide expanse of varieties, ranging between late-ripening shiraz and cabernet sauvignon, to early-ripening chardonnay, merlot, sauvignon blanc and pinot noir.

Riverina produced 17% of the national crush in 2021. It is part of the engine room of the industry, and, coupled with the NSW share of the **Murray Darling/Swan Hill** output of 10% of the total, is of major economic importance.

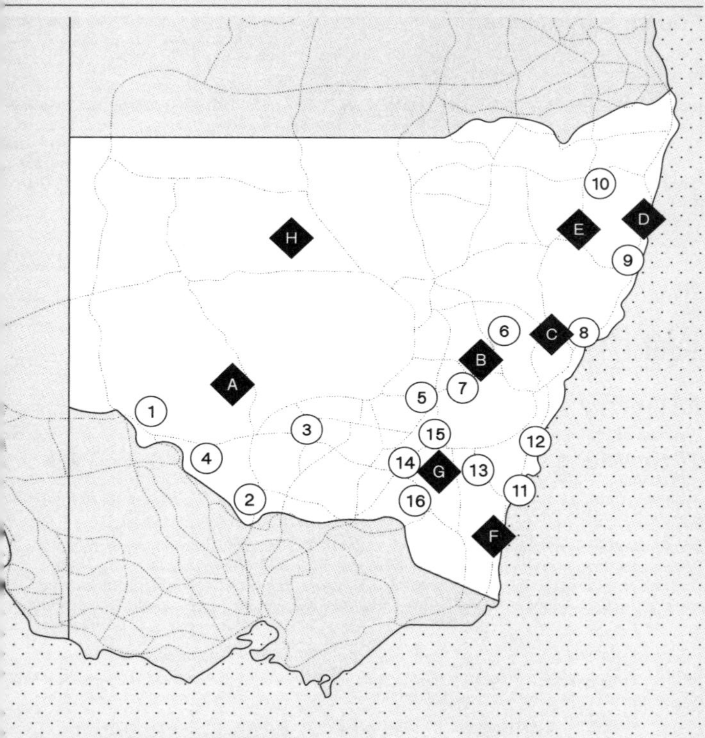

ZONE	REGION
A Big Rivers	1 Murray Darling
	2 Perricoota
	3 Riverina
	4 Swan Hill
B Central Ranges	5 Cowra
	6 Mudgee
	7 Orange
C Hunter Valley	8 Hunter
D Northern Rivers	9 Hastings River
E Northern Slopes	10 New England Australia
F South Coast	11 Shoalhaven Coast
	12 Southern Highlands
G Southern New South Wales	13 Canberra District
	14 Gundagai
	15 Hilltops
	16 Tumbarumba
H Western Plains	

Fourth Wave Wine ★★★★

Suite 22, Level 1, OTP house, 10 Bradford Close, Kotara, NSW 2289 **T** 1300 778 047 www.fourthwavewine.com.au **WINEMAKER** Various **EST.** 2009

Based in the suburbs of Newcastle, Fourth Wave Wine was founded in 2009 by Nicholas and Frances Crampton, boasting wine industry nous; finance and IT skills respectively. Assisted by winemaker and consultant Corey Ryan, Fourth Wave makes wine in 6 countries with a tota production of 300000 dozen bottles packaged under a panoply of brands. A modern-day global negoçiant, if you will. Domestically, brands include Elephant in the Room, Little Giant, Burns and Fuller and Take it to the Grave. (NG)

94 **Tread Softly Yarra Valley Pinot Noir 2020** From the Upper Yarra, early picked, wild fermented, matured in used large-format French oak. Woods Crampton steps out of South Australia to fashion this attractively labelled (and vinified) wine. It's not thin or green; the bright, full, clear crimson hue marking a bargain. Screw cap | 12.2% alc. | To 2023 | $22 | JH

ZONE

Big Rivers

REGION

Murray Darling

Zilzie Wines

544 Kulkyne Way, Karadoc, Vic 3496 **T** (03) 5025 8100 www.zilziewines.com **OPEN** By appt **WINEMAKER** Jonathan Creek **EST.** 1999 **VYDS** 700ha

The Forbes family has been farming since the early 1900s. Zilzie is currently run by Roslyn Forbes and sons Steven and Andrew, the diverse range of farming activities now solely focused on grapegrowing from substantial vineyards. The wines consistently far exceed expectations, given their enticing prices, that consistency driving the substantial production volume in an extremely competitive market. The business includes contract processing, winemaking and storage; the winery is certified organic.

95 **Platinum Edition Arinto 2020** This is a terrific rendition. Pressings fermented in older barrels, free-run juice into stainless steel, then partial transfer to barrel and left on lees to build texture. Spicy, juicy pears, lemon juice, and grated Granny Smith apples. Excellent length, with fine, chalky acidity and grapefruit pith phenolics. It's crisp, very dry and deliciously good. Screw cap | 14% alc. | To 2025 | $35 | JF

REGION

Riverina

Calabria Family Wines

1283 Brayne Road, Griffith, NSW 2680 **T** (02) 6969 0800 www.calabriawines.com.au **OPEN** Mon-Fri 8.30-5, w'ends 10-4 **WINEMAKER** Bill Calabria, Emma Norbiato, Tony Steffania, Jeremy Nascimben, Sam Mittiga **EST.** 1945 **VYDS** 100ha

Calabria Family Wines' 3 Bridges range is anchored on estate vineyards. The operation is moving with the times, increasing its plantings of durif and introducing aglianico, nero d'Avola and St Macaire (once grown in Bordeaux, and on the verge of extinction, this 2ha is the largest planting in the world). Equally importantly, it is casting its net over the Barossa Valley, Hilltops and King Valley premium regions, taking this one step further by acquiring a vineyard in the Barossa Valley and opening a cellar door/restaurant.

96 **Francesco Show Reserve Grand Tawny NV** Judging by the amber hue and gentle waft of rancio complexity, the average age of the wine here is considerable. High-quality spirit is seamlessly integrated into a fray of spiced date, clove, walnut, tamarind, cinnamon and every other sensorial experience of the Moroccan souk. Complex, long and impeccably realised. Sweet, but far from cloying. Screw cap | 19% alc. | $45 | NG

94 **Reserve Eden Valley Riesling 2019** This is a dainty, intensely flavoured high-country riesling. Aromas of squeezed lime juice, orange verbena, cumquat and quince. The acidity is juicy rather than battery-acid hard. The alcohol, à point. The fruit sweetness, spot on. The phenolics, intact after fermenting pressings only, serving up a sluice of pucker and detail. Delicious drinking. Screw cap | 11% alc. | To 2028 | $30 | NG

e Bortoli ★★★★☆

Bortoli Road, Bilbul, NSW 2680 **T** (02) 6966 0100 **www**.debortoli.com.au **OPEN** Mon-Sat 9-5, 9-4 **WINEMAKER** Darren De Bortoli, Julie Mortlock, John Coughlan **EST.** 1928 **VYDS** 367ha

mous among the cognoscenti for its superb Noble One, which in fact accounts for only iny part of its total production, this winery turns out low-priced varietal wines that are ariably competently made. De Bortoli is a founding member of Australia's First Families Wine.

Deen De Bortoli Vat 1 Riverina Durif 2018 A deep crimson. Explosive, packing aromatic punch delivered as violet, blueberry, mulberry, anise, dried tobacco and oodles of coffee bean/mocha oak. Hedonistic, to be sure. But durif's tannic mettle and the oak handling ensure that nothing overwhelms the wine's raw power and joyous drinkability. Screw cap | 15% alc. | To 2026 | $16 | NG

ominic Wines 

:ay Ave, Berri, SA 5343 **T** (08) 8582 5524 **www**.dominicwines.com **OPEN** Mon-Fri 8.30-5 **EMAKER** Linley Schultz **EST.** 2004 **DOZENS** 2100 **VYDS** 200ha

ird-generation vignerons and producers, the Dominic family estate is based at Berri in uth Australia's Riverland. Post-WWII they planted a simple block with rows of shiraz, gordo d mourvèdre, supplying to G Gramp and Son (forerunners to Orlando). Now the family urces fruit from both their own and grower vineyards in the region as well as extending their ach to more than 40 growers from Langhorne Creek, Adelaide Hills and Coonawarra. (TL)

Adelaide Hills Sauvignon Blanc 2020 Easygoing, tangy and tropical, a dash of musk aromatic in there too. A short 4-week rest on lees has added some chalky texture. Nothing too dramatic, yet the citrus-pithy finish does linger well. Screw cap | 12.5% alc. | To 2023 | $18 | TL

icca Terra

Box 305, Angaston, SA 5353 **T** 0411 370 057 **www**.riccaterra.com.au **WINEMAKER** Ashley Ratcliff . 2017 **DOZENS** 10000 **VYDS** 80ha

ien Ashley and Holly Ratcliff purchased an 8ha vineyard in the Riverland it presented the portunity to plant varieties pushing the envelope, such as the rare planting of an ancient lkan variety slankamenka bela. There are now 80ha of varieties, mainly selected for the mate, grown with surface mulches, soil moisture monitoring probes and smart viticultural actices. The wines are made using all of the cutting edge techniques, hand picked into half-nne bins and chilled for 12 hours before transfer to the winery in the Barossa Valley. Ricca rra means rich earth in Italian.

Bullets Before Cannonballs 2020 A blend of tempranillo, lagrein, aglianico and shiraz, percentages unknown, but I'm assuming the former is dominant as it's full of red licorice and cola, with v-shaped tannins (that start with some volume and then taper to a precise end point). This just works. Plump, fleshy, very savoury, with some meaty reduction adding to its shape alongside charred radicchio bitterness on the finish; yet its core is all juicy, ripe fruit. Screw cap | 14.8% alc. | To 2025 | $23 | JF

arran Wines

8 Myall Park Road, Yenda, NSW 2681 **T** (02) 6968 1125 **www**.yarranwines.com.au **OPEN** Mon-Sat 10-5 **NEMAKER** Sam Brewer **EST.** 2000 **DOZENS** 20000 **VYDS** 30ha

orraine Brewer (and late husband John) were grapegrowers for over 30 years and when son am completed a degree in wine science at CSU, they celebrated his graduation by crushing of shiraz, fermenting the grapes in a milk vat. The majority of the grapes from the estate antings are sold but each year a little more has been made under the Yarran banner; along e way a winery with a crush capacity of 150t has been built. Over the past 3 years Sam has cused on improving the quality of the estate-grown grapes, moving to organic conversion. arran was the *Wine Companion 2021* Dark Horse of the Year.

Bendigo Heathcote Hilltops Shiraz 2019 Violet, boysenberry and clove. Plump yet sinewy and savoury enough to evince a modicum of sophistication. This drinks akin to a wine twice its price. My overall impression is one of intuition and an admirably deft touch. Screw cap | 14.2% alc. | To 2023 | $15 | NG

ZONE

Central Ranges

REGION

Cowra

Pig in the House N

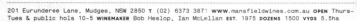

Balcombe Road, Billimari, NSW 2804 **T** 0427 443 598 **WWW**.piginthehouse.com.au **OPEN** Fri-Sun 11-5 by appt **WINEMAKER** Antonio D'Onise **EST.** 2002 **DOZENS** 3000 **VYDS** 25ha

Jason and Rebecca O'Dea established their vineyard on a block of land formerly used as home for 20 free-range pigs. Given its prior use, one would imagine the vines would grow lustily, and it is no surprise that organic certification has been given by Biological Farmers of Australia. The O'Deas have in fact taken the process several steps further, using biodynamic preparations and significantly reducing all sprays. The wines made are good advertisements for organic/ biodynamic farming.

92 **Organic Rosé 2019** A light coral with copper edges. A great colour! A textural and expansive palate boasting a multitude of layers. Poached strawberry, orange zest, a twine of dried herbs and musk notes barrel long down the throat. This is impressive: dry and really thirst slaking. I am unsure whe this was released, but it is drinking very well. Screw cap | 13% alc. | To 2022 | $25 | NG

REGION

Mudgee

Mansfield Wines ★★★

201 Eurunderee Lane, Mudgee, NSW 2850 **T** (02) 6373 3871 **WWW**.mansfieldwines.com.au **OPEN** Thurs-Tues & public hols 10-5 **WINEMAKER** Bob Heslop, Ian McLellan **EST.** 1975 **DOZENS** 1500 **VYDS** 5.5ha

Ian McLellan and family purchased Mansfield Wines from his cousin Peter Mansfield in late 1997. The original plantings, which included chardonnay, frontignac, sauvignon blanc, cabernet sauvignon, merlot and shiraz, were removed, to be replaced by a Joseph's coat patchwork of savagnin, vermentino, petit manseng, parellada, tempranillo, touriga, zinfande and tinta cão, supported by grenache, mourvèdre and pedro ximénez. Sousão and carignan are more recent arrivals.

91 **Monastrell 2018** A delicious wine. Full bodied and burly, with a ferrous tannic mettle that champio balance over dryness, and a sumptuous flow of flavour. Aromas of smoked meat, dark cherry, clove, blood, game, espresso and black volcanic rock. The oak, French and American, a mere adjunct. There is a lot of mass packed into the glass but there is nothing sweet or jammy about it. Screw cap | 14% alc. | To 2025 | $21 | NG

REGION

Orange

Canobolas-Smith  

Boree Lane, off Cargo Road, Lidster via Orange, NSW 2800 **T** (02) 6365 6113 **WWW**.canobolassmithwines.com.au **OPEN** Sat 11-5 **WINEMAKER** Murray Smith **EST.** 1986 **DOZENS** 1000 **VYDS** 6ha

The Smith family, led by Murray Smith, was one of the early movers in Orange. The vineyard has always been dry-grown, gaining strength from the free-draining clay loam derived from basalt soils. The wines are released under 3 labels, the newest of which is The Shine, utilising the golden mean enunciated by Pythagoras, and is reserved for very special wines.

96 **Shine Reserve Chardonnay 2014** A medium yellow colour with glints of green. A shift away from th overly reductive match-struck style of the recent past, now celebrating both the region's altitudina freshness and its proclivity for ripeness. In these hands, this richer vintage is amplified by extende time on lees, wild yeast-inflected shiitake/umami accents offsetting teeming stone-fruit flavours, pungent mineral and nourishing barrel work. The touch, deft, but one of flavour, generosity and thrilling length. Screw cap | 14% alc. | To 2026 | $75 | NG

umulus Vineyards

★★★☆

5 Euchareena Road, Molong, NSW 2866 **T** 1300 449 860 **www**.cumulusvineyards.com.au
EMAKER Debbie Lauritz **EST.** 1995 **DOZENS** 193000 **VYDS** 508ha

e 508ha Cumulus vineyard (at 600m above sea level) is one of the largest single estates NSW. The wines are made at the Robert Oatley winery in Mudgee and are released under e Cumulus, Soaring, Climbing, Rolling, Luna Rosa, Block 50, Head in the Clouds, Alte and kberry labels.

Cumulus Luna Rosa Rosado 2020 An eclectic blend of 85/7/4/4% shiraz/riesling/sangiovese/barbera. Mid coral. Musk stick, sour cherry and dried herb. Cool-fermented to retain freshness alongside effusive fruit. Palpably dry, easy drinking, poised and savoury. A don't-think-just-drink proposition. For the price and vintage challenges, this is very impressive. Screw cap | 12.5% alc. | To 2021 | $13 | NG

ilbert Family Wines 

7 Ulan Road, Mudgee, NSW 2850 **T** (02) 6373 1371 **www**.gilbertfamilywines.com.au **OPEN** Sun–Thurs -4, Fri–Sat 10–5 **WINEMAKER** Simon Gilbert, Will Gilbert **EST.** 2004 **DOZENS** 18000 **VYDS** 25.81ha

e Gilbert Family Wine Company was established in 2004 by 5th-generation winemaker mon Gilbert; 6th-generation Will Gilbert took over the reins in '14. Will draws on extensive d and New World winemaking experience to push boundaries with different techniques and eas to make the Gilbert Family wines from Orange and Mudgee.

Gilbert Orange Riesling 2019 Fermented cool in tank, before draining to neutral wood for completion, stirring and élévage on full lees. Tangerine, tonic, bergamot, lemon oil and quinine. Lime, a given. But so much more! 5% fermented on skins. A little malolactic sneaking across the lo-fi controls. The result, excellent. Scintillating, steely length and cut-glass precision. Screw cap | 11.4% alc. | To 2032 | $28 | NG

ighland Heritage 

59 Mitchell Highway, Orange, NSW 2800 **T** (02) 6363 5602 **www**.highlandheritage.com.au **OPEN** 7 ys 9–5 **WINEMAKER** Luke Steel, Mike Degaris (Consultant) **EST.** 1985 **DOZENS** 4500 **VYDS** 14.4ha

wned and operated by the D'Aquino family, the vineyard, restaurant and cellar door are 125ha located 3km east of Orange, with a heliport offering scenic flights and tours. At an evation of 900m, on deep alluvial and rich basalt soils, the cool to cold climate and long owing season produce elegant reds and crisp, clean whites.

Estate Generations Shiraz 2019 This mid-weighted shiraz packs grace and charm, although 18 months in American oak is an odd way to express it in a climate as ostensibly cool as Orange. Clove, orange zest, ground pepper, maraschino cherry and lilac meander along a frame of gauzy tannins to the point of an easygoing evanescence. Clumsy oak across the finish, but a lovely drink all the same. Screw cap | 13.5% alc. | To 2024 | $22 | NG

atina

9 Summerhill Lane, Orange, NSW 2800 **T** (02) 6362 8336 **www**.patinawines.com.au **OPEN** Fri–Mon -5 **WINEMAKER** Gerald Naef **EST.** 1999 **DOZENS** 2500 **VYDS** 3ha

erald Naef and wife Angie left California in 1981, initially establishing an irrigation farm in orthwest NSW; 20 years later they moved to Orange and by 2006 Gerald was a final-year udent of wine science at CSU. He set up a micro-winery at the Orange Cool Stores, his first ine the trophy-winning '03 Chardonnay.

6 **Museum Release Orange Cabernet Merlot 2006** Of all museum releases here (and I've tasted a few), this is by far the best. A digestible luncheon claret: impeccably poised, medium bodied and immensely savoury. A bow of nourishing tannin, massaged with bottle age and well-appointed oak, drawn taut by high-country freshness. The fruit, bright and rich as it fades into a halcyon senescence. Plum, Asian medicine, tea leaf, currant, mint, tobacco and graphite. A beautiful wine at its apogee. Cork | 13.5% alc. | To 2027 | $65 | NG

Renzaglia Wines  Dark Horse 2022 

38 Bosworth Falls Road, O'Connell, NSW 2795 **T** (02) 6337 5756 **www**.renzagliawines.com.au **OPEN** By appt **WINEMAKER** Mark Renzaglia, Sam Renzaglia **EST.** 2017 **DOZENS** 2500 **VYDS** 3ha

American Mark Renzaglia and his Australian wife Sandy planted their first vineyard in 1997 (1ha of chardonnay, cabernet sauvignon and merlot), Mark making small quantities of his own wines while working as a vineyard manager and winemaker at Winburndale Wines for 11 years. Son Sam has since joined the business too, and a new winery and cellar door have been constructed.

96 **Mount Panorama Estate Chardonnay 2019** These Renzaglia wines are proving a revelation, with th engineering of flavour and structural architecture as finessed as the packaging. No shortage of rip fruit flavours, with dried mango, white peach and nectarine strung across a chassis of salubrious oak, impeccably integrated, imparting riffs on hazelnut, truffle, nougat and chestnut. A masterstro of ripe fruit, sexy oak, pungent mineral and mouth-watering freshness. Generosity far from the madding crowd. A very fine wine. Screw cap | 13% alc. | To 2028 | $50 | NG

Mount Panorama Estate Cabernet Sauvignon 2018 This is exceptional cool-climate cabernet, somehow transcending the green edges of its blended sibling to showcase a sheath of impeccabl tuned tannins, ripe and juicy. This makes all the difference! Spearmint, blackcurrant, olive, chilli, ba leaf and a swathe of firm, saliva-sapping tannins driving a long finish. Already delicious, its precoc belies the depth and longevity herein. Screw cap | 13.8% alc. | To 2035 | $50 | NG | ♥

Ross Hill Wines  

134 Wallace Lane, Orange, NSW 2800 **T** (02) 6365 3223 **www**.rosshillwines.com.au **OPEN** 7 days 10.30-5 **WINEMAKER** Luke Steele **EST.** 1994 **DOZENS** 25000 **VYDS** 18.2ha

Peter and Terri Robson planted their vines on north-facing slopes of the Griffin Road Vineyar in 1994. In 2007 their son James and his wife Chrissy joined the business and the Wallace La Vineyard was planted. The vines are now mature and the winery was NCOS Certified Carbor Neutral in '13. The Barrel & Larder School of Wine and Food (WSET Levels 1 and 2) operates from the extended cellar door.

95 **Pinnacle Series Griffin Road Vineyard Orange Sauvignon Blanc 2019** Among the better sauvignon in the country, more suggestive of the pungent mineral notes of the Loire's better examples than wines from the New World. Aromas of nettle, redcurrant and gooseberry. The plume of acidity, juic and saliva-sapping, bringing the wine to life as much as forcing one to reach for the next glass. Th is benchmark. Screw cap | 12.7% alc. | To 2025 | $30 | NG

ZONE

Hunter Valley

REGION

Hunter

Briar Ridge Vineyard  

593 Mount View Road, Mount View, NSW 2325 **T** (02) 4990 3670 **www**.briarridge.com.au **OPEN** 7 days 10-5 **WINEMAKER** Alex Beckett, Gwyneth Olsen (Consultant) **EST.** 1972 **DOZENS** 9500 **VYDS** 39ha

Semillon and shiraz have been the most consistent performers. Underlying the suitability of these varieties to the Hunter Valley, Briar Ridge has been a model of stability, and has the comfort of substantial estate vineyards from which it is able to select the best grapes.

95 **Stockhausen Hunter Valley Shiraz 2019** This is a fine '19: extract harnessed by inimitable Hunter savouriness, judicious French oak (17% new) and a steady hand. Plenty of whole berries in the mix impart a juiciness, floral lift and an effusive joy. Sour cherry, Damson plum, baking spice and vanill pod. Mid weighted, lithe and long, as the tannins expand with air and the acidity tows the flavours. Delicious. Screw cap | 13.8% alc. | To 2028 | $35 | NG

94 **Wrattonbully Fiano 2020** Let's be clear. Fiano is a top-drawer variety. Noble. Tolerant to drought, with a kaleidoscope of stone fruit, fennel, thyme and pungent mineral that transcends any workhor label. Iterated well in these hands, with proper ripeness, some skin-contact inflection and old barre breadth of texture. Among the best to date. Screw cap | 13.5% alc. | To 2024 | $28 | NG

ıgles Rest Wines ★★★★☆

Maxwells Road, Pokolbin, NSW 2320 **T** 0428 199 888 **WWW**.eaglesrestwines.com.au **OPEN** By appt
EMAKER Xanthe Hatcher **EST.** 2007 **DOZENS** 1000 **VYDS** 20ha

gles Rest has flown under the radar since its establishment in 2007, and still does. The
:ate is planted to 8ha of chardonnay, 7ha shiraz, 3ha semillon and 2ha verdelho.

The Wild Place Hunter Valley Semillon 2019 The flagship wine of this superlative suite. The homegrown trope. Semillon, unadorned. Hand picked and crushed, with the resultant pickup of esters and textural detail, compelling. Lemon balm, tonic, spa salts and barley scents of intensity, thrum and thrill. Top tier. Screw cap | 10.5% alc. | To 2030 | $28 | NG

Maluna Hunter Valley Semillon 2019 A similar dynamic between these 2 semillons as to the 2 chardonnays in the same suite. One, chewier and textually intriguing; the other, a transparent fugue of intensity and weightlessness. This, the latter. Skeletal. Refined. Tonic, citrus zest, grapefruit pulp and a waxy tail. Nascent, still. Loads in store. Prodigious length. Age with immense confidence. Screw cap | 11.5% alc. | To 2034 | $35 | NG

'nest Hill Wines

Wine Country Drive, Nulkaba, NSW 2325 **T** (02) 4991 4418 **WWW**.ernesthillwines.com.au
N 7 days 10-5 **WINEMAKER** Mark Woods **EST.** 1999 **DOZENS** 6000 **VYDS** 12ha

s is part of a vineyard originally planted in the early 1970s by Harry Tulloch for Seppelt
ıes; it was later renamed Pokolbin Creek Vineyard, and later still (in '99) the Wilson family
rchased the upper (hill) part of the vineyard and renamed it Ernest Hill.

Cyril Premium Hunter Semillon 2011 At its zenith and ready to drink. The aromatic fireworks and compelling fruit intensity, in stark contrast to the wine's lightweight and balletic mouthfeel. The complexity lies in the dichotomies. Melted butter on toast, quince, citrus marmalade, tonic, quinine and lemon balm scents, all. As the fruit has expanded with bottle age, the finish has lost some verve. Delicious all the same. Screw cap | 11% alc. | To 2022 | $35 | NG

lenguin Estate

brodale Road, Broke, NSW 2330 **T** (02) 6579 1009 **WWW**.glenguinestate.com.au **WINEMAKER** Robin
der MW, Rhys Eather **EST.** 1993 **DOZENS** 2000 **VYDS** 5ha

ınguin Estate was established by the Tedder family, headed by Robin Tedder MW. The
:kbone of the production comes from almost 30-year-old plantings of Busby clone
nillon and shiraz. Vineyard manager Andrew Tedder, who has considerable experience
h organics and biodynamics, is overseeing the ongoing development of Glenguin's
ıanic program.

Glenguin Vineyard Semillon 2017 Lemon buttered toast, finger lime, quince and lemongrass scents are of a purity and sapid intensity, without the shrillness of other regional expressions. Lightweight but extended time on lees has imparted a welcome creaminess. The long flow, precise but effortless. A fine vintage and a lovely wine. Screw cap | 11% alc. | To 2030 | $35 | NG

·undog Estate

McDonalds Road, Pokolbin, NSW 2320 **T** (03) 7036 1088 **WWW**.gundogestate.com.au **OPEN** 7 days
5 **WINEMAKER** Matthew Burton **EST.** 2006 **DOZENS** 7000 **VYDS** 5ha

tt Burton makes 4 different Hunter Semillons, and Shiraz from the Hunter Valley,
rrumbateman and Hilltops. The cellar door is located in the historic Pokolbin schoolhouse,
‹t to the old Rosemount/Hungerford Hill building on McDonalds Road.

Indomitus Rutilus Canberra District Shiraz 2018 Reminiscent of an Etna red, or lighter southern Rhône. Scant resemblance to shiraz as I know it. The point? A swaggering Australian iteration of place and style: volcanic smoky/rocky/mineral freshness driving dark cherry, nori, root spice, a potpourri of Indian spice and floral scents long and firm. The tannins win me over: expansive, succulent and saliva-sapping. Thrust of structure and parry of fruit, all Murrumbateman. A glimpse of the future. Excellent wine. Screw cap | 14.5% alc. | To 2026 | $40 | NG

Hungerford Hill 

2450 Broke Road, Pokolbin, NSW 2320 **T** (02) 4998 7666 **www**.hungerfordhill.com.au **OPEN** Sun–Thur 10–5, Fri–Sat 10–6 **WINEMAKER** Bryan Currie **EST.** 1967 **DOZENS** 22000 **VYDS** 5ha

Sam and Christie Arnaout purchased Hungerford Hill in December 2016, planning to refocu the 50yo label on its Hunter Valley origin, also adding significant new Lower Hunter vineyar at Sweetwater and Dalwood – the oldest continuously operating vineyard in Australia.

96 **Blackberry Vineyard Hunter Valley Semillon 2013** The 2013 vintage is among the very finest of all semillon vintages. Scintillating aromas of lemongrass, myrtle, curd and tonic. Despite its age, the wine hinges on the cusp of adolescence like a high-wire act, far from full maturity. The salubrious notes are yet to come. But mark my words, the wine's verve, impeccable poise and intensity of fru assure it. Screw cap | 10.4% alc. | To 2033 | $65 | NG

Keith Tulloch Wine  

989 Hermitage Road, Pokolbin, NSW 2320 **T** (02) 4998 7500 **www**.keithtullochwine.com.au **OPEN** 7 days 10–5 **WINEMAKER** Keith Tulloch, Brendan Kaczorowski, Alisdair Tulloch **EST.** 1997 **DOZENS** 10000 **VYDS** 12.7ha

Keith Tulloch is, of course, a member of the Tulloch family, which has played a leading role in the Hunter Valley for over a century. There is the almost obsessive attention to detail, the same almost ascetic intellectual approach, the same refusal to accept anything but the best In April 2019 the winery became the first Hunter Valley winery to become certified carbon neutral under the National Carbon Offset Standard (NCOS).

96 **Field of Mars Block 2A Hunter Valley Semillon 2018** Pointed aromas of lemon drops, citrus balm and verbena. Indelible scents of dried hay and freshly lain tatami mat. Best, the juicy middle stains the palate before running the scales of pumice, a chalky salinity and pungent mineral length. Fine Screw cap | 11.25% alc. | To 2035 | $50 | NG

Lake's Folly 

2416 Broke Road, Pokolbin, NSW 2320 **T** (02) 4998 7507 **www**.lakesfolly.wine **OPEN** 7 days 10–4 while wine available **WINEMAKER** Rodney Kempe **EST.** 1963 **DOZENS** 4500 **VYDS** 13ha

The first of the weekend wineries to produce wines for commercial sale, long revered for its Cabernet Sauvignon and nowadays its Chardonnay. Just as they should, terroir and climate produce a distinct wine style. Lake's Folly no longer has any connection with the Lake family having been acquired some years ago by Perth businessman Peter Fogarty.

97 **Hunter Valley Cabernets 2019** A beautiful wine of exquisite detail and perfume. Currant, mulberry violet, mulch, mint, graphite, anise and black olive. Sage-rolled tannins, impeccably hewn of sinew and fine grained oak. Delicate, sappy and mellifluous. So measured. So classy. Dangerously easy to drink already, it reminds me of a great Chinon. I feel guilty spitting it. Screw cap | 12.5% alc. | To 2032 | $80 | NG | ♥

Leogate Estate Wines 

1693 Broke Road, Pokolbin, NSW 2320 **T** (02) 4998 7499 **www**.leogate.com.au **OPEN** 7 days 10–5 **WINEMAKER** Mark Woods **EST.** 2009 **DOZENS** 30000 **VYDS** 127.5ha

Since purchasing the substantial Brokenback Vineyard in 2009 (a key part of the original Rothbury Estate, with the majority of vines over 50 years old), Bill and Vicki Widin have wast no time. Initially the Widins leased the Tempus Two winery but prior to the '13 vintage they completed the construction of their own winery and cellar door. They have had a string of wine show successes for their very impressive portfolio.

96 **Museum Release Creek Bed Reserve Hunter Valley Semillon 2013** A stellar vintage for the Hunter. The whites are particularly lauded and rightly so. This is an effortless meld of chewiness and pung mineral freshness. Nectarine, quince, beeswax, fennel, finger lime and a regional hint of lemon dr Pulpy, intense and impressively long, pummelling the cheeks while staining the throat. Screw cap 11.5% alc. | To 2032 | $50 | NG

Museum Release Creek Bed Reserve Hunter Valley Semillon 2014 A fine vintage by virtue of consistent ripening and extract, yet not quite up to the complexity and subdued energy of the '13 This said, an easier wine to grasp, perhaps. Waxy and full. White peach, wasabi, white pepper and a pumice-like glint to the chalky acidity. Long and very fine. Screw cap | 11% alc. | To 2028 | $50 | NG

Brokenback Vineyard Hunter Valley Gewürztraminer 2019 The Hunter spools few high-quality expressions of this grape across its humid climate, but perhaps it should try more. The aromas are bang on: grape spice, lychee, orange blossom and crystalline ginger. The palate could be a bit more unctuous and chewy, but that is being churlish. Mid weighted, highly versatile and very good drinking. An unexpected beauty. Screw cap | 13% alc. | To 2024 | $22 | NG

eerea Park ★★★★★

ilion B, 2144 Broke Road, Pokolbin, NSW 2320 **T** (02) 4998 7474 **www**.meereapark.com.au
N 7 days 10-5 **WINEMAKER** Rhys Eather **EST.** 1991 **DOZENS** 10000

s is the project of Rhys and Garth Eather, whose great-great-grandfather, Alexander Munro, ablished a famous vineyard in the 19th century, known as Bebeah. While the range of wines efly focuses on semillon and shiraz, it extends to other varieties (including chardonnay) d also into other regions. It hardly need be said that the quality of the wines, especially h 5 years' cellaring, is outstanding.

Indie Individual Vineyard Hunter Valley Marsanne Roussanne 2019 This is exceptional. Such promise, suggesting more of these great Rhône varieties should be planted in the region. Sumptuous and savoury, with pear, marzipan, dried straw and cheesecloth scents billowing across a full-weighted palate; sewn by a thread of mineral between seams of smart oak. I'd like more phenolics, but excellent all the same. Screw cap | 13% alc. | To 2030 | $30 | NG

istletoe Wines ★★★★★

Hermitage Road, Pokolbin, NSW 2320 **T** (02) 4998 7770 **www**.mistletoewines.com.au **OPEN** 7 days
5 **WINEMAKER** Scott Stephens **EST.** 1989 **DOZENS** 5000 **VYDS** 5.5ha

tletoe Wines, owned by Ken and Gwen Sloan, can trace its history back to 1909, when neyard was planted on what was then called Mistletoe Farm, before disappearing. The ans have long since created a winery business here to stay. All wine is made onsite. The ality and consistency of these wines is irreproachable, as is their price.

Grand Reserve Hunter Valley Shiraz 2019 Crushed, destemmed, open-fermented, matured for 16 months in new and used French oak. Another very good vintage, the picking decision spot on, leaving a skein of freshness running through the perfectly balanced, medium-bodied palate. Blackberry, plum and a regional whisper of earth provide all the flavour one could wish for, the tannins lining up in measured support. Screw cap | 13.5% alc. | To 2040 | $75 | JH

Reserve Hunter Valley Semillon 2019 Hand picked, whole-bunch pressed, a short maturation in tank on gross lees after a cold ferment. Gleaming straw green; the lemon-scented bouquet leads into a generously flavoured palate, with lemon curd and Meyer lemon fruit flavours extended by the backbone of acidity. Now or later enjoyment. Screw cap | 12.2% alc. | To 2030 | $25 | JH

olly Morgan Vineyard  

Talga Road, Rothbury, NSW 2320 **T** (02) 4930 7695 **www**.mollymorgan.com
EMAKER Usher Tinkler **EST.** 1963 **DOZENS** 2000 **VYDS** 7.66ha

s vineyard is named after an exceptionally resourceful woman who was twice convicted d sent to NSW, married 3 times (the last time when she was 60, her husband aged 31). Out his improbable background she emerged as a significant benefactor of the sick, earning soubriquet 'Queen of the Hunter'.

MoMo Hunter Valley Semillon 2019 Youthful Hunter semillon personified: lemongrass, tonic, barley sugar and citrus balm. Broader than most examples, in the best sense. Approachable given the warm year, although I'd wait at least a couple of years. A fine skein of acidity, pulpy fruit and an uncluttered juicy palate of considerable length, auguring well for a very bright future. A beautifully measured wine. Screw cap | 11% alc. | To 2031 | $25 | NG

MoMo Hunter Valley Rosé 2019 Shiraz. A very bright, deep and attractive coral colour. Sappy. Intensely flavoured, despite the moderate alcohol. Rich, even. This level of intensity is clearly a skill at this address, belying the wine's inherent lightness of being. Poached strawberry, thyme, orange blossom and rosehip. A highly versatile rosé that is far from the Provençal mock-ups of the madding crowd. Screw cap | 12.2% alc. | To 2022 | $25 | NG

MoMo Hunter Valley Shiraz 2019 Another uncluttered wine boasting fealty to region and an an easygoing drinkability. Simply put, there is nothing bothering my palate when I taste. Moreover, it tastes of the the sweet Hunter earth. Terracotta, even. Poached cherries, polished leather and a verdant lilt of herb, to boot. Mid weighted, energetic enough and truly exceptional value. Screw cap | 13.5% alc. | To 2026 | $25 | NG

Mount Pleasant

401 Marrowbone Road, Pokolbin, NSW 2320 **T** (02) 4998 7505 **www**.mountpleasantwines.com.au **OPEN** Thurs–Mon 10–4 **WINEMAKER** Adrian Sparks **EST.** 1921 **VYDS** 88.2ha

The glorious Elizabeth and Lovedale Semillons are generally commercially available with 4–5 years of bottle age; they are treasures with a consistently superb show record. Mount Pleasant's individual vineyard wines, together with the Maurice O'Shea memorial wines, add to the lustre of this proud name. Winery of the Year in the *Wine Companion 2017*.

99 **Maurice O'Shea Hunter Valley Shiraz 2018** An utterly stupendous wine, in the same league as Penfolds 1962 Bin 60A. This O'Shea has the complexity of a great tapestry woven centuries ago when time was of no consequence. The sky, the soil and the fruit coalesce into an entity that throbs with intensity and a never-ending kaleidoscope of blackberry, earth and leather flavours. Screw cap | 13.5% alc. | To 2040 | $250 | JH | ♥

97 **1880 Vines Old Hill Vineyard Hunter Valley Shiraz 2018** This is a wine of ascetic, aptly reductive tension. Eking out visceral pleasure over the cerebral is a challenge right now. But it is often the w with youthful wine this good. The transparent, fine-boned, chalky and tensile structural pillars ser as a path into a bright future. For now, think lilac, cherry pip, bergamot and crunchy red berries. Wonderful chewy length. Expands. A truly excellent wine. Takes time to calibrate to its elastic cadence. Somehow reminiscent of fine youthful Burgundy. Screw cap | 13.5% alc. | To 2040 | $135 | NG

Pokolbin Estate

McDonalds Road, Pokolbin, NSW 2321 **T** (02) 4998 7524 **www**.pokolbinestate.com.au **OPEN** 7 days 9- **WINEMAKER** Xanthe Hatcher **EST.** 1980 **DOZENS** 2500 **VYDS** 15.7ha

Pokolbin Estate has a very unusual, but very good, multi-varietal, multi-vintage array of wine always available for sale. The Riesling is true riesling, not misnamed semillon, the latter bein one of their best wines, and wines under screw cap going back 6 or 7 vintages, and single-vineyard offerings to boot, are available.

95 **Phil Swannell Semillon 2013** Possibly the finest vintage for semillon in my lifetime, 2013 boasts concentration of fruit and a relaxed stridency, imparting freshness and detail without any severity. The wines are effortlessly poised, incredibly juicy and have drunk well across their lifetimes. No exception here. At its zenith: lemon butter, toast, Seville orange and hibiscus roll long across the mouth. Delicious. Screw cap | 11.4% alc. | To 2024 | $30 | NG

RidgeView Wines

273 Sweetwater Road, Pokolbin, NSW 2320 **T** (02) 6574 7332 **www**.ridgeview.com.au **OPEN** Wed–Sun 10–5 **WINEMAKER** Darren Scott, Gary MacLean, Mark Woods **EST.** 2000 **DOZENS** 3000 **VYDS** 9ha

Darren and Tracey Scott have transformed a 40ha timbered farm into a vineyard with self-contained accommodation and a cellar door. The greater part of the plantings are 4.5ha of shiraz; cabernet sauvignon, chambourcin, merlot, pinot gris, viognier and traminer make up a somewhat eclectic selection of other varieties.

96 **Museum Release Generations Reserve Hunter Valley Semillon 2013** Arguably the finest Hunter semillon vintage of my drinking lifetime. Of these museum releases, the '07 has the flare, big charisma and an incongruous Euro appeal. The 2013, however, reverts to the tensile drive so fidelitous to the local turf. Lanolin, nettle, bath salts, lemon zest and a bare whiff of toast. Loads of speed. The shift into an aged gear will bring a marvellous wine. All that is required is patience. Screw cap | 11.4% alc. | To 2033 | $65 | NG

Museum Release Generations Reserve Hunter Valley Semillon 2007 This has aged brilliantly. For some, unrecognisable perhaps from the citric verve of youthful expressions. Yet the degree of aged complexity is riveting. Dried hay, raw honey, buttered toast, quinine and apricot pith. This, aside from the acidity, has an uncanny resemblance to aged white Rhône. A beautiful wine, far from the conventional norm, aged or otherwise. Compelling intensity and length. A stunning wine. Screw cap | 11% alc. | To 2024 | $40 | NG

94 **Hunter Valley Verdelho 2018** Possibly the most sophisticated verdelho I have ever tasted. And no, that is not a backhanded put-down. This is very good. Almost exceptional. Taut, mineral and nicely oily, a textural carapace that restrains varietal tendencies toward tropical exuberance. The finish long and effortless. Wonderful persistence. An excellent food wine. All about texture. More European than Australian. Plenty of traction left. Screw cap | 12.9% alc. | To 2025 | $25 | NG

tomp Wine ★★★★☆

‡ Wilderness Road, Lovedale, NSW 2330 **T** 0409 774 280 **www.stompwines.com.au** **OPEN** Thurs–Mon -5 **WINEMAKER** Michael McManus **EST.** 2004 **DOZENS** 1000

chael and Meredith McManus have set up Stomp Winemaking, a contract winemaker signed to keep small and larger parcels of grapes separate through the fermentation and aturation process, thus meeting the needs of boutique wine producers in the Hunter Valley. e addition of their own Stomp label is a small but important part of their business.

Hunter Valley Shiraz 2019 These tannins have been extracted with aplomb: chewy, ripe and savoury; medium bodied as a result. The fruit, Hunter-style earthy but with a pulpy plum, mulberry and black-cherry joyousness. Lively, with a real thrust of extract and parry of structure, coating the palate. Wonderful vinosity, joy and length. Lovely wine. Screw cap | 14% alc. | To 2030 | $35 | NG

homas Wines

Mistletoe Lane, Pokolbin, NSW 2320 **T** (02) 4998 7134 **www.thomaswines.com.au** **OPEN** 7 days 10–5 **NEMAKER** Andrew Thomas **EST.** 1997 **DOZENS** 10 000 **VYDS** 6ha

ter 13 years at Tyrell's Wines, Andrew Thomas left to undertake contract work and to ntinue the development of his own label. The major part of the production comes from ng-term arrangements with growers of old-vine semillon and shiraz. The acquisition of aemore Vineyard in December 2017 was significant, giving Thomas Wines a long-term pply of grapes from one of the Hunter Valley's most distinguished semillon sites. The quality the wines and the reputation of Andrew Thomas have never been higher.

The Cote Individual Vineyard Hunter Valley Shiraz 2019 Very fine. A majestic composition of tannins of noble detail and grit; blue/blackberry fruits, licorice straps and a smear of black olive and bincho charcoal. Feels ethereal, by virtue of the structural bones. All by virtue of a dry-grown vineyard, planted in '71. The finest tannin profile of the bunch. Screw cap | 14% alc. | To 2035 | $35 | NG

Synergy Vineyard Selection Hunter Valley Semillon 2020 Multi-vineyard sources as usual, but there's nothing usual about the depth of varietal fruit expression on the palate. Lemongrass/lemon curd flavours run throughout, Hunter acidity the staff of the long life ahead. Great success in a difficult vintage. Screw cap | 11.5% alc. | To 2035 | $22 | JH | ♥

Sweetwater Individual Vineyard Hunter Valley Shiraz 2019 This vineyard always imparts verve and a thirst-quenching crunch to its wines: this is firmly marked. A boysenberry creaminess to the aroma. Less floral and iodine-lifted. Black olive and some salami smokiness. Yet the tannins run across the palate with detailed precision, not binding the wine too tightly. Long and compelling. Screw cap | 14% alc. | To 2030 | $35 | NG

Synergy Vineyard Selection Hunter Valley Shiraz 2018 Multiple vineyard sources separately vinified. The high-quality vintage shines through the expressive, dark berry-filled bouquet and into a sculpted, medium-bodied palate. Its freshness and savoury fruit/oak/tannin balance guarantee it will develop superbly over decades. Value+. Screw cap | 14.2% alc. | To 2038 | $25 | JH

inklers Vineyard

kolbin Mountains Road, Pokolbin, NSW 2320 **T** (02) 4998 7435 **www.tinklers.com.au** **OPEN** 7 days -5 **WINEMAKER** Usher Tinkler **EST.** 1946 **DOZENS** 7000 **VYDS** 41ha

ree generations of the Tinkler family have been involved with the property since 1942. riginally a beef and dairy farm, vines have been both pulled out and replanted at various ages and part of the adjoining 80+yo Ben Ean Vineyard has been acquired. The majority the grape production is sold to McWilliam's and Tyrrell's. Usher has resigned his roles as ief winemaker at Poole's Rock and Cockfighter's Ghost to take on full-time responsibility Tinklers, and production has been increased to meet demand.

5 **Reserve Hunter Valley Semillon 2017** Youthful semillon, just shuffling from adolescence into puberty, alluding to what we can expect with the iron will and patience required by this classic variety. Bath salts, buttered toast and lemon-drop scents. The palate, balletic and light, is still tense and elemental. Wait! Screw cap | 11.7% alc. | To 2032 | $35 | NG

4 **School Block Hunter Valley Semillon 2019** This is very good, in the typically understated way of a youthful classic. Aromas of lemongrass, verdant herb and citrus balm skitter along a juicy rail of vibrant acidity and a pungent mineral undercarriage. Subtle, but long and finely tuned. Nothing out of place. This will go to very good places for those with patience. Screw cap | 11.5% alc. | To 2032 | $25 | NG

Tyrrell's Wines 

★★★★

1838 Broke Road, Pokolbin, NSW 2321 **T** (02) 4993 7000 **www**.tyrrells.com.au **OPEN** Mon-Sun 9-4 **WINEMAKER** Andrew Spinaze, Mark Richardson, Chris Tyrrell **EST.** 1858 **DOZENS** 220 000 **VYDS** 364ha

One of the most successful family wineries, a humble operation for the first 110 years of its li that has grown out of all recognition over the past 40 years. There are 11 blocks of vines olde than 100 years in the Hunter Valley and the Tyrrell family owns 7 of those blocks. A founding member of Australia's First Families of Wine.

97 **4 Acres Hunter Valley Shiraz 2019** Shiraz of the Year 2022. This oscillates with the 8 Acres as my favourite of these single-vineyard expressions. An apotheosis of Hunter savouriness and a lightne of touch of yore. Truly ethereal. Fragrant, with mottled blue-fruit allusions, lilac, nori and chinotto. Clove, pepper grind and cardamom lace the finish. Yet frankly, words are a waste. The texture, the totem. Detailed tannins of immaculate precision. An airy grace. Elegance personified. Screw cap | 13% alc. | To 2034 | $135 | NG | ♥

ZONE

Southern New South Wales

REGION

Canberra District

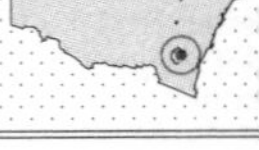

Clonakilla

★★★★

3 Crisps Lane, Murrumbateman, NSW 2582 **T** (02) 6227 5877 **www**.clonakilla.com.au **OPEN** Mon-Fri 11-4, w'ends 10-5 **WINEMAKER** Tim Kirk, Chris Bruno **EST.** 1971 **DOZENS** 20 000 **VYDS** 16ha

The indefatigable Tim Kirk, with an inexhaustible thirst for knowledge, is the winemaker and manager of this family winery founded by his father, scientist Dr John Kirk. It is not at all surprising that the quality of the wines is exceptional, especially the Shiraz Viognier, which has paved the way for numerous others but remains the icon.

97 **Murrumbateman Syrah 2019** This is really astonishing: the flavours, the texture and the depth of t wine without it ever moving much beyond medium bodied. It is not trying to be flash. It's in its ow comfort zone, full of florals, ripe fruit and an array of spices. It's an exercise in texture though. Ver fine, velvety tannins sashay across the palate, which extends out, adding more fruit flavours, savo tones and well-integrated oak along the way. Long, decisive and a pleasure to taste. Screw cap | 14% alc. | To 2039 | $130 | JF | ♥

Collector Wines 

★★★★

7 Murray Street, Collector, NSW 2581 **T** (02) 6116 8722 **www**.collectorwines.com.au **OPEN** Thurs-M 10-4 **WINEMAKER** Alex McKay **EST.** 2007 **DOZENS** 6000 **VYDS** 6ha

Owner and winemaker Alex McKay makes exquisitely detailed wines, bending to the dictate of inclement weather on his doorstep, heading elsewhere if need be. He is known to not spe much, and when he does, his voice is very quiet. So you have to remain alert to appreciate his unparalleled sense of humour. No such attention is needed for his wines, which are consistently excellent, their elegance appropriate for their maker.

96 **Tiger Tiger Chardonnay 2018** This is as much a pure expression of cool Tumbarumba fruit as it is c Alex McKay's winemaking – whole-bunch pressed, fermented in French oak, mlf and aged on lees for about 10 months. It's flinty and fine, with pure grapefruit and lemon and a light, leesy, creamy texture. But it's the laser line of acidity that thrills. Screw cap | 12.9% alc. | To 2030 | $38 | JF

95 **Lamp Lit Canberra District Marsanne 2019** Given its youth, this is tight, flinty and lightly aromatic. different on the palate as the flavours have been ramped up, partly via mlf and partly via toasty ne French barrels – expect creamed honey and texture. There's some tension between the acidity an the oak, ensuring this will unfurl in time. But today it could slake a thirst. Screw cap | 13.3% alc. To 2028 | $32 | JF

Corang Estate 

★★★

533 Oallen Road, Nerriga, NSW 2622 **T** 0419 738 548 **www**.corangestate.com.au **OPEN** By appt **WINEMAKER** Michael Bynon, Alex McKay **EST.** 2018 **DOZENS** 1000 **VYDS** 1ha

This is the nascent business of Michael and Jill Bynon. Michael has been in the wine industry in one role or another for 30 years, attending Roseworthy Agricultural College and moving

›m a marketing career to join the senior corporate ranks. Most impressive of all is that he has ıssed the master of wine tasting examination. Jill was a linguist and marketing professional, ıent in French, having spent much time in France before moving to Australia from her native :otland in 2003.

Hilltops Shiraz 2019 Floral scented, sweetly fruited, lightly spiced and well priced. You want more? Expect a dash of pepper and cinnamon with charry oak in the mix too, but balanced. There's a whiff of prosciutto so it does have appealing savoury tones to tame the intense fruit. Full bodied, plush tannins and a slightly bitter finish. Screw cap | 14.5% alc. | To 2027 | $25 | JF

Hilltops Tempranillo 2019 I love the simplicity of this. It's also an utterly delicious drink-now style full of juicy red cherries with a smattering of woodsy spices. The cranberry tartness of the acidity keeps it lively and fresh. Screw cap | 13.5% alc. | To 2025 | $25 | JF

ake George Winery

3 The Vineyards Road, Lake George, NSW 2581 **T** (02) 9948 4676 **WWW**.lakegeorgewinery.com.au
EN Thurs–Sun 10–5 **WINEMAKER** Nick O'Leary, Anthony McDougall **EST.** 1971 **DOZENS** 2000 **VYDS** 8ha

ıke George Winery was established by legend-in-his-own-lifetime Dr Edgar Riek, who ›ntributed so much to the Canberra District and the Australian wine industry. It has now ıssed into the hands of Sarah and Anthony McDougall, and the 47yo dry-grown chardonnay, not noir, cabernet sauvignon, semillon and merlot plantings have been joined by shiraz, mpranillo, pinot gris, viognier and riesling.

; **Pinot Noir 2018** This sits snugly in come-and-drink-me-now territory. And it has layers and beauty too. Poached cherries and rhubarb, spiced with cinnamon and the orange myrtle of chinotto. The palate is a lesson in elegance – cool and refreshing, with lithe tannins, all light and bright. Screw cap | 13% alc. | To 2026 | $35 | JF

Shiraz 2019 The same lightness of touch as the pinot noir. A fantastic purple-red hue entices, as does the palate. A neat mix of sweet-berried fruit, woodsy spices and oak char give it a savoury edge with grainy, fine tannins. Overall, very satisfying. Screw cap | 13.5% alc. | To 2028 | $35 | JF

1ount Majura Vineyard

Lime Kiln Road, Majura, ACT 2609 **T** (02) 6262 3070 **WWW**.mountmajura.com.au **OPEN** 7 days 10–5
NEMAKER Dr Frank van de Loo **EST.** 1988 **DOZENS** 5000 **VYDS** 9.3ha

ıis tiny vineyard has been significantly expanded since '99. Much attention has been ›cused on tempranillo. The Mount Majura flagship remains the Canberra District Tempranillo, ith volume and quality cementing its place. All the grapes used come from these estate antings. One of the star performers in the Canberra District.

5 **Little Dam Canberra District Tempranillo 2019** The most complete, structured and compelling of the single-site wines. Its own distinct personality comes through with a whorl of dark fruits, tarry and earthy, licorice root and a smidge of sarsaparilla. It's very savoury with exceptional tannins – ripe, textural, with a graininess akin to raw silk, the acidity bright and the finish long. Screw cap | 14.5% alc. | To 2033 | $65 | JF

ıick O'Leary Wines

ı9 Brooklands Road, Wallaroo, NSW 2618 **T** (02) 6230 2745 **WWW**.nickolearywines.com.au
›EN By appt **WINEMAKER** Nick O'Leary **EST.** 2007 **DOZENS** 12 000 **VYDS** 11ha

t the ripe old age of 28, Nick O'Leary had been involved in the wine industry for over a ecade, working variously in retail, wholesale, viticulture and winemaking. His wines have ad extraordinarily consistent success in local wine shows and competitions since the first ıntages, and are building on that early success in spectacular fashion. At the NSW Wine wards '15, the '14 Shiraz was awarded the NSW Wine of the Year trophy, exactly as the '13 hiraz was in the prior year – the first time any winery had won the award in consecutive years.

6 **Tumbarumba Chardonnay 2019** Oh my. This is fabulous. It sparkles in the glass and lights up the palate. It's heady, with the right amount of flinty, smoky sulphides and lovely citrus flavours – grapefruit and lemon, zest and pith. There's tension across the palate, mainly an interplay between toasty oak and creamy lees flavours and acidity. It's tight and will continue to unfurl beautifully over the next few years. Screw cap | 13% alc. | To 2029 | $32 | JF

Heywood Canberra District Shiraz 2019 Seriously. This is too good to be true, especially at this price. A highly perfumed, floral and spicy wine. The palate is assured and medium bodied, dotted with beautiful fruit flavours, superfine tannins and length to behold. Elegant and refined. Screw cap | 13.5% alc. | To 2029 | $35 | JF

Bolaro Canberra District Shiraz 2019 This is made almost identically to the Heywood shiraz (bar the extra 5% whole bunches, capped at 35% here). Both wines are really an expression of their site. This is obviously different yet equally compelling. It's more plush, with darker fruit, more woodsy spices and pepper. The palate is full bodied, with shapely, grainy yet denser tannins and the acidity is bright and encompassing. It is also incredibly vibrant and, quite frankly, rather sexy. Screw cap | 13.5% alc. | To 2035 | $58 | JF | ♥

95 **Canberra District Shiraz 2019** This has found its groove. It offers everything one could want from a cool-climate shiraz: perfume, juicy fruit, the right seasoning of pepper, spice, oak, tangy acidity and a freshness throughout. Terrific wine and excellent value. Screw cap | 13.5% alc. | To 2029 | $30 | JF

Poachers

431 Nanima Road, Springrange, NSW 2618 **T** (02) 6230 2487 **www.poacherspantry.com.au** **OPEN** 7 days 9.30-5 **WINEMAKER** Will Bruce **EST.** 1998 **DOZENS** 3500 **VYDS** 20ha

Poachers Vineyard, owned by the Bruce family, shares its home with the Poachers Pantry, a renowned gourmet smokehouse. The quality of the wines is very good. The northeast-facing slopes, at an elevation of 720m, provide some air drainage and hence protection against spring frosts.

94 **Canberra District Syrah 2019** This is a bit subtle and slinky, yet shows off its spiced cherry, berry, pips and peppered flavours well. The acidity is a bit jangly, but there's a juiciness within. It's very easy to sip away, thanks to a refined, barely medium-bodied palate, covered in lacy tannins. Screw cap | 13% alc. | To 2029 | $30 | JF

Ravensworth

312 Patemans Lane, Murrumbateman, ACT 2582 **T** (02) 6226 8368 **www.ravensworthwines.com.au** **WINEMAKER** Bryan Martin **EST.** 2000 **DOZENS** 2000 **VYDS** 2.6ha

Winemaker, vineyard manager and partner Bryan Martin (with dual wine science and winegrowing degrees from CSU) has a background in wine retail, food and beverage experience in the hospitality industry and teaches part-time. He is also assistant winemaker to Tim Kirk at Clonakilla, after 7 years at Jeir Creek. Judging at wine shows is another string to his bow.

95 **A Long Way Around Margaret River Chenin Blanc 2020** This is wonderful, a wine that defies the odds. Imagine ambrosia. It's a cross between a lemon daiquiri and shiso pickled ginger. It tastes like spiced ginger and fresh ginger in a black tea weakly sweetened with honey – this is obviously dry but the fruit weight lends itself to that sensation. Peppery too. Lovely texture, the phenolics beautifully handled and acidity paramount in harnessing those tannins and energy of this wine. Respect. Screw cap | 12.5% alc. | To 2026 | $28 | JF

94 **The Long Way Around Frankland River Gewürztraminer 2020** The colour is of Turkish delight and so too the aromas and flavours. It's a Middle Eastern extravaganza with musk, rose petals and lemon oil. The palate is soft and textural, until the chewy tannins kick in. They're like fine sandpaper, and there's blood-orange acidity travelling along for the ride, too. Screw cap | 13% alc. | To 2026 | $28 | JF

Shaw Wines

34 Isabel Drive, Murrumbateman, NSW 2582 **T** (02) 6227 5827 **www.shawwines.com.au** **OPEN** 7 days 10-5 **WINEMAKER** Graeme Shaw, Jeremy Nascimben **EST.** 1999 **DOZENS** 12000 **VYDS** 28ha

Graeme and Ann Shaw established their vineyard (cabernet sauvignon, merlot, shiraz, semillon and riesling) in 1998 on a 280ha fine wool-producing property established in the mid- 1800s and known as Olleyville. It is one of the largest privately owned vineyard holdings in the Canberra area. Their children are fully employed in the family business, Michael as viticulturist and Tanya as cellar door manager.

90 **Winemakers Selection Canberra Cabernet Sauvignon 2018** Showing its cool credentials with mint and herbs slinking around blackberries, currants and woodsy spice. It has a refreshing appeal with tannins aplenty, hovering between savoury and fruit flavours. Screw cap | 14% alc. | To 2025 | $20 | JF

NSW SA VIC WA TAS

arrh Wines ⓨ ★★★★

0 Greenwood Road, Murrumbateman, NSW 2582 **T** (02) 6227 1474 **www**.yarrhwines.com.au
EN Fri-Sun 11-5 **WINEMAKER** Fiona Wholohan **EST.** 1997 **DOZENS** 2000 **VYDS** 6ha

ona Wholohan and Neil McGregor are IT refugees; both now work full-time running the Yarrh ines Vineyard and making the wines. Fiona undertook the oenology and viticulture course at SU and has also spent time as an associate judge at wine shows. They spent 5 years moving a hybrid organic vineyard with composting, mulching, biological controls and careful neyard floor management. Yarrh was the original Aboriginal name for the Yass district.

The Brunette Canberra District Sangiovese 2018 Dark, spicy cherries, Mediterranean herbs and radicchio bitterness too. Woodsy spices via oak, which is in check. The palate is pure sangiovese – textural tannins, sinewy and tangy, with refreshing acidity in the driver's seat and leading the way to the finish line. Screw cap | 13.5% alc. | To 2028 | $35 | JF

GION

Gundagai

Nick Spencer Wines

Loch Street, Yarralumla, ACT 2600 (postal) **T** 0419 810 274 **www**.nickspencerwines.com.au
NEMAKER Nick Spencer **EST.** 2017 **DOZENS** 2500

ck Spencer won the biggest wine show trophy in 2009: the Jimmy Watson; in '11 he was a n Evans Tutorial scholar and in '14 was a finalist in the Young Gun of Wine and a finalist in e Gourmet Traveller Winemaker of the Year. His 2 regions of interest are Tumbarumba and undagai – adjoining but very different. The quality of his wines from Gundagai make him the ptain of that ship.

Gundagai Medium Dry Red 2019 60/20/10/5/5% shiraz/cabernet/malbec/tempranillo/touriga, fermented separately and aged in used French oak puncheons. This is really getting its DNA established. It is medium bodied and dry, although there's an abundance of ripe fruits. Tangy and slightly sinewy this vintage, but so refreshing. Loads of baking spices, with bitter herbs, lithe acidity and neat tannins to close. Screw cap | 13% alc. | To 2030 | $35 | JF

GION

Hilltops

Moppity Vineyards

ppity Road, Young, NSW 2594 (postal) **T** (02) 6382 6222 **www**.moppity.com.au
NEMAKER Jason Brown **EST.** 1973 **DOZENS** 30000 **VYDS** 66.54ha

son Brown and wife Alecia, with backgrounds in fine-wine retail and accounting, purchased oppity Vineyards in 2004 when it was already 31 years old. Initially they were content to sell e grapes to other makers, but that changed with the release of the '06 Shiraz, which won p gold in its class at the London International Wine & Spirit Competition. In Nov '09 the '08 len Road Long Road Hilltops Shiraz, made from Moppity Vineyards grapes, won the Jimmy atson Trophy. The Lock & Key range provides exceptional value for money.

Estate Hilltops Shiraz 2019 This reveals a core of black plums, cherry liqueur, earthy and warm, with soy sauce and licorice. It's rich and full bodied, with oak in check, savouriness throughout, supportive tannins and frankly, a bargain. Screw cap | 14% alc. | To 2032 | $35 | JF

South Australia

76292ha | 7 zones | 19 regions

Self-dubbed 'The Wine State', South Australia has seven zones including the Adelaide Super Zone, an odd assembly of three of the seven, not to mention chunks of otherwise nameless land.

When international wine and lifestyle tourists finally return, the region that will be foremost in their minds is the **Barossa Valley**, an easy drive northeast of Adelaide. For many, it is the home of Australia's best shiraz wines, with Penfolds Grange the splendidly opulent ultimate icon. Cabernet sauvignon is often united with shiraz in Australia's definitive blend. À la mode grenache is fresher and more vibrant in its familiar partnership with shiraz and mourvèdre, and flying solo more frequently and confidently than ever.

The cooler temperatures of **Eden Valley** and **High Eden** grow elegant shiraz and bring riesling into the limelight, with flavours of lime and Meyer lemon fruit. This variety is grist for the mill in the **Clare Valley**; here, slate rock, limestone and red earth give riesling its gravitas, likewise shiraz, the second-most widely planted, well in advance of cabernet sauvignon. **Adelaide Hills** is the final region on the Mount Lofty Ranges zone. Pinot noir has the lion's share of red plantings, 3 times greater than shiraz, but thumped by the region's hero of sauvignon blanc, along with chardonnay and pinot gris.

The grouping of the 5 regions in the Fleurieu zone is logical, all enjoying a Mediterranean/maritime climate: an even accumulation of warmth (seasonal and diurnal) with a dry summer and cool nights. **McLaren Vale** spans the expanse between the cool of the Adelaide Hills and the moderating influence of St Vincent Gulf; dark-chocolate-riddled shiraz, satisfyingly generous yet varietally accurate cabernet and the thrill of modern grenache are its mainstays. **Langhorne Creek** is the other important player, and the most underrated region in Australia, producing red wines with rivers of plush shiraz and cabernet sauvignon comprising the majority of the total crush. **Currency Creek** is a scaled-down mirror image of Langhorne Creek.

The Limestone Coast zone of six regions has three big names. **Coonawarra** hung its hat on shiraz until 1955 (1955 Wynns Michael Hermitage a still-superb great Australian shiraz), thereafter on cabernet sauvignon (1963 Mildara

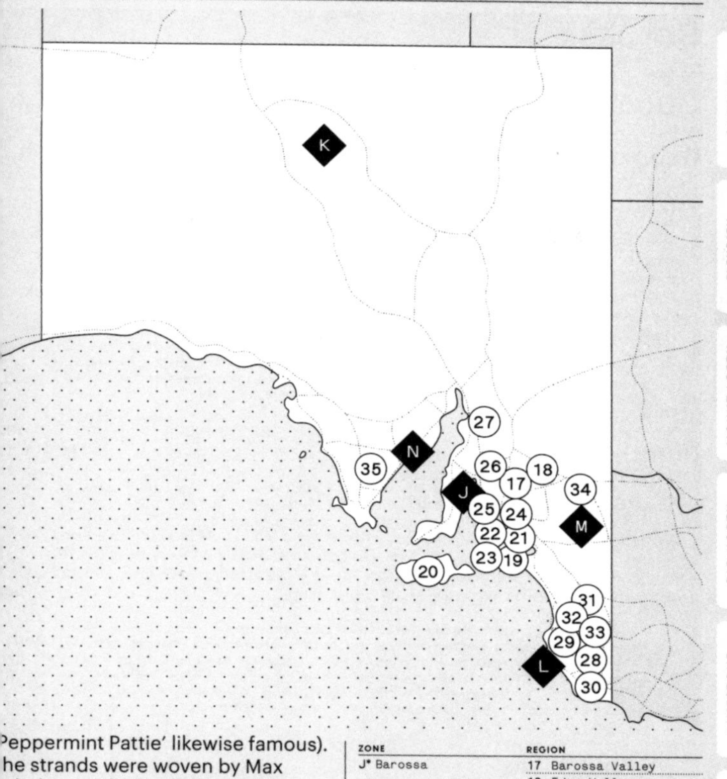

'eppermint Pattie' likewise famous). he strands were woven by Max chubert with the 1962 Bin 60A :oonawarra Cabernet Kalimna hiraz, the all-time greatest red ine. **Padthaway** produces wines f consistent quality and yield cross shiraz, chardonnay, cabernet auvignon and pinot gris/grigio n order of size), plus seven other arieties. **Wrattonbully** is a slimmed-own version of Padthaway, with the ubious distinction of growing more inot gris/grigio than chardonnay, ut neither can challenge the red-vine duo of cabernet sauvignon ull of blackcurrant and plum) and enerous, fleshy shiraz.

ZONE	REGION
J* Barossa	17 Barossa Valley
	18 Eden Valley
Fleurieu	19 Currency Creek
	20 Kangaroo Island
	21 Langhorne Creek
	22 McLaren Vale
	23 Southern Fleurieu
Mount Lofty Ranges	24 Adelaide Hills
	25 Adelaide Plains
	26 Clare Valley
K Far North	27 Southern Flinders Ranges
L Limestone Coast	28 Coonawarra
	29 Mount Benson
	30 Mount Gambier
	31 Padthaway
	32 Robe
	33 Wrattonbully
M Lower Murray	34 Riverland
N The Peninsulas	35 Southern Eyre Peninsula
* Adelaide Super Zone	

ZONE

Barossa

REGION

Barossa Valley

Cooper Burns

★★★★☆

494 Research Road, Nuriootpa, SA 5355 **T** (08) 7513 7606 **www**.cooperburns.com.au **OPEN** Fri–Mon 11–4 **WINEMAKER** Russell Burns **EST.** 2004 **DOZENS** 3000

Established in 2004, Cooper Burns was the side project of Mark Cooper and Russell Burns as they worked their winemaking day jobs at Treasury Wine Estates and Torbreck respectively. In '17 they established their winery at Nuriootpa and Russell left Torbreck to work full-time at Cooper Burns. The old homestead garage was renovated in '19 and now serves as the cellar door within the grounds of the winery.

94 **Barossa Valley Grenache Shiraz Mataro 2019** An elegantly medium-bodied blend in which the lead role of grenache is reinforced by carefully judged whole-bunch fermentation. Dark raspberries and fresh strawberries are fragranced with rose petal and musk, underscored by fine-grained tannins that carry a long and eloquent conclusion. Classy Barossa grenache. Screw cap | 14.5% alc. | To 2024 | $30 | TS

Dutschke Wines

★★★★☆

Lot 1 Gods Hill Road, Lyndoch, SA 5351 **T** (08) 8524 5485 **www**.dutschkewines.com **OPEN** By appt **WINEMAKER** Wayne Dutschke **EST.** 1998 **DOZENS** 5000 **VYDS** 15ha

Winemaker and owner Wayne Dutschke set up business with uncle (and grapegrower) Ken Semmler in 1990 to produce wine. Wayne was crowned Barossa Winemaker of the Year in 2010, inducted into the Barons of Barossa in '13 and is the author of a children's book about growing up in a winery called *My Dad has Purple Hands*.

96 **Oscar Semmler Lyndoch Barossa Valley Shiraz 2018** Lyndoch may not be as revered as the fabled parishes of the northern and western Barossa, but this wine alone is a statement that it should be held in equal if not higher regard. Wayne Dutschke exemplifies that wonderful Barossa juxtapositio of sweet, ripe black fruit density and the refinement of crunchy definition, freshness and violet-infused detail. I've been avidly following, buying and cellaring Oscar for decades and I cannot reca such detail, mineral tannin finesse and undeterred persistence. Screw cap | 14.5% alc. | To 2038 | $75 | TS

Gomersal Wines

203 Lyndoch Road, Gomersal, SA 5352 **T** (08) 8563 3611 **www**.gomersalwines.com.au **OPEN** Wed–Mon 10–5 **WINEMAKER** Barry White **EST.** 1887 **DOZENS** 10200 **VYDS** 20.2ha

The 1887 establishment date has a degree of poetic licence. In 1887 Friedrich W Fromm planted the Wonganella Vineyards, following that with a winery on the edge of the Gomersal Creek in '91; it remained in operation for 90 years, finally closing in 1983. In 2000 a group of friends 'with strong credentials in both the making and consumption ends of the wine industry' bought the winery and re-established the vineyard.

92 **Clare Valley Riesling 2020** A spot-on drink-now wine with citrussy aromatics moving from lemon to orange and a touch of ginger spice. It's not racy as such, although acidity encases the textural pala flavoured with baked apples. Screw cap | 12.5% alc. | To 2027 | $20 | JF

Grant Burge

279 Krondorf Road, Barossa Valley, SA 5352 **T** (08) 8563 7675 **www**.grantburgewines.com.au **OPEN** 7 days 10–5 **WINEMAKER** Craig Stansborough **EST.** 1988 **DOZENS** 400000

Grant and Helen Burge established the eponymous Grant Burge business in 1988. It grew into one of the largest family-owned wine businesses in the valley. In February 2015, Accolade Wines announced it had acquired the Grant Burge brand and the historic Krondorf Winery. The 356ha of vineyards remain in family ownership and will continue to supply premium grapes to the Accolade-owned business.

NSW SA VIC WA TAS QLD

6 **Corryton Park Barossa Cabernet Sauvignon 2018** I have long admired Corryton Park cabernet, less showy and flamboyant than is typical for these parts, and ultimately more sophisticated. It leads out closed and contemplative, with a core of crunchy blackcurrant fruit rising on the mid palate and holding with impressive line and drive. Eloquent, bright acidity and brilliant fine-grained tannins never drop their gaze long into the finish. A cellaring special. Screw cap | 14.6% alc. | To 2043 | $48 | TS

ɜreenock Creek Wines

50 Seppeltsfield Road, Marananga, SA 5355 **T** (08) 8563 2898 **WWW**.greenockcreekwines.com.au
PEN 7 days 11-5 **WINEMAKER** Alex Peel, Peter Atyeo **EST**. 1984 **DOZENS** 4000 **VYDS** 22ha

ounders Michael and Annabelle Waugh deliberately accumulated a series of old dryland, ow-yielding Barossa vineyards back in the '70s, aiming to produce wines of unusual depth of flavour and character. They succeeded handsomely in this aim, achieving icon status and stratospheric prices in the US, making the opinions of Australian scribes irrelevant. The Waughs retired in 2018 and the business was purchased by a group headed by Sydney-based immy Chen.

4 **Barossa Valley Mataro 2020** The savoury, dried sage signature of mataro is well married to the satsuma plums and blackberries of ripe Seppeltsfield, eloquently backed by fine-grained American oak. A long finish of powder-fine tannin and bright acidity carries lingering rhubarb freshness that completely trumps its alcohol. Skilfully composed and great value. Cork | 15% alc. | To 2026 | $30 | TS

Groom

8 Langmeil Road, Tanunda, SA 5352 (postal) **T** (08) 8563 1101 **WWW**.groomwines.com
WINEMAKER Daryl Groom, Lisa Groom, Jeanette Marschall **EST**. 1997 **DOZENS** 2000 **VYDS** 27.8ha

The full name of the business is Marschall Groom Cellars, a venture owned by David and Jeanette Marschall and their 6 children, and Daryl and Lisa Groom and their 4 children. Daryl was a highly regarded winemaker at Penfolds before he moved to Geyser Peak in California. Years of discussion between the families resulted in the purchase of a 35ha block of bare land adjacent to Penfolds' 130yo Kalimna Vineyard.

94 **Bush Block Barossa Valley Zinfandel 2019** Spicy dark fruitcake and fruit-mince spice proclaim zin. Juicy blackberries and black cherries are well set off by nicely composed acidity and fine-ground tannins; dark chocolate oak an eloquent afterthought. Well played. Cork | 14.5% alc. | To 2039 | $30 | TS

Hesketh Wine Company

28 The Parade, Norwood, SA 5067 **T** (08) 8362 8622 **WWW**.heskethwinecompany.com.au
WINEMAKER James Lienert, Keeda Zilm, Andrew Hardy **EST**. 2006 **DOZENS** 40000

Headed by Jonathon Hesketh, this is part of WD Wines Pty Ltd, which also owns Parker Coonawarra Estate, St John's Road and Vickery Wines. Jonathon spent 7 years as the global sales and marketing manager of Wirra Wirra, and 2.5 as general manager of Distinguished Vineyards in NZ. He is also the son of Robert Hesketh, one of the key players in the development of many facets of the SA wine industry.

95 **Jimi's Ferment Limestone Coast Sauvignon Blanc 2019** Inspired by Sancerre and made by the same recipe, to sophisticated and stunning effect! The greatest sauvignons are more about mineral tension, structure and drive than overt fruit. Here, the chalk mineral structure of the Limestone Coast is brilliantly paired with malic acidity for an incredible finish of undeterred line and length. Impeccably engineered for the long haul. Screw cap | 12% alc. | To 2034 | $35 | TS

Hewitson

66 Seppeltsfield Road, Nuriootpa, SA 5355 **T** (08) 8212 6233 **WWW**.hewitson.com.au **OPEN** Mon, Fri, Sat 11-4.30 **WINEMAKER** Dean Hewitson **EST**. 1996 **DOZENS** 25000 **VYDS** 12ha

Dean Hewitson was a winemaker at Petaluma for 10 years, during which time he managed to do 3 vintages in France and one in Oregon, as well as undertaking his master's at the University of California, Davis. It is hardly surprising that the wines are immaculately made from a technical viewpoint.

97 **Monopole Mother Vine Barossa Valley Shiraz 2018** A clonal selection from a single vine planted in 1853, the subsequent plantings necessarily relatively young, but firing on all cylinders. It is a graceful wine with a silky texture, red and purple fruits foremost; the tannins superfine, the finish lingering, the aftertaste fresh. Lovely now or in 20+ years. Diam | 14% alc. | To 2038 | $150 | JH

95 **Gun Metal Eden Valley Riesling 2020** Single vineyard. A replay – at an even higher level – of 2019's drought-induced abysmal yields, yet an even better outcome: depth of flavour with refreshing acidity. Screw cap | 12.5% alc. | To 2030 | $28 | JH

Jacob's Creek

2129 Barossa Valley Way, Rowland Flat, SA 5352 **T** (08) 8521 3000 **www.jacobscreek.com**
OPEN 7 days 10-4.30 **WINEMAKER** Dan Swincer **EST.** 1973 **DOZENS** 5700000 **VYDS** 740ha

Jacob's Creek (owned by Pernod Ricard) is one of the largest-selling brands in the world, and the global success of the base range has had the perverse effect of prejudicing many critics and wine writers who sometimes fail to objectively look behind the label and taste what is in fact in the glass.

97 **1819 The Birth of Johann Barossa Coonawarra Shiraz Cabernet 2018** A blend of monumental promise, declared from the outset in the deepest, vibrant purple hue. Coiled up tight, a powerful core of black fruits calls for considerable time to burst from its shell. French oak offers exacting support, rightly building structure before flavour, setting off superfine, enduring tannins. Line, length and integrity on another plane. Come back in 20 years. Cork | 14.7% alc. | To 2048 | $80 | TS

Kaesler Wines

Barossa Valley Way, Nuriootpa, SA 5355 **T** (08) 8562 4488 **www.kaesler.com.au** **OPEN** 7 days 11-5
WINEMAKER Reid Bosward, Stephen Dew **EST.** 1990 **DOZENS** 20000 **VYDS** 36ha

The first members of the Kaesler family settled in the Barossa Valley in 1845. The vineyards date back to 1893, but the Kaesler family ownership ended in 1968. Kaesler Wines was eventually acquired by a small group of investment bankers (who have since purchased Yarra Yering), in conjunction with former Flying Winemaker Reid Bosward and wife Bindy. Reid's experience shows through in the wines.

94 **Stonehorse Clare Valley Riesling 2017** It's fresh as a spring day, with the florals to prove it. A gently spiced, citrussy spread of Meyer lemon with grapefruit pith. No signs of age, although the palate has softened, the acidity is neat and while it falls short on the finish, it's a lovely drink. Screw cap | 12.5% alc. | To 2025 | $25 | JF

Old Vine Barossa Valley Semillon 2020 Energetic and intense, this is a concentrated, taut and pristine expression of Barossa floor semillon. Wild lemon and Granny Smith apple are accented with subtle varietal lanolin notes, cut with the lively acidity of cool nights that illuminates a bright, long finish. Grand potential. Screw cap | 11.5% alc. | To 2035 | $25 | TS

Langmeil Winery

Cnr Langmeil Road/Para Road, Tanunda, SA 5352 **T** (08) 8563 2595 **www.langmeilwinery.com.au**
OPEN 7 days 10-4 **WINEMAKER** Paul Lindner **EST.** 1996 **VYDS** 33.12ha

Langmeil Winery, owned and operated by the Lindner family, is home to what may be the world's oldest surviving shiraz vineyard, The Freedom 1843. It was planted by Christian Auricht, a blacksmith who fled religious persecution in his native Prussia and sought a new life for his family in Australia. The historic, now renovated, site was once an important trading post and is also the location of the Orphan Bank Vineyard.

90 **Three Gardens Viognier Marsanne Roussanne 2020** Ripe nectarine and grapefruit are brushed with subtle lemon blossom aromatics and subtly underscored with the hazelnut cream nuances of partial barrel maturation. A finish of medium length is braced with a little more firm phenolic grip than it needs, but nonetheless a good result for the price. Screw cap | 13% alc. | To 2022 | $20 | TS

Laughing Jack

194 Stonewell Road, Marananga, SA 5355 **T** (08) 8562 3878 **www.laughingjackwines.com.au**
OPEN By appt **WINEMAKER** Shawn Kalleske **EST.** 1999 **DOZENS** 5000 **VYDS** 38.88ha

The Kalleske family has many branches in the Barossa Valley. Laughing Jack is owned by Shawn, Nathan, Ian and Carol Kalleske, and Linda Schroeter. As any Australian knows, the kookaburra is also called the laughing jackass, and there is a resident flock of kookaburras in the stands of blue and red gums surrounding the vineyards.

5 **Moppa Hill Gold Seam Barossa Valley Cabernet Sauvignon 2018** Serious Barossa cabernet, coiled, tense and enduring. Deep, vibrant purple. Impeccably varietal: tiny, crunchy black/redcurrants, blackberries and cassis. Top-class French oak deployed confidently yet with the utmost care. Bright, natural acid line and fantastic persistence make for a cellaring special. Screw cap | 14.5% alc. | To 2048 | $40 | TS

ʌagpie Estate  

ɔlf Binder, Cnr Seppeltsfield Road/Stelzer Road, Stonewell, SA 5352 **T** (08) 8562 3300 **WW**.magpieestate.com **OPEN** At Rolf Binder **WINEMAKER** Rolf Binder, Noel Young **EST.** 1993 **ɔZENS** 16000 **VYDS** 16ha

partnership between 2 Rhône-philes: Barossa winemaker Rolf Binder and UK wine npresario Noel Young. Fruit is sourced from a group of select growers, with the acquisition f the Smalltown Vineyard in Ebenezer providing estate-grown fruit from the 2017 vintage. ach fruit batch is kept separate, giving the winemakers more blending options. The intent to make wines that have a sense of place and show true Barossa characters, wines that are omplex with a degree of elegance.

2 **Small Town Barossa Valley Shiraz 2019** There's a succulent, rich and fleshy breadth to Rolf Binder's reds, exemplified here in a generous and enticing take on Ebenezer. Packed with licorice and black fruits of all descriptions. The fine, fluffy tannins of pressings unite with dark- and milk-chocolate oak and tangy acidity to bring definition to a luscious and long finish. Screw cap | 14% alc. | To 2024 | $25 | TS

ʌichael Hall Wines 

03 Langmeil Road, Tanunda, SA 5352 **T** 0419 126 290 **www**.michaelhallwines.com **OPEN** Fri–Sat 11–5 r by appt **WINEMAKER** Michael Hall **EST.** 2008 **DOZENS** 2500

or reasons no longer relevant (however interesting) Michael Hall was once a jewellery aluer for Sotheby's in Switzerland. He came to Australia in 2001 to pursue winemaking – lifelong interest. He is now involved full-time with his eponymous brand and the wines are ighly impressive.

6 **Piccadilly and Lenswood Adelaide Hills Chardonnay 2019** Two blocks in Lenswood and Piccadilly Valley provide excellent fruit, wild barrel fermented and matured for 11 months in oak, of which 25% was new. The fruit remains the main focus, delicious white nectarine flavours of the utmost purity, delicately spicy and textured, with energy to spare in the exit. Superb. Screw cap | 13.7% alc. | To 2027 | $50 | TL

4 **Sang de Pigeon Adelaide Hills Chardonnay 2019** Wild-yeast fermented in barrel. Matured on lees for 11 months in a good percentage of new French oak, which has given some gingery spice over to the wine in a good way, without dominating the citrus and white nectarine fruit senses. Finishes with a vibrant upward lift. Screw cap | 13.6% alc. | To 2026 | $30 | TL

Ɔrlando 

arossa Valley Way, Rowland Flat, SA 5352 **T** (08) 8521 3111 **www**.pernod-ricard-winemakers.com **/INEMAKER** Ben Thoman **EST.** 1847 **DOZENS** 10000 **VYDS** 14ha

Ɔrlando is the parent who has been separated from its child, Jacob's Creek. While Orlando is ɔver 170 years old, Jacob's Creek is little more than 45 years old. For what are doubtless sound narketing reasons, Orlando aided and abetted the separation, but the average consumer is ınlikely to understand the logic and, if truth be known, is unlikely to care.

97 **Centenary Hill Barossa Shiraz 2016** The fragrant, exotic spice of century-old Barossa vines is something to behold, heightened magnificently by carefully gauged whole-bunch fermentation. Classy, polished dark chocolate oak sits just below the fruit at every moment throughout a finish of incredible persistence and undeviating line. Quite phenomenal. Screw cap | 14.8% alc. | To 2038 | $70 | TS

96 **Jacaranda Ridge Coonawarra Cabernet Sauvignon 2016** Quintessential Coonawarra cabernet of power and promise. Deep wells of blackcurrant, blackberry and cassis take on strong licorice reflections in 2016, generously bolstered by rich coffee bean and high-cocoa dark chocolate oak. Masterfully assembled, a veritable army of fine tannins carry the finish very straight and long. Cork | 14.5% alc. | To 2046 | $65 | TS

NSW SA VIC WA TAS QLD

Penfolds

★★★★★

30 Tanunda Road, Nuriootpa, SA 5355 P16 **T** (08) 8568 8408 **www.penfolds.com** **OPEN** 7 days 10-5
WINEMAKER Peter Gago **EST.** 1844

Penfolds is the star in the crown of Treasury Wine Estates (TWE) but its history predates the formation of TWE by close on 170 years. Its shape has changed in terms of its vineyards, its management, its passing parade of great winemakers and its wines. There is no other single winery brand in the New or the Old World with the depth and breadth of Penfolds. Retail prices range from less than $20 to $950 for Grange, which is the cornerstone, produced every year, albeit with the volume determined by the quality of the vintage, not by cash flow.

99 **Yattarna Bin 144 Chardonnay 2018** Winner of 2 awards in the *Wine Companion 2022*: White Wine of the Year and one of three joint winners for Chardonnay of the Year. An ultra-cool climate blend of Tasmania, Tumbarumba and Adelaide Hills fruit wastes no time in setting the terms of engagement with a wine of infinite class. The flinty/smoky aromas introducing an almost painful intensity on the mercurial palate, a celebration of white-fleshed stone fruits. It has made light work of 8 months in 100% new French oak. Struts its stuff without a care in the world. Screw cap | 13% alc. | To 2033 $175 | JH | ♥

98 **Reserve Bin A Adelaide Hills Chardonnay 2019** Hand picked, whole-bunch pressed, part direct to barriques for wild ferment and 100% mlf, the balance via tank for brief settling before 8 months in French oak (80% new). A beautifully detailed chardonnay, white peach and pink grapefruit plus supple creamy cashew run through the very long palate. Rubs shoulders with the best in the land. Screw cap | 13% alc. | To 2030 | $125 | JH

96 **Bin 51 Eden Valley Riesling 2020** The low yield and cool conditions from Jan through to harvest hav resulted in a wine humming with the full box and dice of citrus blossoms and flavours; perfectly poised acidity promises a long future. Top class wine. Screw cap | 12% alc. | To 2030 | $40 | JH

Peter Lehmann

★★★★★

Para Road, Tanunda, SA 5352 **T** (08) 8565 9555 **www.peterlehmannwines.com** **OPEN** By appt
WINEMAKER Nigel Westblade, Tim Dolan, Brett Smith, Brooke Blair **EST.** 1979 **DOZENS** 750000

The seemingly indestructible Peter Lehmann (the person) died in June 2013, laying the seeds for what became the last step in the sale of the minority Lehmann family ownership in the company. The Hess Group of California had acquired control in '03 (leaving part of the capita with the Lehmann family) but a decade later it became apparent that Hess wished to quit its holding. Various suitors put their case forward but Margaret Lehmann (Peter's widow) wantec ongoing family, not corporate, ownership. Casella thus was able to make the successful bid in November '14.

97 **Wigan Eden Valley Riesling 2016** Wigan is king of Eden Valley riesling and yet again one of the top releases of the year. Still a magnificent straw green at just 5yo, it's at that magic moment where primary and secondary characters unite in equal measure. All the fresh lime and Granny Smith apple of youth, backed by rising buttery, spicy, roast almond maturity. Brilliant acid line charges an astonishing finish that lasts for 30 seconds. Yes, I timed it! For all it represents, this might just be th bargain of the year. Screw cap | 11% alc. | To 2031 | $35 | TS

VSV Valley View Road Barossa Valley Shiraz 2018 This is a great example of the Barossa Valley at its best, marrying elegance with high-definition shiraz. The palate is long, balanced, and, above all els fresh. Screw cap | 14.5% alc. | To 2038 | $60 | JH

Stonewell Barossa Shiraz 2017 Lehmann's depth of reach into Barossa's finest sites is in evidence here, upholding the style and greatness of its flagship, even in a cooler season. A magnificently full vibrant purple hue, it's packed with compact, dense, crunchy, bright black fruits of all kinds, dresse in a gown of finely woven tannins. High-cocoa dark chocolate French oak has been perfectly tuned to the season. Integrity and persistence define great longevity. Screw cap | 14.5% alc. | To 2042 $100 | TS

96 **Margaret Barossa Semillon 2015** An impossibly pale straw green. Shot with cut grass, fresh lemon, Granny Smith apple skin. Building preserved lemon, buttered toast and subtle nutmeg. Crystalline acidity electrifies an exceedingly long finish. The Hunter is king of dry semillon and Margaret is its only true rival. Screw cap | 10.3% alc. | To 2035 | $35 | TS | ♥

95 **H&V Eden Valley Riesling 2020** Pitch-perfect Eden Valley riesling of impeccable precision. Textboo lime, lemon and Granny Smith apple. This low-yielding season has delivered fantastic concentratio and all the energy of cool nights is captured in shimmering acidity. The skill of the Lehmann team in managing phenolics is exemplified in 2020, making this one of the rieslings of the vintage. Captivating from the outset and it will live long, if you can keep your hands off it! Screw cap | 11% alc. | To 2030 | $25 | TS

94 **The Bond Barossa Grenache 2018** Graceful and accurate Barossa grenache in an enticingly medium-bodied guise. Alluring signature raspberry, poached strawberry and rhubarb fruit is the focus, sensitively and subtly supported by seasoned French oak, building more in texture than flavour. Finely crafted tannins carry a long finish. The definition of Barossa grenache. Screw cap | 14% alc. | To 2025 | $25 | TS

H&V Barossa Valley Cabernet Sauvignon 2019 H&V has been an exciting tier for Lehmann from the outset, and this is a very strong release. A crunchy and compelling cabernet of impressively full, vibrant purple hue. Bright blackcurrant and cassis fruit takes a rightful lead, confidently backed by a chassis of firm, fine tannins, engineered to go the distance. Screw cap | 14.5% alc. | To 2034 | $25 | TS

'urple Hands Wines

tisans Wine Room, 64 Murray Street, Tanunda, SA 5352 **T** 0401 988 185
ww.purplehandswines.com.au **WINEMAKER** Craig Stansborough **EST.** 2006 **DOZENS** 3000 **VYDS** 14ha

ıis is a partnership between Craig Stansborough, who provides the winemaking know-how ıd an 8ha vineyard of shiraz (northwest of Williamstown in a cooler corner of the southern arossa), and Mark Slade, who provides the passion. Don't ask me (James) how this works – lon't know – but I do know they are producing outstanding single-vineyard wines (the 'enache is contract-grown) of quite remarkable elegance.

5 **Old Vine Barossa Valley Grenache 2019** Old bush vines, 35% whole bunch, matured in used puncheons for 10 months. The wine is medium bodied and perfectly balanced, the flavours of red and purple fruit held in a gently savoury net of fine tannins. It's akin to a high-quality Rhône wine with no confection, and will live for years. Screw cap | 14% alc. | To 2029 | $30 | JH

4 **Barossa Valley Shiraz 2018** From the Stansborough vineyard in Williamstown, this is signature southern Barossa shiraz of density and definition, at a party-friendly price. Fantastic accuracy of blackberry, blueberry and black cherry fruit is the hero. Whole bunches and oak have been sensitively played to elevate the fruit profile. Bright acidity and fine tannins draw out a long finish. Screw cap | 14% alc. | To 2028 | $30 | TS

:ogers & Rufus

Eden Valley Road, Angaston, SA 5353 **T** (08) 8561 3200 **www**.rogersandrufus.com
NEMAKER Sam Wigan **EST.** 2009

ıis is a decidedly under-the-bedcover partnership between Robert Hill-Smith and his ımediate family, and Rupert and Jo Clevely – Rupert is the former Veuve Clicquot director Australia but now runs gastro pub group Geronimo Inns in London. Late in 2008 the Hill-niths and Clevelys decided (in their words) 'to do something fun together with a serious dip Euro-styled dry and savoury delicate rosé using 3 site-specific, old, low-yielding, dry-grown 'enache sites from the Barossa floor'.

Grenache of Barossa Rosé 2020 With its pretty, pale salmon hue and understated pear and strawberry hull nuances, Rogers & Rufus defines the elegant end of the Barossa Valley rosé continuum. Primary and graceful, it carries refined and subtle acidity and just the right level of delicate phenolic tension. For those who appreciate that less is indeed more with rosé. Screw cap | 12% alc. | To 2021 | $23 | TS

olf Binder

r Seppeltsfield Road/Stelzer Road, Tanunda, SA 5352 **T** (08) 8562 3300 **www**.rolfbinder.com
EN Mon–Sat 10–4.30, Sun on long weekends **WINEMAKER** Rolf Binder, Christa Deans, Harry ntzarapis **EST.** 1955 **DOZENS** 28000 **VYDS** 110ha

winery steeped in family tradition and Barossa history, Rolf Binder and sister Christa Deans e following their father's philosophy, using primarily estate-grown fruit from their own neyards located in various districts of the Barossa. A vineyard acquisition in the Vine Vale ea has provided the family with centenarian shiraz vines planted in the 1890s, in fact parent nes to the Hanisch Shiraz. In 2019 Rolf and Christa celebrated 25 consecutive vintages, ırely a unique record achievement for a brother/sister winemaking team.

5 **Heysen Barossa Valley Shiraz 2018** Binder's fabled Heysen vineyard has delivered a fantastic and characterful Barossa shiraz in 2018, brilliantly capturing tremendous depth without sacrificing brightness or definition. Crunchy black fruits of all kinds play to a backdrop of fresh licorice straps, wonderfully bright acidity and fine tannin confidence. Good value. Screw cap | 14% alc. | To 2033 | $75 | TS

St Hallett

St Hallett Road, Tanunda, SA 5352 **T** (08) 8563 7000 **www**.sthallett.com.au **OPEN** 7 days 10-5
WINEMAKER Helen McCarthy **EST.** 1944 **DOZENS** 210000

St Hallett sources all their grapes from within the Barossa GI and is synonymous with the region's icon variety – shiraz. Old Block is the ultra-premium leader of the band, supported by Blackwell. The winemaking team continues to explore the geographical, geological and climatic diversity of the Barossa, manifested through individual processing of all vineyards and single-vineyard releases.

96 **Higher Earth Eden Valley Syrah 2018** St Hallett's deep reach into the great sites of the Eden Valley and its blending wizardry forge an exquisite take on this great vintage. At once concentrated and vibrant, spice-laden and enduring. Impeccably constructed tannins draw out a finish of pinpoint detail and lingering persistence. Screw cap | 14.5% alc. | To 2038 | $60 | TS

Saltram 

Murray Street, Angaston, SA 5353 **T** (08) 8561 0200 **www**.saltramwines.com.au **OPEN** 7 days 10-5
WINEMAKER Alex MacKenzie **EST.** 1859 **DOZENS** 150000

There is no doubt that Saltram has taken strides towards regaining the reputation it held 30 o so years ago. Grape sourcing has come back to the Barossa Valley for the flagship wines. The red wines, in particular, have enjoyed great show success over the past decade with No. 1 Shiraz and Mamre Brook leading the charge.

97 **No. 1 Barossa Shiraz 2017** Cool years like these bless the Barossa with brightness, definition, integrity and endurance. Saltram has captured all the focus and poise of the season while upholdin incredible black fruit density. Epic tannins entwine with magnificent natural acidity. High-class French oak sits just behind the fruit at every moment of a very long finish. Screw cap | 14.5% alc. To 2047 | $100 | TS

96 **Pepperjack Premium Cut Barossa Cabernet Shiraz 2018** Richard Mattner unites the big-gun region of SA to celebrate the quintessential Aussie blend. It rejoices in all there is to love about the past, present and future of Australian winemaking. A deep core of blackcurrant and blackberry fruit stretches tall and long, upheld by a fine splay of intricate tannins and bright acidity. Outstanding line and unwavering persistence make for one of the best reds at this price on the shelves today. Screw cap | 14.5% alc. | To 2038 | $40 | TS

Mr Pickwick's Particular Tawny NV Incredible depth and age are proclaimed in a magnificently savoury and complex tawny. Roast nuts, dried fruits and spice of all kinds flow into dark chocolate, caramel, fruit-mince spice and warm hearth. Long age has concentrated acidity, bringing liveliness amid judicious sweetness on a finish of monumental carry. Cork | 19.5% alc. | $75 | TS

94 **Pepperjack Barossa Cabernet Sauvignon 2019** A core of glossy, crunchy blackcurrant fruit is backe by licorice and high-cocoa dark chocolate oak. Varietal definition and endurance are captured in ar exciting interplay between bright acidity and confident, fine-grained tannin that coast effortlessly through a long finish, promising great things in a decade. Screw cap | 14.5% alc. | To 2037 | $30 | TS

Schwarz Wine Company 

PO Box 779, Tanunda, SA 5352 **T** 0417 881 923 **www**.schwarzwineco.com.au **OPEN** At Vino Lokal, Tanunda **WINEMAKER** Jason Schwarz **EST.** 2001 **DOZENS** 5000

The economical name is appropriate for a business that started with 1t of grapes making 2 hogsheads of wine in 2001. The following year half a tonne of grenache was added. In '05, grape sale agreements with another (larger) winery were terminated, freeing up 1.8ha of shiraz and 0.8ha of grenache. From this point on things moved more quickly: in '06 Jason formed a partnership (Biscay Road Vintners) with Peter Schell of Spinifex, giving them total control over production.

95 **The Grower Barossa Valley Shiraz 2019** An impressively full, vibrant purple hue heralds a carefully blended shiraz that unites the districts of the central Barossa Valley. Judicious deployment of whole bunches and seasoned French oak upholds a resolute focus on classy blackberry, black cherry and satsuma plum fruit, nuanced with black pepper and violets. Finely textured tannins and bright acidity carry a finish of impressive line, length and potential. Great value. Screw cap | 14.2% alc. | To 2034 | $30 | TS

eppeltsfield

0 Seppeltsfield Road, Seppeltsfield, SA 5355 **T** (08) 8568 6200 **www**.seppeltsfield.com.au
EN 7 days 10.30-5 **WINEMAKER** Fiona Donald, Charlie Seppelt, Matthew Pick, Henry Slattery
r. 1851 **DOZENS** 50000 **VYDS** 1500ha

ıe historic Seppeltsfield property and its bounty of old fortified wines was originally ıtablished by the Seppelt family in 1851. Warren Randall now owns in excess of 90% of its ıpital. Randall, former sparkling winemaker for Seppelt Great Western in the 1980s, has led revival of Seppeltsfield, gradually restoring the heritage-listed property. The estate's 1888 ravity cellar is back in full operation and a tourism village has been established. The 100 Year ld Paras have no parallel anywhere else in the world and the conjunction of 100 years of evoted stewardship and climate/terroir/varieties have had an outcome that can never, ever, e duplicated.

Para Tawny 2000 The legendary fortified outfit of Seppeltsfield achieves epic levels of complexity even in single-vintage blends. All the profound power, detail and impeccable balance we've come to expect, but what truly sets off the millennium vintage is line and length that hover unwavering for more than 60 seconds. Absolutely splendid. Screw cap | 20.8% alc. | $88 | TS

Para Rare Tawny NV 170 years of legendary history and masterful expertise are woven into the intricate fabric of this phenomenal blend, not to mention one of the finest colletions of old blending material in the country. Its flavour allusions would fill a page, and then some, so I won't even start. Exquisite detail of grand old age, seamlessly united with younger material and perfectly integrated spirit. A mesmerising finish holds undeterred for 90 seconds and counting! Screw cap | 20.2% alc. | $75 | TS

ister's Run

) Box 148, McLaren Vale, SA 5171 **T** (08) 8323 8979 **www**.sistersrun.com.au
INEMAKER Elena Brooks **EST**. 2001

ister's Run is now part of the Brooks family empire, the highly experienced Elena Brooks ıaking the wines. The Stiletto and Boot on the label are those of Elena, and the motto 'he truth is in the vineyard, but the proof is in the glass' is, I (James) would guess, the work of ıarketer extraordinaire husband Zar Brooks.

3 **Bethlehem Block Gomersal Barossa Cabernet Sauvignon 2018** Give this a little air and it will open up before your eyes. It has lovely ripe cabernet fruit in the blackberry spectrum with a delicate waft of mint-choc in the rear. Simple, well-toned fruit and even structures across the palate offer a good-value, easygoing cabernet that is ready to go now and might surprise with a few more years in its quiver. Screw cap | 14% alc. | To 2028 | $23 | TL

2 **Calvary Hill Lyndoch Barossa Shiraz 2018** Rich, chocolatey plum, sweeter Asian and baking spices all weave together in this delicious, straight-up-and-down Barossa shiraz. Whatever oak has been employed offers a backdrop only. Simple pleasures. Screw cap | 14.5% alc. | To 2026 | $23 | TL

'eusner

5 Samuel Road, Nuriootpa, SA 5355 **T** (08) 8562 4147 **www**.teusner.com.au **OPEN** By appt
INEMAKER Kym Teusner **EST**. 2001 **DOZENS** 30000 **VYDS** 120ha

eusner is a partnership between former Torbreck winemaker Kym Teusner and Javier Moll, nd is typical of the new wave of winemakers determined to protect very old, low-yielding, ry-grown Barossa vines. The winery approach is based on lees ageing, little racking, no ning or filtration and no new American oak. As each year passes, the consistency, quality ınd range) of the wines increases; there must be an end point, but it's not easy to guess vhen, or even if, it will be reached.

6 **Avatar Barossa Valley 2019** A longstanding mainstay of the ever-diversifying Teusner stable, Avatar has always been one of my Barossa GMS go-tos. Teusner's mastery in championing fruit and integrity before oak and artefact make for exquisite definition and detail, multi-dextrous food-matching versatility and downright deliciousness. Oh, and nothing is lost in longevity, either. Its true greatness is confirmed by superfine tannins, effortless fruit persistence and impeccable, understated oak support. Screw cap | 14.5% alc. | To 2029 | $40 | TS

4 **Bilmore Barossa Valley Shiraz 2019** I've long marvelled at Kym Teusner's superpower of delivering glossy density with vitality and accuracy. Few in the Barossa do this with such consistency across every varietal and price point. Particularly noble at the value end of the pool. The depth and just-picked freshness of sweet black fruits that he has conjured here is not often seen without spending double the dollars. Long, fine-grained, jubilant and irresistible. Yes, please. Screw cap | 14.5% alc. | To 2025 | $27 | TS

The Willows Vineyard

310 Light Pass Road, Light Pass, SA 5355 **T** (08) 8562 1080 **www.thewillowsvineyard.com.au**
OPEN Wed-Mon 10.30-4.30 **WINEMAKER** Peter Scholz **EST.** 1989 **DOZENS** 6000 **VYDS** 42.74ha

The Scholz family have been grapegrowers for generations and they have over 40ha of vineyards, selling part of the crop. Current-generation winemaker Peter Scholz makes rich, ripe, velvety wines, some marketed with some bottle age.

94 **Barossa Valley Riesling 2020** A tense and refined Barossa floor riesling, thanks partly to cool gully breezes of nearby Eden Valley, partly to early picking and not least to the fanatical expertise of Pete Scholz. The 2020 represents a benchmark at any price and a bargain at $20. Purity of exact lime, lemon and Granny Smith apple, magnificently honed acid line, persistence and phenolic manageme rarely seen in this drought season. Kudos. Screw cap | 11.3% alc. | To 2030 | $20 | TS

Thistledown Wines

c/- Revenir, Peacock Road North, Lenswood, SA 5240 **T** 0405 038 757 **www.thistledownwines.com**
WINEMAKER Giles Cooke MW **EST.** 2010 **DOZENS** 10000

Founders Giles Cooke and Fergal Tynan are UK-based MWs with a collective 40+ years' experience in buying and selling Australian wines. They have been friends since 1998, when they met over a pint of beer on the evening before their first master of wine course. In 2006 they established Alliance Wine Australia, which purchases Australian wines for distribution in the UK; they took the process one step further when Alliance began the Thistledown Wines venture. This focuses on Barossa Valley shiraz, McLaren Vale grenache, and smaller amounts of Adelaide Hills chardonnay.

97 **Sands of Time Old Vine Single Vineyard Blewitt Springs McLaren Vale Grenache 2019** Grenache of the Year 2022. The beauty of this wine belies the label. Among the finest reds in Australia. A turbid mid ruby. Damson plum, strawberry, clove, rosemary, anise and turmeric flavours. A sandy weld of impeccable tannins, drawn taut and long by a beam of saline freshness. Ethereal and transparent. A blessed Australian site and an uncanny semblance to Rayas. Diam | 14.5% alc. | To 2027 | $80 | NG | ♥

96 **Cunning Plan McLaren Vale Shiraz 2019** A full-bodied shiraz that reflects cunning winemaking. Whole-berry fermentation has put a rich gloss on the palate without overloading the tannin structure. The predominantly black berry fruit is shot through with licorice, spice and an airbrush of dark chocolate. Screw cap | 14.5% alc. | To 2039 | $30 | JH

Thorn-Clarke Wines

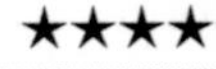

266 Gawler Park Road, Angaston, SA 5353 **T** (08) 8564 3036 **www.thornclarkewines.com.au**
OPEN Thurs-Mon 10-4, Tues-Wed by appt **WINEMAKER** Peter Kelly **EST.** 1987 **DOZENS** 90000 **VYDS** 222ha

Established by David and Cheryl Clarke (née Thorn), and son Sam,Thorn-Clarke is one of the largest family-owned estate-based businesses in the Barossa. Their winery is close to the border between the Barossa and Eden valleys. In all 4 of their vineyards careful soil mapping has resulted in matching of variety and site, with all the major varieties represented. The quality of grapes retained for the Thorn-Clarke label has resulted in a succession of trophy and gold medal–winning wines at very competitive prices.

93 **Sandpiper Eden Valley Riesling 2020** Testimony to Pete Kelly's dexterity with riesling, this is a carefully tuned release, boasting a detail and elegance rarely seen in this vintage. Fresh, pure, signature lemon, lime and Granny Smith apple are graced with subtle nuances of star fruit. Gracefu crystalline acidity glides through a long finish. Enticing from the outset, and poised for a confident future. Screw cap | 11.5% alc. | To 2030 | $22 | TS

91 **Sandpiper Barossa Rosé 2020** It takes a steady hand to craft such elegance and refinement from Barossa mataro. Fresh, vibrant strawberry and raspberry fruit is eloquenty presented with vibrant acid drive that elongates a refreshing finish, sensitively backed with fine-ground tannins. Medium salmon crimson. Pretty and enticing in equal measure. Screw cap | 11.5% alc. | To 2021 | $22 | TS

Torbreck Vintners

348 Roennfeldt Road, Marananga, SA 5352 **T** (08) 8562 4155 **www.torbreck.com** **OPEN** 7 days 10-5
WINEMAKER Ian Hongell, Scott McDonald **EST.** 1994 **DOZENS** 70000 **VYDS** 112ha

Torbreck Vintners was already one of Australia's best-known producers of high-quality red wine when, in Sept 2013, wealthy Californian entrepreneur and vintner Peter Kight (of Quivira ıeyards) acquired 100% ownership of the business. The brand structure remains as before: top quartet led by The Laird (single-vineyard shiraz), RunRig (shiraz/viognier), The Factor iraz) and Descendant (shiraz/viognier).

Hillside Vineyard Barossa Valley Shiraz Roussanne 2019 Inspired by co-fermenting shiraz and viognier, demonstrating that roussanne is equally adept at the counterintuitive art of deepening the colour of shiraz to a profound black purple. Violets and spice elevate a dense core of satsuma plum, compact blackberries and fresh, warm licorice straps. Grand density, magnificently structured with a burst of fine tannins. Superb depth for dollar, with integrity that many Barossa shiraz wines (with another digit in the price tag) could only dream of. Screw cap | 14.5% alc. | To 2027 | $32 | TS

ırkey Flat

hany Road, Tanunda, SA 5352 **T** (08) 8563 2851 **www.**turkeyflat.com.au **OPEN** 7 days 11-5 **EMAKER** Mark Bulman **EST.** 1990 **DOZENS** 20 000 **VYDS** 47.83ha

e establishment date of Turkey Flat is given as 1990 but it might equally have been 1870 thereabouts), when the Schulz family purchased the Turkey Flat Vineyard; or 1847, when vineyard was first planted – to the very old shiraz that still grows there today and the a of equally old grenache. Plantings and varieties have since expanded significantly. The siness is run by sole proprietor Christie Schulz.

Barossa Valley Grenache 2019 Primarily produced from 100+yo estate vines, it is a model of consistent style, quality and supreme value. Its balance is marvellous, appropriate for a wine that makes its statement of juicy red berries, Turkish delight and rose petals without fuss or fanfare. Screw cap | 14.5% alc. | To 2029 | $45 | JH | ♥

Barossa Valley White 2019 Marsanne/roussanne of breathtakingly sophisticated and intellectual heights. Uber-reductive, a veritable keg of gunpowder with lit fuse! Tension, energy and cut like the Barossa floor has never seen. It unites this maelstrom with astonishing coherence, grace and persistence that holds undeviating for a full 30 seconds. And it will live for decades. If you love grand cru Burgundy, you'll adore this. Outclasses its price point by a country mile! Screw cap | 13.1% alc. | To 2034 | $25 | TS

Butchers Block Barossa Valley Red Blend 2019 Grenache, shiraz and mataro from original vines on the estate Bethany vineyard. Marrying the exuberant, fragrant, exotic and herbal lift of whole-bunch fermentation while upholding varietal definition, integrity and graceful palate flow is an art form. Mark Bulman has again shown his talent in this bargain blend. Flamboyant and multi-faceted in its complexity, drawing into a tail of fine-grained texture and polished persistence. Benchmark bargain. Screw cap | 14.5% alc. | To 2024 | $22 | TS

topos

Box 764, Tanunda, SA 5352 **T** 0409 351 166 **www.**utopos.com.au **WINEMAKER** Kym Teusner **EST.** 2015 **ENS** 1500 **VYDS** 20ha

e fates were kind when Neil Panuja, a friend of Kym Teusner's from 'the big smoke', said had the wish (and the cash) to get into fine-wine production and asked that Kym keep an out for something special. Shortly thereafter a vineyard that Kym had coveted from his ginnings in the Barossa Valley came onto the market. The depleted stony soils consistently oduce low yields of high-quality grapes that loudly proclaim their Barossan origin. The actor is the site-driven savoury balance that Kym says he always longs for. The name they ve given the business is the root word of Utopia. Everything is just so right: great vineyard, eat winemaker, great story, great packaging.

Shiraz 2018 Uniting the personalities of Marananga and Greenock, this is a shiraz at once delightfully plush and polished and magnificently structured for the cellar. Waves of deep black fruits, black pastilles and licorice wash with high-cocoa dark chocolate oak. Lively acidity and fantastically defined tannins sweep through a very long finish. One bottle was cork scalped. Screw caps please. Cork | 14.5% alc. | To 2036 | $65 | TS

ION

den Valley

ɔrbes & Forbes

Hooper Road, Strathalbyn, SA 5255 **T** 0478 391 304 **www.**forbeswine.com.au **OPEN** At Taste Eden ley, Angaston **WINEMAKER** Colin Forbes **EST.** 2008 **DOZENS** 1200 **VYDS** 3.2ha

s venture is owned by Colin and Robert Forbes, and their respective partners. Colin says, ave been in the industry for a frightening length of time', beginning with Thomas Hardy &

Sons in 1974. Colin is particularly attached to riesling and the property owned by the partne in Eden Valley has 2ha of the variety (plus 0.5ha each of merlot and cabernet sauvignon and 0.2ha of cabernet franc).

95 **Cellar Matured Eden Valley Riesling 2011** Wonderful mature Eden Valley riesling. The wet and cool 2011 season furnished layers of apricot, persimmon and spice thanks to the onset of botrytis. These have morphed beautifully with the buttery, nutty, honeyed complexity of a decade of age. Held pristine under screw cap, it's maintained a spine of energetic, cool-vintage acidity that draws out a long, crystalline and still energetic finish. Screw cap | 12.5% alc. | To 2026 | $32 | TS

Heathvale

300 Saw Pit Gully Road, via Keyneton, SA 5353 **T** 0407 600 487 www.heathvale.com **OPEN** By appt
WINEMAKER Trevor March, Tony Carapetis (Consultant) **EST.** 1987 **DOZENS** 1200 **VYDS** 9ha

The origins of Heathvale go back to 1865; the vineyards were re-established in 1987 and consisted of shiraz, cabernet sauvignon, riesling, sagrantino and tempranillo. Between 2011 and '12 fundamental changes for the better took place – stylish new labels are but an outwar sign of the far more important changes to wine style, with the winemaking now under the control of consultant Tony Carapetis (Quattro Mano) and the introduction of French oak. The tempranillo is soon to be planted over to shiraz.

95 **Estate Barossa Cabernet Sauvignon 2019** Capturing cabernet of impeccable ripeness and integrit in the challenging drought season of 2019 took tenacity and talent in equal measure. Under the circumstances, this wine is a rare and effortless translation of happy vines. Glorious, polished cass and blackcurrant declare exacting varietal credentials, impeccably framed in fine-grained tannins dark chocolate French oak and perfectly judged acidity. It's a delight from the outset, and will only improve over the medium term. Screw cap | 13.3% alc. | To 2029 | $27 | TS

94 **Estate Barossa Shiraz 2019** Tended and raised with care and sensitivity, here is an Eden Valley shir of presence, fullness and poise. Compact and crunchy, dense blackberry, satsuma plum fruit and licorice take the lead. Oak is sensitively deployed, building structure and persistence more than flavour. Fine-ground tannins furnish a long life. Screw cap | 14.5% alc. | To 2034 | $27 | TS

Henschke

1428 Keyneton Road, Keyneton, SA 5353 **T** (08) 8564 8223 www.henschke.com.au **OPEN** Mon-Sat 9-4.
WINEMAKER Stephen Henschke **EST.** 1868 **DOZENS** 30000 **VYDS** 100ha

Henschke is the foremost medium-sized wine producer in Australia. Stephen and Prue Henschk have taken a crown jewel and polished it to an even greater brilliance. Year on year they have quietly added labels for single vineyards, single varieties or blends. Recognition as Winery o the Year in the 2021 *Companion* was arguably long overdue.

97 **Julius Eden Valley Riesling 2020** Filled with citrus and apple blossom on the notably expressive bouquet that leads into a delicious palate, its elfin grace and purity defying the impact of drought. Forget food matching – this lime- and lemon-infused wine has such elegance and balance it sets it own stage. Screw cap | 12% alc. | To 2035 | $45 | JH

96 **Peggy's Hill Eden Valley Riesling 2020** Delicious riesling in full-on Eden Valley style, lemon blosso aromas swiftly replayed on the juicy yet tightly framed palate. Makes life difficult for the taster such as I, with dozens of wines remaining to be tasted, prohibiting the impulse to swallow just a little bit Screw cap | 12% alc. | To 2030 | $25 | JH

Irvine

63 Valley Road, Angaston, SA 5353 **T** (08) 8564 1110 www.irvinewines.com.au
WINEMAKER Peter Miles **EST.** 1983 **DOZENS** 15000 **VYDS** 111ha

When James (Jim) Irvine established his eponymous winery, he chose a singularly difficult focus for the business: the production of great merlot from the Eden Valley. Throughout the years of establishment, and indeed thereafter, he was a much-in-demand consultant, bobbi up in all sorts of places. Yet when he decided to sell the business in 2014, its potential was greatly increased with the dowry provided by the purchasing Wade and Miles families.

94 **Spring Hill Eden Valley Riesling 2020** Endowed with amiable flesh and spice while upholding impressive tension and zest, this is an impeccably assembled riesling at a fantastic price. Picked a precisely the right instant, shot with exact lime and Granny Smith apple fruit. Fine-tuned phenolic control is tricky at this level of concentration, calling for a steady hand in both the vines and the winery. Screw cap | 12.2% alc. | To 2030 | $24 | TS

eo Buring ★★★★☆

rt Highway, Nuriootpa, SA 5355 **T** 1300 651 650 **WINEMAKER** Tom Shanahan **EST.** 1934

tween 1965 and 2000 Leo Buring was Australia's foremost producer of rieslings, with a h legacy left by former winemaker John Vickery. After veering away from its core business o other varietal wines, it has now refocused on riesling. Top of the range are the Leopold rwent Valley and the Leonay Eden Valley rieslings, supported by Clare Valley and Eden lley rieslings at significantly lower prices, and expanding its wings to Tasmania and WA.

Leonay Eden Valley Riesling 2020 Another epic chapter in the odyssey that is Leonay, possessing an effortless purity, precision and endurance that appear nothing short of supernatural here. All the lemon, lime and Granny Smith apple hallmarks of the greats are here in full measure, but rather than swaying to the tropical mood of the season, it upholds breathtaking dignity, even tilting toward white pepper. Concentration meets elegance. Acid line is mesmerising, driving a finish that holds undeterred and undiminished for a full 45 seconds. Screw cap | 11.5% alc. | To 2045 | $40 | TS | ♥

Eden Valley Dry Riesling 2020 Exotic allusions, intense concentration and bright acid drive make this a quintessential expression of 2020 in the Eden Valley. Glimpses of frangipani and kiwifruit dart about a tense core of pure lime, lemon and Granny Smith apple. It holds drive and presence through a long finish, sustained by enduring acidity, with the concentration and confidence to quash very subtle phenolic structure. What a wine, what a price! Screw cap | 11.5% alc. | To 2027 | $20 | TS

ax & Me  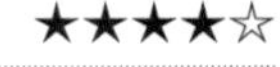

en Valley Hotel, 11 Murray Street, Eden Valley, SA 5235 **T** 0403 250 331 **www**.maxandme.com.au
EN 7 days 12-5 **WINEMAKER** Philip Lehmann **EST.** 2011 **DOZENS** 900 **VYDS** 10.22ha

ax is the name of a German shepherd/whippet cross purchased by Phil Lehmann from the PCA pound and who introduced Phil to his wife-to-be Sarah during a visit to the Barossa. dog lover from way back, she fell in love with Max; Phil made it clear she wouldn't get ax unless she married him (Phil). They converted his vineyard to (non-certified) organic anagement, with no herbicides and only copper/sulphur sprays. The benefits are self-ident, reflected in the high quality of the wines made since '11.

Woodcarvers Vineyard Mirooloo Road Eden Valley Riesling 2020 High-toned blossom/flower scents fill the bouquet. The palate is juicy with Rose's lime juice and crisp, clear acidity to give balance now and join forces with the fruit as the wine gains texture and complexity with prolonged cellaring. Screw cap | 12.9% alc. | To 2032 | $30 | JH

ountadam  

gh Eden Road, Eden Valley, SA 5235 **T** 0427 089 836 **www**.mountadam.com.au **OPEN** By appt
NEMAKER Phil Lehmann **EST.** 1972 **DOZENS** 30000 **VYDS** 148ha

unded by the late David Wynn for the benefit of winemaker son Adam, Mountadam was omewhat surprisingly) purchased by Möet Hennessy Wine Estates in 2000. In 2005, ountadam returned to family ownership when it was purchased by David and Jenni Brown om Adelaide. Phil Lehmann stepped into the role of chief winemaker in 2019, with extensive perience in the Barossa and Eden valleys at Peter Lehmann, Yalumba, Teusner, WD Wines d his own label Max & Me.

Eden Valley Cabernet Sauvignon 2018 Cabernet was evidently in a happy place high in the Mountadam vineyard in '18, displaying an integrity, balance and concentration that can only come from long, slow ripening. It's at once varietal and generous, with a textbook array of red/blackcurrants, cassis, roast capsicum and cedar trailing all the way to the distant horizon. Ripe, fine, confident tannins and seamless, bright acidity guarantee longevity. For all it represents, this is a bargain. Screw cap | 15% alc. | To 2038 | $28 | TS

alumba 

Eden Valley Road, Angaston, SA 5353 **T** (08) 8561 3200 **www**.yalumba.com **OPEN** 7 days 10-5
NEMAKER Louisa Rose (chief), Kevin Glastonbury, Natalie Cleghorn, Sam Wigan, Heather Fraser, ll John, Teresa Heuzenroeder **EST.** 1849 **DOZENS** 930000 **VYDS** 180ha

wned and run by the Hill-Smith family, Yalumba has a long commitment to quality and great sion in its selection of vineyard sites, new varieties and brands. It has always been a serious ayer at the top end of full-bodied Australian reds and was a pioneer in the use of screw caps.

The synergy of the range of brands, varieties and prices is lustrous. A founding member of Australia's First Families of Wine.

97 **Carriage Block Dry Grown Barossa Valley Grenache 2017** The ruby colour is just gaining a little da brick red around the rims, and the red fruits that cover the rainbow of cherry to raspberry notes a just showing the introduction of delicate and delicious sourness. Adults-only palate complexity. There's a clarity and directness to the palate, pure grenache juiciness and a tender touch of tanni finish. The whole picture of this wine is bright and beautiful. Cork | 13.5% alc. | To 2027 | $50 |

96 **Vine Vale Barossa Valley Grenache 2019** The medium-bodied, red-fruited persona of Barossa grenache is compelling, all the more so when lifted by the fragrance and exotic spice of whole-bur fermentation. With the full, glorious detail accurately preserved under screw cap, this is a joyous celebration of dark raspberries, wild strawberries, rosehip and incense. Super-fine tannins are perfectly matched to its fragrant mood. Benchmark. Screw cap | 14% alc. | To 2029 | $40 | TS

The Signature Barossa Cabernet Sauvignon Shiraz 2017 Embracing Yalumba's deep reach in to th great sites of the Barossa, this cool vintage was sourced entirely from the Valley floor. Compact, concentrated and exact, cabernet's varietal integrity takes a bright, fragrant, compelling lead. Impressive black-fruit depth is backed by a splay of superfine, enduring tannins. Testimony to the blending wizardry of Yalumba, this is one of the wines of the vintage and one of the greats of the hallowed Signature lineage. Cork | 14.5% alc. | To 2052 | $65 | TS

94 **FSW Wrattonbully Botrytis Viognier 2020** Viognier's unctuous glacé apricot finds an enticing plac between the honey and exotic spice of botrytis. Carefully handled fermentation makes for a pristi style of impressive line and length. 2020 furnished the acidity to uphold freshness and poise. One of the greatest under this label yet. Screw cap | 10.5% alc. | To 2030 | $30 | TS

ZONE

Fleurieu

REGION

Kangaroo Island

The Islander Estate Vineyards 

78 Gum Creek Road, Cygnet River, SA 5223 **T** (08) 8553 9008 **www**.iev.com.au **OPEN** Thurs-Tues 12-
WINEMAKER Jacques Lurton, Yale Norris **EST.** 2000 **DOZENS** 8000 **VYDS** 10ha

Established by one of the most famous Flying Winemakers in the world, Bordeaux-born and trained and part-time Australian resident Jacques Lurton. The property was ravaged by the terrible bushfire that devastated many (not all) parts of the island in January 2020. The fire consumed the entire vineyard and its infrastructure, the house, the laboratory and the office which became the sacrificial lamb slowing the fire sufficiently to allow the protection of the winery and its stock of bottled wine, and the wines still in barrel and tank. Long-time friend and business partner Yale Norris cut back every vine down to 20cm, hoping that shoots wou appear – many have done so, but far from all. If the regeneration ceases, the entire vineyard will be pulled out and replanted.

94 **Kangaroo Island Cabernet Sauvignon 2019** Here's a story in a bottle. After several years/viticultur challenges, this cabernet came to fruition for the first time in '19. A delicately teased cabernet, wit all the varietal character on the nose, beautiful clarity of flavour, medium-weighted concentration and a coat of classical tannins. But after finally doing its thing in '19, the KI bushfires of '20 destro the block and it sadly won't see the light of day again. Get into it while you can – once in a lifetime Screw cap | 13.5% alc. | To 2028 | $30 | TL

REGION

Langhorne Creek

Bleasdale Vineyards

1640 Langhorne Creek Road, Langhorne Creek, SA 5255 **T** (08) 8537 4000 **www**.bleasdale.com.au
OPEN 7 days 10-5 **WINEMAKER** Paul Hotker, Matt Laube **EST.** 1850 **VYDS** 45ha

This is one of the most historic wineries in Australia; in 2020 it celebrated 170 years of continuous winemaking by the direct descendants of the founding Potts family. Bleasdale has completely revamped its labels and packaging, and has headed to the Adelaide Hills for sauvignon blanc, pinot gris and chardonnay under the direction of gifted winemaker Paul Hotker.

18 Year Old Rare Tawny Langhorne Creek NV A mid to deep amber rather than the heavier tawny expected in a wine of such age. It tells us of the freshness to follow, a hallmark of the wine, with vibrant baking spice, beautifully delicate timbered backdrops, the faintest of nutty rancio just appearing. Importantly, no cloying finish – rather, refreshing, clean and vibrant. Fabulous. Cork | 18.5% alc. | $79 | TL | ♥

Adelaide Hills Riesling 2020 Winemaker Paul Hotker has a way with riesling, far from the centre of the Bleasdale portfolio. There's a tactile feel to the wine that moves from lime juice painted on the surfaces of the mouth, to mouth-watering acidity. Low yields in this vintage is only part of the story. Screw cap | 11% alc. | To 2030 | $30 | JH

Frank Potts Langhorne Creek 2019 A great red blend, 69/17/8/6% cabernet sauvignon/malbec/merlot/petit verdot. Matured for 12 months in 25% new French oak barrels. Understated at first, though very deeply set in its bouquet with the darkest of berries and chocolate, working their layered magic on the palate. The regional imprint of cabernet is in the lead, plump and generous, with masterful integration of tannins. Screw cap | 14% alc. | To 2032 | $35 | TL

Second Innings Langhorne Creek Malbec 2019 Bleasdale can't put a foot wrong with malbec at whatever price point it chooses. This is flooded with plum varietal fruit, but also has the texture and back-palate structure that many malbecs miss out on. Winemaker Paul Hotker is a wiz. Screw cap | 14% alc. | To 2027 | $22 | JH | ♥

Generations Langhorne Creek Malbec 2019 Next-level malbec here, with all its varietal expectations fulfilled. Vibrant purple colour, violets and blue/black fruits, a whiff of iodine and a faint sense of Dutch licorice, without its bitterness. All of it swells on the palate, the tannins settling in underneath, fitting neatly with the flow of the wine. Many years ahead of it – decant for now. Screw cap | 14% alc. | To 2028 | $35 | TL | ♥

·emerton Wines  

Kent Town Road, Langhorne Creek, SA 5255 **T** (08) 8537 3093 **WWW**.bremerton.com.au **OPEN** 7 days
5 **WINEMAKER** Rebecca Willson **EST.** 1988 **DOZENS** 30 000 **VYDS** 120ha

·merton has been producing wines since 1988. Rebecca Willson (chief winemaker) and ·y Willson (marketing manager) were the first sisters in Australia to manage and run a ·ery. With 120ha of premium vineyards (80% of which goes into their own labels), they grow ·ernet sauvignon, shiraz, verdelho, chardonnay, sauvignon blanc, malbec, merlot, fiano, ·ciano and petit verdot.

Old Adam Langhorne Creek Shiraz 2018 Twenty months maturation in French and American oak. Deep and dark from the outset, the best shiraz of the season is steered into this rich, chewy, chocolatey style, the American oak a necessary element. As is the traditional regional stamp, it is earthy and rich with full-bodied intent, yet not overly weighed down by heavy tannin blocks. Will gather itself more completely over the next decade. Diam | 14.5% alc. | To 2030 | $56 | TL

B.O.V. 2017 Only 4 barrels selected across the traditional regional red program, bringing together a blend of 60/20/20% shiraz/cabernet sauvignon/malbec. The nose is fully engaged in its Aussie claret-like mode, oak entwined, and a faint waft of dark mint chocolate. Dried orange even, if you dwell too long, which is easy to do. Full bodied and layered with fine peppery tannins. Drink it now if you are into heavyweight pleasures, or wait another 5 years to watch it even out and open up further. Diam | 14.5% alc. | To 2030 | $14.50 | TL

Special Release Langhorne Creek Shiraz 2020 No added preservatives. Picked ripe yet still vibrant, aged on full solids for 4–5 months to tease out the natural colours and tannins that enable it to fulfil its total, rich shiraz plum fruit experience without other additions needed. The flavour power is spot-on. Ripe and chewy tannins become part of the concentration on the palate. Neatly done. Satisfying. Screw cap | 15% alc. | To 2024 | $24 | TL

Special Release Langhorne Creek Barbera 2019 Powdery dark chocolate, with a layer of crushed crimson, blackberries, seams of savoury spices and fruit flavours on the palate, even a notion of nori seaweed/salines. The variety's natural acidity rocks the finish – while getting there is full of interest. Makes you crave for paté and antipasti treats. Screw cap | 14.5% alc. | To 2025 | $24 | TL

Special Release Langhorne Creek Malbec 2019 With malbec one of Langhorne Creek's finest treats, this sits within the Bremerton Special Release range with a certain pride. To begin, think of the aromas of a dark Negroni, a slice of orange peel included. The flavours follow, without of course the same amaro bitterness, though rich with body and captivating mouth feels. Screw cap | 14.5% alc. | To 2028 | $24 | TL

Lake Breeze Wines Best Value Winery 2022 ★★★★

Step Road, Langhorne Creek, SA 5255 **T** (08) 8537 3017 **www.lakebreeze.com.au** **OPEN** 7 days 10-5
WINEMAKER Greg Follett **EST.** 1987 **DOZENS** 20000 **VYDS** 90ha

The Folletts have been farmers at Langhorne Creek since 1880, and grapegrowers since the 1930s. Part of the grape production is sold, but the quality of the Lake Breeze wines is exemplary, with the red wines particularly appealing.

97 **Langhorne Creek Cabernet Sauvignon 2019** The epitome of signature Langhorne Creek cabernet The quality of the fruit is evident from the outset. It's matured for 20 months in French oak, 40% n yet this is subservient to the black/blueberry aromas and flavours, some regional dark choc-mint adding a tiny whiff behind. Everything knits together perfectly and the varietal tannin structures lie in exact tune with the whole. When it works so well, wines like this just come alive. Screw cap 14% alc. | To 2031 | $29 | TL | ♥

95 **Langhorne Creek Rosato 2020** While you might think this kind of rosé is just a fun summer splash the reality is that 50% of the grenache base for the wine comes from 90yo vines. Aged without oak for 2–3 months on its lees, it displays all the expected white-tipped strawberry flavours, with strikingly next-level spice and pithiness. Worthy of reward. Screw cap | 13% alc. | To 2024 | $19 | TL

Section 54 Langhorne Creek Shiraz 2019 The portion of old-vine fruit from the region's traditiona flood plains plays a major role in this wine, revealed in a sophisticated, mature style of shiraz. Plur and spice, bright and lifted, with some French oak influence providing a calm and secure foundat underneath, the rich tannins tightening everything. An absolute pleasure to drink. Screw cap | 14.5% alc. | To 2028 | $28 | TL

94 **Old Vine Langhorne Creek Grenache 2020** The vibrant garnet colour is the first thing that grabs attention. The rest is all about the rustic appeal of grenache: cherry flesh and skins, crumbled dry earth, and a lively palate where the fruit, spice and tannins are pretty energetic. Makes your mout stand to attention. Lick-your-lips good. Screw cap | 14.5% alc. | To 2028 | $29 | TL

Project Wine

83 Pioneer Road, Angas Plains, SA 5255 **T** (08) 8537 0600 **www.projectwine.com.au**
WINEMAKER Peter Pollard **EST.** 2001 **DOZENS** 155000

Originally designed as a contract winemaking facility, Project Wine has developed a sales a distribution arm that has rapidly developed markets both domestic and overseas. Located in Langhorne Creek, it sources fruit from most key SA wine regions, including McLaren Vale, Barossa Valley and Adelaide Hills. The diversity of grape sourcing allows the winery to produce a wide range of products under the Tail Spin, Pioneer Road, Parson's Paddock, Birc Eye View and Angas & Bremer labels.

92 **Angas & Bremer Langhorne Creek Shiraz 2018** Big, rich, old-school shiraz that's spent 18 months maturing in American oak, 25% new. It's a testament to the fruit involved that it stands up to the sweet vanilla/spice barrel impact. In the end, that's the style and for the price, what you see is wh you get. Screw cap | 14.8% alc. | To 2026 | $25 | TL

Watkins

59 Grants Gully Road, Chandlers Hill, SA, 5159 **T** 0422 418 845 **www.watkins.wine** **OPEN** Fri 1-7 Sat-Sun 11-5 **WINEMAKER** Sam Watkins **EST.** 2019 **DOZENS** 2500 **VYDS** 120ha

Sibling trio Ben, Sam and Jo Watkins, under the guidance of parents David and Ros Watkins, have established Watkins as a new label based at their Chandlers Hill winery and cellar door They are tapping into their well-established estate vineyards there and in Langhorne Creek: both regions' vines are maritime influenced, with afternoon sea breezes tempering summe ripening temperatures. The top-of-the-ridge cellar door overlooks rolling hillside vines on o side and St Vincent Gulf on the other. (TL)

91 **Langhorne Creek Shiraz 2019** Estate grown, 10 parcels in the winery, maturing in a range of most larger, old oak vessels with some newer barrels also in the mix. Rich, ripe shiraz as well as that faint background of mint and chocolate, more milk than dark. Chewy palate textures while the fru lingers. A good-value shiraz with genuine regional expression. Screw cap | 14.2% alc. | To 2025 $20 | TL

Langhorne Creek Cabernet Sauvignon 2019 Estate cabernet, with 10% merlot. Matured in Americ and French barrels. Ripe cabernet fruit characters, some earthiness which expresses itself in a fai mint/eucalyptus forest feel. Not holding back in the tannin department, thick yet soft. Screw cap 14.2% alc. | To 2026 | $20 | TL

cLaren Vale

gove Family Winemakers

mark Avenue, Renmark, SA 5341 **T** (08) 8580 3100 **WWW**.angove.com.au **OPEN** Mon-Fri 10-5, 10-4, Sun & public hols 10-3 **WINEMAKER** Tony Ingle, Paul Kernich, Ben Horley, Amelia Anspach 1886 **DOZENS** 1 million **VYDS** 300ha

nded in 1886, Angove Family Winemakers is one of Australia's most successful wine nesses – a 5th-generation family company with a tradition of excellence and an eye for the re. The McLaren Vale cellar door is nestled in the family's certified organic and biodynamic boys Vineyard on Chalk Hill Road, the Renmark cellar door (home of the St Agnes Distillery) ookmark Avenue.

The Medhyk McLaren Vale Shiraz 2017 Disciplined attention to detail has produced a perfectly balanced medium- to full-bodied palate with supple, juicy and smooth plum and blackberry fruit; a hint of dark chocolate; integrated cedary oak and built-in tannins. It sings from start to finish. Screw cap | 14.5% alc. | To 2042 | $65 | JH | ♥

helion Wine

t Andrews Terrace, Willunga, SA 5172 **T** 0404 390 840 **WWW**.aphelionwine.com.au **OPEN** By appt **MAKER** Rob Mack **EST.** 2014 **DOZENS** 2500

elion Wine is akin to a miniature painting done with single-hair paintbrushes. When you sider the credentials of winemaker Rob Mack, supported by co-founder wife Louise des Mack, great oaks come to mind. Rob has accumulated 2 degrees, scaled the ghts of direct marketing as wine buyer and planner for Laithwaites Wine People, and nt 18 months as production manager for Direct Wines in McLaren Vale. Rob was voted ng Gun of Wine '18 and Aphelion won Best Small Producer at the McLaren Vale Wine w in '19.

Pir Blewitt Springs Chenin Blanc 2020 50% was barrel fermented and left on lees for several months, conferring textural detail as much as imparting a chord of authoritative match-struck tension. Brilliant aromas of lemon drop crystals, cheese rind, quince, dried hay and lanolin. The acidity, pungent, juicy and electrifying, towing this very long like an elastic band pulling the saliva from the back of the mouth, unlike most Australian wines that roll across the front. Exceptional. Screw cap | 13.4% alc. | To 2027 | $35 | NG

Project 5255 Welkin Langhorne Creek Malbec 2020 Part of a creative project out of Langhorne Creek, for which 3 winemakers were offered access to the region's fruit for the first time. From the Wenzel vineyard, 2 separate blocks were co-fermented, then steered via a range of vinification techniques and maturation vessels. The deep purple colour is astounding, aromas of masses of violets, flint, and dark plum cake with baking spices. The palate then turns to pure dark plum and garden herb freshness. High intensity flavours, yet with an ease of flow and fine tannin grip. An exciting malbec expression. Screw cap | 13.5% alc. | To 2030 | $28 | TL

kkers

-220 Seaview Road, McLaren Vale, SA 5171 **T** 0408 807 568 **WWW**.bekkerswine.com **OPEN** Thurs-Sat or by appt **WINEMAKER** Emmanuelle Bekkers **EST.** 2010 **DOZENS** 1500 **VYDS** 18ha

s brings together two high-performing, highly experienced and highly credentialled iness and life partners. Toby Bekkers graduated with an honours degree in applied science griculture from the University of Adelaide, and over the ensuing years has had broad-ging responsibilities as general manager of Paxton Wines in McLaren Vale, and as a leading onent of organic and biodynamic viticulture. Emmanuelle Bekkers was born in Bandol in south of France, and gained 2 university degrees, in biochemistry and oenology, before king for the Hardys in the south of France, which led her to Australia and a wide-ranging eer, including Chalk Hill.

McLaren Vale Grenache 2019 A shimmering light ruby. A textural polyglot, incandescent, lit by its delicate shades of fruit as much as its textural precision and savouriness. Nebbiolo meets pinot on the nose. This is what grenache does at the highest calibre. Sandalwood, Darjeeling, bergamot, crushed rose, pomegranate, tamarind and kirsch. Long and gritty in the best sense. Febrile. Tensile. Would love to see it in bigger oak. A beautiful stain on the memory bank. Screw cap | 14.5% alc. | To 2026 | $90 | NG

Bondar Wines ⚲ ★★★★

148 McMurtrie Road, McLaren Vale, SA 5171 **T** 0147 888 553 **www**.bondarwines.com.au **OPEN** Fri-Mc 11-5 **WINEMAKER** Andre Bondar **EST.** 2013 **DOZENS** 3000 **VYDS** 13.5ha

Andre Bondar and Selina Kelly were in search of a vineyard capable of producing great shir and the Rayner Vineyard had all the answers: a ridge bisecting the land, Blewitt Springs sar on the eastern side; and the Seaview, heavier clay loam soils over limestone on the westerr side. The vineyard has been substantially reworked and includes 10ha of shiraz, with smalle amounts of grenache, mataro, touriga, carignan, cinsault and counoise.

96 **Rayner Vineyard Shiraz 2019** While I am optimistic about grenache in these parts, I often find the style of shiraz monochromatic. Not in these hands. Despite the heat spikes of a warm year, the sa blocks across the vineyard thrived. A cool finish to the season, providing perk. All things done rig picking window, use of bunches (20%) and a long extraction. Mostly older wood. A textural tour de force. Violet, blueberry, nori, peppery acidity and a licorella tannin line so fine that it could be threaded through the eye of a needle. A beautiful wine. Screw cap | 14% alc. | To 2032 | $45

95 **Adelaide Hills Chardonnay 2019** While I find the array of Mediterranean varieties at this estate compelling, this is exceptional chardonnay from the Hills. Riveting! A core of nougat/cashew/var pod/oatmeal cream, with rims of mineral pungency and a frame flecked by stone-fruit references sweet and savoury/sour. A thrilling tussle between extract, energy and structural binds. Screw ca 13% alc. | To 2027 | $35 | NG | ♥

Chalk Hill

58 Field Street, McLaren Vale, SA 5171 **T** (08) 8323 6400 **www**.chalkhillwines.com.au **WINEMAKER** Renae Hirsch **EST.** 1973 **DOZENS** 20000 **VYDS** 89ha

The growth of Chalk Hill has accelerated after passing from parents John and Diana Harvey grapegrowing sons Jock and Tom. Both are heavily involved in wine industry affairs. Furthe acquisitions mean the vineyards now span each district of McLaren Vale, planted to both the exotic (savagnin, barbera and sangiovese) and mainstream (shiraz, cabernet sauvignon grenache, chardonnay and cabernet franc).

98 **Alpha Crucis Old Vine McLaren Vale Grenache 2019** Predominantly 90yo vines in Blewitt Spring 10% whole-bunch ferment, matured in 3rd-use French oak for 11 months. Brilliant crimson hue: an intensely perfumed bouquet floats into the juicy palate of pomegranate, red cherry and spice A gorgeous grenache. Superlative length. Screw cap | 14% alc. | To 2025 | $55 | JH | ♥

97 **Clarendon McLaren Vale Syrah 2018** A fine example of temperate-grown shiraz. The bouquet pulsates with black cherry, spice, licorice and pepper, the palate opening with a fanfare of dark f and finishes with fine-grained tannins. The drinking window is open, and won't close for decades Screw cap | 14% alc. | To 2048 | $48 | JH

94 **Alpha Crucis Titan McLaren Vale Shiraz 2019** For the price, this is very hard to top. Even if it were double, it would be impressive. Dark cherry, violet, bitter chocolate, Dutch licorice and clove. Very regional fruit profile, but discernibly noble and far from the madding crowd by virtue of its lithe, slinky tannin profile and well-applied oak; a welcome belt of savoury restraint. Screw cap 14.5% alc. | To 2028 | $30 | NG

Cooter & Cooter

82 Almond Grove Road, Whites Valley, SA 5172 **T** 0438 766 178 **www**.cooter.com.au **WINEMAKER** James Cooter, Kimberly Cooter **EST.** 2012 **DOZENS** 800 **VYDS** 23ha

The cursive script on the Cooter & Cooter wine labels was that of various Cooter family businesses operating in SA since 1847. Their vineyard, on the southern slopes of Whites Valley, has 18ha of shiraz and 3ha of cabernet sauvignon planted in 1996, and 2ha of old-vi grenache planted in the '50s. They also buy Clare Valley grapes to make riesling.

93 **McLaren Vale Shiraz 2019** Artisanal and rewarding producer delivering wines of great value, amp fruit and – most importantly, somewhere this warm – properly extracted tannins. Boysenberry, mulberry, licorice and blackberry. Juicy, grapey and pulpy, with the teeming fruit galvanised into a savoury whole by that prized slatey tannic kit, gently briary and herbal. Screw cap | 14% alc. To 2028 | $25 | NG

›riole ★★★★★

'feys Road, McLaren Vale, SA 5171 **T** (08) 8323 8305 **www**.coriole.com **OPEN** Mon-Fri 10-5, ıds & public hols 11-5 **WINEMAKER** Duncan Lloyd **EST.** 1967 **DOZENS** 30000 **VYDS** 48.5ha

ıle Coriole was established in 1967, the cellar door and gardens date back to 1860, when original farm houses that now constitute the cellar door were built. The oldest shiraz ning part of the estate plantings was planted in 1917, and since '85, Coriole has been Australian pioneer of sangiovese and the Italian white variety fiano. Coriole celebrated 50th anniversary in 2019, presumably counting from the year of its first commercial e release.

Rubato Reserve McLaren Vale Fiano 2020 Other White of the Year 2022. This is a superb wine. No two ways about it. Possibly the finest fiano in the country, attesting to the nobility of the variety as much as the promise it shows in the Vale. A monument of mineral pungency, offset by a shimmering veil of tangerine, quince, lemon balm, orange verbena, anise and apricot pith. Ripe. Viscous. Real drive. Phenomenal length. Power, vivacity and weightlessness all at once. Stunning! Screw cap | 13% alc. | To 2024 | $50 | NG | ♥

Arenberg  

Osborn Road, McLaren Vale, SA 5171 **T** (08) 8329 4888 **www**.darenberg.com.au **OPEN** 7 days 10-5 **EMAKER** Chester Osborn, Jack Walton **EST.** 1912 **DOZENS** 220000 **VYDS** 197.2ha

:hing, they say, succeeds like success. Few operations in Australia fit this dictum better n d'Arenberg, which has kept its 100+yo heritage while moving into the 21st century with r and élan. d'Arenberg celebrated 100 years of family grapegrowing in '12 on the property t houses the winery and the iconic cube cellar door and restaurant. A founding member of stralia's First Families of Wine.

The Peppermint Paddock Sparkling Chambourcin Graciano NV No lack of punch, nor froth. Delicious in a carnal sort of way: rhubarb, amaro bitters, ground pepper, dill and sour black cherry, all succulent and savoury as a wonderful meld of poise and mindless joy. Mouthfilling and mercifully, perceivably dry. Twin top | 14% alc. | $30 | NG

›dgy Brothers 

Box 655, McLaren Vale, SA 5171 **T** 0450 000 373 **www**.dodgybrotherswines.com **EMAKER** Wes Pearson **EST.** 2010 **DOZENS** 2000

s is a partnership between Canadian-born Flying Winemaker Wes Pearson, viticulturist :er Bolte and grapegrower Peter Sommerville. Wes, among other qualifications, is a sensory alyst at the Australian Wine Research Institute. Peter Bolte has over 35 vintages in McLaren e under his belt and was the original Dodgy Brother. Peter Sommerville's vineyard provides ›ernet sauvignon, cabernet franc and petit verdot for the Dodgy Brothers Bordeaux blend.

Juxtaposed Old Vine Old Block Sherry Vineyard Blewitt Springs Shiraz 2019 The Blewitt Springs postcode is tattooed across the elevated florals, bouncy blue/boysenberry scents and detailed sandy tannins. Elastic tension here, the fruit reverberating as it pulls the saliva from the back of the mouth while making one hungry. Dried seaweed, olive, salami and a satchel of clove, cardamom and pepper, too. Long and energetic. Lithe and sinuous. Frisky and engaging. Fine. Screw cap | 14.5% alc. | To 2028 | $37 | NG

Juxtaposed Old Vine Sandy Corner Block Wait Vineyard Blewitt Springs Shiraz 2019 The duo of single-plot Blewitt Springs shiraz wines under this label is exceptional. There is possibly no better expression of upper-echelon warm-climate shiraz at such a price. Premium pedigree. The salient point of differentiation being the riper, coffee grind/mocha elements of this cuvée and its darker-fruit aspersions. Minimal handling is manifest in juicy acidity and moreish precise tannins. Lots of kombu umami elements, conferring warmth and savouriness. A real pulse and fine length. Screw cap | 14.5% alc. | To 2028 | $37 | NG

Juxtaposed Old Vine McLaren Vale Grenache 2019 A meld of fruit from the subzones that deify elegance when it comes to grenache in the Vale: Blewitt Springs and Clarendon. Savoury overall, with poached strawberry, white pepper and ample spice, strung taut across a briary patina of tannins, sandy and detailed. A spurt of freshness pulls it long. Real pinosity here. Superlative value! Screw cap | 14.3% alc. | To 2025 | $29 | NG

The Dilemma 2019 There is but a handful of producers that I would make my first call in the Vale. Dodgy Bros is entrenched as one of them. 57/43% cabernets sauvignon/franc each from noble single vineyards. We are clearly in the lap of a warm maritime zone, pulling this classic blend off with aplomb. Particularly in gentle hands, such as these. Piercing currant, bell pepper, spearmint, olive and hedgerow scents, splayed across some pliant sage-doused tannins. Screw cap | 13.9% alc. | To 2028 | $29 | NG

DogRidge Wine Company

129 Bagshaws Road, McLaren Flat, SA 5171 **T** (08) 8383 0140 **www.dogridge.com.au** **OPEN** Mon-Fri 11-5, Sat-Sun 12-4 **WINEMAKER** Fred Howard **EST.** 1991 **DOZENS** 18000 **VYDS** 56ha

This McLaren Flat vineyard is home to shiraz and grenache vines planted in the early 1940s as a source for Chateau Reynella fortified wines, and the vineyards now range from 2001 plantings to some of the oldest vines in the immediate district. Quality at one end, value-packed at the other end.

95 **Fortified Viognier NV** This is an idiosyncratic concept by virtue of the variety, historically seldom ever fortified. Excellent! The spirit is high grade and not sticking its alcohol beyond the warm flow chestnut, apricot pith, orange verbena, molasses and crème Catalan. Very long. Poised. Delicious Screw cap | 19% alc. | $25 | NG

DOWIE DOOLE

695 California Road, McLaren Vale, SA 5171 **T** 0459 101 372 **www.dowiedoole.com** **OPEN** 7 days 10 **WINEMAKER** Chris Thomas **EST.** 1995 **DOZENS** 25000 **VYDS** 90ha

DOWIE DOOLE was founded in 1995 by Drew Dowie and Norm Doole. They had been connected to the McLaren Vale community for many years as grapegrowers in the region. Vineyard management is now led by champions of sustainable viticulture practices Dave Gartelmann and Drew Dowie.

93 **McLaren Vale Rosé 2020** A gentle coral. Dry, with rosewater, sour cherry, raspberry, rosehip and cranberry scents popping along saline acid rails flecked with pumice. Finishes with a herbal inflection of rosemary, thyme and a twist of orange. This is a refined rosé serving up dangerous drinkability and impressive length. Screw cap | 12.7% alc. | To 2021 | $25 | NG

92 **C Blanc McLaren Vale Chenin Blanc 2020** As I taste through DOWIE DOOLE's solid suite of white wines, I appreciate the level of acidity; pleasantly fresh, rather than overtly tweaked. Granny Smit apple, lanolin, mint, a melody of citrus and dried pistachio. Supple across the mid palate, with so lees work conferring detail and warmth between the rails of freshness. Screw cap | 12.8% alc. | To 2025 | $25 | NG

Estate McLaren Vale Merlot 2018 Rich, plump, round and inimitably of the region in its saline war finish. Baked plum, Christmas cake, violet, hedgerow, olive and vanillan oak scents bustle about the mouth, the oak serving directives. Few surprises here, but poise and generosity in spades. Screw cap | 14% alc. | To 2027 | $25 | NG

90 **Estate Adelaide Hills Sauvignon Blanc 2020** A solid savvy from the Hills. Fuller bodied, with more ample fruit and attractive texture than most. Greengage, pine, lemon squash, gooseberry and redcurrant scents. Mercifully, no screeching acidity. Nothing overtly sweet/sour. Just a bright flov of dutifully ripe fruit and zesty freshness. Screw cap | 12.4% alc. | To 2021 | $20 | NG

Dune Wine

PO Box 9, McLaren Vale, SA 5171 **T** 0403 584 845 **www.dunewine.com** **WINEMAKER** Duncan Lloyd, Peter Lloyd **EST.** 2017 **DOZENS** 1700 **VYDS** 8ha

This is the project of Duncan and Peter Lloyd (of Coriole fame) using fruit sourced from a single vineyard in Blewitt Springs. The brothers grew up immersed in a world of wine, olive oil, illegal goat's cheese and great food. Both worked in kitchens from the age of 13 and continued to develop a love of good food and wine.

96 **Blewitt Springs McLaren Vale Shiraz 2019** Fermented with a mix of whole-bunch, whole-berry an crushed fruit. This really sings; it proclaims its Blewitt Springs birth with energetic, spicy, savoury notes threaded through predominantly black fruits, backed and lengthened by fine, but firm, tannins. Remarkable wine. Screw cap | 14% alc. | To 2034 | $26 | JH

Field Day

RSD1436 Meadows Road, Willunga, SA 5172 **T** 0428 581 177 **www.monterrawines.com.au** **WINEMAKER** Mike Farmilo, Nick Whiteway **EST.** 2014 **DOZENS** 20000 **VYDS** 15ha

Yet another venture by Canadian-born and raised (but long-term McLaren Vale resident) No Doole (in partnership with Mike Farmilo and Nick Whiteway). Field Day (formerly Loonie Win Co and before that, Monterra) has been a centre of activity in McLaren Vale in recent years.

Monterra Fleurieu Cabernets 2020 A blend of cabernet sauvignon and cabernet franc showing its blackcurrant and leafy aromatic side in a positive light. The is palate given proper diligence via a mouthful of varietal tannins. At this price, you're onto something. Screw cap | 13.5% alc. | To 2026 | $20 | TL

Colab and Bloom Adelaide Hills McLaren Vale Tempranillo 2020 Earthy, mineral, savoury elements coating soft plum and black cherry fruits. Varietal tannins wrap the palate, but they are soft and pliable and their texture is a definite part of this wine's expression. Screw cap | 14% alc. | To 2026 | $22 | TL

›x Creek Wines 

Malpas Road, McLaren Vale, SA 5171 **T** (08) 8557 0000 **WWW**.foxcreekwines.com **OPEN** 7 days 10-5
MAKER Ben Tanzer, Steven Soper **EST.** 1995 **DOZENS** 35000 **VYDS** 21ha

Creek has a winemaking history that dates back to 1984 when Helen and Dr Jim Watts chased a 32ha property in McLaren Vale. The winery has been upgraded to handle the anded production of Fox Creek, the increase a function of demand for the full-flavoured, ust red wines that make up the portfolio.

JSM McLaren Vale Shiraz Cabernet Sauvignon Cabernet Franc 2018 Cabernet franc adds so much to the kit, particularly in this warm-climate blend: a spicy, verdant lift of chilli, spearmint and dill, conferring a degree of refreshment. Otherwise, a salubrious band of cassis, violet, black cherry and anise brushed by well-wrought, sage-doused tannins. A sum far greater than its individual parts! An exercise in poise, effortless drinkability, serious value and great length. Kudos! Screw cap | 14.5% alc. | To 2028 | $29 | NG

›mtree Wines 

Elliot Road, McLaren Flat, SA 5171 **T** (08) 8323 0802 **WWW**.gemtreewines.com **OPEN** Fri-Tues
5 **WINEMAKER** Mike Brown, Joshua Waechter **EST.** 1998 **DOZENS** 90000 **VYDS** 123ha

mtree Wines is owned and operated by husband and wife team Melissa and Mike Brown. e (winemaker) and Melissa (viticulturist) firmly believe it is their responsibility to improve land for future generations, and the vineyards are farmed organically and biodynamically.

Small Batch McLaren Vale Marsanne 2020 By far the truest expression of marsanne I have tasted in Australia. Waxy, understated and effortless in a shy, medium-bodied way. Reliant on phenolics more than freshness: as it should be. Ebbs and flows across conversation and with what is on the plate. Lanolin, apricot pith and scents of dried straw before a tatami room is lain. A striking marsanne of immense purity and authenticity. Cork | 13% alc. | To 2025 | $35 | NG

›ounded Cru 

Ingoldby Road, McLaren Flat, SA 5052 **T** 0438897738 **WWW**.groundedcru.com.au **OPEN** By appt
MAKER Geoff Thompson, Matt Jackman **EST.** 2015 **DOZENS** 18000

ablished as a brand in 2015 with an inaugural release of wines in 2017, Grounded Cru draws t from high-quality vineyards in McLaren Vale, Langhorne Creek and the Adelaide Hills, ions that maker Geoff Thompson believes 'talk to each other' due to a complementary na of mesoclimates, soil types, rainfall, altitude and varying degrees of maritime influence. approach at Grounded Cru is one that seeks textural intrigue over obvious fruit, with opean styling melded to Australian generosity. (NG)

Cru McLaren Vale Grenache 2018 A gentle ruby hue, with orange zest, cherry bon-bon and molten strawberry aromas. Fibrous whole-bunch tannins, beautifully detailed, gently scrub the palate of any excess sweetness. This has a pinosity to it, with a thrust of extract and herbal freshness imparting balance and crunchy length. This address is marked by a consistent and indelible style of fine tannin management, complexity and an easygoing deliciousness. Screw cap | 14.1% alc. | To 2024 | $28 | NG

›donist Wines

e Range Road, McLaren Vale, SA 5171 **T** (08) 8323 8818 **WWW**.hedonistwines.com.au
MAKER Walter Clappis, Kimberly Cooter, James Cooter **EST.** 1982 **DOZENS** 18000 **VYDS** 35ha

ter Clappis has been making wine in McLaren Vale for 40 years, and over that time has n innumerable trophies and gold medals, including the prestigious George Mackey morial Trophy with his 2009 The Hedonist Shiraz, chosen as the best wine exported from tralia that year. The NASAA-certified organic and biodynamic estate plantings are the nerstones of the business.

92 **The Hedonist McLaren Vale Shiraz 2019** Aromas of crushed sooty rock, licorice straps, violet, blueberry and clove. A grind of pepper for lift. Salumi, too. A sumptuous wine that does not fall into the mould of a regional caricature. Plenty rich, but plenty fresh. Effortless, lithe and long. Screw cap | 14% alc. | To 2026 | $25 | NG

The Hedonist McLaren Vale Cabernet Sauvignon 2019 Plenty to like. Currant, red and black. A sheath of crushed mint, graphite and pencil shaving-clad tannins, pliant enough but soft enoug too, to facilitate early access. Pushy length. An easygoing cab with the hallmarks of something considerably more expensive. Screw cap | 14% alc. | To 2027 | $25 | NG

Hickinbotham Clarendon Vineyard

92 Brooks Road, Clarendon, SA 5157 **T** (08) 8383 7504 **www**.hickinbothamwines.com.au **OPEN** By app
WINEMAKER Chris Carpenter, Peter Fraser **EST.** 2012 **DOZENS** 4800 **VYDS** 87ha

Alan Hickinbotham established the vineyard bearing his name in 1971 when he planted dry-grown cabernet sauvignon and shiraz in contoured rows on the sloping site. In 2012 Clarendon and the stately sandstone house on the property were purchased by Jackson Family Wines; it is run as a separate business from Yangarra Estate Vineyard, with different winemaking teams and wines. The vineyards are undergoing biodynamic conversion.

97 **Trueman McLaren Vale Cabernet Sauvignon 2019** Flying winemaker Chris Carpenter is well verse in the sort of tannin management that defines his Californian expressions. Here, the piste is not as smooth, with a bit more edge to the framework; a little more greenery to the aromas. For the bette Cassis, pencil lead and dried tobacco leaf, to boot. The finish, long and thrumming; the tannic gris etching fine grooves of tension with each sip. This will age beautifully. Screw cap | 14.5% alc. | To 2034 | $75 | NG | ♥

96 **The Revivalist McLaren Vale Merlot 2019** This cuvée has shape-shifted. It's a more compact, mid-weighted and savoury experience than previous vintages. Attention to detail is a given here: hand picked, wild fermented and properly extracted. The oak, top-drawer. The tannins, detailed, finely wound, precise and laden with graphite. The length, compelling. Unrivalled by any other merlot bu perhaps, for Blue Poles in Margaret River. Stunning. Screw cap | 13.5% alc. | To 2032 | $75 | NG

The Nest McLaren Vale Cabernet Franc 2019 The quality of fruit, tannic precision and apposite application of oak under this banner are unequalled in Australia. Nobody else gets it quite as right. The budget and gear help, yet it is the viticulture and sites that are the foundation for everything else. Franc from a warm place, salvaging its sappy cavalcade of tannin, crunch and floral lift. Redcurrant, spearmint and chilli powder lace a finely tuned finish marked by a flourish of garden herb. Kerpow! Screw cap | 13.5% alc. | To 2031 | $75 | NG | ♥

Hither & Yon 

17 High Street, Willunga, SA 5172 **T** (08) 8556 2082 **www**.hitherandyon.com.au **OPEN** 7 days 11-4
WINEMAKER Malcom Leask, Richard Leask **EST.** 2012 **DOZENS** 10 000 **VYDS** 78ha

Brothers Richard and Malcolm Leask started Hither & Yon in 2012, the Old Jarvie label added in '16. The historic, tiny cellar door in Willunga has a vintage feel with a café and music event The Hither & Yon labels feature the brand's ampersand, with a different artist creating the artwork for each wine. Old Jarvie (www.oldjarvie.com.au) focuses on blends.

94 **Old Jarvie The Enforcer McLaren Vale Shiraz Malbec Mataro 2019** This blend works very well. Rich, textural and bright. Darker fruit persuasions, a verdant riff of herb and a ferruginous growl of smoked meat and iodine notes dousing the firm backbone of tannin. The choice of oak, smart: use 400L French puncheons. This is compact and dense; yet lithe and strident across the mouth. An innovative blend that makes for delicious drinking. Screw cap | 14.5% alc. | To 2028 | $30 | NG

Hugh Hamilton Wines

94 McMurtrie Road, McLaren Vale, SA 5171 **T** (08) 8323 8689 **www**.hughhamiltonwines.com.au
OPEN 7 days 11-5 **WINEMAKER** Nic Bourke **EST.** 1991 **DOZENS** 18 500 **VYDS** 21.4ha

In 2014, 5th-generation family member Hugh Hamilton handed over the reins to daughter Mary. She developed the irreverent black sheep packaging. The business continues to embrace both mainstream and alternative varieties. The cellar door is lined with the original jarrah from Vat 15 of the historic Hamilton's Ewell winery, the largest wooden vat ever built in the Southern Hemisphere.

95 **The Ruffian Liqueur Muscat NV** Date, orange verbena, cinnamon, molasses and an overall aura of a Moroccan souk. The average age of the blend is modest, rather than extremely old. This promote freshness amid the morass of exotic sweetness and textural detail. Viscous and generous, yet fresh and impressively long. Screw cap | 18% alc. | $30 | NG

kwell ⚲ ★★★★☆

Box 33, Sellicks Beach, SA 5174 **T** 0430 050 115 **WWW**.inkwellwines.com **OPEN** By appt
EMAKER Dudley Brown **EST.** 2003 **DOZENS** 800 **VYDS** 12ha

well was born in 2003 when Dudley Brown bought a rundown vineyard on California Road. inherited 5ha of neglected shiraz, and planted an additional 7ha to viognier, zinfandel and ritage shiraz clones. The 5-year restoration of the old vines and establishment of the new ds like the ultimate handbook for aspiring vignerons, particularly those who are prepared work non-stop. The reward has been rich.

Tangerine McLaren Vale Viogner 2019 A skin-inflected amber expression. Very good it is, too! A moreish phenolic burr corrals viognier's effusive aromas while imparting an umami warmth, savoury and nourishing. Flavours of dried hay and white miso mesh with apricot pith, orange blossom and the curry powder and chutney scents also derived from the skins. Wonderful intensity and life. A zap of volatility for lift. A whole wine, from the attack and middle, to the long, textural finish. Screw cap | 11.6% alc. | To 2026 | $26 | NG

oomilya ⚲

ry Road, McLaren Vale SA 5171 **T** (08) 8323 8000 **WWW**.koomilya.com.au **OPEN** By appt
EMAKER Stephen Pannell **EST.** 2015 **DOZENS** 2000 **VYDS** 13ha

ephen Pannell first experienced the fruit from this vineyard when he made the Jimmy tson trophy-winning 1995 Eileen Hardy Shiraz, a major component of which was sourced m the Koomilya JC Block. Seventeen years later in 2012, Stephen and wife Fiona bought the operty and have embarked on rejuvenating it with organic farming, weeding the native bush d removing olive trees to create biochar to return as charcoal to the soil.

McLaren Vale Shiraz 2017 This is a most distinctive shiraz in the greater regional context, exuding a powerful mix of black fruits with the smells of Australian bush enveloping the fruits. The palate is dense, not with oak but with rich, savoury licorice and definite earthy, mossy, roasted root vegetable notes in there as well. And with all that, there's still a medium-bodied flow through the mouth. Which should be open in awe at the exit because of how astoundingly good this wine is! Screw cap | 14% alc. | To 2030 | $70 | TL | ♥

oyd Brothers

Warners Road, McLaren Vale, SA 5171 **T** (08) 8323 8792 **WWW**.lloydbrothers.com.au **OPEN** 7 days
5 **WINEMAKER** Ross Durbidge **EST.** 2002 **DOZENS** 10 000 **VYDS** 42.4ha

yd Brothers Wine and Olive Company is owned and operated by David and Matthew Lloyd, l-generation McLaren Vale vignerons. Their 25ha estate overlooks the township, and is nted to 20ha shiraz, 2.5ha bushvine grenache and 1ha bushvine mataro (plus 18.9ha of uvignon blanc, chardonnay, pinot gris and shiraz in the Adelaide Hills).

McLaren Vale Grenache Shiraz Mourvèdre 2019 Each variety fermented and aged separately for 14 months in seasoned French wood, including some barriques. A swathe of bitter chocolate and oak-derived vanillans meld with blue fruits, kirsch, anise and clove. Expansive and luxuriant, as much as it is taut and energetic. A complex juxtaposition, with firm, briary tannins to conclude. Screw cap | 14.5% alc. | To 2028 | $35 | NG

inistry of Clouds ⚲

Chapel Hill Road, McLaren Vale, SA 5171 **T** 0417 864 615 **WWW**.ministryofclouds.com.au
N By appt **WINEMAKER** Julian Forwood, Bernice Ong **EST.** 2012 **DOZENS** 5000 **VYDS** 9.6ha

rnice Ong and Julian Forwood say, 'The name Ministry of Clouds symbolises the nquishing of our past security and structure (ministry) for the beguiling freedom, ependence and adventure (clouds) inherent in our own venture'. I doubt whether there are artners in a relatively young wine business with such extraordinary experience in sales and rketing of wine, stretching back well over 20 years.

Clare Valley Riesling 2020 Despite the searing dryness of this mid-weight wine, the extract and compelling vinosity are winning. Low yields, evidently. The extract absorbs the tensile acidity, making for a compact juiciness. Austere in its youth, but far from shrill. Pithy lime, quince, anise, spa salts and pink grapefruit. Stony. Pumice-like. Thirst-slaking and long. Screw cap | 12.4% alc. | To 2032 | $32 | NG

Minnow Creek

42 Frontenac Avenue, Panorama, SA 5041 (postal) **T** 0404 288 108 **www.minnowcreekwines.com.au**
WINEMAKER Tony Walker **EST.** 2005 **DOZENS** 1600

Tony Walker spent 6 years as winemaker at Fox Creek, after 2 previous vintages in Beaujolais and Languedoc. He founded Minnow Creek in 2005, not with any fanfare of (marketing) trumpets, but simply to make very good wines that reflected their place and their variety.

91 **The Silver Minnow Langhorne Creek Pinot Gris 2020** A mid-weighted and highly textural gris. Drawing on the complexity that 40% barrel fermentation bestows, notes of nashi pear granita, quince, ripe apple and jasmine are galvanised by a judicious meld of oak and phenolics. A creamy core of leesy nougatine provides a well-judged counterpoint. Flavour, balance and versatility in spades. Screw cap | 13.5% alc. | To 2022 | $21 | NG

Mr Riggs Wine Company

169 Douglas Gully Road, McLaren Flat, SA 5171 **T** 1300 946 326 **www.mrriggs.com.au** **OPEN** Mon-Fri 9-5 **WINEMAKER** Ben Riggs **EST.** 2001 **DOZENS** 20000 **VYDS** 7.5ha

With over a quarter of a century of winemaking experience, Ben Riggs is well established under his own banner. The vision of the Mr Riggs brand is unpretentious and personal: 'To make the wines I love to drink'. He drinks very well.

95 **The Gaffer McLaren Vale Shiraz 2018** Has all one could wish for in a wine that speaks so clearly of its place, yet does so without bombast. The colour is bright, the bouquet with aromas of plum, spice and dark chocolate, the medium-bodied palate in total synchrony. Screw cap | 14.5% alc. | To 2043 | $25 | JH

94 **Montepulciano d'Adelaide 2019** Predominantly Adelaide Hills–grown fruit from one of the earliest growers of this increasingly exciting variety. There's a captivating purity to this beautifully medium weight wine, with lingering cherry cola-esque aromas and flavours. An even coat of tannins is balanced by prominent fruit. A delicious drink, and one of the higher achievers in this class. Screw cap | 14.5% alc. | To 2028 | $30 | TL

Morgan Simpson

PO Box 39, Kensington Park, SA 5068 **T** 0417 843 118 **www.morgansimpson.com.au**
WINEMAKER Richard Simpson **EST.** 1998 **DOZENS** 1200 **VYDS** 17.1ha

Morgan Simpson was founded by SA businessman George Morgan (since retired) and winemaker Richard Simpson, who is a graduate of CSU. Most of the grapes are sold, the remainder used to provide the reasonably priced, drinkable wines for which Morgan Simpson has become well known: they are available through their website.

92 **Barcore McLaren Vale Shiraz Mataro 2017** $20 buys a nourishing, rich mouthful of wine that is admirably savoury. A ferrous mataro burr across the back end. Loads of anise, sassafras, salami, violet and black cherry, but the firm plane of tannin makes this a winning ticket. Screw cap | 14.8% alc. | To 2025 | $20 | NG

Row 42 McLaren Vale Cabernet Sauvignon 2018 A relaxed and full-bodied maritime cab. Saline and lithe tannins, palpably firm enough to rally the morass of flavours, draw a gentle bow of tension across cassis, olive, dried sage and a potpourri of anise and scrub. Screw cap | 15.4% alc. | To 2026 | $20 | NG

Paralian Wines

21 Eden Terrace, Port Willunga, SA 5171 **T** 0413 308 730 **www.paralian.com.au** **OPEN** By appt
WINEMAKER Skye Salter, Charlie Seppelt **EST.** 2018 **DOZENS** 450

Charlie Seppelt and Skye Salter have covered many miles and worked in many places since they met in 2008 working the vintage at Hardys Tintara in McLaren Vale. By the time they took the plunge and established Paralian Wines in '18 they had accumulated 46 vintages between them, working for others. The name is a noun for someone who lives by the sea.

96 **Marmont Vineyard McLaren Vale Grenache 2020** A stellar vintage in these parts: extract and freshness, a holy duopoly. Fragrant, febrile, mid-weighted of feel, despite the concentration and totem of juicy tannins. Spindly, detailed and drenched in tamarind, turmeric and clove, akin to the sensations of a souk. This is like sucking on an orange mulled with sour cherry and exotica. Long and gorgeous. Value! I am pouring another glass, one-handed, as I finish the note. Screw cap | 14% alc. | To 2027 | $42 | NG

axton

Wheaton Road, McLaren Vale, SA 5171 **T** (08) 8323 9131 **www**.paxtonvineyards.com **OPEN** 7 days -5 **WINEMAKER** Dwayne Cunningham, Kate Goodman (Consultant) **EST.** 1979 **DOZENS** 32 000 **VYDS** 82.5ha

avid Paxton is of one Australia's most successful and respected viticulturists, with a career anning over 40 years. He started his successful premium grower business in 1979 and has en involved with planting and managing some of the most prestigious vineyards in McLaren le, Barossa Valley, Yarra Valley, Margaret River and Adelaide Hills for top global wineries. His incipal focus is on his own operations in McLaren Vale with Paxton Wines, established in '98 a premium shiraz, grenache and cabernet producer.

Quandong Farm Single Vineyard McLaren Vale Shiraz 2019 The first Paxton vineyard to adopt a biodynamic regime. The complex bouquet has sweet dark berry fruits, spice and wood smoke (not bushfire) aromas, and a medium- to full-bodied palate that stays light on its feet in a wealth of licorice, juniper and savoury, earthy notes. Screw cap | 14% alc. | To 2034 | $30 | JH

irramimma

hnston Road, McLaren Vale, SA 5171 **T** (08) 8323 8205 **www**.pirramimma.com.au **OPEN** Mon-Fri -4.30, w'ends & public hols 10.30-5 **WINEMAKER** Geoff Johnston **EST.** 1892 **DOZENS** 50 000 **VYDS** 91.5ha

long-established family-owned company with outstanding vineyard resources, which it is ing to full effect. A series of intense old-vine varietals includes semillon, sauvignon blanc, ardonnay, shiraz, grenache, cabernet sauvignon and petit verdot, all fashioned without er-embellishment.

Stock's Hill McLaren Vale GSM 2018 A delicious GSM, full weighted without being heavy. The wine ably promotes grenache's kirsch-scented generosity, ethereal feel and spice mix of aromas. The oak, a gentle beam across the wine's mid-drift, corralling the fruit as much as staving it off, just enough for the wine to find poise, regional probity and a zone of drinkability. Screw cap | 14.5% alc. | To 2026 | $25 | NG

rimo Estate

Murtrie Road, McLaren Vale, SA 5171 **T** (08) 8323 6800 **www**.primoestate.com.au **OPEN** 7 days 11-4 **NEMAKER** Joseph Grilli, Daniel Grilli, Tom Garrett **EST.** 1979 **DOZENS** 30 000 **VYDS** 34ha

e Grilli has always produced innovative and excellent wines. The biennial release of the seph Sparkling Red (in its tall Italian glass bottle) is eagerly awaited, the wine immediately lling out. Also highly regarded are the vintage-dated extra virgin olive oils.

Joseph The Fronti NV Always delicious, muscat's telltale grapey spice, lychee and orange blossom scents are effusive, morphing into an elixir of rancio/walnut, dried tobacco and peat aromas, bridging a resinous viscosity and dutiful freshness that are more compelling with the virtues of age. The finish, infinite. Screw cap | 19.5% alc. | $50 | NG

ichard Hamilton

9 Main Road, McLaren Vale, SA 5171 **T** (08) 8323 8830 **www**.richardhamiltonwines.com **EN** Mon-Fri 10-5, w'ends & public hols 11-5 **WINEMAKER** Paul Gordon, Greg Foster **EST.** 1972 **ZENS** 25 000 **VYDS** 40.46ha

chard Hamilton has outstanding estate vineyards, some of great age, all fully mature. An perienced and skilled winemaking team has allowed the full potential of those vineyards be realised. The quality, style and consistency of both red and white wines has reached new level; being able to keep only the best parcels for the Richard Hamilton brand is an ormous advantage.

Hut Block McLaren Vale Cabernet Sauvignon 2018 At this meagre price, the wine is stellar. Vale cabernet 101. Think cassis, spearmint, a smear of black olive, sage and sea spray salinity dousing the juicy finish. Lovely drinking with varietal and regional pedigree intact. Screw cap | 14.5% alc. | To 2023 | $22 | NG

Lot 148 McLaren Vale Merlot 2019 A delicious medium-bodied wine, brimming with life and a succulence of fruit that has drawn me back for another whiff before penning this note. Damson plum, verdant herb, a sappy minty lift and a perfect proportion of oak to promote an effusive drinkability. The tannins, tactile enough to confer poise; gentle enough to promote imminent pleasure. Screw cap | 14% alc. | To 2023 | $22 | NG

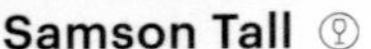

Samson Tall

219 Strout Road, McLaren Vale, SA 5171 **T** 0488 214 680 **www**.samsontall.com.au **OPEN** 7 days 10-5 **WINEMAKER** Paul Wilson **EST.** 2016 **DOZENS** 500

Paul Wilson and Heather Budich purchase grapes from local growers, making the wine in a small winery on their property. The cellar door is a small church built in 1854, the winery and church (with a small historic cemetery) surrounded by gardens and a vineyard. Paul has learned his craft as a winemaker well; all of the wines are well made and the grapes well chosen.

96 **McLaren Vale Grenache 2019** A svelte expression of an uncanny lightness, extrapolated with palpable respect for arguably the finest variety of the region. A winning approach that does not necessarily guarantee old bones, but ensures a joyous ride from youth to middle age. Sour cherry, pomegranate, cranberry, bergamot, thyme, lavender and kirsch. Grenache meets pinot. A splay of impeccably hewn tannins, spindly, herbal and moreish, brings a huge smile to this Rhône lover. Screw cap | 14.5% alc. | To 2025 | $30 | NG

SC Pannell

60 Olivers Road, McLaren Vale, SA 5171 **T** (08) 8323 8000 **www**.pannell.com.au **OPEN** Thurs-Mon 11- **WINEMAKER** Stephen Pannell **EST.** 2004 **DOZENS** 15000 **VYDS** 9ha

Steve Pannell radiates intensity and his extended experience has resulted in wines of the highest quality, right from the first vintage. The Pannells have 2 vineyards in McLaren Vale, th first planted in 1891 with a precious 3.6ha of shiraz. The future for the Pannells is limitless, the icon status of the label already well established.

96 **Smart Clarendon Grenache 2019** Intense aromas of molten cherry liqueur, orange amaro, bergamo and cranberry. A fine vinous pulse, drawing the fore with the aft. Long attenuated filigreed tannins, sandy to be sure, but very fine. This is exceptional grenache that, with a few others, sets the region high tone. Screw cap | 14.5% alc. | To 2026 | $60 | NG

Serafino Wines

Kangarilla Road, McLaren Vale, SA 5171 **T** (08) 8323 0157 **www**.serafinowines.com.au **OPEN** Mon-Fri 10-4.30, w'ends & public hols 10-4.30 **WINEMAKER** Charles Whish **EST.** 2000 **DOZENS** 30000 **VYDS** 121ha

After the sale of Maglieri Wines to Beringer Blass in 1998, Maglieri founder Serafino (Steve) Maglieri acquired the McLarens on the Lake complex originally established by Andrew Garrett. Serafino Wines has won a number of major trophies in Australia and the UK, Steve Maglieri awarded a Member of the Order of Australia in January 2018.

96 **McLaren Vale GSM 2019** Strikingly deep, bright-rimmed hue. The 83/14/3% blend works to perfection, with the red fruits of grenache doing all the lifting, shiraz providing a dab of plum coupled with silky tannins. Truly delicious. Screw cap | 14.5% alc. | To 2030 | $28 | JH

Sherrah Wines

148 McMurtrie Road, McLaren Vale SA 5171 **T** 0403 057 704 **www**.sherrahwines.com.au **OPEN** Fri-Mon 11-5 **WINEMAKER** Alex Sherrah **EST.** 2016 **DOZENS** 3000

I (James) cannot help but pass on some of owner Alex Sherrah's words of wisdom (and I'm not being sarcastic): 'Wine to me is not about tasting blackcurrant and cigar box but how the wine "feels" to drink. Flavour is obviously a big part of this, but how does the wine flow from the front to the back palate? It should transition effortlessly from first smell and sip to swallow aftertaste and lingering influence of tannin and acid. I believe in balance, a great wine should have no sharp edges, it should have beautiful smooth curves from front to back.' Small wonder he makes such wonderful wines.

94 **Skin Party McLaren Vale Fiano 2020** Selectiv' machine-harvested, whole berries open-fermented in shallow vats, initially wild fermented, then overseeded with an aromatic cultured yeast, matured in used hogsheads for 4 months. A great success for a bold exercise, the wine complex but fresh, with no obvious tannins. The bright straw-green colour is another plus. Screw cap | 12% alc. | To 2025 | $30 | JH

hingleback

Stump Hill Road, McLaren Vale, SA 5171 **T** (08) 8323 7388 **WWW**.shingleback.com.au **OPEN** 7 days -5 **WINEMAKER** John Davey, Dan Hills **EST.** 1995 **DOZENS** 150000 **VYDS** 120ha

others Kym and John Davey planted and nurture their family-owned and sustainably anaged vineyard on land purchased by their grandfather in the 1950s. Shingleback has een a success story since its establishment. Its 120ha of estate vineyards are one of the keys that success, which includes winning the Jimmy Watson Trophy in 2006 for the '05 D Block abernet Sauvignon. The well-made wines are rich and full-flavoured, but not overripe (and nce, not excessively alcoholic).

The Gate McLaren Vale Shiraz 2018 Estate-grown fruit. Deep crimson/purple colour; an unusual but extremely attractive wine, with characters normally encountered in cool climates. The intensity of the red/black cherry fruit comes with fine, tailored tannins. The result is a wine of great length, offering pleasure from the first to last sips. Screw cap | 14.5% alc. | To 2035 | $40 | JH

The Bio Project McLaren Vale Fiano 2020 Fiano is a variety that will surely achieve ever greater significance in Australia's varietal landscape. It holds its acidity and its lingering aftertaste wherever it is grown. Its almond and kaffir-lime flavours delicately coat the mouth, the next glass never far away. Screw cap | 12.5% alc. | To 2026 | $25 | JH

hirvington

7 Strout Road, McLaren Vale, SA 5171 **T** (08) 8323 7649 **WWW**.shirvington.com **OPEN** Thurs–Mon -4 **WINEMAKER** Kim Jackson **EST.** 1996 **DOZENS** 950 **VYDS** 23.8ha

ıe Shirvington family began the development of their McLaren Vale vineyards in 1996 ıder the direction of viticulturist Peter Bolte and now have almost 24ha under vine, the ajority to shiraz and cabernet sauvignon, with small additional plantings of grenache and ataro. A substantial part of the production is sold as grapes, the best reserved for the ıirvington wines.

Row X Row McLaren Vale Rosé 2020 Straight-laced grenache. A light coral hue belies the intensity of rosewater, lemon verbena, raspberry and dried thyme flavours. Juicy, but not overtly fruity. A dry and thirst-slaking wine melding European restraint with an effusive Australian joy. Screw cap | 12.8% alc. | To 2021 | $25 | NG

midge Wines

0 Tatachilla Road, McLaren Vale, SA 5171 **T** 0419 839 964 **WWW**.smidgewines.com **OPEN** By appt **NEMAKER** Matt Wenk **EST.** 2004 **DOZENS** 5000 **VYDS** 4.1ha

nidge Wines is owned by Matt Wenk and wife Trish Callaghan. He plans to increase oduction of Smidge to 8000 dozen over the next few years, with winemaking operations McLaren Vale, where Smidge is currently leasing a small winery. Smidge owns the neyard in Willunga that provides the grapes for all the cabernet sauvignon releases and ome of the McLaren Vale shiraz. The vision is to build a modern customised facility on the 'illunga property in the not-too-distant future.

6 **Pedra Branca VP 2018** A port for the big-dry-red drinker due to its contextual restraint. Far from cloying, it reels off thrilling aromas of cherry pith, blackberry, Chinese medicine, lilac, clove, pepper and suede. The tannins are impeccably hewn, chamois of feel. Real thrust of structure and parry of fruit. Immaculate and impressively long. Kudos! Screw cap | 17% alc. | $45 | NG

'hree Dark Horses

)7 Schuller Road, Blewitt Springs, SA 5171 **T** 0405 294 500 **WWW**.3dh.com.au **NEMAKER** Matt Broomhead **EST.** 2009 **DOZENS** 5000 **VYDS** 8.9ha

ıree Dark Horses is the project of former Coriole winemaker Matt Broomhead. After vintages southern Italy (2007) and the Rhône Valley, he returned to McLaren Vale in late 2009 and, ith his father Alan, buys quality grapes, thanks to the many years of experience they both ave in the region. The 3rd dark horse is Matt's grandfather, a vintage regular.

4 **McLaren Vale Grenache 2019** Grenache is the raison d'être of the Vale. And it will get even better! Here is the testing ground: thick and vinous. But paradoxically, lithe and sprightly. Kirsch, black cherry, cardamom, licorice, dried thyme and lavender. A complex potpourri of intrigue and great potential. Screw cap | 14.5% alc. | To 2026 | $25 | NG

Varney Wines

62 Victor Harbor Road, Old Noarlunga, SA 5168 **T** 0450 414 570 **www**.varneywines.com.au **OPEN** Thurs-Mon 11-5 **WINEMAKER** Alan Varney **EST.** 2017 **DOZENS** 1050

Alan Varney is a brilliant winemaker, saying, 'I am not afraid to step out of the box and go wit my intuition ... I only use old seasoned oak with no fining or filtration.' His ability to draw the varietal heart of each wine he makes with alcohol levels between 12% and 14% is extraordinar He has built an environmentally sensitive winery alongside wife Kathrin's restaurant, Victor's Place, overlooking the rolling hills of the Onkaparinga Gorge. Varney Wines were the *Wine Companion 2021* Best New Winery.

96 **McLaren Vale GSM 2018** An exceptional Rhône blend. For the record, I loathe the GSM moniker, seeking wines that sublimate branding and the personality of each component with a juicy mouthf of spicy, Mediterranean herb-doused blue/black-fruit aspersions. This is THAT wine! The tannins, noble, savoury and thirst-slaking. Possibly the finest domestic 'GSM' yet tasted. A mini Gigondas. Screw cap | 14.6% alc. | To 2024 | $32 | NG

95 **Adelaide Hills Chardonnay 2019** A very fine wine, relying as much on phenolic texture as reductive tension and bright acidity. A more complete, textural package as a result. Toasted hazelnut, oatme white peach and tatami. Long, sprightly and effortless. Screw cap | 12.8% alc. | To 2026 | $32 | NG

Entrada McLaren Vale Grenache Mourvèdre Touriga 2019 A 60/30/10% blend, the grenache ex 60yo Blewitt Springs bush vines, all components picked early for vibrancy. Partial whole-bunch fermentation, briefly matured in used oak. Holding its hue well, and delivering a very complex yet juicy palate, jumping with spice and fine, savoury tannins. Screw cap | 13.1% alc. | To 2029 | $25 | JH

Vigna Bottin 

192 Main Road, Willunga SA 5172 **T** 0414 562 956 **www**.vignabottin.com.au **OPEN** Fri 11-4, Sat-Sun 11-5 **WINEMAKER** Paolo Bottin **EST.** 2006 **DOZENS** 1500 **VYDS** 15.22ha

The Bottin family migrated to Australia in 1954 from Treviso in northern Italy, where they were grapegrowers. The family began growing grapes in McLaren Vale in '70, focusing on mainstream varieties for sale to wineries in the region. When son Paolo and wife Maria made a trip back to Italy in '98, they were inspired to do more, and, says Paolo, 'My love for barbera and sangiovese was sealed during a vintage in Pavia. I came straight home to plant both varieties in our family plot. My father was finally happy!' They now trade under the catchy phrase 'Italian Vines, Australian Wines'.

94 **Mclaren Vale Fiano 2019** Great promise. There may be better fiano out there, but this is top tier. A superior wine. Winning because of the optimal ripeness and additional textural intrigue, binding a sea-spray freshness with a savoury chewiness. Aromas of apricot pith, fennel, samphire, pistachio and marzipan. A long driver and an intense player. Delicious wine! Screw cap | 12.9% alc. | To 2024 | $27 | NG

Vintage Longbottom 

15 Spring Gully Road, Piccadilly, SA 5151 **T** (08) 8132 1048 **www**.vintagelongbottom.com **WINEMAKER** Matt Wenk **EST.** 1998 **DOZENS** 48 000 **VYDS** 94.9ha

Kim Longbottom runs her wine business in the Adelaide Hills, where Tapanappa has taken or the responsibility of making 3 tiers of wines. At the top is Magnus Shiraz from Clarendon and Blewitt Springs; the middle is the H Range from the McLaren Vale floor districts; and there is a sparkling range from the Adelaide Hills. Her daughter Margo brings experience in fashion, digital marketing and business administration.

94 **Henry's Drive H Adelaide Hills Sauvignon Blanc 2019** A serious take on Hills sauvignon blanc, away from the familiar wild aromatic style, with 5 months in French oak puncheons, albeit without using the word fumé anywhere on the bottle. The wine expresses initial vanilla and baking spice from the barrel time, while the citrus and herbal elements harmonise on the palate, creating a unique tang, intriguingly rich yet refreshing at the same time. I'm convinced. Screw cap | 12.7% alc. | To 2025 | $28 | TL

Henry's Drive H Adelaide Hills Chardonnay 2019 This has sat for 8 months in French oak puncheor In doing so it has picked up all those good elements of contemporary chardonnay, a touch of oak and barrel character to begin, nothing overblown, then pure fruit expression – trademark Hills whit nectarine – on the palate, a nice little tang of citrus and spice on the finish, keeping it fresh and vibrant. A lovely, balanced approach. Screw cap | 13.5% alc. | To 2026 | $28 | TL

'irra Wirra

3 McMurtrie Road, McLaren Vale, SA 5171 **T** (08) 8323 8414 **WWW**.wirrawirra.com **OPEN** Mon-Sat ·5, Sun & public hols 11-5 **WINEMAKER** Paul Smith, Tom Ravech, Kelly Wellington **EST.** 1894 **:ENS** 140000 **VYDS** 21.5ha

rra Wirra has established a formidable reputation. The wines are of exemplary character, ality and style; The Angelus Cabernet Sauvignon and RWS Shiraz battling each other for premacy, with The Absconder Grenache one to watch. Long may the battle continue under anaging director Andrew Kay and the winemaking team of Paul Smith, Tom Ravech and Kelly ellington, who forge along the path of excellence first trod by the late (and much loved) eg Trott, the pioneering founder of modern-day Wirra Wirra.

Woodhenge Basket-Pressed McLaren Vale Shiraz 2018 Black fruits of many types glide across the palate on a magic carpet of savoury but fine tannins. Its overall balance is perfect. Just lovely. Screw cap | 14.5% alc. | To 2033 | $35 | JH

The Angelus McLaren Vale Cabernet Sauvignon 2018 Fresher, fleet of foot and more detailed than not too long ago. Kudos! A herbal and mineral confluence of sage, graphite and bay leaf laces the tannins, lithe, attenuated and refined. Tapenade and currant, too. The oak is impeccably integrated. Long and seamless. A refined classic, sacrificing neither richness nor the inimitable nori salinity that stamps its regional pedigree. Cellarworthy. Screw cap | 14% alc. | To 2035 | $70 | NG

Church Block McLaren Vale Cabernet Sauvignon Shiraz Merlot 2018 It is lightning fast out of the blocks, the colour bright, the bouquet flowery, the medium-bodied palate with a silky smooth mouthfeel. The fruit flavours are predominantly red cherry/berry-accented, the tannins sewn skilfully into the fabric of the wine. Screw cap | 14.5% alc. | To 2029 | $25 | JH

angarra Estate Vineyard

9 McLaren Flat Road, Kangarilla SA 5171 **T** (08) 8383 7459 **WWW**.yangarra.com.au **OPEN** Mon-Sat -5 **WINEMAKER** Peter Fraser **EST.** 2000 **DOZENS** 15000 **VYDS** 100ha

is is the Australian operation of Jackson Family Wines, one of the leading premium wine oducers in California, which in 2000 acquired the 172ha Eringa Park Vineyard from Normans ines (the oldest vines dated back to 1923). The renamed Yangarra Estate Vineyard is the tate base for the operation and has moved to certified biodynamic status with its vineyards. ter Fraser has taken Yangarra Estate to another level altogether with his innovative nemaking and desire to explore all the possibilities of the Rhône Valley red and white styles. eramic eggs are used in parallel with conventional fermenters. In 2015 Peter was named inemaker of the Year at the launch of the *Wine Companion 2016*.

Old Vine McLaren Vale Grenache 2019 From vines planted in '45 on a deep sandy dune dubbed 'The Beach' by Yangarra. Whole bunches are open-fermented. The bouquet exudes fresh-picked raspberries which form the nucleus of the powerful and intense palate, with grainy tannins that underline the complexity of the wine. Screw cap | 14% alc. | To 2034 | $35 | JH

Hickinbotham Clarendon Grenache 2019 This cuvée is akin to the finest pinot; svelte, detailed and uplifting. Aromas of sour cherry, raspberry, rosewater, mace and orange zest. The superior wine of 2019 here, or at least what I've tasted to date. Stunning. The tannins, growing with air and the next sip. The finish, jitterbug energetic, chiselled and chamois of texture. Long and succulent. Another addition to the Australian stable of finessed world-class grenache. Screw cap | 14.5% alc. | To 2027 | $60 | NG

McLaren Vale Roussanne 2020 Warm vintages service this doyen of white Rhône varieties so well, almost forcing the phenolic amplitude and textural quilt that would otherwise be lacking, at least in this country. This has it in spades. Scintillating aromas of bitter almond, apricot pith, rooibos, pistachio and freshly lain tatami mat. À point! Pucker and freshness; textural detail personified. The French oak (25% new) and lees work, apposite. The finish, long and rippling across the textural crevices. I'd love to drink this in 5 years. Screw cap | 14.5% alc. | To 2027 | $35 | NG

onte's Footstep

e General Wine Bar, 55a Main Road, McLaren Flat, SA 5171 **T** (08) 7286 3088 ww.zontesfootstep.com.au **OPEN** Mon-Sat by appt **WINEMAKER** Brad Rey **EST.** 2003 **DOZENS** 20000 **DS** 214.72ha

onte's Footstep has been very successful since a group of long-standing friends, collectively ith deep knowledge of every aspect of the wine business, decided it was time to do mething together. There has been some shuffling of the deck chairs since, but all achieved ithout any ill feeling from those who moved sideways or backwards. The major change has een a broadening of the regions (Langhorne Creek, McLaren Vale, the Barossa and Clare alleys and elsewhere) from which the grapes are sourced.

94 **Blackberry Patch Fleurieu Cabernet 2019** Fruit from Langhorne Creek and a block in Blewitt Sprin McLaren Vale. Cabernet with 5% tempranillo, finding a delicious companionship with aromas of warm sun-kissed blackberries. There's delicious, pure fruit and a delicate touch of licorice on the palate, leaving you with a sense of honesty and immense satisfaction – a vinous hug, if you will. Screw cap | 14% alc. | To 2028 | $30 | TL

Canto Fleurieu Sangiovese Lagrein 2019 An 87/13% blend with sangio in the lead. Plenty to love here, and no need to dissect each variety's contribution, as the wine works in its own right. Part earthy and savoury, part dark plum and chocolate; with juicy, crunchy tart satsuma plum flavours and lip-smacking tannins that carry the flavours for quite some time. Screw cap | 14% alc. | To 2028 | $30 | TL

ZONE

Mount Lofty Ranges

REGION

Adelaide Hills

Anvers ★★★★

633 Razorback Road, Kangarilla, SA 5157 **T** (08) 7079 8691 **www**.anvers.com.au **OPEN** Sun 11–5
WINEMAKER Kym Milne MW **EST.** 1998 **DOZENS** 10000 **VYDS** 24.5ha

Myriam and Wayne Keoghan's principal vineyard is in the Adelaide Hills at Kangarilla (17ha of sauvignon blanc, chardonnay, shiraz, barbera and gamay). Winemaker Kym Milne has experience gained across many of the wine-producing countries in both northern and southern hemispheres.

95 **Limited Release Adelaide Hills Cabernet Sauvignon 2018** A combo of cooler-climate location and a warmer vintage has worked together to deliver classic cabernet dark berries, with atypical leafy and herbal notes. There are mint aromas, but not dominant. The success of this wine is thanks to its medium weight yet saturation of cabernet flavour, supported by superfine tannins and the very faintest of suggestions of gastronomic bitterness on the finish. Great value. Screw cap | 14.5% alc. | To 2028 | $24 | TL | ♥

Ashton Hills Vineyard

126 Tregarthen Road, Ashton, SA 5137 **T** (08) 8390 1243 **www**.ashtonhills.com.au **OPEN** Fri–Mon 11–
WINEMAKER Stephen George, Liam Van Pelt **EST.** 1982 **DOZENS** 3000 **VYDS** 3ha

Stephen George made Ashton Hills one of the great producers of Pinot Noir in Australia, and by some distance the best in the Adelaide Hills. With no family succession in place, he sold the business to Wirra Wirra in April 2015. (When it was announced, there was a sigh of relief that it should pass to a business such as Wirra Wirra, with undoubted commitment to retainin the extraordinary quality of the wines.) Stephen continues to live in the house on the propert and provide ongoing consulting advice.

98 **Reserve Pinot Noir 2020** As with the Reserve releases we've witnessed over many years, this has a latent power, deep down in the aromatic wells. Say it again – deep down. The fruit has a darker cherry expression, the fragrance in the nose rising gently, savoury forest-like elements on the palat well entwined. The weight is ethereal and exhibits a class, medium-bodied line and length, all of it lingering around the top and sides of your mouth for eons. So special, even tasted in its early stage of a long life. Screw cap | 13.5% alc. | To 2030 | $85 | TL | ♥

97 **Piccadilly Valley Chardonnay 2020** This is straight-out-of-the-blocks pure and delicious chardonna with just the right amount of all the elements fitting exactly together: exact ripeness in the white stone-fruit flavours, citrus acidity, oak-encouraged creaminess and finishing pithy texture. Purity, refreshment, A-list. Screw cap | 12.5% alc. | To 2028 | $40 | TL

Reserve Pinot Noir 2019 A darker, more earthy and foresty feel here than the Estate version, and a different proportional mix of clones. The cherry sense is blacker fruit, while the acidity and mouthfeel are ramped up, evenly, to be more powerful once you engage. Likewise the aromatics, nose and palate, are poised, waiting to find their lift in time. Experience says this wine will be on another level in 5 years. Screw cap | 13.5% alc. | To 2030 | $80 | TL

atlin Wines ★★★★★

; Sydney Road, Nairne, SA 5252 **T** 0411 326 384 **www**.catlinwines.com.au **WINEMAKER** Darryl Catlin , 2013 **DOZENS** 2000

rryl Catlin grew up in the Barossa Valley with vineyards as his playground, picking bush-vine enache for pocket money as a youngster. Stints in various facets of the industry led to him tablishing his own business in 2013.

Nellie Margaret Adelaide Hills Chardonnay 2017 Great to have a chardonnay released with time allowed for development, and even then there are fresh, green tinges to the pale gold. Oak has gifted some vanilla spice to the familiar darker stone fruits that tingle a little on the palate as the fresh citrus elements wash in, leaving an even line of acidity and pith. Everything feels really well balanced and in place. Screw cap | 12% alc. | To 2026 | $30 | TL

Pudding and Pie Adelaide Hills Pinot Noir 2020 Lightly coloured in the glass, highly fragrant and carrying just a little mystery in its savoury offsets – a little nice nebbiolo-like funk. Slightly sour cherry, with an earthy outer layer, Middle Eastern spice notes and a pleasing light grip. It's tasty and moreish. Bang on. Screw cap | 12% alc. | To 2026 | $30 | TL

hain of Ponds

'he Parade West, Kent Town, SA 5067 **T** (08) 7324 3031 **www**.chainofponds.com.au **WINEMAKER** Greg ick **EST.** 1985 **DOZENS** 20000

s years since the Chain of Ponds brand was separated from its then 200ha of estate ieyards, which were among the largest in the Adelaide Hills. It does, however, have long-'m contracts with major growers. Prior to the 2015 vintage, Greg Clack came onboard as l-time chief winemaker. In May '16 Chain of Ponds closed its cellar door and moved to ject Wine's small-batch processing facility at Langhorne Creek, where it also sources fruit ' its budget range.

Innocence Adelaide Hills Rosé 2020 Three vineyards/varieties suited to the world of rosé – 47/40% pinot noir/sangiovese from 2 Hills sites, the remaining 13% grenache from Langhorne Creek. Enticing red fruit and petal aromas, with good strawberry flavours, dry and spicy with a mouth-filling textural layer to add a bit of presence. Screw cap | 13% alc. | To 2022 | $20 | TL

harlotte Dalton Wines 

:tory 9, 89-91 Hill Street, Port Elliot, SA 5212 **T** 0466 541 361 **www**.charlottedaltonwines. ı.au **OPEN** Fri-Mon 11-3 (7 days 26 Dec-26 Jan) **WINEMAKER** Charlotte Hardy **EST.** 2015 **DOZENS** 1200

ıarlotte Hardy has been making wines for 20 years, with a star-studded career at Craggy ıge (NZ), Château Giscours (Bordeaux) and David Abreu (California), but has called SA me since 2007. Her winery is part of her Basket Range house, which has been through ıny incarnations since starting life as a pig farm in 1858.

Project 5255 Langhorne Creek Fiano 2020 Made for a unique Langhorne Creek collaboration titled Project 5255, giving 3 winemakers outside of Langhorne Creek the opportunity to create a one-off wine with Langhorne Creek fruit. Winemaker Charlotte Hardy has been gifted fiano from Bremerton's vineyard in Langhorne Creek in a low-cropping year. Fermented slowly over winter in older French barrels, no sulphur added until a week before bottling in November. A textured style, with oak offering a subtle wooded nature to the nose, before a delicious lemon-curd-like flavour swirls across the palate. This is one of the more attention-grabbing fianos witnessed this year. Screw cap | 13% alc. | To 2024 | $35 | TL | ♥

Love Me Love You Adelaide Hills Shiraz 2019 Ripe with satsuma plum notes, and a great dusting of white pepper. Juicy, fleshy, tangy with sticky tannins. Rolls delightfully through the mouth. Screw cap | 13% alc. | To 2026 | $32 | TL

oates Wines

; Tynan Road, Kuitpo, SA 5172 **T** 0417 882 557 **www**.coates-wines.com **OPEN** W'ends & public hols -5 **WINEMAKER** Duane Coates **EST.** 2003 **DOZENS** 2500

ane Coates has a bachelor of science, a master of business administration and a master of nology from the University of Adelaide; for good measure he completed the theory component the MW program in 2005. Having made wine in various parts of the world, and in SA, he is more ın qualified to make and market Coates wines. The key is organically grown grapes.

96 **Adelaide Hills The Riesling 2020** An exercise in how to make riesling (too often shrill, battery acid-dry and brittle in this country) into a phalanx of optimally ripe fruit, the sort of juicy acidity tha pulls the saliva from the back of the mouth with an elastic cadence and real textural intrigue. Class and complexity, the DNA. Kaffir lime, sure. Better, quince paste, tangerine, lemon meringue and a pungent mineral undercurrent. The older oak, servicing an expansive breadth that stains the cheel Thrilling length! Excellent wine. Screw cap | 12% alc. | To 2028 | $35 | NG | ♥

Adelaide Hills The Reserve Chardonnay 2019 Real vibrato here, as an underlying mineral tension plays off the creamy vanilla-pod oak, subsuming nectarine and melon elements in the name of savouriness. Wild mushroom scents. Dried hay. Nougatine and toasted hazelnuts. As generous as it is tensile. An exceptional mid-weighted chardonnay with no expense spared, built for mid-term ageing. Screw cap | 13% alc. | To 2030 | $45 | NG | ♥

Adelaide Hills The Blanc de Blancs 2016 A pleasure bomb that shifts the paradigm, for the better. Made akin to a great grower champagne. The soft, natural acidity, mitigated with the crescendo of oak and lees. Palate-staining, every crevice of the mouth filled with leesy nourishment. The underlying current is forceful, creamy and endless. A tour de force of Australian fizz. Diam | 12% alc. | $60 | NG | ♥

95 **McLaren Vale The Syrah 2019** This is McLaren Vale meeting the northern Rhône on its own terms. Full bodied, but savoury. Sweetness of obvious fruit, mercifully avoided. The clutch of reduction handled deftly, imparting tension and a sense of freshness across the mid palate. This is how to do it! Dried nori, jamon, tapenade salinity and violets. There's a core of unadulterated blueberry sweetness tempered by clove, cardamom and a skein of peppery acidity threaded long. Screw cap | 14% alc. | To 2028 | $30 | NG

Coulter Wines

6 Third Avenue, Tanunda, SA 5352 (postal) **T** 0448 741 773 **www**.coulterwines.com
WINEMAKER Chris Coulter **EST.** 2015 **DOZENS** 800

Chris Coulter had a 22-year previous life as a chef, but fell in love with wine in the early 1990s and managed to fit in a vintage at Coldstream Hills as a cellar rat. In 2007 he undertook a winemaking degree and secured work with a number of reputable labels. Coulter Wines was born in the '15 vintage as a side project, making wines from another universe – nothing other than SO_2 is added, movements are by gravity and the wine is unfiltered where practicable. He purchases and hand-picks grapes from vineyards mainly in the Adelaide Hills.

95 **C1 Adelaide Hills Chardonnay 2020** An immaculate balancing act of bright and vibrant chardonna fruit with the lightest touch of empathetic oak, finishing with delicious and encouraging, mouth-watering textures. Screw cap | 12.7% alc. | To 2026 | $30 | TL

CRFT Wines

45 Rangeview Drive, Carey Gully, SA 5144 **T** 0413 475 485 **www**.crftwines.com.au **OPEN** Fri-Sun 12
WINEMAKER Candice Helbig, Frewin Ries **EST.** 2012 **DOZENS** 1000 **VYDS** 1.9ha

Life and business partners NZ-born Frewin Ries and Barossa-born Candice Helbig crammed multiple wine lives into a relatively short period, before giving up secure jobs and establishing CRFT in 2013. The core focus is on small-batch single-vineyard Adelaide Hills pinot noir, chardonnay and grüner veltliner. The Arranmore vineyard was purchased in 2016, gaining NASAA organic certification in 2019, and wines are made with a minimal-intervention approach.

94 **Arranmore Vineyard Adelaide Hills Grüner Veltliner 2020** One of 3 Grüners from this creative Hills couple; 50% whole-bunch pressed with 2 days skin contact, wild fermentation and lees influence. Swelling with white peach and pear, the texture verging on an oiliness, though cut with lines of Meyer lemon and gentle, finishing acidity. Quite delicious, and a definite statement. Screw cap | 13% alc. | To 2024 | $30 | TL

Longview Vineyard Adelaide Hills Grüner Veltliner 2020 This Macclesfield district variation has subtle green pear notes to begin. There's a wave of tempered minerally acidity as you first sip, mor earthy than the others, with lemon/lime elements on the palate. It finishes with mouthfilling textur and complex lingering flavours and textures. Well realised. Screw cap | 13.5% alc. | To 2024 | $30 | TL

Deviation Road 

207 Scott Creek Road, Longwood, SA 5153 **T** (08) 8339 2633 **www**.deviationroad.com **OPEN** 7 days 10-5 **WINEMAKER** Kate Laurie **EST.** 1999 **DOZENS** 8000 **VYDS** 11.05ha

In '04 Hamish and Kate Laurie purchased their property at Longwood, which is the current home to 4ha of shiraz and pinot noir, the winery and tasting room. Disgorging equipment n Kate's family's Manjimup winery, originally imported from Champagne, was shipped to Adelaide Hills in '08 enabling the first Deviation Road traditional method sparkling wine ase. Hamish and Kate consistently produce wines that represent the cool-climate terroir he Adelaide Hills.

Beltana Adelaide Hills Blanc de Blancs 2014 Winner of 2 awards in the *Wine Companion 2022*: Sparkling Wine of the Year and Sparkling White of the Year. Opens with aromas of apple and lemon cream streusel bun. With a fine pithy mousse, the palate is compelling, with all the citrus/lemon chardonnay excitement it can muster. This is added to by a subtle aldehydic complexity that expresses itself in a light quinine character. Totally engaging. Always among the finest – this is next level. Diam | 12.5% alc. | $95 | TL | ♥

eoff Weaver

.lpin Lane, Mitcham, SA 5062 (postal) **T** (08) 8272 2105 **www**.geoffweaver.com.au **MAKER** Geoff Weaver **EST**. 1982 **DOZENS** 3000 **VYDS** 12.3ha

is the business of one-time Hardys chief winemaker Geoff Weaver. The Lenswood eyard was established between 1982 and '88, and invariably produces immaculate riesling sauvignon blanc and long-lived chardonnays. The beauty of the labels ranks supreme.

Single Vineyard Adelaide Hills Sauvignon Blanc 2020 To have been able to get these grapes off the Lenswood vineyard (impacted by a disastrous bushfire in December 2019) was a miracle to start with. Geoff Weaver's sauvignon blancs stand alone in their purity and delicacy. As does this iteration, not tempted by wild and exotic aromatics, rather a gently spicy white peach flavour, juicy and absolutely comfortable in its own skin. Screw cap | 12.5% alc. | To 2024 | $25 | TL

Single Vineyard Adelaide Hills Sauvignon Blanc 2019 A wine that stands tall to show us how great both the Hills and sauvignon blanc can be in Geoff Weaver's gentlemanly hands. The nose and palate are all about well-mannered varietal pungency, gooseberry and ginger, with fabulous, pithy texture and a reverb of exciting flavours on the finish. Simply terrific. Screw cap | 13% alc. | To 2024 | $25 | TL

Lenswood Riesling 2020 Working a new way with the riesling in this vintage, the wine was fermented and spent 7 months in old barrels with lees contact, leaving a delicate 5g/L RS in the final wine. The barrel characters offer some cream and spice to the apple and custard apple flavours; the sugars are benign yet textural and in context. Screw cap | 12.5% alc. | To 2025 | $30 | TL

eenhill

Greenhill Road, Summertown, SA 5141 **T** (08) 8390 1615 **www**.greenhillwines.com.au **OPEN** Fri-10-5 or by appt **WINEMAKER** Paul Henschke **EST**. 2010 **DOZENS** 800 **VYDS** 1.5ha

ated on a former strawberry farm, Greenhill Wines is a winery, vineyard, cellar door and run by Drs Paul and Penny Henschke. Paul creates a range of estate pinot-based sparkling es as well as estate and Piccadilly Valley-sourced white and red table wines. Being a wine robiologist, Paul likes to exploit yeast in creative ways to enrich flavour complexity. Penny duces a range of Mediterranean foods to complement the wine tasting experience. (TL)

Blanc de Noir Brut 2017 Pinot meunier. From the tiny Summertown estate of Drs Paul and Penny Henschke, with a minimum 18 months on lees and disgorged on demand. This is the epitome of purity, the faintest of apple/aldehyde, all the character and complexity of traditional method sparkling, with lively sherbet brightness on the palate and excellent fine talc mouthfeel. A delicate touch yielding a lovely aperitif wine. Diam | 12% alc. | $29 | TL

Brut Rosé 2013 Lightly blushed pinot noir that's spent 6.5 years on lees, delicately expressed and with some earthy, savoury notes now showing in the beginning, but coming to life in the sipping; its bright red fruit flavours irrepressible. Diam | 12% alc. | $29 | TL

hndorf Hill Winery

ain Road, Hahndorf, SA 5245 **T** (08) 8388 7512 **www**.hahndorfhillwinery.com.au **OPEN** 7 days **WINEMAKER** Larry Jacobs **EST**. 2002 **DOZENS** 6000 **VYDS** 6.5ha

y Jacobs and Marc Dobson, both originally from South Africa, purchased Hahndorf Hill ery in 2002. Before migrating, Larry had given up a career in intensive care medicine in 8 when he bought an abandoned property in Stellenbosch and established the near-iconic derbosch Wines. It was purchased at the end of '96 and the pair eventually found their to Australia and Hahndorf Hill. In 2006, their investment in the winery and cellar door was arded by induction into the South Australian Tourism Hall of Fame.

BAROSSA
FLEURIEU
MOUNT LOFTY RANGES
FAR NORTH
LIMESTONE COAST
LOWER MURRAY
THE PENINSULAS

95 **White Mischief Adelaide Hills Grüner Veltliner 2020** Small bunches started the ball rolling for a v with an excellent mouthfeel and a faint white-pepper varietal marker. The length and drive on the finish give the wine serious gravitas. Attention to vinification detail is its own reward. Screw cap | 13% alc. | To 2023 | $24 | JH | ♥

GRU Adelaide Hills Grüner Veltliner 2020 A well-defined middle path between a restrained fruit expression and more savoury lines. Typical notes of cut celery and white pepper, subtle citron an Granny Smith apple flavours. An immaculately tempered palate with a dash of spice and grapefru pithy acidity. Pleasing and complex textures deliver a fulfilling wine on many counts. Screw cap | 12.5% alc. | To 2025 | $29 | TL

Adelaide Hills Rosé 2020 39/26/22/13% tempranillo/shiraz/pinot noir and, uniquely, trollinger. Free-run juices co-fermented to a quite zingy style, lively acidity throughout, a bouquet of garde herbs and crunchy white strawberry bits. A top summer buster. Screw cap | 12.5% alc. | To 2022 | $24 | TL

94 **Adelaide Hills Pinot Grigio 2020** Fresh and zesty. Floral and field grassy to begin, with terrific pit and chalkiness in the feels. Familiar Pink Lady apple flavours get a little tickle from faint, spicy mu notes. A gentle tang in the mid palate sends this wine on its summery, refreshing way. Screw cap | 12.5% alc. | To 2022 | $25 | TL

Head in the Clouds

36 Neate Avenue, Belair, SA 5052 **T** 0404 440 298 **www**.headinthecloudswines.com **WINEMAKER** Ashl Coats **EST.** 2008 **DOZENS** 300

Head in the Clouds is a family-run microbusiness that, by virtue of its size, is able to lavish attention to detail on sourcing its intake of contract-grown grapes and on the vinification of its wines. The wines are distributed statewide by Glenn Beale.

91 **Adelaide Hills Pinot Grigio 2020** With 10% pinot blanc, which punches well above its weight even in this tiny proportion. Savoury senses like fennel and sea air mix with a light honeyed and blosso note to begin. The palate is crisp yet spicy and lifted. Quite moreish. Don't serve it too cold. Screw cap | 12.6% alc. | To 2023 | $20 | TL

Heirloom Vineyards

PO Box 39, McLaren Vale, SA 5171 **T** (08) 8323 8979 **www**.heirloomvineyards.com.au **WINEMAKER** Elena Brooks **EST.** 2004

Another venture for winemaker Elena Brooks and her husband Zar. They met during the 200 vintage and one thing led to another, as they say. The lofty aims of Heirloom are 'to preserv the best of tradition, the unique old vineyards of SA, and to champion the best clones of each variety, embracing organic and biodynamic farming'. The quality of the wines has bee consistently very good.

96 **McLaren Vale Shiraz 2019** Dashing, slick and transfixing. Inky blackberry, black cherry and satsur plum fruit delivering density with impressive definition, lifted by violet perfume and set to a grand foundation of fresh licorice. Elena Brooks' signature fine-ground tannins carry a long finish Screw cap | 14.5% alc. | To 2034 | $40 | TS

Honey Moon Vineyard

135 Church Hill Road, Echunga, SA 5153 **T** 0438 727 079 **www**.honeymoonvineyard.com.au **OPEN** By appt **WINEMAKER** Jane Bromley, Hylton McLean **EST.** 2004 **DOZENS** 800 **VYDS** 1.2ha

Jane Bromley and Hylton McLean planted 0.7ha of pinot noir (clones 777, 114 and 115) and 0.5ha of shiraz (selected from 2 old vineyards known for their spicy fruit flavours). The moor a striking feature of the landscape, particularly at harvest time when, as a full moon, it appe as a dollop of rich honey in the sky – hence the name.

96 **EBVR Adelaide Hills 2018** EBVR stands for Early Bottled Vintage Red, a fortified take on what used be known here as Vintage Port. 63% tinta roriz (tempranillo), 31% shiraz and 6% McLaren Vale touri nacional. Made traditionally, it exudes blackberry-liqueur-meets-chocolate aromatics, with the gr art of integrating wood-aged brandy spirit to be virtually invisible. Sweetness is restrained and the fruit chocolate flavours refuse to disappear. Delicious. Diam | 20% alc. | $60 | TL

Jericho Wines

13 Moore Street, Willunga, SA 5172 (postal) **T** 0410 519 945 **www**.jerichowines.com.au **WINEMAKER** Neil Jericho, Andrew Jericho **EST.** 2012 **DOZENS** 5000

is venture the whole family is involved. The winemaking team consists of father and son, and Andrew Jericho. Wife Kaye is an experienced vintage widow, eldest daughter Sally marketing and accounting degrees (she worked for Wine Australia for 10 years). Youngest Kim was torn between oenology, hospitality and graphic design; he opted for the latter, ce designing the highly standout label and Jericho branding.

Limited Release Average 24 Years Age Tawny NV A blend of tawny across 6 barrels that Neil Jericho bought in his early career, along with his own fruit-cum-tawny that he crafted between regions, growing a family and realising the importance of the idiom to the Australian wine narrative. Emphasised, surely, by his experience at Taylor Fladgate in Portugal and later at Campbells and Brown Brothers. Moroccan souk: date, tamarind and clove. Darjeeling tea. Walnut. Ginger. Rancio cheesecloth, varnish and nostril stinging lift. Very fine. Cork | 19.8% alc. | $85 | NG | ♥

Kuitpo Lockett Vineyard Adelaide Hills Fumé Blanc 2019 Shattering stereotypes and striking a pose of immense promise and strident energy into a misbegotten category! Powerful scents of hedgerow, spruce, resin, quince, cheesecloth, nettle and durian. A rail of new oak, the beam of guidance. Mineral and thick and gristly and pungent. Long. Palate-staining. Intense. Côtat-like. Groundbreaking. Diam | 13.5% alc. | To 2027 | $42 | NG | ♥

Selected Vineyards Adelaide Hills Rosé 2020 A gorgeous colour: faint coral with a subtle copper hue. Poached strawberry, musk stick and a hint of kirsch pour along juicy acid rails, pulling the saliva out of the mouth. Crunchy, smoky, gently tannic and persistent, this is an exceptional rosé, attesting to just how exciting this category is in Australia. Screw cap | 13.2% alc. | To 2021 | $26 | NG

Linea

Shipsters Road, Kensington Park, SA 5068 (postal) **T** (08) 8431 3556 **www**.lalinea.com.au
MAKER Peter Leske **EST.** 2007 **DOZENS** 4000 **VYDS** 6.64ha

Linea is a partnership between experienced wine industry professionals Peter Leske Nepenthe) and David LeMire MW. Peter was among the first to recognise the potential of pranillo in Australia and his knowledge of it is reflected in the 3 wine styles made from the ety: a dry rosé, a dry red blended from several Adelaide Hills vineyards, and Sureno, made elect vintages from specific sites at the southern end of the Hills.

Adelaide Hills Mencia 2019 Only a handful are crafting this variety at the moment, hopefully more will see its pleasantries. Cherry and dusty white pepper, a most desirable palate weight and flow. Very distinctive tannins that start in the juice then rise and gently pucker. Encourages follow-up pours. I'll have mine with a char-grilled steak and bearnaise. Screw cap | 13% alc. | To 2025 | $29 | TL | ♥

Prova

Main Street, Hahndorf, SA 5245 **T** (08) 8388 7330 **www**.laprova.com.au **OPEN** 1st w'end of the th 11-5 or by appt **WINEMAKER** Sam Scott **EST.** 2009 **DOZENS** 5000

n Scott's great-grandfather worked in the cellar for Max Schubert and passed his owledge down to Sam's grandfather. It was he who gave Sam his early education. Sam olled in business at university, continuing the casual retailing with Booze Brothers – which d started while at school – afterwards picking up experience all over until '06, when he ved to Bird in Hand winery. This is where Andrew Nugent indicated that it was about time took the plunge on his own account and this he has done.

Colpevole Adelaide Hills Nebbiolo 2018 All the mysteries of nebbiolo unveiled here. There's a faint petrichor note and roast root vegetables to start, then some cherry. As expected, a complete wraparound of varietal tannins coat the mouth, but allow the fruit and savoury weave to remain true to the finish. Stylish and very moreish. Screw cap | 14.1% alc. | To 2030 | $45 | TL

Adelaide Hills Pinot Grigio 2020 Orchard florals suggest a pretty wine, and this is that. But the energy here is astounding, with fabulous grapefruit-like acidity and pith. It's already exciting the palate in that sense, yet there's an underlying layer of apple turnover flavour as well, bringing even more joy. Screw cap | 12.5% alc. | To 2023 | $26 | TL

Adelaide Hills Nebbiolo Rosato 2020 Rosé of the Year 2022. Pink with copper tinges. The nose is a little earthy, along with its red fruits, and then you get a rush of crunchy, zingy red and white berries, a peppery spice and salivating finish, leaving the palate thirsty for more and more. Fantastic rosé. Screw cap | 12.8% alc. | To 2024 | $26 | TL | ♥

Limestone Coast Dolcetto 2020 You've got to love a wine with aromas that strike you with as much personality as this. Crushed blueberry, with handfuls of kitchen herbs, and a distinctive dark-berried sweet spot on the palate, textured up with pith and lightly puckery tannins. Heaps of energy, and just a little twist of darker amaro bitters to finish. Smashing. Screw cap | 13.5% alc. | To 2026 | $26 | TL

94 **Adelaide Hills Fiano 2020** There's a slate-like note to begin, mineral to the nose, with Winemaker Sam Scott's signature skill of creating vibrant lift as well as textural foundations. Lemon fruit and first, then a blanched nut mouthfeel. Salines, often typical in the variety, season the palate as the wine lingers. Screw cap | 13.5% alc. | To 2023 | $28 | TL

Adelaide Hills Sangiovese 2019 Wild-yeast fermented, over a month on skins, the search for 'grip tannins' kept under tight control. Pickled cherry, spice and finely etched tannins on the long, wel balanced palate add up to a wine that will fervently embrace virtually any Italian dish. Screw cap 14% alc. | To 2026 | $26 | JH

Lobethal Road Wines  

2254 Onkaparinga Valley Road, Mount Torrens, SA 5244 **T** (08) 8389 4595 **www**.lobethalroad.com **OPEN** Thurs-Mon 11-5 **WINEMAKER** Michael Sykes **EST.** 1998 **DOZENS** 7500 **VYDS** 10.5ha

Dave Neyle and Inga Lidums bring diverse, but very relevant, experience to the Lobethal R vineyard; the lion's share planted to shiraz, with smaller amounts of chardonnay, tempranil sauvignon blanc, graciano, pinot gris and roussanne. The property is managed with minima chemical input.

93 **Adelaide Hills Sauvignon Blanc 2020** From the spiritual home (in Australia) of elegant, fine-bone sauvignon blanc springs this pretty little thing. Juniper berry, white currant, hints of cassis, greer apple, white pear and sugar snap peas. The palate is whippy, persistent, deceptively concentrate and very long. Compelling wine for the price. Screw cap | 12% alc. | To 2024 | $25 | EL

92 **Adelaide Hills Pinot Gris 2020** The acidity (assuming due to elevated sites) gives a little zing on th palate, while the summer nashi pears, sugar snap peas and juniper berry flesh out things around The oak is felt from the mid palate onwards which does distract a bit, but otherwise a lovely wine with good length. Screw cap | 13.1% alc. | To 2025 | $25 | EL

Longview Vineyard 

154 Pound Road, Macclesfield, SA 5153 **T** (08) 8388 9694 **www**.longviewvineyard.com.au **OPEN** Wed-Sun 11-4, Mon-Tues by appt **WINEMAKER** Michael Sykes, Paul Hotker **EST.** 1995 **DOZENS** 200 **VYDS** 59ha

With a lifelong involvement in wine and hospitality, the Saturno family has been at the helm of Longview since 2007. A new cellar door and kitchen was unveiled in '17, adding to 16 accommodation suites, a popular function room and unique food and wine events in the vineyard.

94 **Macclesfield Grüner Veltliner 2020** One of the leading Adelaide Hills proponents of this variety, here deciding on free-run juice only, with lees returned later to soften and enrich the otherwise crisply structured palate. There's a slate-like sense to start, grapefruit and green pear, then add a dash of varietally typical white pepper, with an interesting parsnip-like line in the exit. Plenty to b captivated by. Screw cap | 12.5% alc. | To 2024 | $30 | TL

Nebbiolo Rosato 2020 An all-nebbiolo pinkie with the palest of copper hues, focusing on one of Longview's major varietal assets. The fragrance here is so captivating – orange peel and cut whit strawberry tops, reverbing in the mouth with exciting tang, a peppery spice energy, and penetrat acidity. Mouth freshener of the highest calibre. Screw cap | 13% alc. | To 2022 | $26 | TL

Mike Press Wines 

PO Box 224, Lobethal, SA 5241 **T** (08) 8389 5546 **www**.mikepresswines.com.au **WINEMAKER** Mike Pre **EST.** 1998 **DOZENS** 12 000 **VYDS** 22.7ha

Mike and Judy Press established their Kenton Valley Vineyards in 1998, when they purchase 34ha of land in the Adelaide Hills at an elevation of 500m. They produce high-quality sauvignon blanc, chardonnay, rose, pinot noir, merlot, shiraz, cabernet merlot and cabernet sauvignon, which are sold at mouth-wateringly low prices.

94 **Single Vineyard Adelaide Hills Pinot Noir Rosé 2020** Estate-grown fruit. Very bright fuchsia colou The bouquet surges out of the glass, all strawberries, fresh and poached. The palate moves onto another plane, powerful and arresting. A pinot noir masquerading as a rosé. The price is downrig ludicrous. Screw cap | 12% alc. | To 2023 | $13 | JH

Jimmy's Block Single Vineyard Adelaide Hills Shiraz 2018 A single-vineyard, single-block variatic that is a step up from the producer's standard estate shiraz, named after the favourite parcel of his (vineyard manager) son. The nose is classic cooler-climate blueberry to crimson plum with a display of peppery spice, all spilling into the palate with plenty of brightness and vitality, backed with good upright structure and length. Very smart at this rate. Screw cap | 14% alc. | To 2026 $16 | TL

It Lofty Ranges Vineyard ★★★★★

ris Road, Lenswood, SA 5240 **T** (08) 8389 8339 **www**.mtloftyrangesvineyard.com.au **OPEN** Fri-Sun ublic hols 11-5 **WINEMAKER** Peter Leske, Taras Ochota **EST.** 1992 **DOZENS** 3000 **VYDS** 4.6ha

Lofty Ranges is owned and operated by Sharon Pearson and Garry Sweeney. Nestled gh in the Lenswood subregion of the Adelaide Hills at an altitude of 500m, the very steep rth-facing vineyard is pruned and picked by hand. The soil is sandy clay loam with a rock se of white quartz and ironstone, and irrigation is kept to a minimum to allow the wines to splay vintage characteristics.

Home Block Lenswood Riesling 2020 A fabulous expression of this variety. High-toned white orchard florals and cut yellow and green citrus fruits, with brilliant acidity and pithy minerality in the mouth. It's even spicy, with length, line and glorious tangy flavour retention. A real riesling pleasure. Screw cap | 12.5% alc. | To 2026 | $30 | TL

urdoch Hill ★★★★★

) Mappinga Road, Woodside, SA 5244 **T** (08) 7200 5018 **www**.murdochhill.com.au **OPEN** Thurs-Mon -4 **WINEMAKER** Michael Downer **EST.** 1998 **DOZENS** 5000 **VYDS** 17.3ha

ittle over 20ha of vines have been established on the undulating, gum tree-studded untryside of Charlie and Julie Downer's 60yo Erika property, 4km east of Oakbank. Son chael, with a bachelor of oenology degree from the University of Adelaide, is winemaker.

Adelaide Hills Sauvignon Blanc 2020 The aromatic bouquet has a suite of nettle, herb and fresh-cut-grass notes that play directly to the lively and fresh palate, there picked up with gooseberry and citrus fruit. The finish is clean and brightly polished, the wine at its best now. Screw cap | 12% alc. | To 2022 | $24 | JH

Adelaide Hills Pinot Noir 2020 Perfume lifts from the glass, earthy, spicy and a delicate aperol note. The palate is in the winemaker's preferred style, juicy and gently flowing, light to medium weight, a soft grip to finish. Ethereal is the word. Screw cap | 13% alc. | To 2026 | $30 | TL

epenthe  

Jones Road, Balhannah, SA 5242 **T** (08) 8398 8899 **www**.nepenthe.com.au **OPEN** 7 days 10-5 **NEMAKER** James Evers **EST.** 1994 **DOZENS** 44000 **VYDS** 93ha

epenthe quickly established its reputation as a producer of high-quality wines, but founder Tweddell died unexpectedly in 2006 and the business was purchased by Australian ntage Limited, then McGuigan Wines (Barossa Valley). The Nepenthe winery has since been urchased by Peter Leske and Mark Kozned, and provides contract winemaking services via eir Revenir venture. Nepenthe has 93ha of close-planted vines in the Adelaide Hills, with an otic array of varieties.

Altitude Adelaide Hills Pinot Gris 2020 Classical pear and apple to begin, orchard florals as well. A 6-week stint on lees has imparted some creamy texture to the palate, with the pomme fruits and a dash of citrus continuing throughout. Perfectly acceptable and good value. Screw cap | 13.5% alc. | To 2023 | $20 | TL

Altitude Adelaide Hills Sauvignon Blanc 2020 All the good sauvignon blanc feels in here, tropical fruits, passionfruit, a smattering of lime. What attracts, too, is a well-tempered palate that doesn't rely on simplistic acidity, but rather finds a satisfying textural feel. Screw cap | 13.6% alc. | To 2023 | $20 | TL

ew Era Vineyards 

Box 391, Woodside SA 5244 **T** 0413 544 246 **www**.neweravineyards.com.au **NEMAKER** Robert Baxter, Iain Baxter **EST.** 1988 **DOZENS** 1500 **VYDS** 15ha

ne New Era vineyard is situated over a gold reef that was mined for 60 years until 1940, hen all recoverable gold had been extracted. The vineyard was mostly contracted to oster's; much of the production is sold to other winemakers in the region. The small nount of wine made has been the subject of favourable reviews.

Adelaide Hills Grüner Veltliner 2020 Devastated by the December 2019 Hills bushfires, 2t of grüner fruit was donated to New Era by the Saturno lads at Longview Vineyard in Macclesfield. One portion went to tank for a crisp and crunchy vibe, the other underwent wild fermentation in barrels for a richer element, then blended together. This is a delicate, pithy, yellow-citrus-natured wine. The variety's trademark white pepper is there in the background, while other attractive notes pop out as well – a grapefruit tang offset by a faint honey cornflake. A brilliant mouth-watering finish. What a success. Screw cap | 12.5% alc. | To 2024 | $25 | TL

Nova Vita Wines

11 Woodlands Road, Kenton Valley, SA 5235 **T** (08) 8356 0454 **www**.novavitawines.com.au
OPEN Wed–Sun 11–5 **WINEMAKER** Mark Kozned **EST.** 2005 **DOZENS** 20000 **VYDS** 49ha

The name Nova Vita reflects the beginning of Mark and Jo Kozned's new life, the firebird on the label coming from their Russian ancestry – it is a Russian myth that only a happy or lucky person may see the bird or hear its song. They are building a new winery and cellar door at the Woodlands Ridge Vineyard.

94 **Firebird Adelaide Hills Cabernet Sauvignon 2018** Sourced from an estate vineyard in the far northern districts of the Hills, settled and rested for close to 2 years in a range of new and older, small and larger oak vessels. This offers an attractive, gentile style of cabernet, unmistakably blackcurrant, with a subtle roasted red capsicum layered into it. The flavours weave well together, the palate quite lively and the tannins relaxed; a faint bitterness built into the finish of this medium-bodied style. Screw cap | 14.5% alc. | To 2028 | $30 | TL

Ochota Barrels

Merchants Road, Basket Range, SA 5138 **T** 0400 798 818 **www**.ochotabarrels.com
WINEMAKER Taras Ochota **EST.** 2008 **DOZENS** 900 **VYDS** 0.5ha

Taras Ochota has been a talisman for a new generation of Australian winemakers, creating with wife Amber an exciting portfolio of wines from small, beloved Adelaide Hills blocks as well as neighbouring districts such as McLaren Vale. They set up Ochota Barrels in 2008 and garnered much more than a cult following. Tragically, Taras died in October 2020. The 2021 vintage was managed by Amber, with assistance of Taras' dad Yari and Louis Schofield, as well as long-time winemaking mentor Peter Leske. (TL)

96 **Control Voltage +5VOV Chardonnay 2020** Sourced from a single vineyard in the Piccadilly Valley, with focused terroir expression. Smells of delicate bath powders one moment, soft lime and mint gels the next. Totally seductive. The palate is energised and mineral, with subtle lemon zest and Pink Lady apple suggestions, tonic quinine and spice. Has fabulous thrust and a mouth-watering finish. A bloody marvel. Cork | 13.6% alc. | To 2026 | $60 | TL

Paracombe Wines

294b Paracombe Road, Paracombe, SA 5132 **T** (08) 8380 5058 **www**.paracombewines.com **OPEN** By appt
WINEMAKER Paul Drogemuller **EST.** 1983 **DOZENS** 15000 **VYDS** 22.1ha

Paul and Kathy Drogemuller established Paracombe Wines in 1983 in the wake of the devastating Ash Wednesday bushfires. The winery is located high on a plateau at Paracombe, looking out over the Mount Lofty Ranges, and the vineyard is run with minimal irrigation and hand pruning to keep yields low.

93 **Adelaide Hills Pinot Blanc 2020** Lots to like here, from an alluring aroma that carries multiple suggestions, sea spray and white citrus blossom among them. It all flows onto the palate in a neatly balanced, fresh, savoury and saline style that begs for the company of top-shelf seafood. Screw cap | 11% alc. | To 2022 | $23 | TL

The Reuben 2016 The epitome of Australian bordeaux blending: 37/32/23/6/2% cabernet sauvignon/merlot/cabernet franc/malbec/shiraz. A well-woven, understated yet classic aromatic introduction, similarly expressed on the palate. Complex and confident, a distinctive energy and freshness as well. Recommended at such an attractive price. Screw cap | 14.6% alc. | To 2026 | $25 | TL

92 **Adelaide Hills Shiraz 2016** Well crafted and balanced evenly, with classic cool-climate spice over dark fruits. Medium to full bodied, settled into its skin with 5 years of age on it, the 30% new oak integrated. And great value. Screw cap | 14.6% alc. | To 2026 | $25 | TL

Pike & Joyce

730 Mawson Road, Lenswood, SA 5240 **T** (08) 8389 8102 **www**.pikeandjoyce.com.au **OPEN** 7 days 11–4
WINEMAKER Steve Baraglia, Andrew Kenny **EST.** 1998 **DOZENS** 5000 **VYDS** 18.5ha

This is a partnership between the Pike family (of Clare Valley fame) and the Joyce family, related to Andrew Pike's wife, Cathy. The Joyce family have been orchardists at Lenswood fo er 100 years and also have extensive operations in the Riverland. The wines are made at the es' Clare Valley winery.

Beurre Bosc Adelaide Hills Pinot Gris 2020 Lovely familiar varietal pear and apple aromas. There's a little squeeze of lemon over the same fruit profile on the palate, giving a note of acidity. A medium-bodied palate, structured by a small portion of barrel ferment and a dash of peppery spice on the finish. Tasty and well crafted. Screw cap | 13% alc. | To 2023 | $25 | TL

rotero

Olivers Road, McLaren Vale SA 5171 **T** (08) 8323 8000 **www**.protero.com.au **OPEN** By appt
IEMAKER Stephen Pannell **EST.** 1999 **DOZENS** 3000 **VYDS** 13.2ha

rrounded by native bush, twice in 20 years the Protero vineyard has been surrounded by e and twice it has survived (including a week after the Pannells bought the property in cember 2019). Nebbiolo remains a passion, but Stephen poses the questions each year: at is Australian nebbiolo? How does it translate? 'We shouldn't attempt to replicate the nes of Piedmont, but rather create a unique style of nebbiolo that speaks of our place.' (TL)

Gumeracha Adelaide Hills Nebbiolo 2018 You might just want to stay with the aromas forever and a day, captivating, lifted, generous in their mix of dried orange, garden rose beds, leaf stem and petal, followed by a completely different savoury, mineral, amaro bitters-toned palate. Nebbiolo tannins as expected, fitting comfortably into the matrix. A fascinating, long-term journey ahead. Screw cap | 14% alc. | To 2030 | $38 | TL

iposte

Box 256, Lobethal, SA 5241 **T** 0412 816 107 **www**.timknappstein.com.au **WINEMAKER** Tim Knappstein
. 2006 **DOZENS** 14000

n Knappstein is a 3rd-generation vigneron, his winemaking lineage dating back to 1893 the Clare Valley. He made his first wines at the family's Stanley Wine Company and tablished his own wine company in the Clare Valley in 1976. After the sale of that company '81, Tim relocated to Lenswood in the Adelaide Hills to make cool-climate wines led by pinot ir and chardonnay. His quest has now been achieved with consistently excellent wines flected in the winery's 5-star rating since the *Wine Companion 2012*.

The Cutlass Single Vineyard Adelaide Hills Shiraz 2019 Adelaide Hills and shiraz are having a public love affair, exemplified by this wine's brightly flavoured pepper, spice and cherry fruits, on a very complex palate that's just within medium-bodied bounds. Its 50% whole-bunch fermentation adds fine, savoury tannins to the long finish. Screw cap | 13.5% alc. | To 2027 | $28 | JH

haw + Smith

6 Jones Road, Balhannah, SA 5242 **T** (08) 8398 0500 **www**.shawandsmith.com **OPEN** 7 days 11-5
NEMAKER Martin Shaw, Adam Wadewitz **EST.** 1989 **VYDS** 56ha

ousins Martin Shaw and Michael Hill Smith MW already had unbeatable experience when ey founded Shaw + Smith as a virtual winery in 1989. In '99 Martin and Michael purchased e 36ha Balhannah property, building the superbly designed winery in 2000 and planting ore sauvignon blanc, shiraz, pinot noir and riesling. It is here that visitors can taste the wines appropriately beautiful surroundings.

M3 Adelaide Hills Chardonnay 2020 The first thing that strikes you is an elegance that is so fundamental to the style and respectful to the elite fruit within. The faintest of oak lifts adds a complexity to start, but the energy and concentration of the fruit become the prime focus on the palate. It's all about chardonnay's finest flavours and a vibrant acidity to drive it long into the future. Screw cap | 13.5% alc. | To 2030 | $49 | TL | ♥

Adelaide Hills Sauvignon Blanc 2020 A lightness of touch now marks this wine, less wild-tropical-fruit punch and more grapefruit/citrus, both aromatic partners creating a superbly balanced aromatic pattern that is enhanced by a short maturation on lees to develop the most delicious, powdery mouthfeel. Always a style leader, now offering next-level varietal sophistication. Screw cap | 12.5% alc. | To 2023 | $29 | TL | ♥

Adelaide Hills Riesling 2020 From a high Lenswood vineyard, half whole-bunch pressed, half crushed. The blend sat on lees for 4 months to develop a delicate Granny Smith/Pink Lady apple textural pithiness that fits perfectly with those same fruit flavours and pure orchard floral aromatics. Delicious, mouth-awakening, aperitif styling. Screw cap | 11.5% alc. | To 2028 | $33 | TL | ♥

Sidewood Estate  ★★★★

6 River Road, Hahndorf, SA 5245 **T** (08) 8388 1673 **www**.sidewood.com.au **OPEN** Wed-Mon 11-5, Fri-Sat 11-8.30 **WINEMAKER** Darryl Catlin **EST.** 2004 **VYDS** 90ha

Sidewood Estate was established in 2004. It is owned by Owen and Cassandra Inglis who operate it as a winery and cidery. Significant expenditure on regeneration of the vineyards was already well underway when Sidewood invested over $12 million in the expansion of the winery, increasing capacity from 500t to 2000t each vintage and implementing sustainable improvements including 100kW solar panels, water treatment works and insulation for the winery. The expansion includes new bottling and canning facilities capable of handling 6 million bottles of wine and cider annually. A multimillion-dollar restaurant, cellar door and cidery was opened in 2020.

97 **Oberlin Adelaide Hills Pinot Noir 2019** One of 3 single-clone pinots in this range. 100% whole bunches and wild ferment. Alluring crimson colours in the glass, sophisticated cherry aromas tha want to be swallowed up by the stems. Starts out a little reserved but builds on the palate with rea power and depth. Dark cherry and raspberry notes in abundance, with layers and layers unfolding the bottle for hours. Totally engaging. Screw cap | 13.5% alc. | To 2028 | $40 | TL

96 **Mappinga Shiraz 2018** Finely sculpted, with sophisticated balance of flavour and structure, delici concentration of blacker fruits and berries, with fresh acidity, lip-smacking tannins, and white-pepper-led spices. Ticks all the boxes. Screw cap | 14.5% alc. | To 2030 | $60 | TL

95 **Adelaide Hills Sauvignon Blanc 2020** A fragrant blossom-filled bouquet, with tropical notes feedi through to a lively, juicy palate that presents a dual stream of citrus and passionfruit flavours. Has effortless charm that many sauvignon blancs lack. Ready now. Screw cap | 12% alc. | To 2022 | $22 | JH

Adelaide Hills Chardonnay 2020 Styled to be most respectful to the best that Hills fruit can offer, sourced across the best estate and grower blocks. Multi-clonal and cleverly steered through a ran of barrel sizes (25% new). It's all about crisp, ripe stone fruit and subtle citrus-focused chardonnay with delightfully balanced oak sitting in support, developing a creamy palate while holding excell length. Great value. Screw cap | 13% alc. | To 2025 | $24 | TL

Adelaide Hills Shiraz 2019 Quintessential Adelaide Hills shiraz. Dark berries and aromatic garden herbs, swirling fruit with a classy Amaro bitters edge and fine tannins providing a gently chewines A terrific expression of region and variety. Screw cap | 14% alc. | To 2028 | $26 | TL

94 **Adelaide Hills Pinot Blanc 2020** Steered towards the fresh and crisp side of the variety's capaciti with gentle treatment in hand picking, wild fermentation to start, then straight to barrel. It all contributes to a clear, citrus sense, specifically yellow grapefruit in its aromatics and flavours. A tiny sprinkle of sugariness for balance, some pithiness and bright acidity for textural feels. Mouth-watering. A top aperitif. Screw cap | 12.7% alc. | To 2023 | $24 | TL

Silver Lining 

60 Gleneagles Road, Mount Osmond, SA 5064 **T** 0438 736 052 **www**.silverliningwine.com.au **WINEMAKER** Leigh Ratzmer, Marty Edwards **EST.** 2020 **DOZENS** 1200

The name alone says a lot about the positive and life-affirming attitude of this new venture by Marty Edwards, whose love of the Adelaide Hills was nurtured by his family's pioneering involvement with The Lane Vineyard in Hahndorf. They have all left that business now but af being diagnosed with Parkinson's Disease in 2012, Marty (previously an elite navy clearance diver) decided he still had a lot more to give. He focused on his health and young family, but couldn't give up his passion for Hills vineyards and wines. Silver Lining Wines was the result with proceeds going to Parkinson's Disease research with the aim of helping others on the same challenging journey as this inspiring vigneron. (TL)

94 **Adelaide Hills Chardonnay 2020** From the Macclesfield district. This chardonnay is cast in a tight and linear style, clear and crisp with delicate opening lines that rise to burst with typical Hills whit stone fruit and lemon-like acidity. After a short time in new and seasoned French barrels there's a faint background of lemon-zested cream biscuit. It's delicious. Deceptively so. Screw cap | 13% alc. | To 2028 | $30 | TL

Tapanappa 

15 Spring Gully Road, Piccadilly, SA 5151 **T** (08) 7324 5301 **www**.tapanappa.com.au **OPEN** 7 days 11-4 **WINEMAKER** Brian Croser **EST.** 2002 **DOZENS** 2500 **VYDS** 16.7ha

Tapanappa was founded by Brian Croser in 2002. The word Tapanappa is probably derived from the local Aboriginal language and likely translates to 'stick to the path'. Through panappa, Brian is continuing a career-long mission of matching the climate, soil and ›ology of distinguished sites to the right varieties, and then developing and managing the neyards to optimise quality. Tapanappa is dedicated to producing unique 'wines of terroir' om its 3 distinguished sites in SA with its winery located in the heart of the Piccadilly Valley.

Foggy Hill Vineyard Pinot Noir 2019 A darker note of berry here – blueberry and black cherry. It's fully fragrant, with the stems adding their woody spice and seasoning. What happens on the palate is unique, the structure of the wine taking your senses deeper into the flavour well, where a gastronomic heart of subtle amaro-like bitters dwells. Learned palates will want to sit on this and watch it unfold for hours, if not years. Cork | 13% alc. | To 2030 | $55 | TL | ♥

enafeate Creek Wines

71 Gawler-One Tree Hill Road, One Tree Hill, SA 5114 **T** (08) 8280 7715 **www**.tcw.com.au
EN Fri-Sun & public hols 11-5 **WINEMAKER** Larry Costa, Michael Costa **EST.** 2002 **DOZENS** 3000
DS 1ha

rry Costa, a former hairdresser, embarked on winemaking as a hobby in 2002. The property situated on the rolling countryside of One Tree Hill in the Mount Lofty Ranges. The business ew rapidly, and now Michael Costa, Larry's son, with 18 vintages under his belt and Flying inemaker stints in southern Italy and Provence, has joined his father as co-owner of the ısiness. The red wines have won many medals over the years.

One Tree Hill Basket Press Montepulciano 2017 In the house style, a big red wine with an incredibly expressive nose: dark fruit, crushed and mulled with plenty of sweet spice, prunes, blackberries and dark mint chocolate. The aromas all follow through on the palate, structurally balanced to match the fuller-bodied feel, with acidity and tannins all in play. A demonstrative wine suited to the campfire and rustic cooking. Screw cap | 14.5% alc. | To 2028 | $30 | TL

he Other Wine Co 

6 Jones Road, Balhannah, SA 5242 **T** (08) 8398 0500 **www**.theotherwineco.com **OPEN** At Shaw + Smith
NEMAKER Martin Shaw, Adam Wadewitz **EST.** 2015 **DOZENS** 1000

is is the venture of Michael Hill Smith and Martin Shaw, established in the shadow of naw + Smith but with an entirely different focus and separate marketing. The name reflects e wines, which are intended for casual consumption; the whole focus being freshness ombined with seductive mouthfeel. The concept of matching variety and place is one thout any particular limits and there may well be other wines made by The Other Wine Co years to come.

Adelaide Hills Shiraz 2020 From an Adelaide Hills vineyard outside Shaw + Smith's usual remit, this time from the Echunga district, vinified in neutral concrete vats using a mix of whole berries and 15% whole bunches. A lighter-bodied style, redolent with bright plum fruit, offset with a subtle background of wood and stems, underpinned by a gentle spice and earthiness. Quite delicious and immensely drinkable. Screw cap | 13% alc. | To 2024 | $26 | TL

McLaren Vale Grenache 2020 Initial earthy, almost ironwork-like notes and bush herbals lead into a juicy style, a little ripper. It's fresh and vibrant, but then gathers an encouraging mouthfeel with powdery, earthy tannins. Very likeable. Screw cap | 13.5% alc. | To 2025 | $27 | TL

omich Wines 

King William Road, Unley, SA 5061 **T** (08) 8299 7500 **www**.tomich.com.au **OPEN** By appt
NEMAKER Randal Tomich **EST.** 2002 **DOZENS** 40 000 **VYDS** 85ha

triarch John Tomich was born on a vineyard near Mildura, where he learnt firsthand the skills d knowledge required for premium grapegrowing. He completed postgraduate studies winemaking at the University of Adelaide in 2002 and embarked on the master of wine vision course from the Institute of Masters of Wine. His son Randal is a cutting from the old ne (metaphorically speaking), having invented new equipment and techniques for tending e family's vineyard in the Adelaide Hills, resulting in a 60% saving in time and fuel costs.

Woodside Vineyard Adelaide Hills Pinot Noir 2019 At this price, this is a very smart wine. It brings cherry and plum to the flavour wheel, deliciously balanced spice suggesting a note of fennel and thyme, even a light touch of mint, sliding easily through its subtly sticky, grippy tannin curtains to finish. All-round pinot goodness, at a very attractive price. Screw cap | 13% alc. | To 2026 | $30 | TL

Totino Estate

982 Port Road, Albert Park, SA 5014 (postal) **T** (08) 8349 1200 www.totinowines.com.au
WINEMAKER Don Totino, Damien Harris **EST.** 1992 **DOZENS** 15000 **VYDS** 29ha

Don Totino migrated from Italy in 1968, and at the age of 18 became the youngest barber in Australia. He soon moved on, into general food and importing and distribution. Festival City, as the business is known, has been highly successful, recognised by a recent significant award from the Italian government. In 1998 he purchased a rundown vineyard at Paracombe in the Adelaide Hills, since extending the plantings. Various family members, including daughter Linda, are involved in the business.

93 **Adelaide Hills Cabernet Sauvignon 2017** No mistaking the cabernet here. In a cooler year from the northern Paracombe district of the region, it has ripened slowly, delivering concentrated cassis wit spice and the cedar of oak maturation. Drinking well now in this traditional style and will repay well with cellaring for 5–10 years. Screw cap | 14% alc. | To 2030 | $25 | TL

Turon Wines

1760 Lobethal Road, Lobethal, SA 5241 **T** 0423 956 480 www.turonwines.com.au **OPEN** By appt
WINEMAKER Turon White **EST.** 2013 **DOZENS** 800 **VYDS** 2ha

This is the thoroughly impressive venture of newlyweds Turon and Alex White. Turon has a minimal-intervention approach to winemaking, being confident enough to stand back and let the wine develop and be itself, but equally being prepared to intervene if needs must. They have built a winery at their property in Lenswood and turned it into a cooperative, where young winemakers can work together, sharing equipment, resources and knowledge. They called the venture the Hills Handcrafted Collective, with wines to be released a bit further down the track. Given the quality of the wines released under the Turon Wines label, one is tempted to say the sky's the limit. As it is, it was one of the top new wineries in the *Wine Companion 2019*.

93 **Artist Series Adelaide Hills Field Blend 2020** Here we have sauvignon blanc, grüner veltliner and chardonnay, the 3 most lauded whites of the Hills region. Do they get on together? They absolutely do. Attractive white orchard florals and exciting palate zing, lemony and saline and tonic water in th flavour zone. Technically whizz bang and simply yum. Screw cap | 12.9% alc. | To 2024 | $25 | T

Uraidla

30 Swamp Road, Uraidla, SA 5142 www.uraidlawines.com.au **WINEMAKER** Frank Virgara **EST.** 2016

Third-generation Uraidla boy Frank Virgara continues family tradition, following in the footste of his father Girolamo and grandfather, local market gardeners, fruit and vegetable retailers and well-known owners and operators of the fruit mart in the nearby Stirling township. Hills-based winemaker Turon White has sourced fruit from the Virgara vineyards and has been engaged as winemaker for the new releases of Momo wines under the Uraidla banner. (TL)

95 **Momo Adelaide Hills Chardonnay 2020** Textbook modern Australian chardonnay. The oak offers gingery spice and faint charriness and lees character as toasted nuttiness. The rich stone fruits sit comfortably just at the surface, lingering all the way through the palate. Well done. Screw cap | 13.5% alc. | To 2026 | $35 | TL

Wicks Estate Wines

21 Franklin Street, Adelaide, SA 5000 (postal) **T** (08) 82120004 www.wicksestate.com.au
WINEMAKER Adam Carnaby **EST.** 2000 **DOZENS** 25000 **VYDS** 53.96ha

Tim and Simon Wicks had a long-term involvement with orchard and nursery operations at Highbury in the Adelaide Hills prior to purchasing their property at Woodside in 1999. They planted fractionally less than 54ha of sauvignon blanc, shiraz, chardonnay, pinot noir, cabernet sauvignon, tempranillo and riesling. Wicks Estate has won more than its fair share o wine show medals over the years, the wines priced well below their full worth.

95 **Adelaide Hills Cabernet Sauvignon 2012** Museum Release. Well reviewed when first released with just 2 years under its belt. This Tim Knappstein-steered Hills cabernet is peaking now at 8 years, releasing astonishingly intense cabernet aromatics in full crushed-blackberry/currant mode. Unmistakably varietal. The concentration of those sweet fruits and peppery spice on the palate just adds more thrills, with the tannins smoothing off, round and supportive. Extraordinary value. Screw cap | 14.5% alc. | To 2025 | $25 | TL

'ine Architect ★★★★

. Murray Street, Tanunda, SA 5352 **T** 0439 823 251 **www**.winearchitect.com.au **OPEN** Wed-Thurs , Fri 2-late, or by appt **WINEMAKER** Natasha Mooney **EST.** 2006 **DOZENS** 3000

is is a reasonably significant busman's holiday for Natasha Mooney, a well-known and highly ented winemaker whose 'day job' (her term) is to provide winemaking consultancy services some of SA's larger wineries. This allows her to find small, unique parcels of grapes that ght otherwise be blended into large-volume brands. She manages the arrangements so ıt there is no conflict of interest, making wines that are about fruit and vineyard expression. e aims for mouthfeel and drinkability without high alcohol, and for that she should be loudly plauded. Wines are released under La Bise (named for the southerly wind that blows across rgundy) and The Thief? labels.

La Bise Whole Bunch Pressed Adelaide Hills Pinot Gris 2020 From the renowned Amadio Vineyard at Kersbrook, whole-bunch pressed juice kept on full solids for a week before fermentation. Full flavoured pear – heading in the Buerre Bosc direction – with a delicate musk note there too. Delicious, mouth-watering texture and spice on the palate. All round goodness. Screw cap | 12.9% alc. | To 2024 | $22 | TL

O Wine Co

Wicks Road, Kuitpo, SA 5172 **T** 0402 120 680 **www**.xowineco.com.au **WINEMAKER** Greg Clack, :e Horstmann **EST.** 2015 **DOZENS** 1800

eg Clack is chief winemaker at Chain of Ponds in the Adelaide Hills – this remains his y job, nights and days here and there devoted to XO. Its raison d'être revolves around ıall-batch, single-vineyard wines chiefly made from grenache, barbera, chardonnay and may. The winemaking minimises wine movements, protecting freshness.

Single Vineyard Small Batch Adelaide Hills Barbera 2020 From the Kuitpo district, 10% whole bunch, wild ferment, matured on lees and stirred in older French barrels. Total purity in the nose – cherry with thyme, sweetly lifted on the palate, while kept tight underneath with neatly integrated and sympathetic tannins. Delicious all the way. Screw cap | 14% alc. | To 2026 | $32 | TL

Single Vineyard Games Night McLaren Vale Grenache Shiraz 2019 Sourced from a vineyard just southwest of the Willunga township, a small percentage of whole bunch in both varieties, the shiraz seeing one new oak barrel during maturation. And it's that cedary oak note that really lifts this wine to start, crimson cherry juices as well. Everything works nicely together here, the palate with lovely easy grip and deliciously upbeat. Lovely. Screw cap | 14.5% alc. | To 2025 | $27 | TL

ɪION

ıdelaide Plains

ıld Plains

High Street, Grange, SA 5023 (postal) **T** 0407 605 601 **www**.oldplains.com **NEMAKER** Domenic Torzi, Tim Freeland **EST.** 2003 **DOZENS** 4000 **VYDS** 12ha

d Plains is a partnership between Tim Freeland and Dom Torzi, who have acquired some of e last remaining small parcels of old-vine shiraz, grenache and cabernet sauvignon in the delaide Plains region. Wines made from these vines are sold under the Old Plains label. Pinot is, riesling and a sparkling pinot noir/chardonnay are sourced from the Adelaide Hills and ıld under the Longhop brand.

Longhop Adelaide Plains Cabernet Sauvignon 2017 No heavy-handed winemaking needed to showcase the cabernet aromas and fruit power here, in what was an unusually (and beneficially) cool year for this variety in this place. All the varietal thrills – blackcurrant, blackberry and some plum fruitcake notes, with a fulfilling palate and tannin-supported structure. Great value. Screw cap | 14.5% alc. | To 2026 | $20 | TL

irgara Wines

3 Heaslip Road, Angle Vale, SA 5117 **T** (08) 8284 7688 **www**.virgarawines.com.au **OPEN** Mon-Fri -5, w'ends 11-5 **WINEMAKER** Tony Carapetis **EST.** 2001 **DOZENS** 50000 **VYDS** 118ha

1962 the Virgara family migrated to Australia from southern Italy. Through hard work, in ɹe course they purchased land (1967) and became market gardeners, acquiring an existing neyard in Angle Vale in the early '90s. The plantings have since been expanded to almost

120ha. In 2001 the family purchased the former Barossa Valley Estates winery and today the 2nd generation of the Virgara family run the estate, employing ex-Palandri (and before that, Tahbilk) winemaker Tony Carapetis.

91 **Legacy Adelaide Sauvignon Blanc 2020** Although grown on the Adelaide Plains north of Adelaide (not a district renowned for crisp white wines) this vineyard is shaded from afternoon sun by a hug gum tree, the fruit picked at night at its coolest. Ripe fruit-salad notes with plenty of tangy acidity a mouth-watering expression. Screw cap | 13.7% alc. | To 2022 | $15 | TL

REGION

Clare Valley

Atlas Wines

PO Box 458, Clare, SA 5453 **T** 0419 847 491 **www.atlaswines.com** **WINEMAKER** Adam Barton **EST.** 2008 **DOZENS** 8000 **VYDS** 24ha

Before establishing Atlas Wines, owner and winemaker Adam Barton had an extensive winemaking career. He now has 6ha of shiraz and 2ha of cabernet sauvignon grown on a stony ridge on the eastern slopes of the region, and sources small batches from other distinguished sites in the Clare and Barossa valleys. The quality of the wines is extraordinaril good and consistent.

95 **172° Watervale Riesling 2020** A compelling wine, yet starts a little subdued, revealing candied lemon and orange blossom, with a smidge of creamed honey. Then the palate unfurls with finesse offering texture, fine acidity and a daikon radish crunch to the finish. Screw cap | 12% alc. | To 2030 | $30 | JF

Gaelic Cemetery Vineyard

Gaelic Cemetery Road, Stanley Flat, SA 5453 **T** (08) 7081 5955 **www.gaeliccemeteryvineyard.com** **OPEN** By appt **WINEMAKER** Adam Clay **EST.** 2005 **DOZENS** 2000 **VYDS** 16.8ha

Gaelic Cemetery Vineyard was planted in 1996, adjacent to the historic cemetery of the region's Scottish pioneers. Situated in a secluded valley of the Clare hills, the low-cropping vineyard, say the partners, 'is always one of the earliest ripening shiraz vineyards in the regi and mystifyingly produces fruit with both natural pH and acid analyses that can only be described as beautiful numbers'.

96 **Premium Clare Valley Riesling 2019** Upholding a magnificently pale, bright straw-green hue, this is a riesling that is embarking on its long journey, slow and distinguished. Signature lime, lemon and Granny Smith apple are still the theme, with 2 years' age drawing out the first nuances of warr spice and honey. Focused acidity holds a finish of outstanding line and precision, promising great endurance. Screw cap | 11.5% alc. | To 2034 | $38 | TS

Grosset

King Street, Auburn, SA 5451 **T** 1800 088 223 **www.grosset.com.au** **OPEN** 10-5 Wed-Sun (Spring) **WINEMAKER** Jeffrey Grosset, Brent Treloar **EST.** 1981 **DOZENS** 11000 **VYDS** 21ha

Jeffrey Grosset wears the unchallenged mantle of Australia's foremost riesling maker. Grosset's pre-eminence is recognised both domestically and internationally; however, he merits equal recognition for the other wines in his portfolio: Semillon Sauvignon Blanc from Clare Valley/Adelaide Hills, Chardonnay and Pinot Noir from the Adelaide Hills and Gaia, a Bordeaux blend from the Clare Valley. These are all benchmarks. His quietly spoken manner conceals a steely will.

97 **G110 Clare Valley Riesling 2019** A new wine and what's it like? Outrageously good. The palate sets apart as does its savouriness – it's not a fruity clone. It is spicy, with a beeswax note and layered. It has length and line with some phenolic grip, the acidity driving it. It's long, defined and yes, it is a exceptional wine. Screw cap | 12.8% alc. | To 2034 | $105 | JF

96 **Polish Hill Clare Valley Riesling 2020** This wine retains the energy and drive of Polish Hill, yet its fr concentration and ripeness has softened out any hard edges. It's beautifully fragrant, subtle even and the palate is long and pure with pith-like texture and excellent length. Lovely drink and ready now. Screw cap | 12.9% alc. | To 2030 | $65 | JF

m Barry Wines ⚲ ★★★★★

Craig Hill Road, Clare, SA 5453 **T** (08) 8842 2261 **www**.jimbarry.com **OPEN** 7 days 10-4
IEMAKER Tom Barry, Ben Marx, Simon Mussared, Derrick Quinton **EST**. 1959 **DOZENS** 80000 **VYDS** 380ha

e patriarch of this highly successful wine business, Jim Barry, died in 2004, but the business ntinues under the active involvement of the 2nd and 3rd generations. In November '16, Jim rry Wines released the first commercial assyrtiko grown and made in Australia. A founding ember of Australia's First Families of Wine. Winery of the Year in the *Wine Companion 2020*.

Loosen Barry Wolta Wolta Dry Clare Valley Riesling 2017 A magnificent wine. The aromas and flavours are nothing like Clare riesling. And yet it is just that. Beautiful aromatics and delicate flavours from lemon blossom, gardenia to flint and wet stones. Smoky, savoury with squirts of finger lime and a fine layer of ginger cream. Quite ethereal. Texture is its marker. Although the label says it's dry, it feels off-dry, so it has a viscosity, amazing length and definition. Respect. Screw cap | 12.5% alc. | To 2040 | $120 | JF | ♥

Loosen Barry Wolta Wolta Dry Clare Valley Riesling 2018 This is the second incarnation of this collaborative wine and a very fine follow-up. It's quite savoury with a touch more phenolics adding to its shape. It does have the same texture and off-dry feel that seems to be defining this wine. It's pure, it's energetic, it's something special yet again. Screw cap | 12.5% alc. | To 2038 | $120 | JF

Lodge Hill Clare Valley Shiraz 2018 A very impressive wine at this price: the colour deep and bright, the expressive bouquet with earthy/spicy nuances to black fruits. The medium-bodied palate has an extra level of depth aided by supple tannins and a twitch of oak. The value cannot be gainsaid. Screw cap | 14% alc. | To 2038 | $25 | JH

The McRae Wood Clare Valley Shiraz 2018 The flavours, the savouriness and the feel of this wine are all appealing. Lots of detail with nothing overt. The palate lends itself to cocoa-powder tannins, the oak is integrated and there's a depth of flavour. It comes out as a complete wine. Screw cap | 14% alc. | To 2033 | $60 | JF

Jim's Garden Clare Valley Riesling 2020 A new addition to the Jim Barry riesling portfolio. The slaty, spicy bouquet gives no warning of the intensity of the attack on the palate that continues without hesitation through to the lingering aftertaste. Lime, spice and mineral are the players in a powerful wine. Screw cap | 12% alc. | To 2020 | $25 | JH

Clare Valley Assyrtiko 2020 Delicate aromatics at first. A puff of Mediterranean herbs and lemon blossom, but of course all the action is on the palate. Steely, tight and linear, with wet stone and lime juice. The acidity is pure talc and the finish pristine. Lip-smacking and delicious. Screw cap | 12.5% alc. | To 2028 | $35 | JF

Single Vineyard Kirribilli Coonawarra Cabernet Sauvignon 2019 So fragrant, with the purity of fruit shining through in cassis, blackberries and mulberries. Yes, it has a brightness of youth, but what sets it apart is its lovely tannins and savoury outlook. Elegant and complete. Screw cap | 13.7% alc. | To 2038 | $35 | JF

4 **The Cover Drive 2018** Made from estate vineyards in Clare Valley and Coonawarra. Has excellent colour through to the rim, with austere, brooding, dark berry aromas, adding tapenade/bay leaf notes to the flavour mix. Screw cap | 14% alc. | To 2030 | $22 | JH

irrihill Wines  

8 Farrell Flat Road, Clare, SA 5453 **T** (08) 8842 1233 **www**.kirrihillwines.com.au **OPEN** 7 days -4 **WINEMAKER** Andrew Locke **EST**. 1998 **DOZENS** 35000 **VYDS** 600ha

ie Kirrihill story started in the late 1990s. The aim was to build a business producing emium wines from temperate vineyards that represent the unique characters of the Clare alley. Grapes are sourced from specially selected parcels of Kirrihill's 600ha of vineyards.

5 **E.B.'s The Settler Clare Valley Riesling 2020** Pristine and pure. It starts out subtle, and teases with some white florals, wet stones and daikon radish. Then slowly, more citrus accents, with lemon balm and lime. It's juicy, with superfine acidity lengthening out the palate. Screw cap | 12% alc. | To 2030 | $35 | JF

iz Heidenreich Wines 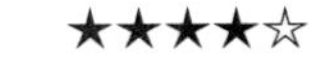

) Box 783, Clare, SA 5453 **T** 0407 710 244 **www**.lizheidenreichwines.com
INEMAKER Liz Heidenreich **EST**. 2018 **DOZENS** 2000 **VYDS** 6ha

1936 Liz Heidenreich's grandfather planted vines at Vine Vale; those vines are still in roduction, still owned and managed by the Heidenreich family. After 15 years as an itensive care nurse, Liz decided to follow her family heritage and enrolled in a post-graduate inemaking degree course at the University of Adelaide. The red wines she makes are from ie family-owned old vines in the Barossa Valley, while her other focus of riesling comes from the Clare Valley, more particularly O'Leary Walker, where she makes small parcels of fruit an also undertakes the contract winemaking of Peter Teakle wines.

95 **Barossa Valley Shiraz 2018** Made in a more restrained style, eschewing overripe fruit. It's a lovely wine. More red fruit upfront, with orange juice freshness; earthy with red licorice and smells of joss sticks. Fuller-bodied tannins, quite pliant, with a succulence that makes it very appealing. Screw cap | 14.3% alc. | To 2030 | $30 | JF

Barossa Valley Grenache 2019 Very nice wine. Deep, earthy, awash with dark fruits, woodsy spices and oak flavour, which needs to settle. Full bodied and savoury, with sandpaper-fine tannins and excellent length. This is going to hang around for some time. Compelling now though, if you let it breathe. Screw cap | 14.3% alc. | To 2033 | $30 | JF

94 **Watervale Clare Valley Riesling 2020** A pure and pristine riesling. Gentle. It slips in some florals, chalky acidity and lime zest. A bit more comes out in time. Lemony bath salts and wet stones. It ha a quiet presence. A lovely drink. Screw cap | 11.7% alc. | To 2029 | $24 | JF

Macaw Creek Wines

Macaw Creek Road, Riverton, SA 5412 **T** (08) 8847 2657 **www**.macawcreekwines.com.au **OPEN** By appt **WINEMAKER** Rodney Hooper **EST.** 1992 **DOZENS** 8000 **VYDS** 10ha

The Macaw Creek brand was established in '92 with wines made from grapes from other regions. Rodney Hooper is a highly qualified and skilled winemaker with experience in many parts of Australia and in Germany, France and the US. The wines are certified organic and free of preservatives.

95 **Mount Lofty Ranges Cabernet Shiraz 2017** Matured 18 months in a range of oaks, adding some love background cedar and spice notes. The fruit aromatics and flavours are true to form, a blackberry and cassis lift to begin, with riper plum flowing onto the palate. Given the power and the fruit here, the tannin feel is proportionately spot on. Great value. Screw cap | 14% alc. | To 2030 | $21 | TL

Mary's Myth

144 Johnsons Road, Balhannah, SA 5242 **T** 0447 608 479 **www**.marysmyth.com.au **WINEMAKER** Alister McMichael **EST.** 2018 **DOZENS** 550

This is the as-yet small venture of 3 childhood friends: Alister McMichael, Evan Starkey and Millie Haigh. Alister grew up in the Adelaide Hills, absorbed Old World treatment of riesling in the Mosel Valley, was exposed to minimalistic vinification approaches plus biodynamic/organic inputs in the northern Canterbury district of NZ, then was off to the very cool Finger Lakes of Upstate New York. Finally back in the Adelaide Hills, Mary's Myth was conceived; the name inspired by the discovery that each of their grandmother's names was Mary.

92 **Clare Valley Riesling 2020** A unique riesling, utilising a specific Austrian yeast and kept on its light lees for 4 months, together encouraging a citrus-like sugar candy note, somewhere between musk sticks and lemon sherbet, with a delicate honeysuckle feel too. Palate texture is more familiar, with a soft pithy feel. Different, yes. And attractive because of it. Screw cap | 12.5% alc. | To 2025 | $22 | TL

Mount Horrocks

The Old Railway Station, Curling Street, Auburn, SA 5451 **T** (08) 8849 2243 **www**.mounthorrocks.com **OPEN** W'ends & public hols 10-5 **WINEMAKER** Stephanie Toole **EST.** 1982 **DOZENS** 3500 **VYDS** 9.4ha

Owner/winemaker Stephanie Toole has never deviated from the pursuit of excellence in the vineyard and winery. She has 3 vineyard sites in the Clare Valley, each managed using natura farming and organic practices. The attention to detail and refusal to cut corners is obvious in all her wines. The cellar door is in the renovated old Auburn railway station.

96 **Watervale Riesling 2020** Wow. This is so good it's hard to put down. Beautiful poise and yet quite energising. A heady mix of white flowers, quince and lemon/lime, with a biscuity flavour, too. The acidity is fine and pure, gliding along the palate to a most resounding finish. Screw cap | 13% alc. | To 2030 | $38 | JF

Alexander Vineyard Clare Valley Shiraz 2018 Excellent, full crimson/purple colour. A wine that is all about high-quality shiraz picked at precisely the right moment. Equal amounts of blackberry and plum drive the bouquet and medium-bodied palate with consummate ease, oak and tannins in dutiful support. Screw cap | 14% alc. | To 2038 | $50 | JH

ked Run Wines

★★★★★

5 Horrocks Righway, Sevenhill, SA 5453 **T** 0408 807 655 **www**.nakedrunwines.com.au
EMAKER Steven Baraglia **EST.** 2005 **DOZENS** 1500

ked Run is the virtual winery of Jayme Wood, Bradley Currie and Steven Baraglia; their ls ranging from viticulture through to production, and also to the all-important sales and rketing (and not to be confused with Naked Wines).

The First Clare Valley Riesling 2020 Pristine, pure and very classy. A beautifully balanced wine of lemon blossom, tangerine and a hint of bath salts, plus beeswax and an array of spices. It's flavoursome, almost textural, as there's a succulence across the palate. Ultimately though, this is all about refinement, with the acidity present yet delicate. Screw cap | 11.5% alc. | To 2030 | $24 | JF

Place in Time Sevenhill Clare Valley Riesling 2016 Revealing the right amount of aged characters, from lime marmalade on buttered toast to baked ricotta and lemon curd. It's in the complex zone, with some weight and richness throughout. The acidity is still at the forefront, though, so it's lively, frisky even. An excellent, compelling wine. Alas, just 64 dozen made. Screw cap | 12% alc. | To 2028 | $40 | JF

Hill 5 Clare Valley Shiraz Cabernet 2019 Apparently the aim of this wine is to let the fruit be the hero. Well that has been achieved. It is so delicious and lively, with red plums, blackberries, currants and a flutter of baking spices. It's juicy, medium bodied, with textural tannins and enjoyment stamped all over it. Oh, and a bargain too! Screw cap | 14% alc. | To 2027 | $24 | JF

The Aldo Barossa Valley Grenache 2019 Fruit from winemaker Steve Baraglia's family vineyard, planted by his grandfather 80 years ago. It's made in a juicy, fresh style, but not at all simple. Quality shines through. Heady aromatics, all cherry and sarsaparilla, with lots of earthiness and a dash of pepper so it's not tutti-frutti. It's slinky across the medium-bodied palate, to the point where the grainy tannins kick in and the glass empties. Screw cap | 14% alc. | To 2027 | $24 | JF

'Leary Walker Wines 

3 Horrocks Highway, Leasingham, SA 5452 **T** 1300 342 569 **www**.olearywalkerwines.com
N Mon–Sat 10–4, Sun & public hols 11–4 **WINEMAKER** David O'Leary, Nick Walker, Jack Walker, e Broadbent **EST.** 2001 **DOZENS** 20000 **VYDS** 45ha

vid O'Leary and Nick Walker together had more than 30 years' experience as winemakers rking for some of the biggest Australian wine groups when they took the plunge in 01 and backed themselves to establish their own winery and brand. The vineyards were rtified organic in 2013. O'Leary Walker also has a cellar door in the Adelaide Hills at Oakwood Road, Oakbank at the heritage-listed former Johnson Brewery established in 43 (7 days 11–4).

Polish Hill River Armagh Shiraz 2018 Very good colour through to the rim; the bouquet has a complex array of licorice and tantalising warm spices. The palate is full bodied and intense, yet so balanced it doesn't muffle a classic Clare Valley shiraz filled with blackberry and black cherry fruit. Screw cap | 14.5% alc. | To 2038 | $35 | JH

Polish Hill River Armagh Cabernet Sauvignon 2018 Cabernet in Clare takes on its own meaning, its own structure and flavour (providing the producer gets it right). It's right on, here. Everything is in its place, from dark spiced fruits, spread of mint chocolate, woodsy spices and tannins. There's a freshness, too, refreshing acidity and smooth tannins. Screw cap | 14% alc. | To 2030 | $35 | JF

aulett Wines 

2 Jolly Way, Polish Hill River, SA 5453 **T** (08) 8843 4328 **www**.paulettwines.com.au **OPEN** 7 days -5 **WINEMAKER** Neil Paulett, Jarrad Steele **EST.** 1983 **DOZENS** 35000 **VYDS** 79.5ha

e Paulett story is a saga of Australian perseverance, commencing with the 1982 purchase of property with 1ha of vines and a house, promptly destroyed by the terrible Ash Wednesday shfires the following year. The winery and cellar door have wonderful views over the Polish ll River region, the memories of the bushfires long gone.

Polish Hill River Riesling 2020 Pristine, linear and tight. Flavours of lemon, lime, even grapefruit in the mix, with wafts of wet stone and ginger powder. It's long and energising, the acidity ensuring it lengthens out and lingers long. Screw cap | 12.5% alc. | To 2028 | $30 | JF

Pikes

★★★★

233 Polish Hill River Road, Sevenhill, SA 5453 **T** (08) 8843 4370 **www**.pikeswines.com.au **OPEN** 7 days 10-4 **WINEMAKER** Andrew Pike **EST.** 1984 **DOZENS** 50000 **VYDS** 130ha

Pikes is a family affair, established in the 1980s by Andrew, Neil and Cathy Pike with support from their parents Merle and Edgar. A generation on, Neil Pike has retired after 35 years as chief winemaker and Andrew's sons Jamie and Alister have come on board (Jamie to overse sales and marketing, Alistair to run the craft brewery that opened in '14). The award-winning Slate restaurant opened in '18, alongside a new tasting room. (TS)

98 **The Merle Clare Valley Riesling 2020** Pikes' flagship, but also a Clare Valley flagship. It's not often a 6-month-old riesling can be described as luscious, but that's the impact of this wine. It's citrus focused, of course, and it also has keynote acidity, but it's the honeyed mouthfeel and flavour that hits the jackpot. Screw cap | 12% alc. | To 2035 | $52 | JH | ♥

96 **Traditionale Clare Valley Riesling 2020** Elegance is the cornerstone of this lovely riesling, with a flawless serenade of citrus allsorts, its spine of acidity a contradiction in terms, because it's almos sweet – an illusion, of course. An each-way proposition for now or later consumption. Screw cap 12% alc. | To 2035 | $25 | JH

Rieslingfreak

103 Langmeil Road, Tanunda, SA 5352 **T** 0439 336 250 **www**.rieslingfreak.com **OPEN** Sat 11-4 or by appt **WINEMAKER** John Hughes, Belinda Hughes **EST.** 2009 **DOZENS** 7500 **VYDS** 40ha

The name of John Hughes' winery leaves no doubt about his long-term ambition: to explore every avenue of riesling, whether bone-dry or sweet, coming from regions across the wine world, albeit with a strong focus on Australia. The wines made from his Clare Valley vineyarc offer dry (No. 2, No. 3, No. 4 and No. 10), off-dry (No. 5 and No. 8), sparkling (No. 9) and fortified (No. 7) styles.

97 **No. 2 Polish Hill River Riesling 2020** From the Polish Hill River. Bright straw green, it's an utterly delicious wine which has aromas and flavours that seem to change in quick succession, with Meye lemon, white peach and Granny Smith apple in full song. Its mouthfeel and the length of the finish are both exceptional. Screw cap | 12% alc. | To 2033 | $37 | JH

96 **No. 6 Clare Valley Aged Release Riesling 2015** Ah, the joy of riesling as it garners age! Heady, with toasted and buttered brioche, spread with lime marmalade. It's still very fresh, bright and even a touch austere, with puckering acidity. It is starting to dry out on the finish, so best to enjoy this sooner rather than later. Screw cap | 12% alc. | To 2023 | $42 | JF

95 **No. 4 Eden Valley Riesling 2020** Does this riesling know how to charm, or what? It's a delight! All heady, with florals, citrus flavours, stone fruit and tangy acidity in tow, yet there's texture too. The finish is refreshingly dry. It incorporates the allure of the region, the decisiveness of the variety an the expertise of its maker. Screw cap | 12% alc. | To 2030 | $27 | JF | ♥

Tim Adams

156 Warenda Road, Clare, SA 5453 **T** (08) 8842 2429 **www**.timadamswines.com.au **OPEN** 7 days 10-4. **WINEMAKER** Tim Adams, Brett Schutz **EST.** 1986 **DOZENS** 60000 **VYDS** 195ha

Tim Adams and partner Pam Goldsack preside over a highly successful business. In 2009 th took a giant step forward with the acquisition of the 80ha Leasingham Rogers Vineyard from CWA, followed in '11 by the purchase of the Leasingham winery and winemaking equipment (for less than replacement cost). The winery is now a major contract winemaking facility for the region.

93 **Clare Valley Shiraz 2018** Gee these wines are great value. This is a rich and ripe rendition, yet there a lovely evenness across the full-bodied palate abetted by supple tannins. No harsh edges, just rip plump fruit and its spice friends having a party. The finish is warm and almost cuddly. It's definitely winter drink. Screw cap | 14.8% alc. | To 2028 | $26 | JF

92 **Clare Valley Riesling 2020** This starts out shy with more lemon barley water and saline flavours. Soft across the palate although neat acidity in the mix. It's refreshing, thoroughly enjoyable and dangerously easy to drink. Screw cap | 12% alc. | To 2028 | $24 | JF

m Gramp ★★★★

3 Mintaro Road, Watervale, SA 5452 **T** (08) 8843 0199 **www**.timgrampwines.com.au
N W'ends 12–4 **WINEMAKER** Tim Gramp **EST.** 1990 **DOZENS** 6000 **VYDS** 16ha

n Gramp has quietly built up a very successful business, and by keeping overheads to a nimum, provides good wines at modest prices. Over the years, estate vineyards (shiraz, sling, cabernet sauvignon, grenache and tempranillo) have been expanded significantly.

Watervale Riesling 2020 Reserved at first but it soon speeds up to reveal all the vitality, lemon flavouring, spice and lifting acidity that stamps this as a Watervale riesling. Refreshing now but will go some distance. Screw cap | 12% alc. | To 2029 | $21 | JF

Watervale Riesling 2019 Mid straw hue and already offering aged flavours from baked ricotta to buttered toast with lime marmalade. Lots of lime juice across the palate, crisp acidity and it is refreshing. Drink this in the short term. Screw cap | 12.5% alc. | To 2025 | $21 | JF

ickery Wines

elvidere Road, Nuriootpa, SA 5355 **T** (08) 8362 8622 **www**.vickerywines.com.au
EMAKER John Vickery, Keeda Zilm **EST.** 2014 **DOZENS** 10 000 **VYDS** 18ha

n Vickery's interest in, love of and exceptional skills with riesling began with Leo Buring in at Chateau Leonay. Over the intervening years he became the uncrowned but absolute narch of riesling makers in Australia until, in his semi-retirement, he passed the mantle on Jeffrey Grosset. Along the way he had (unsurprisingly) won the Wolf Blass Riesling Award the Canberra International Riesling Challenge 2007 and had been judged by his peers as stralia's Greatest Living Winemaker in a survey conducted by *The Age*'s Epicure in '03. His w venture has been undertaken in conjunction with Phil Lehmann, with 12ha of Clare and en valley riesling involved and wine marketer Jonathon Hesketh moving largely invisibly in background.

The Reserve Zander Kosi Block Eden Valley Riesling 2018 It's really, really hard to put this wine down. Expect to be wooed by the fragrance as much as the palate. A perfect blend of freshness and pulsing acidity, with some complexity of age starting to unfurl: preserved lemons with ginger spice, candied lime jellies, buttered toast and lime marmalade. But not too much. It has some way to go. Screw cap | 12% alc. | To 2033 | $32 | JF

Eden Valley Riesling 2020 Immediately enticing, with a bouquet of lavender, lime blossom and wafts of ginger cream and white pepper. It feels almost luscious and juicy as it fills the palate, then the fine line of acidity brings everything together neatly, finishing long. Screw cap | 12% alc. | To 2030 | $23 | JF

The Reserve Castine Hay Shed Block Watervale Riesling 2018 Already revealing toasty characters of baked ricotta and lime marmalade, as if kissed by the sun. They're adding an extra depth to the wine now, but perhaps without the acid drive to shift it into long-term drinking. That's OK. Make the most of it now. Screw cap | 12.5% alc. | To 2028 | $32 | JF

endouree

douree Road, Clare, SA 5453 **T** (08) 8842 2896 **WINEMAKER** Tony Brady **EST.** 1895 **DOZENS** 2000
S 12ha

iron fist in a velvet glove best describes these extraordinary wines. They are fashioned h commitment from the very old vineyard (shiraz, cabernet sauvignon, malbec, mataro d muscat of Alexandria), with its unique terroir, by Tony and Lita Brady, who rightly see emselves as custodians of a priceless treasure. The 100+yo stone winery is virtually changed from the day it was built; this is in every sense a treasure beyond price.

Clare Valley Shiraz 2019 This has a density, richness and ripeness, yet a beauty, too. Wafts of spice and Aussie bush aromas, with baking spices slipping through plums and blackberries. There's a buoyancy throughout, and bright fruit across the palate; the oak steadfast as a support and seasoning. The palate is perfectly shaped, fuller bodied, with expansive, textural tannins and acidity working in unison. Screw cap | 13.6% alc. | To 2039 | $65 | JF

Clare Valley Shiraz Mataro 2019 A 55/45% shiraz/mataro combo means the mataro is buffering or softening out the tannins so they feel ripe and velvety. A neat confluence of bright, dark fruit, savoury inputs via oak and more besides. Dark chocolate and mint, hazelnut-skin tannins, charcuterie and cedary oak. Its youthful vibrancy, while enticing, will be tamed in time. Screw cap | 13.6% alc. | To 2042 | $50 | JF

Clare Valley Cabernet Malbec 2019 With no straight cabernet this vintage, this ends up as 70/30 cabernet/malbec. While shiraz and malbec are good friends, cabernet and malbec are lovers. Thi the wine that smells of Wendouree: the bush, the winery and the vineyards resplendent with gnar centenarian and 'younger' vines. Plush, ripe fruit, all currant and blackberry accented, perfumed with aniseed, wild herbs and dark chocolate studded with mint. Lovely tannins and time on its sid If you can wait. If you can get some. Screw cap | 13.9% alc. | To 2039 | $60 | JF

Woodvale ★★★★

PO Box 54, Watervale, SA 5453 **T** 0417 829 204 **www**.woodvalevintners.com.au
WINEMAKER Kevin Mitchell **EST.** 2014 **DOZENS** 3000 **VYDS** 7ha

This is the personal venture of Kevin Mitchell and wife Kathleen Bourne; the main targets are what Kevin describes as 'modest, sustainable growth, working with the varieties that Clare does so well: riesling, shiraz, cabernet sauvignon, mataro, semillon, pinot gris, and of cours grenache'. Given he is a 3rd-generation Clare Valley grapegrower, procuring grapes from mates to supplement the estate should not be a problem.

95 **Watervale Riesling 2020** This falls into place very quickly, offering pure Watervale charm. The lemons and limes, the light dusting of spice and herbs and the neat line of acidity take it to a long finish. Screw cap | 12% alc. | To 2028 | $25 | JF

ZONE

Limestone Coast

REGION

Coonawarra

Bailey Wine Co

PO Box 368, Penola, SA 5277 **T** 0417 818 539 **www**.baileywineco.com **WINEMAKER** Tim Bailey **EST.** 201
DOZENS 750

After 2 decades living and working in Coonawarra, Tim Bailey decided to take a busman's holiday by establishing his own small wine business. Tim has a simple philosophy: 'Find great growers in the regions and let the vineyard shine through in the bottle.' Thus he sources Clare Valley riesling, Grampians shiraz, Adelaide Hills chardonnay and Coonawarra cabernet sauvignon.

95 **Hyde Park Vineyard Grampians Shiraz 2018** Enticing dark purple hue and no denying its DNA – Grampians through and through. While ultimately a savoury drink, it has a core of plump, juicy fruit spiced with cinnamon, pepper and Aussie bush seasoning. Full bodied, the palate lengthene by layers of smoky meaty nuances, roasted hazelnuts and amazingly velvety, tamed tannins. Screw cap | 14% alc. | To 2033 | $30 | JF

Balnaves of Coonawarra

15517 Riddoch Highway, Coonawarra, SA 5263 **T** (08) 8737 2946 **www**.balnaves.com.au **OPEN** Mon-Fr 9-5, w'ends 11.30-4.30 **WINEMAKER** Pete Bissell **EST.** 1975 **DOZENS** 10000 **VYDS** 74.33ha

Grapegrower, viticultural consultant and vigneron, Doug Balnaves has over 70ha of high-quality estate vineyards. The wines are invariably excellent, often outstanding; notable for their supple mouthfeel, varietal integrity, balance and length – the tannins are always fine ar ripe, the oak subtle and perfectly integrated. Coonawarra at its best.

95 **Shiraz 2019** A lot is packed into this wine, yet it takes everything in its stride and comes out as a more mid-weighted offering. Dark sweet fruits abound. So, too, spices, dark chocolate, coffee grounds and a sprinkle of crushed bay leaves. The tannins have some grit, yet are shapely and ripe. Oak adds some sweet, cedary seasoning, and is well incorporated. Screw cap | 14.5% alc. To 2033 | $30 | JF

ellwether

83 Riddoch Highway, Coonawarra, SA 5263 **T** 0417 080 945 **www**.bellwetherwines.com.au
N 7 days 12-4 **WINEMAKER** Sue Bell **EST.** 2008 **DOZENS** 2500

rmer Constellation chief winemaker Sue Bell received a $46000 wine industry scholarship m the Grape & Wine Research Development Council to study the wine industry in relation other rural industries in Australia and overseas, and its interaction with community and ciety. She also became Dux of the Len Evans Tutorial, her prize an extended trip through rdeaux and Burgundy. The next stroke of good fortune was that the beautiful stone Glen y shearing shed in Coonawarra (built in 1868) came on the market – which these days is her nery and welcoming cellar door.

Wrattonbully Malbec 2018 A malbec pulsating with complex, mouthfilling dark berry/plum fruit, a savoury/earthy regional carpet adding further weight to a wine full of character. Screw cap | 13.8% alc. | To 2030 | $30 | JH

owen Estate

59 Riddoch Highway, Coonawarra, SA 5263 **T** (08) 8737 2229 **www**.bowenestate.com.au
N Mon-Fri 10-5, w'ends 10-4 **WINEMAKER** Emma Bowen **EST.** 1972 **DOZENS** 12000 **VYDS** 33ha

gional veteran Doug Bowen presides over one of Coonawarra's landmarks, but he has nded over full winemaking responsibility to daughter Emma, 'retiring' to the position of culturist. In May 2015 Bowen Estate celebrated its 40th vintage with a tasting of 24 wines iraz and Cabernet Sauvignon) from 1975 to 2014.

Coonawarra Cabernet Sauvignon 2019 This is on the riper spectrum, but it doesn't stray into OTT territory. There's a lot of flavour, sure, but it comes out complete and balanced. Awash with currants and blackberries, mint chocolates and freshly rolled tobacco. Textural tannins have some poise and the finish is fresh and long. Screw cap | 14.7% alc. | To 2030 | $32 | JF

ollick Estates

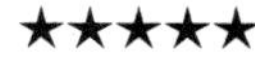

Racecourse Road, Penola, SA 5277 **T** (08) 8737 2318 **www**.hollick.com **OPEN** 7 days 11-5, lic hols 11-4 **WINEMAKER** Trent Nankivell **EST.** 1983 **DOZENS** 40000 **VYDS** 87ha

ablished in 1983 by the Hollick family, Hollick Estates' vineyard, winery, restaurant and lar door overlooks Coonawarra. The classic Coonawarra varieties of cabernet sauvignon, raz and chardonnay are made, along with The Nectar (botrytis riesling), barbera d tempranillo.

The Nectar Coonawarra 2019 Mid gold hue; heady, with saffron poached pears in honey syrup and sprinkled with fresh herbs and spices. The palate is soft, easy and unctuous, with dabs of orange marmalade and fresh lemon. The riesling's acidity coats the sweetness, allowing botrytis flavours to shine. A lovely, gorgeous and complete wine. 375ml bottle. Screw cap | 10.5% alc. | To 2026 | $25 | JF

oonara

Church Street, Penola, SA 5277 **T** (08) 8737 3222 **www**.koonara.com **OPEN** Mon-Thurs 10-5, -Sat 10-6, Sun 10-4 **WINEMAKER** Peter Douglas **EST.** 1988 **DOZENS** 10000 **VYDS** 9ha

vor Reschke planted the first vines on the Koonara property in 1988. Peter Douglas, merly Wynns' chief winemaker before moving overseas for some years, has returned to the trict and is consultant winemaker. After 10 years of organic viticulture practises, Koonara's eyards in Coonawarrra were certified organic in 2017.

Emily May Mount Gambier Pinot Noir Rosé 2020 Pale rose gold hue; it's soft and light, full of squishy red berries, strawberries with some vanilla cream plus a snip of fresh herbs. You'd call this a gentle rosé and it doesn't disappoint. Screw cap | 11% alc. | To 2022 | $20 | JF

NSW
SA
VIC
WA
TAS
QLD

Leconfield ★★★★

15454 Riddoch Highway, Coonawarra, SA 5263 **T** (08) 8323 8830 **www**.leconfieldwines.com **OPEN** 7 days 11-4 **WINEMAKER** Paul Gordon, Greg Foster **EST.** 1974 **DOZENS** 25000 **VYDS** 43.7ha

Sydney Hamilton purchased the unplanted property that was to become Leconfield in 1974 When he acquired the property and set about planting it he was 76 and reluctantly bowed to family pressure to sell Leconfield to nephew Richard in '81. Richard has progressively increased the vineyards to their present level, over 75% dedicated to cabernet sauvignon – for long the winery's specialty.

95 **Coonawarra Cabernet Franc 2019** All hail cabernet franc. So under-appreciated as a varietal, and yet Leconfield knows how to weave some magic. Aromatics to swoon over and the sweetly-fruitec core comes packaged in spice, potpourri and fresh bay leaves, with a savoury overlay. It enjoys a plushness, a softness across the palate, complete with fine tannins. Gorgeous now, but will garne more complexity in time. Screw cap | 14.5% alc. | To 2034 | $30 | JF

Lindeman's (Coonawarra) ★★★★

Level 8, 161 Collins Street, Melbourne, Vic 3000 (postal) **T** 1300 651 650 **www**.lindemans.com **WINEMAKER** Brett Sharpe **EST.** 1965

Lindeman's Coonawarra vineyards have assumed a greater importance than ever thanks to the move towards single-region wines. The Coonawarra Trio of Limestone Ridge Vineyard Shiraz Cabernet, St George Vineyard Cabernet Sauvignon and Pyrus Cabernet Sauvignon Merlot Malbec are all of exemplary quality.

96 **Coonawarra Trio Limestone Ridge Vineyard Shiraz Cabernet 2018** An excellent rendition this vintage, with its 73/27 shiraz/cabernet split. If anything, it's almost a pared-back wine, full bodied sure, yet with refinement, too. Expect dark plums and cassis, cedary oak and a sprinkle of mint. B the tannins, wow – supple and velvety. Screw cap | 13.7% alc. | To 2033 | $70 | JF

Coonawarra Trio St George Vineyard Cabernet Sauvignon 2018 This vintage has handed out an impressive Coonawarra Trio and one of the best St George wines. Of course, this is destined to garner more complexity in time, but it's hard not to open it now and enjoy its youthful exuberance A classy interplay of sweet and savoury, well-pitched oak, with distinct regional choc/eucalypt/m flavours acting as seasoning across the shapely palate. Exemplary tannins and a persistent finish. Screw cap | 14.5% alc. | To 2035 | $70 | JF

Parker Coonawarra Estate ★★★★

15688 Riddoch Highway, Penola, SA 5263 **T** (08) 8737 3525 **www**.parkercoonawarraestate.com.au **OPEN** 7 days 10-4 **WINEMAKER** James Lienert, Andrew Hardy, Keeda Zilm **EST.** 1985 **DOZENS** 30000 **VYDS** 20ha

Parker Coonawarra Estate is at the southern end of Coonawarra, on rich terra rossa soil over limestone. Cabernet sauvignon is the dominant variety (17.45ha), with minor plantings of merlot and petit verdot. It is now part of WD Wines, which also owns Hesketh Wine Compan St John's Road, Vickery Wines and Ox Hardy. Production has risen substantially since the change of ownership.

96 **Kidman Block 2019** A lovely shiraz from a lovely vintage. Excellent dark garnet with a shot of purp Deep, earthy, savoury flavours wash over black plums and cherries. Fuller bodied, with beautiful tannins – plush, ripe and velvety soft. A long persistent finish completes a compelling wine. Screw cap | 14.5% alc. | To 2034 | $65 | JF

Penley Estate ★★★★

McLeans Road, Coonawarra, SA 5263 **T** (08) 8736 3211 **www**.penley.com.au **OPEN** 7 days 10-4 **WINEMAKER** Kate Goodman, Lauren Hansen **EST.** 1988 **DOZENS** 48000 **VYDS** 111ha

In 1988 Kym, Ang and Bec Tolley joined forces to buy a block of land in Coonawarra – Penle Estate was underway. In 2015 Ang and Bec took full ownership of the company. They have made a number of changes, welcoming general manager Michael Armstrong and, even mc importantly, appointing Kate Goodman as winemaker. In December '17, Penley also opened cellar door in the main street of McLaren Vale.

97 **Helios Coonawarra Cabernet Sauvignon 2019** Despite the hefty 1.6kg bottle, this wine is anything but weighty. An excellent dark garnet hue, it's resplendent with pure cabernet aromas and flavou A latent power and beauty at the same time, with exceptional tannins, long and finely chiselled. Cork | 14.5% alc. | To 2044 | $150 | JF

Chertsey Coonawarra 2018 A 3-way bet of 70/20/10% cabernet sauvignon/merlot/cabernet franc. They must be magic numbers, because this is an enchanting outcome. The aromas are like perfume: all floral, blackberries and exotic spices. But it is the palate that really puts on the charm. Medium bodied, exquisite tannins and vivacious, yet elegant throughout. Screw cap | 14% alc. | To 2033 | $75 | JF

uarisa Wines

3 Slopes Road, Tharbogang, NSW 2680 (postal) **T** (02) 6963 6222 **www**.quarisa.com.au
NEMAKER John Quarisa **EST.** 2005

hn and Josephine Quarisa have set up a very successful family business using grapes om various parts of NSW and SA, made in leased space. Production has risen in leaps and unds, doubtless sustained by the exceptional value for money provided by the wines.

Mrs Q Adelaide Hills Sangiovese 2019 Full-tilt sangio here. Dark plums, anise, black olive tapenade all throw their lot into this satisfying expression. The variety's typical tannins are well managed within the whole matrix. Screw cap | 14.5% alc. | To 2027 | $19 | TL

ymill Coonawarra 

ddoch Highway, Coonawarra, SA 5263 **T** (08) 8736 5001 **www**.rymill.com.au **OPEN** 7 days 11-5
NEMAKER Shannon Sutherland **EST.** 1974 **DOZENS** 50000 **VYDS** 140ha

2016 the Rymill family sold the winery, vineyards and brand to a Chinese investor. The anagement, vineyard and winery teams have remained in place and new capital has anced moves to improve the vineyards and winery. The winery building also houses the llar door and art exhibitions, which, together with viewing platforms over the winery, make a must-see destination for tourists.

Classic Release Cabernet Sauvignon 2018 This is pure Coonawarra, showing plenty of class. Cassis and blackcurrants are inflected with tobacco, mint and woodsy spices. It's more medium bodied, very fresh and lively. Tannins are pitch-perfect – ripe, savoury and slightly grainy. It feels nicely polished, but not fabricated. Screw cap | 14.2% alc. | To 2033 | $32 | JF

ynns Coonawarra Estate 

morial Drive, Coonawarra, SA 5263 **T** (08) 8736 2225 **www**.wynns.com.au **OPEN** 7 days 10-5
NEMAKER Sue Hodder, Sarah Pidgeon **EST.** 1897

rge-scale production has not prevented Wynns (an important part of TWE) from producing cellent wines covering the full price spectrum from the bargain-basement Riesling and iraz through to the deluxe John Riddoch Cabernet Sauvignon and Michael Shiraz. Even th steady price increases, Wynns offers extraordinary value for money.

Johnsons Single Vineyard Cabernet Sauvignon 2019 There's an opulence to the 2018 vintage reds and yet Wynns always manages to coat the wines with a layer of elegance. It helps to have access to the oldest cabernet vines in Coonawarra, Johnson's Block planted in 1954. This is only the 2nd release as a single-vineyard wine. It's all about precision, from a core of ripe fruit, its length to beautifully shaped silk-coated tannins. Screw cap | 13.3% alc. | To 2032 | $90 | JF

Black Label Cabernet Sauvignon 2019 The 64th vintage. A wine of provenance. A wine of excellence. It ages superbly, yet is flattering when young. Perfect fruit at its core, with gentle flavours of cassis, blackberries and blueberries. It has depth, length and line, thanks to the fine, detailed tannins. Classy cabernet. This is up there as one of the finest to date. Bravo. Cork | 13.8% alc. | To 2043 | $45 | JF

Harold Single Vineyard Cabernet Sauvignon 2018 In a way, this captures the very essence of Coonawarra cabernet. It has all the heady aromas and flavours from blackberries/currants, black olives to dried herbs, pulled together by a sheath of tannins. And yet, it is distinctly Wynns – or rather, Harold. It has elegance. The oak is completely absorbed into the wine and those tannins are so finely plied. A bit like a Stradivarius violin – this is finely tuned and polished. It is the pick of the 2018 cabernets. Screw cap | 13.4% alc. | To 2038 | $80 | JF

John Riddoch Limited Release Cabernet Sauvignon 2018 Tasting young John Riddoch simply throws a spotlight on its quality as the cornerstone, because this wine evolves into something special with age. It's a majestic wine. Full bodied and deep, with an abundance of tannins, but all in place, with a brightness to the acidity. There's nothing harsh here. Earthy flavours, cedary oak and excellent fruit make it a bit of a tease: it is rather easy to open a bottle to enjoy now, yet its best years are ahead of it. Screw cap | 14% alc. | To 2045 | $150 | JF | ♥

Mount Benson

Cape Jaffa Wines ★★★★

459 Limestone Coast Road, Mount Benson via Robe, SA 5276 **T** (08) 8768 5053 **www**.capejaffawines com.au **OPEN** 7 days 10-5 **WINEMAKER** Anna and Derek Hooper **EST.** 1993 **DOZENS** 10000 **VYDS** 22.86ha

Cape Jaffa was the first of the Mount Benson wineries. Cape Jaffa's fully certified biodynamic vineyard provides 50% of production, with additional fruit sourced from a certified biodynamic grower in Wrattonbully. Having received the Advantage SA Regional Award in '09, '10 and '11 for its sustainable initiatives in the Limestone Coast, Cape Jaffa is a Hall of Fame inductee.

95 **Epic Drop Mount Benson Shiraz 2019** This is a compelling wine, with dark fruit doused in black pepper, baking spices and a dusting of cocoa. It's fuller bodied and comes with a glossy sheen across the palate, bolstered by ripe, pliant tannins. It's quite delicious. Crack it open now to enjoy vibrancy, although it will add more complexity in time. Screw cap | 14.5% alc. | To 2030 | $29 |

94 **Upwelling Mount Benson Cabernet Sauvignon 2018** A medium-bodied wine with just the right amount of varietal charm introduced by currants and blackberries, with fresh herbs, but it's also savoury. Tannins are lovely – fine and shapely and overall, this is delicious. Screw cap | 14.5% alc. | To 2033 | $29 | JF

Norfolk Rise Vineyard

Limestone Coast Road, Mount Benson, SA 5265 **T** (08) 8768 5080 **www**.norfolkrise.com.au **WINEMAKER** Alice Baker **EST.** 2000 **DOZENS** 20000 **VYDS** 130ha

Norfolk Rise Vineyard is by far the largest and most important development in the Mount Benson region. The 46 blocks of plantings allow a range of options in making the 6 single-variety wines in the portfolio. The business has moved from the export of bulk wine to bottled wine, which gives significantly better returns to the winery.

90 **Limestone Coast Shiraz 2019** A sprinkling of black pepper and bold fruit distinguishes this well-priced red. It's supple with shapely tannins and a certain vivacity that makes it appealing. A red to enjoy now, without any more thought. Screw cap | 14.5% alc. | To 2024 | $19 | JF

Wangolina

8 Limestone Coast Road, Mount Benson, SA 5275 **T** (08) 8768 6187 **www**.wangolina.com.au **OPEN** 7 days 10-4 **WINEMAKER** Anita Goode **EST.** 2001 **DOZENS** 4000 **VYDS** 11ha

Four generations of the Goode family have been graziers at Wangolina Station, but Anita Goode has broken with tradition by becoming a vigneron. She has planted sauvignon blanc shiraz, cabernet sauvignon, semillon and pinot gris.

93 **A Series Limestone Coast Tempranillo 2019** Give this time to open up, revealing a flood of flavour from morello cherries, dark plums to sarsaparilla, thick hoisin sauce and boot polish. A dense, full-bodied palate with chewy tannins. It's a little rough and raw, in need of more time or hearty fare, b it's a solid offering. Screw cap | 14% alc. | To 2028 | $25 | JF

GION

Mount Gambier

oola Road

★★★★

ivate Mail Bag 14, Mount Gambier, SA 5291 **T** 0487 700 422 **www**.coolaroad.com
NEMAKER John Innes **EST.** 2013 **DOZENS** 1000 **VYDS** 103.5ha

omas and Sally Ellis are the current generation of the Ellis family, who have owned the Coola azing property on which the vineyard is now established for over 160 years. As the largest neyard owner in the region, they decided they should have some of the grapes vinified to ing further recognition to the area. If global warming should increase significantly, the very ol region will stand to gain.

Single Vineyard Mount Gambier Pinot Noir 2017 Very good colour; has excellent varietal expression engendered by a cool vintage in a very cool region. Red and dark cherry fruit has a silky web of spicy/savoury complexity. A really attractive pinot at a giveaway price. Screw cap | 12.5% alc. | To 2030 | $28 | JH

GION

Wrattonbully

érite Wines

Box 167, Penola, SA 5277 **T** 0437 190 244 **www**.meritewines.com **WINEMAKER** Mike Kloak **EST.** 2000 **ZENS** 2000 **VYDS** 40ha

érite Wines was established in 2000. It was the end of Mike Kloak and Colleen Miller's otracted search for high-quality viticultural land, with a particular focus on the production merlot utilising recently released clones that hold the promise of producing wine of a ality not previously seen.

Wrattonbully Merlot Rosé 2020 Refreshing as a spring or summer's day. Either way, this is delicious. A pale ruby with a copper tinge. It's tangy with clementine and cranberries, lightly spiced, and the lemony acidity leaves a crisp finish. Screw cap | 13.4% alc. | To 2023 | $24 | JF

erre à Terre

Spring Gunny Rd, Piccadilly, SA 5151 **T** 0400 700 447 **www**.terreaterre.com.au
EN At Tapanappa **WINEMAKER** Xavier Bizot **EST.** 2008 **DOZENS** 4000 **VYDS** 20ha

would be hard to imagine 2 better-credentialled owners than Xavier Bizot (son of the late ristian Bizot of Bollinger fame) and wife Lucy Croser (daughter of Brian and Ann Croser). erre à terre' is a French expression meaning down to earth. In 2015, Terre à Terre secured the uit from one of the oldest vineyards in the Adelaide Hills, the Summertown Vineyard, which ll see greater quantities of Daosa and a Piccadilly Valley pinot noir.

Crayeres Vineyard Wrattonbully Sauvignon Blanc 2019 Sauvignon Blanc of the Year 2022. Cold-settled for 2 months, a technique developed by Brian Croser, but rarely duplicated. Fermentation in used 600L demi-muids, then matured on full lees for 8 months. The result is very complex, but the fruit is undaunted, with layers of lemon curd, citrus and a whisper of honey. Screw cap | 13.1% alc. | To 2025 | $50 | JH | ♥

22 151ha | 6 zones | 21 regions

If you look at a map of mainland Australia, you will see that viticulture in all states other than Victoria hugs the coastline, leaving vast areas of empty land devoid of vines. Victoria may only have six zones, but it has 21 contiguous regions evenly spread across the state.

Pride of place goes to the Port Phillip Zone, within one hour's drive from Melbourne. First up, the **Yarra Valley**, with fragrant red berry and spice pinot noir and intense, elegant chardonnay accounting for the lion's share of plantings, and smaller amounts of worthy shiraz and cabernet sauvignon attesting to the variations in altitude, aspect and soil. **Mornington Peninsula**'s maritime climate sees the majority of plantings given over to delicately framed pinot noir and chardonnay; pinot gris/grigio is the mouse that roared, with the cost per tonne inexplicably dwarfing Yarra Valley chardonnay and pinot noir. **Macedon Ranges** and **Sunbury** also fall in the pinot noir and chardonnay school, Macedon's cool climate propelling both varieties to ever greater heights. **Geelong** has several highly rated producers of cabernet sauvignon and powerful chardonnay and pinot noir, shiraz in similar vein.

Gippsland is a zone with no regions the only such example in this book - and one world-famous winery, Bass Phillip, which has made one of Australia's greatest pinot noirs since 1984.

To the Central Ranges. **Bendigo** is largely red wine country, led by faintly minty shiraz, next cabernet sauvignon, then merlot. The ubiquitous pinot gris/grigio is the top white variety. **Heathcote** has 15 red varieties planted, with shiraz in the lead, the wine with a beguiling warmth from the fruit (if not the alcohol). The white varieties are dominated largely by chardonnay: lay down your glasses. The wild and windswept **Strathbogie Ranges** plantings reflect its more than 600m altitude – pinot noir and chardonnay are the game here, followed by shiraz.

The North East Victoria zone has five regions, the hot **Rutherglen** the odd man out, producing gloriously rich fortified muscat and muscadelle (aka tokay, the name changed due to EU requirements). In terms of both quality and style these have no equivalent elsewhere in the world. Historic **Beechworth** is a halfway house up the mountains, chardonnay made famous by Giaconda. The **King Valley** and

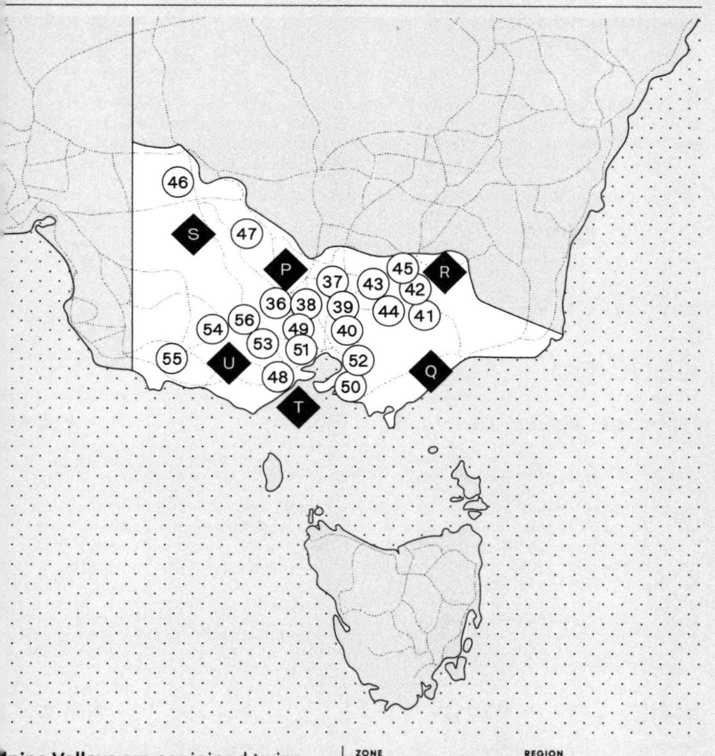

lpine Valleys are conjoined twins oth with vineyards at very different titudes but the runaway success of rosecco, comprising almost half f total plantings.

ne Western Victoria zone has ree cool regions that dominate, d by the **Grampians**. Majestic, eeply coloured and infinitely omplex shiraz makes up the bulk f plantings. **Henty** is the coldest egion on the mainland; Seppelt rumborg Vineyard and Crawford iver are responsible for the vast ajority of the glorious, long-lived esling. **Pyrenees** hits the sweet spot ith its shiraz (one-third of plantings) aving the best of both climate orlds (cool and temperate), spice nd licorice joining black fruits.

ZONE	REGION
P Central Victoria	36 Bendigo
	37 Goulburn Valley
	38 Heathcote
	39 Strathbogie Ranges
	40 Upper Goulburn
Q Gippsland	
R North East Victoria	41 Alpine Valleys
	42 Beechworth
	43 Glenrowan
	44 King Valley
	45 Rutherglen
S North West Victoria	46 Murray Darling
	47 Swan Hill
T Port Phillip	48 Geelong
	49 Macedon Ranges
	50 Mornington Peninsula
	51 Sunbury
	52 Yarra Valley
U Western Victoria	53 Ballarat
	54 Grampians
	55 Henty
	56 Pyrenees

Handpicked Wines ★★★★

80 Collins St, Melbourne VIC 3000 **T** (03) 7036 1088 **WWW**.handpickedwines.com.au **OPEN** Mon-Fri 11-10, w'ends 10-10 **WINEMAKER** Peter Dillon, Jonathon Mattick **EST.** 2001 **DOZENS** 100000 **VYDS** 83ha

Handpicked Wines is a multi-regional business with a flagship vineyard and winery on the Mornington Peninsula and vineyards in the Yarra Valley, Barossa Valley and Tasmania. They also make wines from many of Australia's leading fine-wine regions. The cellar door in Sydney's CBD brings the wines together in a stylish retail and hospitality venue.

96 **Collection Tasmania Pinot Noir 2019** From estate vineyards on either side of the Tamar Valley. Very good colour. The Tamar Valley produces pinot noir with more depth and power than any other Tasmanian district. This wine is a high-quality example, with mouth-coating satsuma plum and more cherry fruit. Will richly repay prolonged cellaring. Screw cap | 13.5% alc. | To 2034 | $60 | JH

ZONE

Central Victoria

REGION

Bendigo

Harcourt Valley Vineyards  ★★★

3339 Calder Highway, Harcourt, Vic 3453 **T** (03) 5474 2223 **WWW**.harcourtvalley.com.au **OPEN** Sun 12-4 **WINEMAKER** Quinn Livingstone **EST.** 1975 **DOZENS** 2500 **VYDS** 4ha

Harcourt Valley Vineyards (planted 1975) has the oldest planting of vines in the Harcourt Valley. Using 100% estate-grown fruit, Quinn Livingstone (2nd-generation winemaker) is making a number of small-batch wines. Minimal fruit handling is used in the winemaking process. The tasting area overlooks the vines, with a large window that allows visitors to see the activity in the winery.

92 **Barbara's Bendigo Shiraz 2018** Belying its modest price point, this shiraz hails from a top year and shows the kind of fruit concentration and depth we might expect. A lifted dusty, earthy bouquet w blackberry fruits. Brings wild berry fruit and local bush spice with generous flavour to the palate, highlighted by fine tannins and a long finish. Screw cap | 14.9% alc. | To 2028 | $25 | JP

Sutton Grange Winery  ★★★★

Carnochans Road, Sutton Grange, Vic 3448 **T** (03) 8672 1478 **WWW**.suttongrange.com.au **OPEN** Sun 11-5 **WINEMAKER** Melanie Chester **EST.** 1998 **DOZENS** 6000 **VYDS** 12ha

The 400ha Sutton Grange property is a horse training facility acquired in 1996 by Peter Sidwell, a Melbourne businessman with horseracing and breeding interests. A lunch visit to the property by long-term friends Alec Epis and Stuart Anderson led to the decision to plant shiraz, merlot, cabernet sauvignon, viognier and sangiovese. The winery is built from WA limestone.

95 **Fairbank Syrah 2019** Fairbank shows the other side of the syrah coin, the plummy, juicy, sweet-fruited side that offers excellent drinking early, with the promise of some medium-term ageing. Brilliant purple hues, bright, jubey, cassis, plum and concentrated spice. Balance, texture and goo length on display, together with some signature bush mint. It's all here. Screw cap | 14% alc. | To 2033 | $35 | JP

Water Wheel  

Bridgewater-Raywood Road, Bridgewater-on-Loddon, Vic 3516 **T** (03) 5437 3060 **WWW**.waterwheelwine.com **OPEN** Mon-Fri 9-5, w'ends 12-4 **WINEMAKER** Bill Trevaskis, Amy Cumming **EST.** 1972 **DOZENS** 35000 **VYDS** 136ha

Peter Cumming, with more than 2 decades of winemaking under his belt, has quietly built on the reputation of Water Wheel year by year. The winery is owned by the Cumming family, which has farmed in the Bendigo region for more than 50 years, with horticulture and viticulture special areas of interest. Water Wheel continues to make wines that over-deliver at their modest prices.

4 **Bendigo Viognier 2019** A complex, barrel-fermented viognier that reveals a dab winemaking hand. Everything is nicely in place (not easy with this grape, which can tend towards the oily) from the spring blossom, orange peel and ripe stone fruits through to the spicy, citrussy and restrained palate. It's a winner. Smooth and totally hedonistic. Screw cap | 14.6% alc. | To 2026 | $24 | JP

GION

Goulburn Valley

Box Grove Vineyard

55 Avenel-Nagambie Road, Tabilk, Vic 3607 **T** 0409 210 015 **WWW**.boxgrovevineyard.com.au
PEN By appt **WINEMAKER** Sarah Gough **EST.** 1995 **DOZENS** 2500 **VYDS** 28.25ha

his is the venture of the Gough family, with industry veteran (and daughter) Sarah Gough anaging the vineyard, winemaking and marketing. Having started with 10ha each of shiraz nd cabernet sauvignon under contract to Brown Brothers, Sarah decided to switch the cus of the business to what could loosely be called 'Mediterranean varieties'. These days hiraz and prosecco are the main varieties, with smaller plantings of pinot gris, primitivo, ermentino, roussanne, sousão, grenache, nebbiolo, negroamaro, mourvèdre and viognier.

4 **Prosecco 2020** Pulses with the kind of light savouriness not often seen in prosecco, built around preserved lemon and acacia together with nashi pear and crunchy apple. Lemon zip and bubble is spot on. Crown seal | 11.2% alc. | To 2024 | $25 | JP

Brave Goose Vineyard

Box 852, Seymour, Vic 3660 **T** 0417 553 225 **WWW**.bravegoosevineyard.com.au **OPEN** By appt
NEMAKER Nina Stocker **EST.** 1988 **DOZENS** 500 **VYDS** 6.5ha

he Brave Goose Vineyard was planted in 1988 by former chairman of the Grape & Wine esearch and Development Corporation, Dr John Stocker and wife Joanne. The brave goose question was the sole survivor of a flock put into the vineyard to repel cockatoos and foxes. wo decades on, Jo and John handed the reins of the operation to their winemaker daughter ina and son-in-law John Day.

4 **Central Victoria Cabernet Sauvignon 2019** Ah, Central Victoria can most definitely make excellent, 94 cabernet! Here's strong proof, with a velvety, rich youngster with a lot of love to give. Cassis, dried leaf and loamy earth aromas. Smooth as she goes on the well-structured palate, delivered with easy tannins and drinkability. Screw cap | 14% alc. | To 2026 | $28 | JP

Dalfarras

Box 123, Nagambie, Vic 3608 **T** (03) 5794 2637 **WWW**.dalfarras.com.au **OPEN** At Tahbilk:
n-Fri 9-5, w'ends & public hols 10-5 **WINEMAKER** Alister Purbrick, Alan George **EST.** 1991
ZENS 8750 **VYDS** 20.97ha

he project of Alister Purbrick and artist wife Rosa (née Dalfarra), whose paintings adorn the bels of the wines. Alister is best known as winemaker at Tahbilk, the family winery and home, ut this range of wines is intended to (in Alister's words) 'allow me to expand my winemaking orizons and mould wines in styles different from Tahbilk'.

Prosecco 2020 Explores the delights of the prosecco grape under $20 and it turns out there are many. Lively, persistent bead and mousse. Aromas of lemon sorbet, apple and cut pear. Gathers a full head of steam and zestiness on the palate. Fresh and invigorating in its youth. Cork | 11% alc. | To 2024 | $19 | JP

Four Sisters

9 O'Dwyers Road, Tabilk, Vic 3608 **T** (03) 5736 2400 **WWW**.foursisters.com.au
NEMAKER Alan George, Jo Nash, Alister Purbrick **EST.** 1995 **DOZENS** 40000

he 4 sisters who inspired this venture were the daughters of the late Trevor Mast, a eat winemaker who died before his time. The business is owned by the Purbrick family he owner of Tahbilk). It orchestrates the purchase of the grapes for the brand, and also cilitates the winemaking.

90 **Central Victoria Shiraz 2018** Keeps true to its Central Victorian identity with generosity, solid shiraz fruit and spice with a touch of the local bay-leaf/eucalyptus character. A friendly, approachable style. Measured, too, with firm structure on display. Smart wine, smart price. Bronze medal Perth Royal Wine Show '20. Screw cap | 14.5% alc. | To 2025 | $17 | JP

Central Victoria Merlot 2018 Crushed, destemmed, cultured-yeast fermentation, 12 months in mix of new/1–5yo French and American oak. A lot of warm and aromatic merlot fruit on display, nicely handled with sympathetic oak. Ripe cassis, mulberry, stewed plum in this fruit-forward style. Variet leafiness is a plus as is the sinewy tannin structure. All-round excellent value. Bronze medal Perth Royal Wine Show '20. Screw cap | 14% alc. | To 2023 | $17 | JP

McPherson Wines

199 O'Dwyer Road, Nagambie, Vic 3608 **T** (03) 9263 0200 **www**.mcphersonwines.com.au **WINEMAKER** Jo Nash **EST.** 1968 **DOZENS** 500000 **VYDS** 262ha

McPherson Wines is, by any standards, a substantial business. Made at various locations fror estate vineyards and contract-grown grapes, they represent very good value across a range labels. Winemaker Jo Nash has been at the helm for many years and co-owner Alistair Purbri (Tahbilk) has a lifetime of experience in the industry. Quality is unfailingly good.

92 **Don't tell Gary Shiraz 2019** What's not to like? Deep and expressive purple hues. Ripe blueberry, blackberry vibrancy and punch with licorice strap, chocolate and warm, spiced oak. Generous and cuddly. Jo Nash certainly knows her shiraz. Screw cap | 14.5% alc. | To 2027 | $24 | JP

90 **Bella Luna Fiano 2020** Fiano is kicking goals at a number of price points. Here is a great-value example that exudes personality+. The grape's signature apple and fleshy pear combines with quince, lemon rind and grapefruit pith. A gently textured palate finishes with bright acid crunch. Plenty to enjoy here for $19. Screw cap | 12% alc. | To 2024 | $19 | JP

Tahbilk

254 O'Neils Road, Tabilk, Vic 3608 **T** (03) 5794 2555 **www**.tahbilk.com.au **OPEN** Mon-Sat 9-5, Sun 11-5 **WINEMAKER** Alister Purbrick, Neil Larson, Alan George **EST.** 1860 **DOZENS** 120000 **VYDS** 221.5ha

A winery steeped in tradition (with National Trust classification) and which should be visited at least once by every wine-conscious Australian. It makes wines – particularly red wines – utterly in keeping with that tradition. The essence of that heritage comes in the form of their tiny quantities of shiraz made from vines planted in 1860. A founding member of Australia's First Families of Wine. *Wine Companion 2016* Winery of the Year.

96 **Museum Release Marsanne 2015** Just look at that straw-yellow colour! So youthful and just 6 years old! This is marsanne at its best, on the long road to a glorious future. It just gets better and better with each year, all without a skerrick of oak. Honeysuckle, buttered toast, jasmine and pear skin scents envelope the senses. The acidity tastes young and bright, belying the wine's age. What valu lies here. Silver medal Alternative Varieties Wine Show '20. Screw cap | 12.5% alc. | To 2030 | $26 | JP | ♥

95 **Cane Cut Marsanne 2018** Marsanne gets to showcase its versatility at Tahbilk. Here, it knocks the dessert-style sweetie out of the park with its complexity and adroit winemaking. Striking gold/gree hue. Orange peel, nougat, stone fruit and candied-fruit aromas transform into utter lusciousness o the palate. Smooth as glass. Can take chilling. 500ml. Screw cap | 11% alc. | To 2026 | $26 | JP

Grenache Mourvèdre Rosé 2020 Cast with a Rhône eye but delivered in a very Australian style wit pristine, juicy, crunchy fruit to the fore. Bright confectionery pink. Red cherry, raspberry, strawber boiled lolly with pomegranate tartness that puckers just so. The degree of acidity/tannin meets the fruit and then just a little bit more. Got the balance just right. Screw cap | 12% alc. | To 2025 | $22 | JP | ♥

REGION

Heathcote

Bull Lane Wine Company

PO Box 77, Heathcote, Vic 3523 **T** 0427 970 041 **www**.bulllane.com.au **WINEMAKER** Simon Osicka **EST.** 2013 **DOZENS** 500

After a successful career as a winemaker with what is now TWE, Simon Osicka, together with viticulturist partner Alison Phillips, returned to the eponymous family winery just within the eastern boundary of the Heathcote region in 2010. Spurred on by a decade of drought impacting on the 60yo dry-grown vineyard, and a desire to create another style of shiraz, mon and Alison spent considerable time visiting Heathcote vineyards with access to water the lead-up to the '10 vintage. After the weather gods gave up their tricks of '11, Bull Lane as in business.

4 **Heathcote Shiraz 2019** Runs the gauntlet of aromas and flavours. Fragrant violet, red fruits, black cherry and musky spice. Flows smoothly and long across an elegant palate. A well-defined Heathcote shiraz that punches well above its weight. Screw cap | 14.5% alc. | To 2027 | $29 | JP

davue Estate 

0 Northern Highway, Heathcote, Vic 3523 **T** 0429 617 287 **WWW**.idavueestate.com **OPEN** W'ends .30-5 **WINEMAKER** Andrew Whytcross, Sandra Whytcross **EST.** 2000 **DOZENS** 600 **VYDS** 5.7ha

wners and winemakers Andrew and Sandra Whytcross produce award-winning wines; the neyard managed by Andy, the winery run using normal small-batch winemaking techniques. ne Barrelhouse cellar door is adorned with music paraphernalia and guitars, and regularly olds blues music events.

4 **Blue Note Heathcote Shiraz 2017** Telltale Heathcote hues: so dark and impenetrable. A generous, youthful shiraz with lots of fruit and spice to latch on to from blackberry, mulberry, a touch of tart cranberry, kitchen spices and licorice. Layered oak is well judged, tannins are fine. Plenty to enjoy here at a fair price. Screw cap | 14% alc. | To 2025 | $30 | JP

asper Hill

Drummonds Lane, Heathcote, Vic 3523 **T** (03) 5433 2528 **WWW**.jasperhill.com.au **OPEN** By appt **NEMAKER** Ron Laughton, Emily McNally **EST.** 1979 **DOZENS** 2000 **VYDS** 26.5ha

ne red wines of Jasper Hill, crafted by father–daughter team Ron Laughton and Emily cNally, are highly regarded and much sought after. The low-yielding dry-grown vineyards e managed organically and tended by hand. As long as vintage conditions allow, these are onderfully rich and full-flavoured wines.

5 **Lo Stesso Heathcote Fiano 2020** Jasper Hill's Emily McNally's personal label is always thought provoking and edgy. The savoury, textural appeal of the Italian fiano grape is turned up to 11 with a most captivating wine. Poached pear, baked apple, wild honey, a peep of nettle, herb, all rolled into a stunning wine that builds through to the finish. Screw cap | 13.5% alc. | To 2026 | $30 | JP

ennedy

ple Park, 224 Wallenjoe Road, Corop, Vic 3559 (postal) **T** (03) 5484 8293 **WWW**.kennedyvintners. m.au **WINEMAKER** Glen Hayley, Gerard Kennedy **EST.** 2002 **DOZENS** 3000 **VYDS** 29.2ha

aving been farmers in the Colbinabbin area of Heathcote for 27 years, John and Patricia ennedy were on the spot when a prime piece of red Cambrian soil on the east-facing slope Mt Camel Range became available for purchase. They planted 20ha of shiraz in 2002. As ey gained knowledge of the intricate differences within the site, further plantings of shiraz, mpranillo and mourvèdre followed in '07.

4 **Pink Hills Heathcote Rosé 2020** A 100% mourvèdre-based rosé, with an established reputation; barrel fermented in old French oak. Pretty light copper in hue, it doesn't stray far from a solid core of ripe summer berries and dusty spice. Dry but not stark, it loosens on the palate with a sweet fruit liveliness, finishing smooth. Screw cap | 13.5% alc. | To 2024 | $24 | JP

erindoc Vintners 

Box 77, Tooborac, Vic 3522 **T** (03) 5433 5188 **WWW**.merindoc.com.au **WINEMAKER** Steve Webber, rgio Carlei, Bryan Martin **EST.** 1994 **DOZENS** 1800 **VYDS** 35ha

ephen Shelmerdine has been a major figure in the wine industry for over 25 years, like his mily (who founded Mitchelton Winery) before him, and has been honoured for his many rvices to the industry. Substantial quantities of the grapes produced are sold to others; a nall amount of high-quality wine is contract-made.

3 **Merindoc Heathcote Riesling 2019** Soft acidity (yes, it's a thing) makes a big impression here, contributing delicious approachability while also acting as a launch pad for a lively citrus intensity. Apple blossom, jasmine, lime cordial, freshly cut apple. Juicy and spicy. Screw cap | 11.5% alc. | To 2026 | $27 | JP

Paul Osicka

Majors Creek Vineyard at Graytown, Vic 3608 **T** (03) 5794 9235 **www.paulosickawines.com.au**
OPEN By appt **WINEMAKER** Simon Osicka **EST.** 1955 **VYDS** 13ha

The Osicka family arrived from Czechoslovakia in the early 1950s. Vignerons in their own country, their vineyard in Australia was the first new venture in central and southern Victoria for over half a century. With the return of Simon Osicka to the family business, there have been substantial changes. Paul Osicka, Simon's father, passed away in 2019 after 50 vintage and over 60 years of involvement in the vineyards.

95 **Heathcote Majors Creek Vineyard Shiraz 2019** The maker reported low yields from small bunches and tiny berries in 2019, evident in the concentration of fruit flavour here. The big man, Simon Osicka, delivers nuance like few others, the juxtaposition of black cherry and fennel here, the dollop of lilting spice and anise there, and all the while a quiet, driving power and intensity, but als elegance. A wine for contemplation in a COVID-weary world. Screw cap | 14.5% alc. | To 2034 | $35 | JP

Majors Creek Vineyard Heathcote Cabernet Sauvignon 2019 Cabernet sauvignon has always beer a strength at Paul Osicka Wines, often taking a starring role in many vintages. Clearly, resolutely cabernet from the outset, with restrained fruit and a tight focus on structure and tannins that go ar go. It's still early days, with assured blackcurrant, wild berries, toasted spices and baked earth whi are set to shine for some time. Screw cap | 14.5% alc. | To 2032 | $35 | JP

Sanguine Estate

77 Shurans Lane, Heathcote, Vic 3523 **T** (03) 5433 3111 **www.sanguinewines.com.au**
OPEN W'ends & public hols 10-5 **WINEMAKER** Mark Hunter **EST.** 1997 **DOZENS** 15000 **VYDS** 26ha

The Hunter family have 21.5ha of shiraz and a 'fruit salad block' of chardonnay, viognier, verdelho, merlot, tempranillo, petit verdot, lagrein, nebbiolo, grenache, cabernet sauvignon and cabernet franc. Low-yielding vines and the magic of the Heathcote region have produce Shiraz of exceptional intensity, which has received rave reviews in the US and led to the 'sold out' sign being posted almost immediately upon release.

95 **Progeny Heathcote Shiraz 2019** It is clear that we have here a shiraz specialist who pays close attention to style and quality at every price point. A $25 shiraz, Progeny hits above its weight in complexity and fruit vibrancy, all with just a relatively light dusting of oak (9 months in French oak and only 10% new). A serious wine, deep, impenetrable 'Heathcote purple' in hue. Hits high notes of violets, blackberry, briar, bramble and spice. Oak is ne'er to be seen but its warm, textural affect on the palate is. A hint of mint gives you a glimpse of the local terroir. Delicious. Screw cap | 14.8% alc. | To 2028 | $25 | JP

Tellurian

408 Tranter Road, Toolleen, Vic 3551 **T** 0431 004 766 **www.tellurianwines.com.au**
OPEN W'ends 11-4.30 or by appt **WINEMAKER** Tobias Ansted **EST.** 2002 **DOZENS** 7000 **VYDS** 32ha

The vineyard is situated on the western side of Mt Camel at Toolleen, on the red Cambrian so that has made Heathcote one of the foremost regions in Australia for the production of shira (Tellurian means 'of the earth'). Viticultural consultant Tim Brown not only supervises the certified organic Tellurian estate plantings, but also works closely with the growers of grape purchased under contract for Tellurian.

96 **Sommet Heathcote Shiraz 2017** Sourced from the highest point of the Tellurian vineyard, this is a flagship shiraz of some stature. Looks and feels the Heathcote part, with astounding deep colour, natural balance, the blackest of berries and tilled red earth resonating throughout. Fragrant and flavoursome, with savoury, fine tannins and a hint of bay leaf to finish. A top wine from a top year. Screw cap | 14.5% alc. | To 2030 | $75 | JP | ♥

94 **Heathcote Marsanne 2019** This is definitely a richer, more expressive style of marsanne but doesn' it carry it well! Bright golden hues. A world of spice aromas with jasmine, wild honey, nougat, marzipan. Complex, but there is also a lightness. The fleshy palate is buoyed and brightened by a flinty edge and juicy acidity. Quite a quality statement for the variety. Screw cap | 13.9% alc. | To 2025 | $29 | JP

'inea Marson ★★★★☆

1 Heathcote-Rochester Road, Heathcote, Vic 3523 **T** 0430 312 165 **www**.vineamarson.com
'EN W'ends **WINEMAKER** Mario Marson **EST.** 2000 **DOZENS** 2500 **VYDS** 7.12ha

wner–winemaker Mario Marson has over 35 years of experience in Australia and overseas. 1999 he and his wife, Helen, purchased the Vinea Marson property on the eastern slopes the Mt Camel Range. They have planted shiraz and viognier, plus Italian varieties of ıngiovese, nebbiolo, barbera and refosco dal peduncolo. Marson also sources northeastern alian varietals from Porepunkah in the Alpine Valleys.

5 **Prosecco 2019** An exceptional vintage in 2019 delivers not only a delicious drink but a complex one. Complexity and prosecco are not mutually exclusive. Honeysuckle, apple blossom, grapefruit and mandarin skin. Flows seamlessly with a quiet savouriness. There's lemon curd, crab apple and poached pear, with a gentle sweetness. Another top prosecco from this maker. Crown seal | 11% alc. | To 2023 | $32 | JP

Vanted Man

:hool House Lane, Heathcote, Vic 3523 **T** (03) 9639 6100 **www**.wantedman.com.au
NEMAKER Shadowfax, Adrian Rodda, Mark Walpole **EST.** 1996 **DOZENS** 2000 **VYDS** 8.19ha

ıe Wanted Man vineyard was planted in 1996 and was managed by Andrew Clarke, producing nks Creek's Heathcote Shiraz. That wine was sufficiently impressive to lead Andrew and partner eter Bartholomew (a Melbourne restaurateur) to purchase the vineyard in 2006 and give it its wn identity. The quirky Ned Kelly label is the work of Mark Knight, cartoonist for the *Herald Sun*.

4 **White Label Heathcote Marsanne Rousanne 2017** A bright, fresh, zippy Rhône blend that combines the prettiness of marsanne with the palate weight and strength of roussanne. Delicious aromas of honeysuckle, citrus, tarte tatin and buttered toast. Gaining bottle complexity as it ages with stone fruits, almond meal, nougat and wet stone. Brisk acidity ties it together beautifully. Gently savoury, too. Screw cap | 13% alc. | To 2026 | $27 | JP

Vren Estate 

39 Heathcote-Rochester Road, Mt Camel, Vic 3523 **T** (03) 9972 9638 **www**.wrenestate.com.au
'EN W'ends & public hols 10-5 **WINEMAKER** Michael Wren **EST.** 2017 **DOZENS** 10 000 **VYDS** 14.5ha

ichael Wren, winemaker and owner of Wren Estate, has been making wine for over 15 years cross multiple continents. For 10 years he was a Flying Winemaker for one of Portugal's top ineries, Esporao, and was particularly struck by the use of lagares for top-quality wines. agares are low, wide, open red-wine fermenters that allow foot treading (or stomping) with e level of must little more than knee deep. The consequence is the very soft, yet high, xtraction of colour, flavour and soft tannins. The red wine fermenters in the Wren winery are eplicas of the traditional lagares.

4 **Heathcote Marsanne 2019** The alcohol gives you a clue to style here, early picked and delicate. It displays the variety's pretty honeysuckle and jasmine florals, in tandem with its citrus, acacia and lemon balm herbals. The palate is fresh and alive, with emerging texture and a wealth of citrus/pear/honeysuckle/spice flavour. A wine to watch. Screw cap | 12.9% alc. | To 2029 | $25 | JP

EGION

Strathbogie Ranges

Elgo Estate

020 Upton Road, Upton Hill, Vic 3664 **T** (03) 5798 5563 **www**.elgoestate.com.au **OPEN** By appt
INEMAKER Grant Taresch, Suzanne Taresch **EST.** 2000 **DOZENS** 10 000 **VYDS** 100ha

lgo Estate, owned by the Taresch family, is located high in the hills of the Strathbogie Ranges, 25km northeast of Melbourne, a stone's throw from the southern end of the Heathcote egion. Elgo Estate is committed to sustainable viticulture reflecting and expressing the haracteristics of this cool-climate region.

3 **Allira Strathbogie Ranges Riesling 2020** Acid hounds will flock to this wine. The lemon-zesty acidity defines this fine-edged riesling in large part, giving it tension and energy. It's quite a thing to enjoy in its youth but it's also there for the journey ahead. Lime, lemon zest, Granny Smith apple, grapefruit all entwined and beautifully engaged by bracing acidity. This is how Strathbogies' quartz delivers riesling. So exciting. Screw cap | 13.4% alc. | To 2030 | $19 | JP

Maygars Hill Winery

53 Longwood-Mansfield Road, Longwood, Vic 3665 **T** 0402 136 448 **www**.maygarshill.com.au
OPEN By appt **WINEMAKER** Contract **EST.** 1997 **DOZENS** 900 **VYDS** 3.2ha

Jenny Houghton purchased this 8ha property in 1994, planting shiraz (1.9ha) and cabernet sauvignon (1.3ha). The name comes from Lieutenant Colonel Maygar, who fought with outstanding bravery in the Boer War in South Africa in 1901 and was awarded the Victoria Cross. In World War I he rose to command the 8th Light Horse Regiment, winning yet further medals for bravery.

95 **Shiraz 2019** An excellent follow-up to the superb '18 shiraz, with concentration and style. Deep purple hue. Still youthful and in development mode, but sporting typical 'bogies balance and structure. Sweet, ripe black cherry, bracken, abundant woody spices and baked earth. The palate has a dense but smooth texture, with a touch of lasting elegance. Screw cap | 14% alc. | To 2027 | $30 | JP

94 **Cabernet Sauvignon 2019** Sings loudly where it hails from, a telltale bay-leaf/eucalyptus thread very much in evidence. It is without doubt an attractive feature, a potent sense of Central Victorian terroir. Good varietal intensity, too: cassis and black cherry, dried bay leaf, a touch of peppermint, violet, leafy. Sinewy mouthfeel. Fine, edgy tannins are quite pronounced, providing structure and potential for further ageing. Screw cap | 13% alc. | To 2029 | $30 | JP

Wine Unplugged

2020 Upton Road, Upton Hill, Vic 3664 (postal) **T** 0432 021 668 **www**.wineunplugged.com.au
WINEMAKER Callie Jemmeson, Nina Stocker **EST.** 2010 **DOZENS** 5000

Nina Stocker and Callie Jemmeson believe that winemaking doesn't have to have barriers: what it does need is quality, focus and a destination. With a strong emphasis on vineyard selection and a gentle approach to their small-batch winemaking, the wines are a true reflection of site. The wines are released under the pacha mama, La Vie en Rose, Cloak & Dagger, Motley Cru and Harvest Moon labels.

95 **pacha mama Yarra Valley Chardonnay 2018** Smoky sulphides at play here, so it smells of chicken soup at first, all savoury and umami-like. There is the requisite white stone fruit and citrus elements too, but very much behind the scenes. Also tucked in neatly, the acidity and perfectly integrated oak. Screw cap | 13% alc. | To 2028 | $30 | JF

pacha mama Pinot Gris 2019 Opens with the telltale varietal inputs of ginger-spiced poached pear, apples, fresh pears too, and a fleck of aniseed. There is a juiciness and tang with lemon/tangerine notes, then it glides into richer territory, with creamy lees adding texture and flavour. Screw cap | 13% alc. | To 2024 | $28 | JF

pacha mama Heathcote Shiraz 2019 Outrageous colour – vibrant black/purple and what's so appealing with this wine is its beautifully tamed tannins. They have shape but are not at all brutish, giving definition to the fuller-bodied wine. In the mix, dark, sweet fruit, Chinese five-spice, charry wood flavours and a guarantee of an excellent drink. Screw cap | 14% alc. | To 2028 | $30 | JF

Wine x Sam

69-71 Anzac Avenue, Seymour, Vic 3660 **T** 03 57 990 437 **www**.winebysam.com.au **OPEN** Fri-Sun 9-4
WINEMAKER Sam Plunkett, Mark Hickin, Sophie Fromont **EST.** 2012 **DOZENS** 70000 **VYDS** 10.2ha

Since 1991 Sam Plunkett and partner Bron Dunwoodie have changed shells as often as a lively hermit crab: 1991, first estate vineyard established and mudbrick winery built; 2001, created a new winery at Avenel; 2004, purchased the large Dominion Wines in partnership with the Fowles family; 2011, Fowles purchased the Plunkett family's shareholding, except 7ha of shiraz and 3.2ha of chardonnay. Winemaking moved to the Taresch family's Elgo Estate winery. Within 2 years the Plunkett interests had leased the entire Elgo winery, now making the Elgo wines as well as their own brands. A large contract make for Naked Wines saw production increase, and a few blinks of the eye later, production is now 70000 dozen.

94 **The Victorian Strathbogie Ranges Riesling 2019** Riesling is always a strength with this maker. Maybe a little more forward in comparison to last year. Zesty, sherbet fresh with apple blossom, talc and musk, fine citrus and spice. Shimmies over the tongue with an added note of lemon butter texture. Finishes with lingering, mouth-watering acidity. Screw cap | 11.8% alc. | To 2025 | $24 | JP

ION

Ipper Goulburn

os Ritchie Wines

ınolia House, 190 Mount Buller Road, Mansfield, 3722 **T** 0444 588 276 **www**.rosritchiewines.com **N** Fri 5-8, w'ends & public hols 11-4 **WINEMAKER** Ros Ritchie **EST.** 2008 **DOZENS** 2000 **VYDS** 7ha

s Ritchie and husband John work with local growers, foremost the Kinlock, McFadden, nbertop and Baxendale vineyards, the last planted by the very experienced viticulturist Jim xendale (and wife Ruth) high above the King River Valley. All vineyards are managed with nimal spray regimes. The cellar door is located at the historic Magnolia House at Mansfield, en on select weekends, hosting seasonal wine dinners and special events.

Barwite Vineyard Riesling 2020 Incredible value. So young and yet revealing so much in readiness for a long life ahead. A jasmine and spring blossom fragrance, teeming with lemon sorbet, green apple and a gently spicy lift. A kind of slatey minerality inhabits the palate in league with fast-paced chalky acidity. In a difficult year, out pops a stunner. Screw cap | 13% alc. | To 2030 | $26 | JP

ırradindi Wines

8 Murrindindi Road, Murrindindi, Vic 3717 **T** 0438 305 314 **www**.mrhughwine.com **EMAKER** Hugh Cuthbertson **EST.** 1979 **DOZENS** 90000 **VYDS** 70ha

ırrindindi Vineyards was established by Alan and Jan Cutherbertson as a minor ersification from their cattle property. Son Hugh Cutherbertson (with a long and high-ofile wine career) took over the venture and in 2015 folded the business into his largest stomers to create Yarradindi Wines. The main focus now is export to China with distribution ganisations in Hangzhou, shipping 1 million bottles annually.

Mr Hugh Sipping Bliss Digestif NV In another time this would have been called a tawny port and was made in the dry, nutty Portuguese style. No ordinary digestif, the name doesn't go anywhere near revealing the seriousness of this fortified or its richness and utter complexity. Reveals its age in the walnut brown colour and deep scent of molasses, dried fruit, caramel, coffee. Flows seamlessly and long across the palate. An absolute beauty in the glass. 375ml. Screw cap | 18% alc. | $35 | JP

E

;ippsland

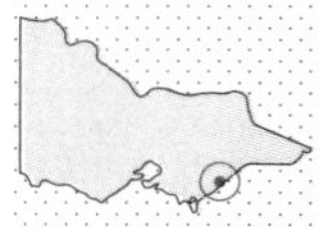

aileys of Glenrowan

Taminick Gap Road, Glenrowan, Vic 3675 **T** (03) 5766 1600 **www**.baileysofglenrowan.com.au **N** 7 days 10-5 **WINEMAKER** Paul Dahlenburg, Elizabeth Kooij **EST.** 1870 **DOZENS** 15000 **VYDS** 144ha

ıce 1998 Baileys has undergone an expansion in the vineyard and the construction of OOOt capacity winery. The cellar door has a heritage museum, winery viewing deck, ntemporary art gallery and landscaped grounds preserving much of the heritage value. e vineyards and winery have been steadily undergoing conversion to organic since 2011, ducing the first full range of certified organic table wines from the 2019 vintage. Baileys d plenty to celebrate for its 150th anniversary in 2020.

Founder Series Classic Topaque NV Baileys turned 150 in '20, celebrating a proud fortified wine history, manifest in this wine of some finesse. Lifted, super-fresh and raisiny, malty in aroma. Filigree-fine on the tongue, with the lasting presence of butterscotch, smoky lapsang souchong tea, licorice block, honey and a touch of Asian spice. Clean as a whistle on delivery. Combines freshness and complexity. Vino-Lok | 17% alc. | $30 | JP

CENTRAL VICTORIA | GIPPSLAND | NORTH EAST VICTORIA | NORTH WEST VICTORIA | PORT PHILLIP | WESTERN VICTORIA

Lightfoot & Sons  

717 Calulu Road, Bairnsdale, Vic 3875 **T** (03) 5156 9205 www.lightfootwines.com **OPEN** Mon-Fri 11-5 **WINEMAKER** Alastair Butt, Tom Lightfoot **EST.** 1995 **DOZENS** 10000 **VYDS** 29.3ha

Brian and Helen Lightfoot first established a vineyard on their Myrtle Point farm in the late '90s. The soils were found to be similar to that of Coonawarra, with terra rossa over limestor In the early days, most of the grapes were sold to other Victorian winemakers, but with the arrival of Alistair Butt (formerly of Brokenwood and Seville Estate) and sons Tom and Rob taking over the business around 2008, the focus has shifted to producing estate wines. (TS)

95 **Myrtle Point Vineyard Gippsland Chardonnay 2019** While the colour is a mid straw gold, it's fresh and a pretty smart wine. White stone fruit, splashes of citrus and lots of spices, but the real pleasu is the palate. Fuller bodied, with a silky, slippery texture. Screw cap | 13.6% alc. | To 2026 | $30 | JF

Narkoojee 

220 Francis Road, Glengarry, Vic 3854 **T** (03) 5192 4257 www.narkoojee.com **OPEN** 7 days 10.30-4.30 **WINEMAKER** Axel Friend **EST.** 1981 **DOZENS** 5000 **VYDS** 13.8ha

Narkoojee, originally a dairy farm owned by the Friend family, is near the old gold-mining tow of Walhalla and looks out over the Strzelecki Ranges. The wines are produced from the estat vineyards, with chardonnay accounting for half the total. Former lecturer in civil engineerin and extremely successful amateur winemaker, Harry Friend, changed horses in 1994 to take joint control of the vineyard and winery with son Axel, and they haven't missed a beat since; their skills show through in all the wines.

95 **Tumbarumba Chardonnay 2018** Another reminder of how good fruit from Tumbarumba is, with this morphing into a yin-and-yang wine. It's flavoursome with stone fruit, lemon curd and a leesy, nutty richness. Yet its fine acidity, linearity, length and freshness keep it reined in. Screw cap | 12.5% alc. | To 2028 | $27 | JF

Taminick Cellars  

339 Booth Road, Taminick via Glenrowan, Vic 3675 **T** (03) 5766 2282 www.taminickcellars.com.a **OPEN** Mon-Sat 9-5, Sun 10-5 **WINEMAKER** James Booth **EST.** 1904 **DOZENS** 2000 **VYDS** 19.7ha

Peter Booth is a 3rd-generation member of the Booth family, who have owned this winery since Esca Booth purchased the property in 1904. James Booth, 4th generation and current winemaker, completed his wine science degree at CSU in 2008. The red wines are massively flavoured and very long-lived, notably those from the 9ha of shiraz planted in 191 Trebbiano and alicante bouschet were also planted in 1919; the much newer arrivals include nero d'Avola.

94 **Durif 2017** A journey into the durif darkness, a place inhabited by the grape's propensity (when se free) for blackberries, bramble berry, tar and red earth. But, it's not for long. What is both apparen on the nose and upfront on the palate melds into an attractive, well-appointed durif with lifted aromatics of violet and spice. Quite a rich and varied little adventure. Screw cap | 13.8% alc. | To 2031 | $22 | JP

ZONE

North East Victoria

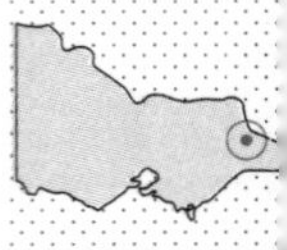

Kooyonga Creek  

2369 Samaria Road, Moorngag, Vic 3673 **T** (03) 9629 5853 www.kooyonga.com.au **OPEN** Fri-Sun 11- or by appt **WINEMAKER** Luis Simian **EST.** 2011 **DOZENS** 5000 **VYDS** 7.5ha

When you read the name of this winery, you expect to find it somewhere on or near the Mornington Peninsula. In fact it's a very long way to North East Victoria, where Barry and Pam Saunders planted 7.5ha of vineyards on their farm and released the first wines under the name Kooyonga Chapel in 2003.

Cabernet Sauvignon 2017 A warm, earthy cabernet to curl up with. A wine without pretence, just good old-fashioned richness of blackberry, plum, earth, leather and a central core of sweet spice. Yes, it's big for a cabernet but not unwieldy, courtesy of smooth, far-reaching tannins. Screw cap | 14.5% alc. | To 2030 | $20 | JP

t Pilot Estate 

Shannons Road, Byawatha, Vic 3678 **T** 0419 243 225 **WWW**.mtpilotestatewines.com.au
N By appt **WINEMAKER** Marc Scalzo **EST.** 1996 **DOZENS** 600 **VYDS** 13ha

chlan and Penny Campbell have planted shiraz, cabernet sauvignon, viognier and durif. The eyard is planted on deep, well-drained granitic soils at an altitude of 250m near Eldorado, km from Wangaratta and 35km from Beechworth.

Reserve Viognier 2017 This smart viognier is definitely worthy of your attention, striking the always delicate balance between richness of fruit and brightness of acidity in the grape. Baked apple, nougat, orange peel, earthy, toasted spice and nuts fill the senses with a deep complexity. It works beautifully on the palate, getting the textural tone and pitch just right. Juicy acidity whets the appetite. Screw cap | 13.7% alc. | To 2027 | $35 | JP

ION

lpine Valleys

lly Button Wines

Camp Street, Bright, Vic 3741 and 61 Myrtle Street, Myrtleford, Vic 3737 **T** (03) 5755 1569
w.billybuttonwines.com.au **OPEN** 7 days 12-6 **WINEMAKER** Jo Marsh, Glenn James, Alex Phillips, an Wallace **EST.** 2014 **DOZENS** 6000

Marsh makes light of the numerous awards she won during her studies for her degree in icultural science (oenology) at the University of Adelaide, followed by a contested position Southcorp's Graduate Recruitment Program. She has set up a grower network in the Alpine leys and makes a string of excellent wines. Billy Button also shares a cellar door with Bush ck Wines in the heart of Myrtleford.

The Beloved Alpine Valleys Shiraz 2018 A deeply coloured young wine with plenty of personality, the result of a lot of obvious love and attention to detail. Super-fragrant and approachable first up, with blackberry, blueberry, wood smoke and aniseed. Proceeds with confidence and effortless balance with lashings of fruit, sage and a touch of undergrowth savouriness winding along a long path of ripe tannins. Screw cap | 14.5% alc. | To 2028 | $32 | JP

The Affable Alpine Valleys Barbera 2019 An interesting follow-up to the excellent '18 release, with greater ripeness evident, pushing the already plush style into luxuriant territory. Black cherries, wild raspberries, dried herbs and a dusty earthiness greet the drinker, but while the fruit intensity rises in '19, the same degree of medium-bodied structure and fineness is also evident, thanks to some juicy, fresh acidity. Screw cap | 14.5% alc. | To 2026 | $32 | JP

The Clandestine Alpine Valleys Schioppettino 2019 Jo Marsh is among the most curious and talented winemakers going. Thanks to her intellectual curiosity, we are blessed with wines like this, a rarity whose home is in Italy's northeast. A finely appointed wine of some delicacy and poise. Florals to the fore on the bouquet. Violet, bramble and rose mingle with black cherry, redcurrant and baking spices. Glides across the tongue to an easy conclusion. Compelling in its understatement. Screw cap | 13.5% alc. | To 2026 | $32 | JP

apsted Wines 

7 Great Alpine Road, Gapsted, Vic 3737 **T** (03) 5751 9100 **WWW**.gapstedwines.com.au
N Thurs-Mon 10-5 **WINEMAKER** Michael Cope-Williams, Toni Pla Bou, Matt Fawcett **EST.** 1997
ENS 250000 **VYDS** 256.1ha

well as the substantial estate plantings, Gapsted sources traditional and alternative grape ieties from the King and Alpine valleys. The quality of the wines made for its own brand s led to the expansion of production not only under that label, but also under a raft of osidiary labels.

Tobacco Road King Valley Sangiovese Rosé 2020 How fresh and lively is this? Palest pink blush in hue. Pulses with bright acidity, red apple, raspberry and cherry crunch throughout. Little wonder the sangiovese grape is increasingly employed in the service of rosé. Summer fruits from start to finish on the palate with just a light creaminess. Screw cap | 12.5% alc. | To 2024 | $16 | JP

REGION

Beechworth

Eldorado Road ★★★★

46-48 Ford Street, Beechworth, Vic 3747 **T** (03) 5725 1698 **www**.eldoradoroad.com.au **OPEN** Fri-S 11-5 **WINEMAKER** Paul Dahlenburg, Ben Dahlenburg, Laurie Schulz **EST.** 2010 **DOZENS** 1500 **VYDS** 4ha

Paul Dahlenburg (nicknamed Bear), Lauretta Schulz (Laurie) knew about the origins of this vineyard, which was in a state of serious decline after years of neglect. Its owners were awa of its historic importance and were more than happy to lease it. Four years of tireless work reconstructing the old vines has resulted in tiny amounts of exceptionally good shiraz; they have also planted a small area of nero d'Avola and durif.

95 **Quasimodo Nero d'Avola Shiraz Durif 2018** An unusual blend but, my, does it work a treat! A fragr and delicious red of an easy presence and impressive balance. Cherry fruit aromas, dark blood plums, sweet oak spice, hints of anise, chocolate. A soft, engaging wine, supple and ripe in tannir Screw cap | 13.6% alc. | To 2026 | $29 | JP | ♥

Fighting Gully Road

Kurrajong Way, Mayday Hill, Beechworth, Vic 3747 **T** 0407 261 373 **www**.fightinggully.com.au **OPEN** By appt **WINEMAKER** Mark Walpole, Adrian Rodda **EST.** 1997 **DOZENS** 3500 **VYDS** 8.3ha

Mark Walpole (who began his viticultural career with Brown Brothers in the late 1980s) and partner Carolyn De Poi found their elevated north-facing site south of Beechworth in 1995. In 2009 they were fortunate to lease the oldest vineyard in the region, planted by the Smith family in 1978 to chardonnay and cabernet sauvignon. Mark says, 'We are now making wine in a building in the old and historic Mayday Hills Lunatic Asylum – a place that should be full of winemakers!'

97 **Black Label Smith's Vineyard Beechworth Chardonnay 2018** From vines planted in '78, fermentec and matured for 18 months in new and used French oak, partial mlf. The power, intensity and dep of the wine comes from the low yield of these venerable vines. Ripe white nectarine/peach is offs by flinty acidity. Screw cap | 13% alc. | To 2030 | $65 | JH

95 **Beechworth Pinot Noir 2019** Medium crimson. Fragrant and high-toned florals join forces with alluring forest berries, thyme and sage. Not an easy year for the region, but it's hard to see this in such a confident youngster, full of life and energy. Tight across the palate, with a lilting tomato leafiness, it's assured of developing further. Screw cap | 13.5% alc. | To 2027 | $35 | JP | ♥

Black Label La Longa Beechworth Sangiovese 2018 According to the maker, La Longa is a test of patience, with extended time in new and seasoned barriques, followed by more time in large 160 wooden cask and, finally, bottle ageing before release. Strikes a wild pose, with baked earth, wild thyme, dried herbs, glazed cherries and Szechuan pepper. Supple tannins meld with warm, ripe fruit, but underlying it all is firm, toasty oak. Screw cap | 14% alc. | To 2030 | $32 | JP

Giaconda ★★★★

30 McClay Road, Beechworth, Vic 3747 **T** (03) 5727 0246 **www**.giaconda.com.au **OPEN** By appt **WINEMAKER** Rick Kinzbrunner, Nathan Kinzbrunner **EST.** 1982 **DOZENS** 3500 **VYDS** 4ha

These wines have a super-cult status and, given the small production, are extremely difficul to find; they are sold chiefly through restaurants and via their website. All have a cosmopoli edge befitting Rick Kinzbrunner's international winemaking experience. The Chardonnay is one of Australia's greatest.

99 **Estate Vineyard Chardonnay 2018** It's so difficult to avoid comparisons with Montrachet, except t say both have profoundly deep and long palates. Of course, there's high-quality French oak and t requisite acidity to freshen the finish, but the ultimate quality lies in the freakish length of the win Screw cap | 13.5% alc. | To 2038 | $130 | JH | ♥

Virago

5a Ford Street, Beechworth, Vic 3747 **T** 0411 718 369 **www**.viragobeechworth.com.au **OPEN** By app **WINEMAKER** Karen Coats, Rick Kinzbrunner **EST.** 2007 **DOZENS** 175 **VYDS** 1ha

Karen Coats was a tax accountant but has now completed the bachelor of wine science at CSU. It was her love of nebbiolo and the Beechworth region that made Virago Vineyard her new office of choice. Prue Keith is an orthopaedic surgeon but devotes her free time ıatever is not occupied by mountain biking, skiing and trekking to the peaks of mountains) Virago Vineyard. The inimitable Rick Kinzbrunner has a more than passing interest in ɔbiolo, so it was inevitable that he would be the consultant winemaker.

Nebbiolo 2017 An excellent year on full display, giving rise to a dark and brooding nebbiolo of wild rosemary, thyme, saltbush, incense, black cherry and mandarin skin. A most complex and accomplished wine of intrigue and discovery – such is nebbiolo's power – finishing firm, with a savoury tannin presence. `Diam | 14% alc. | To 2035 | $50 | JP`

ION

ing Valley

rown Brothers

Milawa-Bobinawarrah Road, Milawa, Vic 3678 **T** (03) 5720 5500 **www**.brownbrothers.com.au **N** 7 days 9-5 **WINEMAKER** Joel Tilbrook, Cate Looney, Geoff Alexander, Katherine Brown, Canning, Simon McMillan **EST.** 1889 **DOZENS** 1 million **VYDS** 570ha

ɔwn Brothers draws upon a considerable number of vineyards spread throughout a range of e climates – from very warm to very cool. In 2010 Brown Brothers took a momentous step, quiring Tasmania's Tamar Ridge for $32.5 million. In May '16 it acquired Innocent Bystander d stock from Giant Steps, and with it a physical presence in the Yarra Valley. It is known for diversity of varieties with which it works, and the wines represent good value for money. servedly one of the most successful family wineries – its cellar door receives the greatest mber of visitors in Australia. A founding member of Australia's First Families of Wine.

Patricia Pinot Noir Chardonnay Brut 2014 78/22% pinot noir/chardonnay, on lees for 6 years. Fruit from the Whitlands Plateau, one of the highest vineyards in Australia, and possessing a rare vitality for a 6yo sparkling. Patricia's signature purity of fruit expression and exhilarating acidity. A persistent, fine bubble. Lemon zest, straw, apple custard and Nice biscuit. Youthful exuberance with grapefruit, citrus, almond meal and a clean creaminess. `Cork | 12.5% alc. | $47 | JP`

Premium King Valley Prosecco Brut NV A premium prosecco – why not? A drier prosecco than usual, bringing gravitas to the style, with a smarter, tighter line and length. No simple lemonade characters here, but rather some depth in aroma and flavour. Granny Smith apples, grapefruit, pear skin, preserved lemon. Zesty, bright on the palate but settles into a citrus-infused, lemon-tart line of flavour with a waxy mouthfeel. Definitely a step up in poise and elegance for the variety. `Agglomerate | 11.5% alc. | To 2026 | $25 | JP`

al Zotto Wines

n Road, Whitfield, Vic 3733 **T** (03) 5729 8321 **www**.dalzotto.com.au **OPEN** 7 days 10-5 **EMAKER** Michael Dal Zotto, Daniel Bettio **EST.** 1987 **DOZENS** 60000 **VYDS** 46ha

e Dal Zotto family is a King Valley institution; ex-tobacco growers, then contract apegrowers, they are now 100% focused on their Dal Zotto wine range. They are producing reasing amounts of Italian varieties of consistent quality from its substantial estate eyard; they were the pioneers of prosecco in Australia with the first planting in 1999. The lar door is in the centre of Whitfield, and is also home to their Trattoria (open weekends).

Pucino Col Fondo King Valley Prosecco 2019 A return to the traditional Italian style of prosecco – a revelation when compared to some commercial, sweet styles going. Lightly cloudy lemon colour, with the soft scent of honeysuckle, fresh apple, lemon sorbet and musky florals. Fresh and vital and full of a fine complexity, almost delicate, with a touch of savoury earth. Dry and lemony, with enlivening acidity. A captivating taste experience. `Crown seal | 11.3% alc. | $30 | JP`

zzini

King Valley Road, Whitfield, Vic 3768 **T** (03) 5729 8278 **www**.pizzini.com.au **OPEN** 7 days 10-5 **EMAKER** Joel Pizzini **EST.** 1980 **DOZENS** 30000 **VYDS** 85ha

e Pizzini family have been grapegrowers in the King Valley for over 40 years. Originally ch of the then riesling, chardonnay and cabernet sauvignon grape production was sold, t since the late '90s the focus has been on winemaking, particularly from Italian varieties. zini's success has enabled an increase in vineyard holdings to 85ha.

Pietra Rossa King Valley Sangiovese 2018 Sangiovese is a natural in the King Valley. Here's the evidence. Rich, glossy red hue. Bright, ripe black cherry, raspberry, plum and spice aromas jump. Takes a serious turn on the palate with texture, depth of flavour, light savouriness and smoky, toasty oak tannins, tapering lean and dry into the finish. `Screw cap | 13.8% alc. | To 2028 | $28 | JP`

REGION

Rutherglen

All Saints Estate

205 All Saints Road, Wahgunyah, Vic 3687 **T** 1800 021 621 **www**.allsaintswine.com.au **OPEN** Sun-F 10-5, Sat 10-5.30 **WINEMAKER** Nick Brown **EST.** 1864 **DOZENS** 22000 **VYDS** 47.9ha

The winery rating reflects the fortified wines, including the unique releases of Museum Muscat and Muscadelle, each with an average age of more than 100 years (and table wines) The 1-hat Terrace Restaurant makes this a must-stop for any visitor to North East Victoria, as does the National Trust–listed property with its towering castle centrepiece.

97 **Rare Rutherglen Muscat NV** Utter deliciousness and just a touch decadent. That olive glimmer giv away the old age: the average age of the wines in the blend is 35 years old. An aromatic treat of raisins, prunes, cracked walnut, roasted coffee beans and salted toffees. Hugely complex but als with a real touch of elegance and clean driving power. 375ml. Vino-Lok | 18% alc. | $120 | JP

Grand Rutherglen Muscat NV Average age in oak is 25 years. The house certainly has a marvellou legacy of old wines to call upon for its fortified program. The scent is heavenly, like inhaling the dessert counter at Alain Ducasse Le Chocolat in Paris. Intense dark chocolate, caramel, coffee be toasted hazelnut and dried fruits. So harmonious, so decadent and so, so lasting in the mouth. 375ml. Vino-Lok | 18% alc. | $75 | JP

95 **Durif 2018** All Saints Estate sees the beauty and elegance in the durif grape – yes, it most definite exists – and produces a style that can overcome any varietal prejudice. With forest-floor notes, wild berries, violets, top spice nuances and vanilla, it's an arresting introduction. Smooth palate, yet retains the grape's robust nature and power. Sensitive handling and winemaking on show. Screw cap | 14% alc. | To 2028 | $32 | JP

Arlo Vintners

8 Jones Road, Rutherglen, Vic 3685 **T** 0431 037 752 **www**.arlovintners.com **WINEMAKER** Dan Bettio Lennie Lister **EST.** 2016 **DOZENS** 400 **VYDS** 2.5ha

Dan Bettio and Lennie Lister are the owners of Arlo Vintners, each with over 20 years experience working in wine, chiefly in North East Victoria. Their business plan is close to a template for others to adopt. Its credo is to select vineyards with something special about th region and adopt small-batch winemaking to produce 100 dozen bottles of each of their win

94 **Old Vine Glenrowan Shiraz 2018** Glenrowan shiraz in all of its medium-bodied, velvety-tannined, fruit-forward beauty. Lifted aromatics, briar, mulberry, native pepper. Fine display of red/blue fruits with well-managed oak (a feature with this producer) falling away to a soft, quiet conclusior Screw cap | 13.6% alc. | To 2026 | $29 | JP

Campbells

4603 Murray Valley Highway, Rutherglen, Vic 3685 **T** (02) 6033 6000 **www**.campbellswines.com.au **OPEN** 7 days 10-5 **WINEMAKER** Julie Campbell **EST.** 1870 **DOZENS** 36000 **VYDS** 72ha

Campbells has a long and rich history, with 5 generations of the family making wine for ove 150 years. There have been spectacular successes in unexpected quarters (white table win especially riesling) and expected success with muscat and topaque. Scores of 99 points from Robert Parker and 100 points from Wine Spectator put Campbells in a special position A founding member of Australia's First Families of Wine.

97 **Isabella Rare Rutherglen Topaque NV** Deep, dark amber, displaying charactertistic Campbells aromatics, Isabella is a treat for the tastebuds and the mind, a wine of living history. The aroma is powerfully luscious and concentrated in plum pudding, orange peel, treacle, raisin. Lush and harmonious to taste, with hints of Saunders malt, viscous honey and dried fruits, all edged in a clean, lively spirit. Flows long, hitting the sweet-and-mellow spot. 375ml. Screw cap | 18% alc. | $140 | JP

Merchant Prince Rare Muscat NV Mesmerising! Merchant Prince is one of the most complex tasti experiences you can have. Such is the depth and age of Campbells fortified stocks; few producer can compete. Dense, deep in colour and super-concentrated, Merchant Prince seems to pour in slow motion. Molasses, dried fruits, soaked raisins and toasted nuts meld and weave their way through the palate, rising in sweet intensity. Clean pair of heels to close. A fortified masterclass. 375ml. Screw cap | 18% alc. | $140 | JP

96 **Grand Rutherglen Topaque NV** Burnished walnut colour. A laid-back approach, mellow even, witr luscious sweetness tempered by cold-tea notes in tandem with raisined fruit, chocolate panforte

and toasted nuts. So much here: layer upon layer of flavour that fills all senses. But that balance of clean spirit keeps things tight and fresh. So much class on display. 375ml. Screw cap | 17.5% alc. | $70 | JP

Grand Rutherglen Muscat NV Superb fruit is the building block here. The colour of treacle accompanies the scent of fig, dried fruits, nougat and orange peel. As intense as it is in aroma and on the palate, there is an incredible freshness, too, the mark of a great fortified. Layer upon layer of raisiny fruitcake goodness, walnut, quince paste, toffee. All class. Screw cap | 17.5% alc. | $70 | JP

Bobbie Burns Rutherglen Shiraz 2018 This release marks the 49th vintage for Bobbie Burns. The secret to its longevity is its honesty, which is nicely expressed here. It is right in the medium-weighted, down to earth, totally accessible, classic Aussie shiraz style. Solid in dark fruits, discreet in oak, awash in tingling, woodsy spice and melded together by fine tannins. Length is assured, the pleasure factor high. Screw cap | 14.5% alc. | To 2029 | $23 | JP

ıambers Rosewood

:ly Street, Rutherglen, Vic 3685 **T** (02) 6032 8641 **www**.chambersrosewood.com.au
Mon-Sat 9-5, Sun 10-5 **WINEMAKER** Stephen Chambers **EST.** 1858 **DOZENS** 5000 **VYDS** 50ha

ımbers' Rare Muscat and Rare Muscadelle (previously Topaque or Tokay) are the greatest ll in the Rutherglen firmament and should be treated as national treasures; the other wines ıe hierarchy also magnificent. Stephen Chambers (6th generation) comes into the role as emaker, but father Bill is seldom far away.

Old Vine Rutherglen Muscat NV Slowly moving up a notch in age, complexity, depth of flavour and stickiness. Suffice to say, this is a fortified brimming with a seamless beauty and richness of expression. Layers of dried fig, dates, honey cake, toffee and raisin set a fresh and lively pace, aided by neutral spirit. Amazing value. 375ml. Screw cap | 18% alc. | $25 | JP

Old Vine Rutherglen Muscadelle NV Equivalent to the Classic Rutherglen Muscat classification, this amber beauty retains the essence of muscadelle flavour – roasted nuts, tea leaves, malt and toffee – within a smoothly honed, deep, sweet palate of some obvious complexity. The blender's art is right here on display to be celebrated. 375ml. Screw cap | 18% alc. | $30 | JP

orris

Mia Road, Rutherglen, Vic 3685 **T** (02) 6026 7303 **www**.morriswines.com **OPEN** Mon-Sun 10-4
EMAKER David Morris **EST.** 1859 **DOZENS** 100000 **VYDS** 96ha

e of the greatest of the fortified winemakers, ranking an eyelash behind Chambers sewood. The art of these wines lies in the blending of very old and much younger material. se Rutherglen fortified wines have no equivalent in any other part of the world (with the ıourable exception of Seppeltsfield in the Barossa Valley).

Old Premium Rare Topaque NV A masterclass from Australia's greatest fortified maker, David Morris, right here. The depth of complexity and intensity lays bare the art of the blender and the depth and quality of the source material. Dried fruit, malt, fruitcake, caramel toffees, licorice, roasted hazelnut and so much more infused in an enveloping umami warmth. 500ml. Screw cap | 17.5% alc. | $90 | JP

Old Premium Rare Liqueur Rutherglen Muscat NV A rich baroque tapestry of aromas and flavours of great complexity. Immense concentration and depth on display but realised with real grace and elegance. The superlatives flow but they are needed. Plum pudding, chocolate, coffee bean, walnut and fruit peel combine with toasty elements and dried dates, all smoothy honed and lifted by neutral spirit. The finish stays with you. 500ml. Screw cap | 17% alc. | $90 | JP

Cellar Reserve Grand Liqueur Rutherglen Topaque NV Deep, dark molasses in hue. Lifted and fresh aromas – a key to quality in aged fortifieds – of fruitcake, roasted nuts, cold tea and coffee grounds. So smooth across the palate; and complex, aided by a low-strength neutral spirit which allows the aged flavours to soar. 500ml. Screw cap | 17.3% alc. | $50 | JP

Cellar Reserve Grand Liqueur Rutherglen Muscat NV Varied vine ages in play here, planted in 1965, 1974, 1982 and 2002, contributing varying degrees of flavour complexity. When combined with age, neutral spirit and judicious blending, they smash it out of the park! What a stunner. A rich, velvety fabric of fig, butterscotch, toffee, walnut, panforte. Flavours go and go. Astoundingly complex and, importantly, fresh. 500ml. Screw cap | 17.3% alc. | $50 | JP

Classic Rutherglen Topaque NV Manages to combine elegance and freshness with a richness of flavour, not an easy task. A lovely delicacy pervades this wine, of freshly roasted coffee beans, mocha, golden syrup, honey and that thread of cold tea so emblematic of the grape and style. A mix of age, clean neutral spirit here and, always, the seamless Morris style. What value! 375ml. Screw cap | 17.5% alc. | $25 | JP

Classic Rutherglen Muscat NV A vibrant, fresh example of the classic style. Golden brown in hue, lifted fragrance of nougat, orange peel, toffee and dark malt biscuit. That sweet maltiness runs deep on the palate with a luscious intensity. Silken palate texture. A top quality classic classification statement. 500ml. Screw cap | 17.5% alc. | $25 | JP

Black Label Rutherglen Muscat NV What a steal. Amazing quality right here. The wealth and dep of the Morris fortified solera system is evident even at the entry-level muscat. Butterscotch, drie fruits, honey and a hint of rose petal combine with a luscious palate with developing nuttiness. Sweetness freshened nicely by the neutral spirit. 500ml. Screw cap | 17.3% alc. | $20 | JP

Pfeiffer Wines ★★★★

167 Distillery Road, Wahgunyah, Vic 3687 **T** (02) 6033 2805 **www.pfeifferwines.com.au**
OPEN Mon-Sat 9-5, Sun 10-5 **WINEMAKER** Chris Pfeiffer, Jen Pfeiffer **EST.** 1984 **DOZENS** 20000
VYDS 33ha

Family-owned and run, Pfeiffer Wines occupies one of the historic wineries (built in 1885) t abound in North East Victoria, which makes it worth a visit on this score alone. In 2012 Chr Pfeiffer was awarded an Order of Australia Medal (OAM) for his services to the wine industr The arrival of daughter Jen, by a somewhat circuitous and initially unplanned route, has dramatically lifted the quality of the table wines, led by the reds.

97 **Rare Rutherglen Topaque NV** A muscadelle of unusual age averaging 25 years old, with world-class silken, supple qualities and complexity. Here, the fortified blender's art reaches its pinnacl Immense concentration is on display and yet it is still so fresh, thanks to sensitive fortification using neutral spirit. Cold-brew coffee, dark chocolate, malt biscuit, dried fruits and more. Luscic umami texture, with treacle-like richness that sticks to the sides of the mouth. Glorious! 500ml. Screw cap | 17.5% alc. | $123 | JP

Rare Rutherglen Muscat NV The blender's art moves up a notch with Rare. Only the best barrel samples from the best parcels of base wine from the best vintages make the grade. Average age here is 25 years. The colour is darker again, a warm walnut. The wine is thicker, slower to move around the glass, stickier. Coffee grounds, soused raisins, rum-and-raisin chocolate, orange pee and toasted hazelnuts, beautifully alive. A rare taste to savour. 500ml. Screw cap | 17.5% alc. | $123 | JP

96 **Christopher's Rutherglen VP 2018** Deep purple hue. The 5 Portuguese varieties bring lifted aromatics of rose, violet, black cherry, raspberry – so pretty – which become entwined on the palate in rich layers of spice, licorice and chocolate with a brandy twist. Intense but not heavy. Quite the opposite. It's way, way too early to even contemplate opening. Give it 10 years at least. Screw cap | 18.5% alc. | $30 | JP

95 **Seriously Fine Pale Dry Apera NV** Jen Pfeiffer keeps the dry apera fires burning, an art on the wa in Australia. Seriously good apera, so complex, fresh, alive and super-dry. Almond kernel, tart green apple, salted citrus, orange peel. That salty tang is irresistible. Finishes long and clean, lip smackingly so. 500ml. Screw cap | 16% alc. | $29 | JP

Classic Rutherglen Topaque NV With an average age of 13 years, the progression of flavour intensity starts to become more noticeable, concentrated, yet, importantly, there is also a sense youthful freshness. Mahogany coloured with sweet golden syrup, salted caramel, orange peel a nougat aromas. The sweetness is cut nicely by spiced, toasted nuts. Clean spirit makes it shine. Excellent value. 500ml. Screw cap | 17.5% alc. | $29 | JP

Classic Rutherglen Muscat NV Combining freshness with age, Classic is lively in dried fig, orang peel, aromatic bergamot and malt. Bright and lively in neutral spirit, yet can retreat into some hic depths of a quiet intensity. 500ml. Screw cap | 17.5% alc. | $29 | JP

94 **Rutherglen Topaque NV** Trademark topaque characters here, from the scent of cold tea and butterscotch through to honey cake. A top introduction to the fortified classification system with this entry-level topaque that shows good balance of flavour and freshness. 500ml. Screw cap | 17.5% alc. | $20 | JP

Valhalla Wines ★★★★

163 All Saints Road, Wahgunyah, Vic 3687 **T** (02) 6033 1438 **www.valhallawines.com.au**
OPEN 7 days 10-4 **WINEMAKER** Anton Therkildsen **EST.** 2001 **DOZENS** 1400 **VYDS** 2.5ha

Anton Therkildsen uses traditional winemaking methods, making and cellaring the wines in their straw-bale winery. Sustainable viticulture practices are used, with minimal use of sprays and annual planting of cover crops between the rows. Rainwater harvesting, recycl packaging, a worm farm and the composting of grape skins and stalks complete the pictu

95 **Rutherglen Riesling 2017** Mouth-wateringly good! Boasts one of the prettiest floral bouquets go around – white flowers, orange blossom – and fine-edged citrus notes of grapefruit, lime leaf. Pl of verve and drive powering this youngster. Lime pith and lemon juice with developing spice ma it one to watch as it develops. Screw cap | 12.2% alc. | To 2028 | $25 | JP

Rutherglen Marsanne 2018 This white Rhône variety arrived in Rutherglen some time ago and seems to enjoy the warm climate, contributing a ripe, clean, well-focused citrussy edge to this w Jasmine, beeswax, lemon-curd bouquet. The grape's gentle acidity guides the palate with an aln Chablis-like nougat/apple/lemon drive. Bravo. Screw cap | 13.2% alc. | To 2027 | $28 | JP

IE

lorth West Victoria

ION

Aurray Darling

rentham Estate ★★★★

31 Sturt Highway, Trentham Cliffs, NSW 2738 **T** (03) 5024 8888 **www**.trenthamestate.com.au
EN 7 days 10-5 **WINEMAKER** Anthony Murphy, Shane Kerr, Kerry Morrison **EST.** 1988 **DOZENS** 60000
DS 38.66ha

markably consistent tasting notes across all wine styles from all vintages attest to the pertise of ex-Mildara winemaker Tony Murphy, a well-known and highly regarded producer. e estate vineyards are on the Murray Darling. The value for money is unfailingly excellent. 2018 Trentham Estate celebrated its 30th anniversary.

The Family Vermentino 2020 Nothing welcomes summer more than a beach view and a glass of vermentino. Crack this open to enjoy a mix of citrus, a sprinkling of herbs with a kiss of lemon salt. Crisp, dry and refreshing. Screw cap | 12.5% alc. | To 2022 | $18 | JF

The Family Frizzante Maestri 2020 An outrageous dark purple hue, slightly fizzy and full of gorgeous sweet fruit flavour. Disco in a glass! Lots of fresh black cherries and sweet cherry essence, balanced with refreshing acidity. Nothing too serious, just a cheery drink. Chill this right down to boogie on. Screw cap | 9.5% alc. | To 2021 | $18 | JF

The Family Moscato 2020 Full of spring white flowers and lemon blossom, juicy and grapey with spicy moscato flavours. Some dried mango and pears too. Sweet and vibrant. Nice fizz. Hits the spot. Screw cap | 6% alc. | To 2021 | $18 | JF

ION

Swan Hill

ndrew Peace Wines  

rray Valley Highway, Piangil, Vic 3597 **T** (03) 5030 5291 **www**.apwines.com **OPEN** Mon-Fri 8-5,
t 12-4 **WINEMAKER** Andrew Peace, David King **EST.** 1995 **DOZENS** 180000 **VYDS** 270ha

e Peace family has been a major Swan Hill grapegrower since 1980, moving into nemaking with the opening of a $3 million winery in '96. Their planting of sagrantino nong other varieties) is the largest of only a few such plantings in Australia.

Full Moon Victoria Shiraz Sagrantino 2019 Just 13% sagrantino, yet its amaro tang and richness come to the fore, so too the 30% new French and American oak barriques, aged 1 year. And yet, there's a suppleness across the full-bodied palate. Ripe fruit, baking spices galore and it all seems to work. Screw cap | 14.5% alc. | To 2028 | $20 | JF

IE

Port Phillip

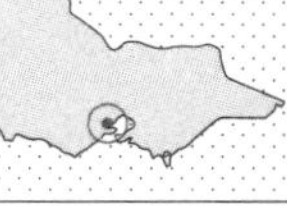

ION

Geelong

ellarine Estate  ★★★★

70 Portarlington Road, Bellarine, Vic 3222 **T** (03) 5259 3310 **www**.bellarineestate.com.au
EN 7 days 11-4 **WINEMAKER** Julian Kenny **EST.** 1995 **DOZENS** 1050 **VYDS** 10.5ha

is business runs parallel with the Bellarine Brewing Company, also situated in the nery, and the extended operating hours of Julian's Restaurant. The vineyard is planted to ardonnay, pinot noir, shiraz, merlot, viognier and sauvignon blanc.

First Blush Geelong Rosé 2019 Deep salmon hue. Woodsy notes, earth and raspberries indicate a serious bent to the rosé style. The palate confirms, with a depth of fruit flavour, layers of dark fruits, musky strawberry and orange rind with tannic edge and so clean and dry. Screw cap | 13.2% alc. | To 2025 | $28 | JP

Ceres Bridge Estate ★★★★

84 Merrawarp Road, Stonehaven, Vic 3221 **T** (03) 5271 1212 **www**.ceresbridge.com.au **OPEN** By appt **WINEMAKER** Scott Ireland, Sam Vogel **EST.** 1996 **DOZENS** 400 **VYDS** 7.4ha

Challon and Patricia Murdock began the long, slow and very frustrating process of establishing their vineyard in 1996. They planted 1.8ha of chardonnay in that year, but 50% c the vines died. They persevered by planting 1.1ha of pinot noir in 2000, and replanting in '01 In '05 they signified their intention to become serious by planting shiraz, nebbiolo, sauvignc blanc, viognier, tempranillo and pinot grigio.

95 **Paper Mill Chardonnay 2019** The winemaker has risen to the challenge of a hot vintage with a chardonnay that gives every impression of being immune to its effects. Brisk in filigreed acidity wi a palate delivering elegance and precision, it remains cool under pressure. Lemon drop, grapefrui pith, juicy white peach and apple blossom. In for the long haul. Screw cap | 13.5% alc. | To 2031 $30 | JP

Paper Mill Shiraz 2019 In the tradition of Paper Mill shiraz, with another lively adventure. Scented, pure black-cherry pastille, raspberry, pomegranate and ferrous, earthy notes. Supple and succule with attractive savouriness and loose-knit tannins, there are strong building blocks in place for a bright future. Screw cap | 13.5% alc. | To 2031 | $30 | JP

Clyde Park Vineyard ★★★★

2490 Midland Highway, Bannockburn, Vic 3331 **T** (03) 5281 7274 **www**.clydepark.com.au **OPEN** 7 day 11-5 **WINEMAKER** Terry Jongebloed **EST.** 1979 **DOZENS** 6000 **VYDS** 10.1ha

Owned by Terry Jongebloed and Sue Jongebloed-Dixon, Clyde Park Vineyard has significan mature plantings of pinot noir, chardonnay, sauvignon blanc, shiraz and pinot gris, and the quality of its wines is consistently exemplary.

96 **Single Block B3 Bannockburn Chardonnay 2020** There's a lot more going on here than your avera chardonnay, a deep complexity for one thing. Nougat, honeysuckle, grilled hazelnuts, lemon butte and musky spice, long and smooth across the palate, launch the drinker into another orbit. Hard tc believe it's just starting its journey. What a road ahead awaits. Screw cap | 12.5% alc. | To 2035 $75 | JP

Dinny Goonan

880 Winchelsea-Deans Marsh Road, Bambra, Vic 3241 **T** 0438 408 420 **www**.dinnygoonan.com.au **OPEN** 7 days Jan, w'ends & public hols Nov-Jun **WINEMAKER** Dinny Goonan, Angus Goonan **EST.** 1990 **DOZENS** 1500 **VYDS** 5.5ha

The genesis of Dinny Goonan dates back to 1988, when Dinny bought a 20ha property near Bambra, in the hinterland of the Otway Coast. Dinny had recently completed a viticulture diploma at CSU and initially a wide range of varieties was planted in what is now known as th Nursery Block, to establish those best suited to the area. As these came into production Din headed back to CSU, where he completed a wine science degree.

95 **Single Vineyard Riesling 2020** A strong suit with this producer, riesling takes on a wide-ranging complexity in 2020 against a positively zesty exuberance of flavour. A challenging vintage is put t rest. This wine rocks. Fragrant lime citrus, lemon drop, touch of spice, nashi pear running free acr a fleshy palate. Tingly acidity. Screw cap | 12.5% alc. | To 2031 | $30 | JP

Lethbridge Wines

74 Burrows Road, Lethbridge, Vic 3222 **T** (03) 5281 7279 **www**.lethbridgewines.com **OPEN** Mon-Fri 11-3, w'ends 11-5 **WINEMAKER** Ray Nadeson, Maree Collis **EST.** 1996 **DOZENS** 10000 **VYDS** 7ha

In founder Ray Lethbridge's words,'Our belief is that the best wines express the unique charact of special places'. As well as understanding the importance of terroir, the partners have buil a unique strawbale winery, designed to recreate the controlled environment of cellars and caves in Europe. Winemaking is no less ecological: hand-picking, indigenous-yeast fermentati small open fermenters, pigeage (foot-stomping) and minimal handling of the wines throughout the maturation process are all part and parcel of the highly successful Lethbridge approach

95 **Dr Nadeson Riesling 2020** After time away from sourcing riesling from Henty, Ray Nadeson is bac with a new source from the region and renewed zip in his winemaking step. You can understand w The energy on display is thrilling; rapier-like acidity matched with a quiet depth of fruit intensity. Lemon zest, lime, apple, nougat saline and don't forget the spice. All humming along in off-dry unison. And still so, so young. Screw cap | 9.7% alc. | To 2026 | $35 | JP

akdene

Grubb Road, Wallington, Vic 3221 **T** (03) 5256 3886 **www**.oakdene.com.au **OPEN** 7 days 10-4
EMAKER Robin Brockett, Marcus Holt **EST.** 2001 **DOZENS** 8000 **VYDS** 32ha

rnard and Elizabeth Hooley purchased Oakdene in 2001. Bernard focused on planting the ieyard while Elizabeth worked to restore the 1920s homestead. Much of the wine is sold ough the award-winning Oakdene Restaurant and cellar door. The quality is exemplary, as he consistency of that quality; Robin Brockett's skills are on full display.

Liz's Single Vineyard Bellarine Peninsula Chardonnay 2019 This wine has a reputation for generosity of flavour and the 2019 vintage doesn't disappoint. Arrives with a bang! Take a long inhale of all that stone fruit, dried peach, orange peel, honeysuckle and pear. Keep that thought, because there's more to behold on the palate and this time it comes with delicious texture and length. Coastal saline sea-spray notes hover, providing added zing. Screw cap | 13.6% alc. | To 2028 | $35 | JP

Bellarine Peninsula Chardonnay 2019 Fermented and matured for 10 months in new and used French barriques. Gleaming straw-green hue. The quality of the fruit is obvious; the wine already in the saddle; the gait smooth and supple; white stone fruit, citrussy acidity and creamy cashew in harmony. Screw cap | 13.4% alc. | To 2029 | $24 | JH

anta & D'Sas

Pincott Street, Newtown, Vic 3220 **T** 0417 384 272 **www**.santandsas.com.au
IEMAKER Andrew Santarossa, Matthew Di Sciascio **EST.** 2014 **DOZENS** 9000

nta & D'Sas is a collaboration between the Santarossa and Di Sciascio families. Andrew ntarossa and Matthew Di Sciascio met while studying for a bachelor of applied science ine science). Wines are released under the Valentino label (fiano, sangiovese and shiraz), dicated to Matthew's father; the remaining wines simply identify the region and variety.

King Valley Prosecco NV A confident, assured prosecco, clean and bright, persistent in mousse and nicely encapsulating the grape's lively green apple, pear, musky florals and aromatics. Super-brisk through to the finish. Crown seal | 11% alc. | To 2021 | $24 | JP

cotchmans Hill

) Scotchmans Road, Drysdale, Vic 3222 **T** (03) 5251 3176 **www**.scotchmans.com.au **OPEN** 7 days .30-4.30 **WINEMAKER** Robin Brockett, Marcus Holt **EST.** 1982 **DOZENS** 50000 **VYDS** 40ha

tablished in 1982, Scotchmans Hill has been a consistent producer of well-made wines ider the stewardship of long-term winemaker Robin Brockett and assistant Marcus Holt. e wines are released under the Scotchmans Hill, Cornelius, Jack & Jill and Swan Bay labels. change of ownership in 2014 has resulted in significant vineyard investment.

Bellarine Peninsula Shiraz 2018 15% whole bunches, wild fermentation, 10 months in French oak. A highly expressive, fragrant and complex bouquet carries onto the savoury/spicy palate with wild blackberry, licorice and black peppercorn flavours. The tannins are very good, adding to texture and length. Screw cap | 14.5% alc. | To 2040 | $42 | JH

hadowfax

Road, Werribee, Vic 3030 **T** (03) 9731 4420 **www**.shadowfax.com.au **OPEN** 7 days 11-5
NEMAKER Alister Timms **EST.** 2000 **DOZENS** 10000 **VYDS** 28ha

nce an offspring of Werribee Park and its grand mansion, Shadowfax is now very much its vn master. It has 10ha of mature vineyards at Werribee; plus 5ha of close-planted pinot noir, ia of chardonnay and 2ha of pinot gris at the Little Hampton Vineyard in Macedon; and 3ha pinot noir, 2ha of chardonnay and 1ha of gewürztraminer elsewhere in Macedon.

Little Hampton Pinot Noir 2019 Such a solid performer. It's wonderfully fragrant; all florals, exotic spices, cherries and cola. Unencumbered by new oak flavour (aged in used French hogsheads and puncheons), it's all about the purity of fruit and drive across a fuller-bodied palate. It's laced with velvety tannins and the finish is long as it is fresh. Screw cap | 13% alc. | To 2033 | $65 | JF

K Road Shiraz 2019 The dark crimson hue is delightful, and it gets better from there as the flavours unfurl. Purple plums, currants dipped in cocoa and flecked with herbs and tapenade. Very complex. Full bodied and, while aged in 50% new French puncheons, the oak isn't demanding – it adds to the savouriness and grainy tannins. Screw cap | 14% alc. | To 2035 | $45 | JF

Spence

760 Burnside Road, Murgheboluc, Vic 3221 **T** (03) 5265 1181 **www**.spencewines.com.au **OPEN** 1st Su each month **WINEMAKER** Peter Spence, Scott Ireland **EST.** 1997 **DOZENS** 1300 **VYDS** 3.2ha

Peter and Anne Spence were sufficiently inspired by an extended European holiday – which included living on a family vineyard in Provence – to purchase a small property and establis vineyard and winery. They have planted 3.2ha on a north-facing slope in a valley 7km south Bannockburn, the lion's share to 3 clones of shiraz. The vineyard attained full organic status 2008, since then using only biodynamic practices.

95 **Geelong Shiraz 2019** A strong follow-up to the 2018 shiraz, walking a similar path of cool-climate spiciness and medium-bodied elegance. Enticing right off the bat, with an arresting fragrance of black cherry, blueberry, stewed plum, dried herbs and black pepper. Flavours and texture glide on the palate, swept along with grainy, ripe tannins. A treat is in store for the drinker here. Screw cap | 13.8% alc. | To 2034 | $30 | JP

REGION

Macedon Ranges

Bindi Wines

★★★★

343 Melton Road, Gisborne, Vic 3437 (postal) **T** (03) 5428 2564 **www**.bindiwines.com.au
WINEMAKER Michael Dhillon, Stuart Anderson (Consultant) **EST.** 1988 **DOZENS** 2000 **VYDS** 6ha

One of the icons of Macedon. The Chardonnay is top-shelf, the Pinot Noir as remarkable (albeit in a very different idiom) as Bass Phillip, Giaconda or any of the other tiny-production icon wines. The addition of Heathcote-sourced shiraz under the Pyrette label confirms Bind as one of the greatest small producers in Australia. Winemaker Michael Dhillon was named Winemaker of the Year in the *Wine Companion 2022*.

97 **Quartz Chardonnay 2019** Wow. This made my heart skip a beat. It races along but not too fast, as does reveal a complex combo of citrus, lemon balm, subtle lees influence and a spark of flint. The oak is beautifully integrated, offering support, as do the grapefruit pith-like phenolics. It's long, pu and simply sensational. Screw cap | 13% alc. | To 2033 | $100 | JF | ♥

Dixon Pinot Noir 2019 A blend of fruit off the original vineyard planted in 1988 and the Kaye vineya planted in 2001. It's morphed into a complete and compelling wine. Fragrant with florals and warr earth. There's a depth of flavour, with dark cherries, amaro and bitter Italian herbs that slip across the fuller-bodied palate. Two key elements here; freshness within and beautiful, plush tannins. Wh a wine. Screw cap | 13.5% alc. | To 2034 | $65 | JF

Original Vineyard Pinot Noir 2019 Its riff is savoury, full of wood smoke, earthy and autumnal tune In the mix, black cherries infused with menthol and Middle Eastern spices. The palate is an exercis in texture. It is caressed by ribbons of velvety tannins, bright acidity and a finish that is as long as pure. A seamless wine. Diam | 13% alc. | To 2033 | $85 | JF

Block 5 Pinot Noir 2019 Pinot Noir of the Year 2022. This is the finest 2019 pinot noir across all regions that I have tasted. I bow to its elegance, its structure and, indeed, its beauty. It's a perfect amalgam of fragrance, flavour and shape, with the latter bolstered by plush tannins covered in ra silk. There's a vitality, an energy that lifts this – it is a wine unencumbered by obvious winemaking. The site speaks. Time to listen. Diam | 13% alc. | To 2035 | $125 | JF | ♥

96 **Kostas Rind Chardonnay 2019** The tension in this is fabulous. Taut as a snare drum, yet intense in flavour. It starts off on a citrus theme, with lemons and a touch of tangerine, tempered by a layer of nutty, leesy richness – just a smidge – this is a linear offering. It finishes long and persuasive. A delicious drink. Screw cap | 13% alc. | To 2030 | $65 | JF

Dhillon Col Mountain Heathcote Shiraz 2014 The wine's colour and freshness belie its age. It has morphed into a complete wine. Fragrant and earthy, with a dusting of exotic spices – woodsy one too, with dark fruit certainly in the picture. Plush, ripe tannins glide effortless across the fuller-bodied palate. Diam | 14% alc. | To 2028 | $75 | JF

Cobaw Ridge

31 Perc Boyers Lane, Pastoria, Vic 3444 **T** (03) 5423 5227 **www**.cobawridge.com.au
OPEN W'ends 12-5 **WINEMAKER** Nelly Cooper, Alan Cooper **EST.** 1985 **DOZENS** 1000 **VYDS** 5ha

Cobaw Ridge is planted to chardonnay and syrah; lagrein and close-planted, multi-clonal pinot noir are more recent arrivals to thrive. Cobaw Ridge is fully certified biodynamic, and winery operations are carried out according to the biodynamic calendar.

Chardonnay 2018 Wow. Exquisite wine. There's a lot of flavour here, yet it runs on the pure energy of its fine acidity. It initially works off a citrus theme, juicy, tangy and zesty. There's a certain amount of sulphide flint adding another layering of complexity, but it's not overt. Neither is the oak, which has absorbed this wine as its own. Leesy, nutty characters add to the palate, which is moreish, savoury and very complete. Diam | 13.5% alc. | To 2030 | $58 | JF

urly Flat 

3 Collivers Road, Lancefield, Vic 3435 **T** (03) 5429 1956 **www**.curlyflat.com **OPEN** Fri-Mon 12-5
NEMAKER Matt Harrop, Ben Kimmorley **EST.** 1991 **DOZENS** 6000 **VYDS** 13ha

unded by Phillip Moraghan and Jenifer Kolkka in 1991, Jenifer has been the sole owner of urly Flat since 2017. The focus has always been on the vineyard, a dedicated team ensuring uality is never compromised. Matt Harrop is now overseeing production.

Central Macedon Ranges Pinot Noir 2019 Central focuses on the oldest plantings from 1992 of MV6 made via 40% whole bunches, wild-yeast fermented and aged in French oak, 27% new, for 16 months. Deep, dark and serious. It's stern, with an abundance of dark cherries, pips, forest floor and woodsy spices. Full-bodied, with raw-silk tannins, yet a vitality within as it sashays to a convincing finish. Screw cap | 13% alc. | To 2034 | $53 | JF

Western Macedon Ranges Pinot Noir 2019 Fruit comes off vineyards on the coolest, western blocks. Clones 115 and 144, 17% whole bunches in the wild ferment and aged in used French oak for 16 months. There's a prettiness, an alluring fragrance of rose petals that gives way to more obvious cherry nuances. It's just shy of full bodied, with textural, fine-grained tannins, crunchy acidity and a moreish element. Compelling wine. Screw cap | 14% alc. | To 2033 | $53 | JF

ranite Hills 

31 Burke and Wills Track, Baynton, Vic 3444 **T** (03) 5423 7273 **www**.granitehills.com.au
EN 7 days 11-5 **WINEMAKER** Llew Knight, Rowen Anstis **EST.** 1970 **DOZENS** 5000 **VYDS** 11.5ha

anite Hills is one of the enduring classics, having pioneered the successful growing of esling and shiraz in an uncompromisingly cool climate. The Rieslings age superbly, and the iraz was the forerunner of the cool-climate school in Australia.

Knight Macedon Ranges Riesling 2020 This charms with its citrus accents from grapefruit, lemon and tangerine. It has a depth across the palate, juicy, natural acidity and a purity throughout. A lovely wine now and for quite some time to come. Screw cap | 12.5% alc. | To 2032 | $27 | JF

Knight Macedon Ranges Grüner Veltliner 2020 This is one very smart grüner. White pepper, lemon rind, juicy grapefruit and poached pears with powdered ginger. It has plenty of energy and fine natural acidity zipping across the palate. Talk about a thirst-quencher. Screw cap | 13% alc. | To 2024 | $27 | JF

ig Zag Rd

1 Zig Zag Road, Drummond, Vic 3446 **T** (03) 5423 9390 **www**.zigzagwines.com.au
EN Thurs-Mon 10-5 **WINEMAKER** Henry Churchill, Harriet Churchill, Gilles Lapalus **EST.** 1972
ZENS 1500 **VYDS** 4.5ha

nry and Harriet Churchill, Brits with a background in sustainable agriculture, took over the g Zag vineyard from Eric and Anne Bellchambers in 2018. With a new baby in tow, Henry and rriet were then 'new to winemaking, viticulture and parenting'. The focus is on regenerative rming, and they have launched a 2nd label, 'Kind Folk', for experimental wines, including an nber wine, a barrel-fermented rosé and a pet nat. (TS)

Macedon Ranges Riesling 2019 New owners. New labels. New energy. Opaque straw hue with wafts of lemon blossom and just-cut herbs of an Alpine persuasion. Flavours of lemon drops, white pepper and radish. The palate has texture and depth, citrus comes into play, with lemon and mandarin. It tastes slightly off-dry, although there's no shortage of acidity, so it feels racy and refreshing to the last drop. Screw cap | 12% alc. | To 2028 | $25 | JF

Macedon Ranges Shiraz 2019 This is certainly showing off its cool-climate credentials with a heady fragrance, florals, a flash of pepper, aniseed and mint. Some tart and tangy Angelina plums and cherries in the mix. Medium bodied, nicely savoury, with a fine emery board of tannins and crunchy, raspberry acidity. A fresh style, yet some substance too. Screw cap | 13% alc. | To 2026 | $27 | JF

Mornington Peninsula

Crittenden Estate 

25 Harrisons Road, Dromana, Vic 3936 **T** (03) 5981 8322 **www**.crittendenwines.com.au **OPEN** 7 days 10.30-4.30 **WINEMAKER** Rollo Crittenden, Matt Campbell **EST.** 1984 **DOZENS** 10000 **VYDS** 4.8ha

Garry Crittenden was a pioneer on the Mornington Peninsula, establishing the family vineyar over 30 years ago and introducing a number of avant-garde pruning and canopy manageme techniques. Much has changed – and continues to change – in cool-climate vineyard management. Crittenden has abandoned the use of synthetic fertilisers in the vineyard, focusing on biological soil health using natural tools such as compost and cover crops.

95 **Peninsula Pinot Gris 2019** The real deal. Pinot gris as it should be: flavoursome, luscious, textural and brimming with poached pears, grated nashi and loaded with powdered and fresh ginger. Some clotted cream and lemon curd on the palate. Nothing cloying. Quite delicious. Screw cap | 13% alc. | To 2024 | $34 | JF

Dexter Wines

210 Foxeys Road, Tuerong, Vic 3915 (postal) **T** (03) 5989 7007 **www**.dexterwines.com.au **WINEMAKER** Tod Dexter **EST.** 2006 **DOZENS** 1800 **VYDS** 7.1ha

Tod Dexter travelled to the US with the intention of enjoying some skiing; having done that, he became an apprentice winemaker at Cakebread Cellars, a well-known Napa Valley establishment. After 7 years he returned to Australia and the Mornington Peninsula, and began the establishment of his vineyard in 1987; spurred on by turning 50 in 2006 (and at the urging of friends), he and wife Debbie established the Dexter label. The quality of his wines has been impeccable, the Pinot Noir especially so.

97 **Mornington Peninsula Chardonnay 2019** The bright straw-green hue heralds a beautifully handled wine. The fragrant bouquet of fused fruit and oak is increased on the harmonious, perfectly balanced palate. There's ultimate detail to the wine, with white peach all the way through to the finish and aftertaste. Screw cap | 13.5% alc. | To 2030 | $40 | JH

Foxeys Hangout 

795 White Hill Road, Red Hill, Vic 3937 **T** (03) 5989 2022 **www**.foxeys-hangout.com.au **OPEN** W'end & public hols 11-5 **WINEMAKER** Tony Lee, Michael Lee **EST.** 1997 **DOZENS** 14000 **VYDS** 3.4ha

After 20 successful years in hospitality operating several cafes and restaurants (including one of Melbourne's first gastropubs in the early 1990s), brothers Michael and Tony Lee planted their first vineyard in '97 at Merricks North. The venture takes its name from the tale of 2 fox hunters in the '30s hanging the results of their day's shooting in opposite branches of an ancient eucalypt, using the tree as their scorecard.

96 **Red Lilac Single Vineyard Mornington Peninsula Chardonnay 2019** A laser beam of acidity leads this tight, persuasive wine. Everything is just so: its citrus tones, the spice, the layer of creamy lees and nuttiness with some nougatine flavouring too. A classy chardonnay. Screw cap | 13.5% alc. | To 2030 | $50 | JF

Mornington Peninsula Shiraz 2019 This has an intensity of flavour and lots of concentration, followed by ribbons of finely textured tannin. And yet, this is a neatly composed wine. It is medium bodied and laced with wonderful spice, especially pepper and dried juniper berries. It's rather elegant. There's a brightness to the fruit, savoury in outlay and compelling all the way through. Screw cap | 13.5% alc. | To 2030 | $45 | JF

95 **The Red Fox Mornington Peninsula Pinot Noir 2019** Modest colour; cooking spices frame the bouquet, contributing even more of the palate's message. In Foxeys' usual style, fine tannins are also centre stage, together with exotic dark berry fruits. Second place in Foxeys' hierarchy, but nonetheless impressive. Screw cap | 13.5% alc. | To 2030 | $29 | JH

Garagiste

72 Blaxland Ave, Frankston South, Vic 3199 **T** 0439 370 530 **www**.garagiste.com.au **WINEMAKER** Barnaby Flanders **EST.** 2006 **DOZENS** 2200 **VYDS** 6ha

rnaby Flanders was a co-founder of Allies Wines in 2003, with some of the wines made der the Garagiste label. Allies has now gone its own way and Barnaby has a controlling erest in the Garagiste brand. The focus is on the Mornington Peninsula. The grapes are nd-sorted in the vineyard and again in the winery.

Terre Maritime Mornington Peninsula Chardonnay 2019 Barnaby Flanders manages to weave magic into his wines. Although a less esoteric explanation is his attention to detail in the vineyard right through to the winemaking. Precise and reasoned. All that combines to a truth: Garagiste crafts some of the finest, most exhilarating wines, from the Peninsula and beyond. Terre Maritime is a case in point. Complex, silky, flinty, flavoursome, long ... and the list goes on. Screw cap | 13% alc. | To 2032 | $75 | JF

Merricks Mornington Peninsula Chardonnay 2019 A cracking wine that's so flavoursome, yet manages to stay on a tight leash thanks to its acidity. Flinty, smoky and spicy, with lots of grapefruit. The palate is injected with lemon curd and cedary/lemon-balm François Frère fragrance (20% new puncheons). It has length and definition. Complex and thoughtful. Screw cap | 13% alc. | To 2029 | $45 | JF

Merricks Cuve Béton Mornington Peninsula Pinot Noir 2019 Barnaby Flanders' same exacting standard in the vineyard and winemaking is applied to this compelling wine. The key difference between this and his other pinots is ageing in concrete on lees for 10 months. The palate is extraordinary; the tannins have a completely different shape, round and giving. It's plush and rich in bright fruit, and lightly spiced. An epic, fabulous drink. Screw cap | 13.5% alc. | To 2032 | $45 | JF

Terre de Feu Mornington Peninsula Pinot Noir 2019 Garagiste's flagship pinot comes out strong: 22 days on 100% whole bunches, fermented wild, as always, and aged in French oak hogsheads, 25% new, for 10 months. It's perfumed and richly flavoured, yet ultimately it's about structure and definition. Somewhat firm and closed, but has all the hallmarks for longevity. Screw cap | 13.5% alc. | To 2035 | $75 | JF

Le Stagiaire Mornington Peninsula Chardonnay 2020 Fruit from 3 disparate vineyards from Merricks, Balnarring and Tuerong. It's in the drink-me-now zone and neatly balanced. Full of bright citrus flavours, white stone fruit on the verge of ripeness, a spark of flint, smoky, a smidge of leesy texture, and saline, thirst-quenching acidity to close. Screw cap | 13% alc. | To 2027 | $30 | JF

Mornington Peninsula Aligote 2019 Aligoté is the third (but these days rare) variety of Burgundy. It's like a lemon daquiri without rum's alcohol punch. Savoury, with a dash of lemon/lime flavour, but texture and acidity are the real drivers. Tangy, smoky and super dry on the finish. This is compelling. Screw cap | 13% alc. | To 2026 | $35 | JF

erri Greens

Paringa Road, Red Hill South, Vic 3937 **T** 0438 219 507 **www**.kerrigreens.com **OPEN** Sat 11-5, n 12-4 **WINEMAKER** Tom McCarthy, Lucas Blanck **EST.** 2015 **DOZENS** 1000

erri Greens (named after a local surf break) is a story of serendipity. It's what happens when young vignerons become colleagues, then friends and now partners in a boutique label at offers excellence and energising wines. Organics, sustainability and treading gently are nportant considerations. What's really exciting is that this young team is respectful of a wine gion that nurtures them, yet not afraid to shake things up. Bravo. (JF)

Ohne Mornington Peninsula Gewürztraminer 2020 Oh my, Ohne is so good. It's more lemon than lychee, but heady aromas of the variety play true. Cinnamon, kaffir lime leaves, rosewater and Turkish delight in the mix, but what sets this apart from many other renditions is that it's not heavy or oily. There is a smidge of texture across the palate, but the fine acidity elevates and tightens, then puts it into cruise control. Screw cap | 12% alc. | To 2026 | $28 | JF

Murra Mornington Peninsula Pinot Noir 2019 Fruit off the steep Duke vineyard in Red Hill, with vines edging 30+ years and eschewing herbicides/synthetic fertilisers. This is a charmer. Rose petals, sweet red cherries and baking spices flow through onto a barely-medium-bodied palate. It's energetic. There's a fineness within, with filigreed tannins and refreshing acidity to close. Screw cap | 13.2% alc. | To 2028 | $32 | JF

Iontalto

Shoreham Road, Red Hill South, Vic 3937 **T** (03) 5989 8412 **www**.montalto.com.au **PEN** 7 days 11-5 **WINEMAKER** Simon Black **EST.** 1998 **DOZENS** 12000 **VYDS** 47ha

ohn Mitchell and family established Montalto in 1998, but the core of the vineyard goes ack to '86. It is planted to pinot noir, chardonnay, pinot gris, riesling, shiraz, tempranillo and auvignon blanc. Intensive vineyard work opens up the canopy, with yields of 3.7–6.1t/ha. 'ines are released in 3 ranges: the flagship Single Vineyard, Montalto estate wines and ennon Hill.

96 **Single Vineyard The Eleven Mornington Peninsula Chardonnay 2019** A refined, elegant style and lip-smackingly delicious. It's the acidity, it's the drive, it's the length. It works off a citrus theme wi grapefruit, lemon and mandarin, with a dab of smoky, flinty reduction and enough spicy oak and creamy lees to add some extra seasoning. Linear and pure. Excellent wine. Screw cap | 13% alc. To 2030 | $60 | JF

95 **Pennon Hill Mornington Peninsula Shiraz 2019** I've said it elsewhere that 2019 is a terrific shiraz vintage on the peninsula. Here's another wonderful example. It's really savoury, with some meaty reduction, but there is certainly a core of good fruit, spiced up with herbs and tapenade. Textural tannins, ripe yet raspy, hold sway on the fuller-bodied palate. Looks great now and even better with food. Screw cap | 13.6% alc. | To 2030 | $34 | JF

Moorooduc Estate

501 Derril Road, Moorooduc, Vic 3936 **T** (03) 5971 8506 **www**.mooroodücestate.com.au **OPEN** 7 days 11-5 **WINEMAKER** Dr Richard McIntyre, Jeremy Magyar **EST.** 1983 **DOZENS** 6000 **VYDS** 14ha

Richard McIntyre has taken Moorooduc Estate to new heights, having completely mastered the difficult art of gaining maximum results from wild-yeast fermentation. Starting with the 2010 vintage, there was a complete revamp of grape sources and hence changes to the tiered structure of the releases: the entry-point wines under the Devil Bend Creek label; the mid-priced Chardonnay and Pinot Noir are now sourced from multiple sites. The single-vineyard Robinson Pinot Noir and Chardonnay, Garden Vineyard Pinot Noir and McIntyre Shiraz are priced a little below the ultimate 'Ducs' (The Moorooduc McIntyre Chardonnay and Pinot Noir).

96 **Robinson Vineyard Chardonnay 2019** There's always a lot of class to this chardonnay. It has flavou aplenty, yet everything is reined in by fine and tight acidity. It's also flinty, spicy and tangy. The oak is a mere part of the overall profile, not at all dominating. Long, pure and utterly refreshing. Screw cap | 13% alc. | To 2029 | $60 | JF

Paringa Estate

44 Paringa Road, Red Hill South, Vic 3937 **T** (03) 5989 2669 **www**.paringaestate.com.au **OPEN** 7 days 11-5 **WINEMAKER** Lindsay McCall, Jamie McCall **EST.** 1985 **DOZENS** 15000 **VYDS** 30.5ha

Schoolteacher-turned-winemaker Lindsay McCall became known for an absolutely exceptional gift for winemaking across a range of styles but with immensely complex pinot noir and shiraz leading the way. The wines have an unmatched level of success in the wine shows and competitions that Paringa Estate is able to enter; the limitation being the relativel small production of the top wines in the portfolio.

96 **Estate Shiraz 2019** Outrageous colour – wonderful deep purple, with a rich red rim. This is magnificent. Dark fruits infused with black pepper, woodsy spices and juniper set the flavour profi The full-bodied palate is complex and detailed. Oak adds another layer of depth, yet there's a controlled vibrancy and freshness throughout. Screw cap | 14% alc. | To 2033 | $50 | JF

95 **Peninsula Shiraz 2019** A vibrant garnet/purple hue; a core of ripe plums, with a flash of cloves, cinnamon, all warm spices and florals. The palate is savoury, with an appealing succulence bolstered by supple tannins and terrific freshness. It seems vintage '19 suits shiraz from this regior Screw cap | 13.5% alc. | To 2029 | $29 | JF

Phaedrus Estate

220 Mornington-Tyabb Road, Moorooduc, Vic 3933 **T** (03) 5978 8134 **www**.phaedrus.com.au **OPEN** W'ends & public hols 11-5 **WINEMAKER** Ewan Campbell, Maitena Zantvoort **EST.** 1997 **DOZENS** 3000 **VYDS** 2.5ha

Since Maitena Zantvoort and Ewan Campbell established Phaedrus Estate, they have gained a reputation for producing premium cool-climate wines. Their winemaking philosophy bring art and science together to produce wines showing regional and varietal character with minimal winemaking interference.

94 **Mornington Peninsula Shiraz 2019** Sultry, smoky reduction is interspersed with ripe fruit here and it works brilliantly. Super-fragrant, with really cool-climate flavours, even in this warmer vintage: violets, pepper, iodine and bay leaves. It's compelling, with shapely tannins and some grunt, too, y it just falls a tad short – a minor quibble though, as it's a ripper. Screw cap | 13.5% alc. | To 2033 $28 | JF

uealy Winemakers 

Bittern-Dromana Road, Balnarring, Vic 3926 **T** (03) 5983 2483 **WWW**.quealy.com.au **OPEN** 7 days
5 **WINEMAKER** Kathleen Quealy, Tom McCarthy **EST.** 1982 **DOZENS** 8000 **VYDS** 8ha

thleen Quealy and Kevin McCarthy were among the early waves of winemakers on e Mornington Peninsula. They challenged the status quo – most publicly by introducing ornington Peninsula pinot gris/grigio (with great success). Behind this was improvement and versification in site selection, plus viticulture and winemaking techniques that allowed their isiness to grow significantly. Son Tom stepped up as head winemaker in 2019. Lucas Blanck anages the certified organic estate vineyards; the leased vineyards are moving towards 0% organic management.

Pinot Grigio 2020 It has the spice, the crunchy pear, the saline, lemony tang and crisp natural acidity to seal it with a big grigio stamp of approval. So refreshing and delicious. Screw cap | 12.9% alc. | To 2024 | $35 | JF

Tussie Mussie Vineyard Late Harvest Pinot Gris 2019 Starting off with a gorgeous burnished copper/orange hue, it gets better. Burnt toffee, lemon brittle and cardamom-infused crème brûlée plus apricot jam. And yet, the acidity lifts the rich flavours, tempers the sweetness and lets the silky luscious texture continue. Superb. Screw cap | 11.5% alc. | To 2026 | $35 | JF

Lina Lool Amber 2019 This is an elixir. Golden Delicious apples, quince, spice, pink grapefruit with lemon/lime acidity. A complex wine with beautifully handled phenolics. It gave me goose bumps. Screw cap | 13.2% alc. | To 2026 | $35 | JF

corpo Wines  

Old Bittern-Dromana Road, Merricks North, Vic 3926 **T** (03) 5989 7697 **WWW**.scorpowines.com.au
EN 1st w'end each month or by appt **WINEMAKER** Paul Scorpo **EST.** 1997 **DOZENS** 6000 **VYDS** 17.3ha

ul Scorpo has a background as a horticulturist/landscape architect, working on major ojects ranging from private gardens to golf courses in Australia, Europe and Asia. His family s a love of food, wine and gardens, all of which led to them buying a derelict apple and erry orchard on rolling hills between Port Phillip and Western Port bays.

Eocene Single Vineyard Chardonnay 2019 Tight as a drum, shot with racy acidity. And no shortage of very flinty sulphides, which would be too much funky reduction, if not for the weight and richness of fruit to balance. Complex, assured, rich, textural, savoury and compelling. Screw cap | 14% alc. | To 2029 | $75 | JF

abby Lake Vineyard  

-112 Tuerong Road, Tuerong, Vic 3937 **T** (03) 5974 3729 **WWW**.yabbylake.com **OPEN** 7 days 10-5
NEMAKER Tom Carson, Chris Forge, Luke Lomax **EST.** 1998 **DOZENS** 3350 **VYDS** 50ha

is high-profile wine business was established in 1998 by Robert and Mem Kirby (of Village oadshow), who had been landowners in the Mornington Peninsula for decades. The arrival of e hugely talented Tom Carson as group winemaker in 2008 added lustre to the winery and s wines, making the first Jimmy Watson Trophy–winning pinot noir in 2014 and continuing to itz the Australian wine show circuit with single-block pinot noirs.

Single Vineyard Mornington Peninsula Syrah 2019 Aside from the striking deep garnet hue that immediately beckons, this starts out a bit shy. Let it be. Let it breathe. It will then unfurl to reveal a savoury, refined wine. Dark fruit, a dusting of pepper and licorice, mocha, warm earth and Aussie bush aromas. It works off a medium-bodied palate with the most exquisite tannins. Top of the class. Screw cap | 14% alc. | To 2032 | $36 | JF

Red Claw Mornington Peninsula Pinot Noir 2019 Hand picked and sorted, open-fermented with 25% whole bunches, matured in used French puncheons. Bright crimson-purple; the fragrant bouquet weaves a tapestry of red berry blossom, with a darker note picked up on the complex palate and its long finish. Screw cap | 14% alc. | To 2029 | $30 | JH

Yal Yal Estate ★★★

15 Wynnstay Road, Prahran, Vic 3181 (postal) **T** 0416 112 703 **www**.yalyal.com.au
WINEMAKER Rollo Crittenden **EST.** 1997 **DOZENS** 2500 **VYDS** 7ha

In 2008 Liz and Simon Gillies acquired a vineyard in Merricks, planted in 1997 to 1.6ha of chardonnay and a little over 1ha of pinot noir. It has since been expanded to 7ha, half devoted to chardonnay, half to pinot noir.

91 **Yal Yal Rd Mornington Peninsula Rosé 2019** Entices from the moment this is poured, starting with its pastel pink/copper hue. Lightly aromatic. The palate offering both texture (thanks to barrel fermentation and ageing in used French oak) and pleasure, as it complements the spiced red fruits and ginger cream flavours. Screw cap | 13.5% alc. | To 2022 | $23 | JF

REGION

Sunbury

The Hairy Arm 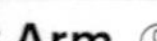

18 Plant Street, Northcote, Vic 3070 **T** 0409 110 462 **www**.hairyarm.com **OPEN** By appt
WINEMAKER Steven Worley **EST.** 2004 **DOZENS** 1000 **VYDS** 3ha

Steven Worley graduated as an exploration geologist, then added a master of geology degree, followed by a postgraduate diploma in oenology and viticulture. The Hairy Arm started as a university project in '04, and has grown from a labour of love to a commercial undertaking. Steven has an informal lease of 2ha of shiraz at Galli's Sunbury vineyard, which he manages, and procures 1ha of nebbiolo from the Galli vineyard in Heathcote.

95 **Merrifolk Cote Nord Sunbury Syrah 2019** Merrifolk is a new label aimed at an earlier-drinking style, although this is an impressive wine in anyone's book. Excellent dark purple; awash with intensely flavoured black plums, laced with licorice root, coffee cream and meaty nuances. Full bodied, with luscious and expansive tannins, the palate glossy. It's a richer, riper style, more shiraz than syrah. Screw cap | 14.5% alc. | To 2029 | $26 | JF

94 **Merrifolk Valhalla Shiraz Nebbiolo 2019** 65% Sunbury shiraz, 35% Heathcote nebbiolo. A good combo that's knitted well. Dark fruit, licorice and bitumen, with intense woodsy spices, especially cardamom and clove. Full bodied and plush. The tannins have some grip, yet roll through quite effortlessly. A bargain at this price. Screw cap | 14% alc. | To 2029 | $26 | JF

REGION

Yarra Valley

B Minor

100 Long Gully Road, Healesville, Vic 3777 **T** 0433 591 617 **www**.bminor.com.au **WINEMAKER** Various
EST. 2019 **DOZENS** 5000

B Minor was originally a small artisan wine brand created in 2010 focusing on producing fresh creative wines specifically targeting on-premise and specialty retail venues in the US and Australia. Its original philosophy was to create an international brand. In 2020, QiQi Fu bought out a partner in B Minor and runs the business, enlisting Best's Wines as a contract winemaker.

95 **Grampians Shiraz 2019** Reveals a vibrant energy which is more than enough to revitalise tired tastebuds. Deep, dense purple. Fresh picked blueberries, black plums, spice, cedar and that irresistible touch of local bush mint/bayleaf. Palate is velvety, ripe, and plush. A mighty smart and lively young shiraz with a big future. Diam | 14.5% alc. | To 2036 | $33 | JP

Dappled Wines

1 Sewell Road, Steels Creek, Vic 3775 **T** 0407 675 994 **www**.dappledwines.com.au **OPEN** By appt
WINEMAKER Shaun Crinion **EST.** 2009 **DOZENS** 800

Owner and winemaker Shaun Crinion was introduced to wine in 1999, working for his winemaker uncle at Laetitia Winery & Vineyards on the central coast of California. His career since then has been nothing short of impressive. His longer-term ambition is to buy or establish his own vineyard.

97 **Les Verges Single Vineyard Yarra Valley Chardonnay 2019** From the red soil Upper Yarra D'Aloisio Vineyard at Seville. Wild-yeast barrel fermentation in French oak, no additions other than SO_2.

The bouquet is complex, fruit and oak both contributing, the palate with grapefruit and white peach persisting throughout the long journey. Compelling. Screw cap | 13% alc. | To 2030 | $45 | JH

Appellation Upper Yarra Valley Pinot Noir 2019 Good depth of colour; the bouquet has fragrant spiced plum and forest berries, the impressive, deeply robed palate following precisely in the tracks of the bouquet. The volume of flavour and mouthfeel suggests even more spicy complexity will follow in the next 2–3 years. Screw cap | 13.5% alc. | To 2030 | $30 | JH

Champs de Cerises Single Vineyard Upper Yarra Valley Pinot Noir 2019 Hand picked, wild-yeast fermented with 30% whole bunches, SO_2 the only addition, the slight turbidity confirming no filtration or fining. A spiced plum bouquet signals a wine of substantial depth and complexity, the texture and structure first class. Diam | 13.5% alc. | To 2030 | $45 | JH

Appellation Yarra Valley Chardonnay 2019 Hand picked, whole-bunch pressed, wild fermented in French oak, part new. White peach and nectarine are the cornerstones of a supple and creamy chardonnay that sits up and welcomes you. Classic each-way proposition, drink now or later. Screw cap | 13% alc. | To 2029 | $30 | JH

CB Wine

Gembrook Road, Hoddles Creek, Vic 3139 **T** 0419 545 544 **www**.dcbwine.com.au
EMAKER Chris Bendle **EST.** 2013 **DOZENS** 1300

B is a busman's holiday for Chris Bendle, currently a winemaker at Hoddles Creek Estate, ere he has been since 2010. He previously made wine in Tasmania, NZ and Oregon, so he he right person to provide wines that are elegant, affordable and reward the pleasure of nking (Chris's aim); the wines also offer excellent value.

Yarra Valley Pinot Noir 2019 While it has some maraschino cherries and pips, it's deep, earthy and flavoursome, largely working off a savoury theme. A youthfulness yet some soul too. The textural palate, with its emery board tannins, is underscored by some meaty reduction. It just works. Screw cap | 13.5% alc. | To 2027 | $24 | JF

e Bortoli (Victoria)

nacle Lane, Dixons Creek, Vic 3775 **T** (03) 5965 2271 **www**.debortoli.com.au **OPEN** 7 days 10–5
EMAKER Stephen Webber, Sarah Fagan, Andrew Bretherton **EST.** 1987 **DOZENS** 350 000 **VYDS** 520ha

guably the most successful of all Yarra Valley wineries, not only in terms of the sheer volume production but also the quality of its wines. The wines are released in 3 quality (and price) oups: at the top Single Vineyard, then Estate Grown and in 3rd place Villages.

Lusatia Chardonnay 2018 A bit like a Ferrari 812 Superfast that can go from zero to 100 in 2.9 seconds, this chardonnay seems to race across the palate, leaving a trail of flavour in its wake. It's pure acidity driving this. Of course there's more in the midst: the citrus, the flint and the smidge of nougatine. A complex, fantastic wine. Screw cap | 12.7% alc. | To 2030 | $90 | JF

Melba Reserve Yarra Valley Cabernet Sauvignon 2017 The trio of high-end cabernets are exceptional. This Reserve is an essay in texture and beautiful cabernet flavours. Cassis, warm earth, wood smoke, tar and baking spices. The medium-bodied palate is caressed by cocoa-powder-like tannins and terrific length. Lovely today but will reward more with cellaring. Diam | 13.5% alc. | To 2035 | $40 | JF

The Estate Vineyard Dixons Creek Yarra Valley Chardonnay 2019 If you had to pick a chardonnay that punches above its weight given its price point, this surely is it. Stamped with Yarra cool, so there's flint and a citrus theme happening. Lemon blossom and juicy tangy fruit across a rather tight and linear palate. It's certainly not lean, as there are dabs of leesy texture and a refreshing saline tang to the finish. Screw cap | 13% alc. | To 2028 | $30 | JF

enton

whill Vineyard, 160 Old Healesville Road, Yarra Glen, Vic 3775 **T** 0402 346 686
w.dentonwine.com **OPEN** By appt **WINEMAKER** Luke Lambert **EST.** 1997 **DOZENS** 2500 **VYDS** 31.3ha

ading Melbourne architect John Denton and son Simon began the establishment of the eyard with a first stage planting in 1997, completing the plantings in 2004. The name ewhill derives from the fact that a granite plug 'was created 370 million years ago, sitting ove the surrounding softer sandstones and silt of the valley'. This granite base is most usual in the Yarra Valley, and, together with the natural amphitheatre that the plug created, s consistently produced exceptional grapes.

Yarra Valley Nebbiolo 2017 As far as Australian nebbiolo goes, this is rock 'n' roll. It has the tar-and-roses thing going on, with chinotto, blood orange zest and a sprinkling of fresh herbs. The palate is the clincher, though, with oak a background player, simply offering the right support. Ribbons of furry tannins are let loose, while the high-toned acidity weaves everything back into respectful submission. Diam | 13.5% alc. | To 2035 | $55 | JF

Dominique Portet ★★★★

870 Maroondah Highway, Coldstream, Vic 3770 **T** (03) 5962 5760 **WWW**.dominiqueportet.com
OPEN 7 days 10–5 **WINEMAKER** Ben Portet, Tim Dexter **EST.** 2000 **DOZENS** 15000 **VYDS** 9ha

Dominique Portet was one of the first Flying Winemakers, commuting to Clos du Val in the Napa Valley where his brother was also a winemaker. After retiring from Taltarni, he moved to the Yarra Valley, a region he had been closely observing since the mid 1980s. In 2000 he found the site he had long looked for and built his winery and cellar door. Son Ben is now executive winemaker, leaving Dominique with a roving role as de facto consultant and brand marketer.

97 **Single Vineyard Yarra Valley Cabernet Sauvignon Malbec 2019** 93/7% cabernet/malbec. Hand-picked fruit, berry sorted and crushed. On skins for 22 days. Matured 14 months in French oak (30% new). Bright, clear colour; this is about as good as one could get from the Yarra Valley in a medium-bodied frame, its purity is wonderful. A drop-dead bargain. Screw cap | 13.5% alc. | To 2034 | $38 | JH | ♥

96 **Single Vineyard Yarra Valley Rosé 2020** Hand picked, whole-bunch pressed, fermented in used Fre oak, matured for 6 months. Pale salmon pink; a perfumed spice and blossom bouquet introduces a complex and perfectly balanced silky palate with a delicious spread of red berry and stone-fruit flavours guarded by gently cleansing acidity. Screw cap | 13.5% alc. | To 2024 | $38 | JH | ♥

95 **Fontaine Yarra Valley Chardonnay 2020** This is DP's drink-young chardonnay. It's a beauty and a bargain, full of white stone fruit with layers of citrus and rich, creamy flavours. There's some refinement as the acidity keeps it fresh, lively and on track. One of the best in this style and shoul be rewarded accordingly. Screw cap | 13% alc. | To 2025 | $24 | JF

Fontaine Yarra Valley Cabernet Sauvignon 2019 Quite what a classy Yarra Valley cabernet-domina blend (86/6/5/2/1% cabernet sauvignon/merlot/cabernet franc/petit verdot/malbec) is doing at th price is beyond me. It is elegant, medium bodied and finely structured, the suite of red/blackcurra fruits given 12 months in French oak (20% new). Screw cap | 13% alc. | To 2034 | $22 | JH

Emilian

PO Box 20 Kalorama, Vic 3766 **T** 0421 100 648 **WWW**.emilian.com.au **WINEMAKER** Robin Querre **EST.** 20
DOZENS 300

Robin Querre is the 4th generation of a family involved in winemaking since 1897, variously i Saint-Émilion and Pomerol, France. Robin commenced studies in medicine at the University of Bordeaux, but changed to oenology in 1990. He studied under some of the Bordeaux greats and worked vintages at Chateau Canon and Moueix, as well as at Rudd Estate in the Napa Valley. This led Robin to work in research, travelling to Australia, Germany, Austria, Switzerland, England, Japan and Israel. He and wife Prue also make small quantities of very good wine in the Yarra Valley.

95 **Single Vineyard Strathbogie Nebbiolo Rosé 2020** As refreshing as a spring day. This has the right amount of aromatics and flavour, the right amount of freshness and texture and the right amount of acidity and charm to warrant another glass. With friends, another bottle. Top-notch rosé. Screw cap | 12.5% alc. | To 2023 | $25 | JF

Single Parcel Yarra Valley Pinot Noir 2020 While this has the same lightness of touch as its single-vineyard sibling, there's more depth here. Still ethereal, with wafts of spiced cherries, rhubarb and warm earth. Silk-like tannins, a gentle palate, fine acidity and a finish that impresses. Screw cap | 13% alc. | To 2026 | $35 | JF

94 **Single Vineyard Dixons Creek Yarra Valley Pinot Noir 2020** Wow, what a pretty wine. It's delicate and soft, with some sweet cherries, chinotto and spice. Lighter framed, with no hard edges, barely-there tannins and a light veil of acidity. It feels like halfway between a rosé and a pinot noir. Quite a revelation. It's not complex, but it doesn't matter. I could drink a lot of this. Screw cap | 12.5% alc. | To 2024 | $27 | JF

First Foot Forward

6 Maddens Lane, Coldstream, Vic 3770 **T** 0402 575 818 **WWW**.firstfootforward.com.au **OPEN** By appt
WINEMAKER Martin Siebert **EST.** 2013 **DOZENS** 500

Owner and winemaker Martin Siebert's daytime job is at Tokar Estate, where he has been chi winemaker for a number of years. In 2013 he had the opportunity to purchase pinot noir and chardonnay from a mature vineyard in The Patch – he says that so long as the fruit is availabl he will be purchasing it, adding other wines from the Yarra Valley to broaden the offer to quality-focused restaurants and specialty wine stores around Melbourne.

Amphora Ferment Single Vineyard Yarra Valley Sauvignon Blanc 2020 Attention to detail on the sorting table is what makes this an exceptional wine. It's pristine and pure, with a line of juicy acidity. Citrussy and savoury, crisp and crunchy. Love it. Screw cap | 12.8% alc. | To 2025 | $25 | JF

Upper Yarra Valley Chardonnay 2020 There's a lot to enjoy here: tangy citrus flavours, and lightness of touch across the palate, yet there's texture and definition, too. A very good price for very cool Yarra chardy. Screw cap | 13% alc. | To 2027 | $28 | JF

Upper Yarra Valley Pinot Noir 2020 While showing the exuberance of youth, this is shaped by raw silk tannins and a smoothness across a light- to medium-bodied palate. It's full of cherries, spice and wild herbs, with refreshing squirts of citrus, especially blood orange and zest. Refreshing, tangy and hard to put down. Screw cap | 13.8% alc. | To 2028 | $28 | JF

Upper Yarra Valley Chardonnay 2019 A go-to chardonnay that offers the right amount of flavour, juiciness and enjoyment. Full of tangy lemon and grapefruit, with creamed honey and lavender, a savoury palate and mouth-watering acidity. It's linear, but not so tight that it can't be enjoyed now. Screw cap | 13.5% alc. | To 2027 | $28 | JF

embrook Hill  

nching Place Road, Gembrook, Vic 3783 **T** (03) 5968 1622 **www**.gembrookhill.com.au **OPEN** By appt
EMAKER Andrew Marks **EST.** 1983 **DOZENS** 1500 **VYDS** 5ha

mbrook Hill's northeast-facing vineyard is in a natural amphitheatre; the low-yielding ıvignon blanc, chardonnay and pinot noir are not irrigated. The minimal approach to ıemaking produces wines of a consistent style with finesse and elegance.

Yarra Valley Sauvignon Blanc 2019 50% stainless-steel fermentation, 50% left on the lees for 5 months in used French oak. One of my go-to sauvignon blancs because it's so delicious and refreshing, yet complex and deep. It incorporates texture, with a vibrancy and brightness of fruit. Expect citrus, white pepper, chalky acidity and decent length. Screw cap | 12% alc. | To 2026 | $32 | JF

elen's Hill Estate  

Ingram Road, Lilydale, Vic 3140 **T** (03) 9739 1573 **www**.helenshill.com.au **OPEN** 7 days 10–5
EMAKER Scott McCarthy **EST.** 1984 **DOZENS** 15000 **VYDS** 53ha

len's Hill Estate is named after the previous owner of the property, Helen Fraser. It produces ıbels: Helen's Hill Estate and Ingram Road, both made onsite. The winery, cellar door mplex and elegant 140-seat restaurant command some of the best views in the valley.

Winemakers Reserve Single Vineyard Yarra Valley Chardonnay 2017 Hand picked, whole-bunch pressed, fermented in French oak, 35% mlf, matured for 9 months. A selection of the 5 best barrels. Gleaming bright straw green; ravishingly complex and intense grapefruit/white peach flavours, integrated oak adding its voice in the background. A very special wine. Diam | 12.6% alc. | To 2029 | $100 | JH

Winemakers Reserve Single Vineyard Yarra Valley Pinot Noir 2017 A vivid stage for the great '17 vintage, 60% MV6, 20% Pommard and 20% Dijon clone 115. Hand picked, lightly crushed, fermented for 10 days on skins, matured for 10 months in French oak (40% new), this wine is a selection of the 5 best barrels. A truly lovely pinot, purity and elegance its corner posts, a marriage of intensity and detail, finishing with the opening of the peacock's tail. Diam | 12.5% alc. | To 2032 | $100 | JH

The Empress Reserve Single Clone Chardonnay 2018 Hand-picked, whole-bunch pressed, fermented in French puncheons (30% new), 30% mlf, matured for 8 months. Bright, light straw-green; has all the elegance and length that puts Yarra Valley chardonnay on a par with Margaret River as the best Australian regions for chardonnay. White peach and nashi pear fruit flavours are dominant, the oak subtle, the acidity fresh. Screw cap | 12.5% alc. | To 2028 | $60 | JH

First Light Single Clone Yarra Valley Pinot Noir 2017 A single block of MV6, whole-berry ferment (no whole bunches), matured for 11 months in French puncheons (40% new). Very much in the style of the cool vintage; elegant, savoury and very long in the mouth. Wild strawberry/cherry fruit is dusted with spices, dried herbs and cedary oak. A strong sense of place. Screw cap | 12.8% alc. | To 2029 | $60 | JH

Ingram Road Single Vineyard Yarra Valley Chardonnay 2019 Hand picked, whole-bunch pressed, wild-yeast fermented in French barriques, partial mlf for 8 months. There's a tangy, lively edge to the white-stone-fruit flavour and citrus-tinged acidity. A remarkably good chardonnay at any price, let alone this. While it's ready now, it will age with grace. Screw cap | 12.5% alc. | To 2030 | $22 | JH

Hill Top Single Vineyard Yarra Valley Syrah 2019 Exceptional colour, vivid crimson/purple on the rim, heralds a perfectly balanced shiraz of medium-plus body. The fruit, oak and tannins are all singing from the same page. Black fruits (both berry and stone fruit) and fine-spun tannins deliver great length. Diam | 14% alc. | To 2039 | $35 | JH

Ingram Road Single Vineyard Heathcote Shiraz 2019 Crushed and destemmed, open-fermented, 14 days on skins, matured for 10 months in French oak (10% new). A great example of why Heathcote is regarded as one of the foremost regions in Australia for shiraz. This overflows with supple blackberry fruit, rounded tannins and a clean finish. Exceptional value. Screw cap | 13.7% alc. | To 2034 | $22 | JH

Lana's Single Vineyard Yarra Valley Rosé 2020 100% cabernet sauvignon. Hand picked, whole-bunch pressed. No time on skins, cold-settled, then fermented in aged barriques for 30 days. Salmon-pink hue; the perfumed bouquet of spiced strawberries heralds a rosé with the lot, with powerful and complex fruit. Very astute winemaking. Screw cap | 12% alc. | To 2022 | $28 | JH

Hoddles Creek Estate ★★★★

505 Gembrook Road, Hoddles Creek, Vic 3139 **T** (03) 5967 4692 **www**.hoddlescreekestate.com.au
OPEN By appt **WINEMAKER** Franco D'Anna, Chris Bendle **EST.** 1997 **DOZENS** 30000 **VYDS** 33.3ha

The D'Anna family established their vineyard on a property that had been in the family since 1960. The vines (chardonnay, pinot noir, sauvignon blanc, cabernet sauvignon, pinot gris, merlot and pinot blanc) are pruned and harvested by hand. A 300t, split-level winery was bu in 2003. Son Franco is the viticulturist and inspired winemaker.

98 **Road Block Chardonnay 2018** From an east-facing contoured vineyard that catches all the mornin sun. Perfectly ripened white stone fruit with a quick squeeze of Meyer lemon. Has been fermented and matured in French oak in such a way as to leave the gorgeous fruit centre stage, the palate of endless length. Screw cap | 12.5% alc. | To 2030 | $60 | JH

Lone Star Creek Vineyard

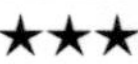

75 Owens Rd, Woori Yallock, Vic 3139 **T** 0414282629 **www**.lonestarcreekwines.com.au
WINEMAKER Franco D'Anna **EST.** 1997 **DOZENS** 800 **VYDS** 22ha

Situated on the border of Woori Yallock and Hoddle's Creek, this cool-climate upper Yarra fruit was sold to wineries including Hoddle's Creek Estate, so when the time came to start producing wine under the Lone Star Creek Vineyard label, enlisting Hoddle's Creek's own Franco D'Anna as winemaker must have seemed an obvious choice. The vineyard is not subject to strictly organic management, but the philosophy with both the viticulture and winemaking is one of minimal intervention throughout the entire process. The current range of wines are very moderately priced, all things considered. (SC)

93 **Chardonnay 2019** Wild-yeast fermented, 9 months on lees in new and used French oak barriques. Has complexity on the bouquet, with grilled nuts, stone fruit, vanilla and some chalky minerality a part of the picture. It gives the impression of being a little lean on the palate, but the texture and acidity propel it along and it sustains well on the finish. Cool-climate elegance on show, you coul say. Screw cap | 12.5% alc. | To 2029 | $24 | SC

Red 2020 60% pinot noir, all destemmed and 40% syrah with 25% whole bunches, fermented separately. It's part of the light dry red movement in the Yarra. This is just right. Savoury yet juicy, light and bright with enough textural tannins and lively acidity to go another round. Or three. Screw cap | 13% alc. | To 2025 | $27 | JF

92 **Sauvignon Blanc 2019** Barrel fermented and aged on lees in older French barriques for around 6 months prior to bottling. Really interesting and attractive combination of smoky/flinty characte and almost tropical fruit on the bouquet. Brisk with acidity and racy along the palate, but textural as well, from the oak maturation. Likely to be even better with a little more time in the bottle. Grea value. Screw cap | 12% alc. | To 2025 | $20 | SC

Chardonnay 2020 Lots of zest appeal here, taking off with all manner of citrus flavours and lemon blossom florals too. There's texture with some lees influence imparting grilled nuts and creamy c A shapely wine with soft acidity gently leading it to the finishing line. Screw cap | 12.5% alc. | To 2026 | $25 | JF

Pinot Gris 2020 A lovely copper/pink blush; lots of crunchy red apples and pears too. Spicy with a squirt of lemon juice throughout. While it has texture, it's quite a tight gris. Screw cap | 12.5% alc. | To 2023 | $22 | JF

Pinot Gris 2019 Some skin contact and lees ageing in oak. Distinctly bronze-pink in colour, almost like a pale rosé. Pear and red apple on the bouquet and something that makes me think of green mango. Quite generous in flavour and mouthfilling without being sweet-fruited; the soft acidity keeps things tight and provides the freshness on the finish. Deftly made and very good drinking. Screw cap | 12.5% alc. | To 2025 | $22 | SC

Mandala

1568 Melba Highway, Dixons Creek, Vic 3775 **T** (03) 5965 2016 **www**.mandalawines.com.au
OPEN Mon-Fri 10-4, w'ends 10-5 **WINEMAKER** Charles Smedley, Don Pope **EST.** 2007 **DOZENS** 10500
VYDS 29ha

Mandala is owned by Charles Smedley, who acquired the established vineyard in 2007. The vineyard has vines up to 25 years old, but the spectacular restaurant and cellar door compl more recent addition. The vineyards are primarily at the home base in Dixons Creek. re is a separate 4.4ha vineyard at Yarra Junction planted entirely to pinot noir with an ressive clonal mix.

Yarra Valley Fumé Blanc 2020 The inaugural release, made from hand-picked fruit, whole clusters pressed to old oak, wild fermented and aged 9 months. It's a really good outcome. Cunchy citrussy flavours, passionfruit pith, pine needle and basil coolness are matched to a more textural palate. Plenty of acidity ensures a delicious drink right now. Screw cap | 12.6% alc. | To 2023 | $30 | JF

edhurst  

6 Medhurst Road, Gruyere, Vic 3770 **T** (03) 5964 9022 **WWW**.medhurstwines.com.au
Thurs-Mon & public hols 11-5 **WINEMAKER** Simon Steele **EST.** 2000 **DOZENS** 6000 **VYDS** 12ha

lhurst focuses on small-batch production and also provides contract winemaking services. visual impact of the winery has been minimised by recessing the building into the slope of and locating the barrel room underground. The building was recognised for its architectural ellence at the Victorian Architecture Awards. The arrival of Simon Steele (his loss much urned by Brokenwood) has enhanced the already considerable reputation of Medhurst.

Estate Vineyard Chardonnay 2020 Wowee. This is a bit of rock'n'roll. All citrus tones, with flint, fennel and daikon. It's complex and savoury, with lots of texture. Brilliant acidity wraps it up tightly. Moreish and utterly delicious. Screw cap | 13% alc. | To 2032 | $44 | JF

Estate Vineyard Rosé 2020 A pastel pink copper blush entices. Lightly spiced and delicately flavoured with redcurrants and a squeeze of blackberries. There's some texture and savouriness, a succulence and juiciness. It's refreshing to the very last drop and the joy continues. Top rosé. Screw cap | 13% alc. | To 2023 | $25 | JF

ount Mary 

lstream West Road, Lilydale, Vic 3140 **T** (03) 9739 1761 **WWW**.mountmary.com.au
MAKER Sam Middleton **EST.** 1971 **DOZENS** 4500 **VYDS** 18ha

unt Mary was one of the foremost pioneers of the rebirth of the Yarra Valley after 50 years hout viticultural activity. From the outset they produced wines of rare finesse and purity. ay its star shines brighter than that of any of the 169 producers in the Yarra Valley. Winery he Year in the *Wine Companion 2018*.

Yarra Valley Quintet 2019 A quintet of 44% cabernet sauvignon, 30% merlot, 16% cabernet franc and 5% each of malbec and petit verdot, all in harmony. Heady aromatics, the fruit pristine and lightly spiced. But it's the medium-bodied palate that really woos: focused and seamless with superfine yet detailed tannins. Of course it has the beauty and charm of youth but age will send this to another level. Did I mention elegance? Tick. Cork | 13% alc. | To 2039 | $165 | JF | ♥

Yarra Valley Chardonnay 2019 There must be some magic dust landing on Mount Mary, or rather, its chardonnay site. Latterly, this has just been rockin' it. No different this year: a pristine, refined and ultra-elegant wine. A harmonious offering of citrus and light, creamy leesy flavours, spice and vanilla-pod oak. The succulence via acidity ensures it lingers long. I got goosebumps tasting this. Screw cap | 13% alc. | To 2035 | $120 | JF

akridge Wines  

Maroondah Highway, Coldstream, Vic 3770 **T** (03) 9738 9900 **WWW**.oakridgewines.com.au
7 days 10-5 **WINEMAKER** David Bicknell, Tim Perrin **EST.** 1978 **DOZENS** 35000 **VYDS** 61ha

nemaker David Bicknell has proved his worth time and again as an extremely talented emaker. At the top of the Oakridge brand tier is 864, all Yarra Valley vineyard selections, y released in the best years; next is the Oakridge Vineyard Series; and the Over the oulder range, drawn from all of the sources available to Oakridge. The estate vineyards Oakridge Vineyard, Hazeldene Vineyard and Henk Vineyard.

864 Single Block Release Drive Block Funder & Diamond Vineyard Yarra Valley Chardonnay 2019 One of three joint winners for Chardonnay of the Year 2022. It might have a smidge more volume and ripeness compared with the exemplary 2017, but this is a very fine follow up. The same DNA. It's about harnessing the power. Expect citrus, flint and form. Length, precision and a mineral drive. The devil is in the details, according to winemaker Dave Bicknell. This wine is the embodiment – indeed the reward – of that. Screw cap | 14% alc. | To 2030 | $90 | JF | ♥

Vineyard Series Willowlake Yarra Valley Chardonnay 2019 All the chardonnays in the Vineyard Series are made identically, so capturing the essence of the place is paramount. This is so good. Flinty, fine, citrussy, long and pure. An ethereal style, yet so much going on. It's hard to pick a favourite in this range. They are all expressive. Today it's Willowlake, tomorrow ... who knows? Screw cap | 13.2% alc. | To 2030 | $44 | JF

Vineyard Series Henk Yarra Valley Chardonnay 2019 A north-facing vineyard at Woori Yallock in the Upper Yarra. It comes with no shortage of flavour or drive. Lemon blossom, struck match, ginger spice and savoury, leesy notes. Feeling fuller and richer on the palate at first, it is pulled through a tight vortex by a silk-thread of acidity. Compelling and equally delicious. Screw cap | 13.3% alc. | To 2029 | $44 | JF

95 **Garden Gris Yarra Valley 2019** The 2nd offering of this textural, lightly tannic and thoroughly appealing gris. It's a beauty. Cloudy pastel ruby and smells of watermelon and rind, Turkish delig and freshly pickled Japanese ginger in red shiso. It's refreshing and obviously phenolic, but all neatly played. The natural acidity adds to its succulence as it finishes dry and brimming with life Screw cap | 11.6% alc. | To 2025 | $30 | JF

Yarra Valley Rosé 2020 A trio of pinots noir, meunier and gris fermented in old casks makes for a fab rosé with a very pale pastel copper hue. There's texture, flavour and a dry finish. In between, dabs of spicy red fruits, lemon zest and unripe pear, as in crunchy and textural. It's a top-notch r Screw cap | 12.5% alc. | To 2023 | $30 | JF

Light Dry Red Yarra Valley 2020 With the Yarra Valley cornering the Light Dry Red market, here's another ripper and it won't break the budget. 50/50% pinot/shiraz. Loaded with bright, poppy fr doused in pepper, spice and all things nice. It's just shy of medium bodied, with crunchy acidity grainy tannins. Fitting the style brief brilliantly, it eschews any serious intent, other than crafting delicious drink. Screw cap | 14% alc. | To 2026 | $30 | JF

94 **Yarra Valley Pinot Noir 2019** A similar feel or DNA to the Light Dry Red and you know what that means? It's a delicious drink. Full of bright, juicy cherries and pips, laced with woodsy spices anc a dash of Angostura bitters. Smoky and sultry, too. Just shy of full bodied, textural and plush, wit slightly grainy tannins. Lively and fresh. Get into this now. Screw cap | 14% alc. | To 2026 | $30 | JF

Rochford Wines

878-880 Maroondah Highway, Coldstream, Vic 3770 **T** (03) 5957 3333 **www**.rochfordwines.com.au **OPEN** 7 days 9-5 **WINEMAKER** Kaspar Hermann, Kelly Healey **EST.** 1988 **DOZENS** 20000 **VYDS** 26ha

This Yarra Valley property was purchased by Helmut Konecsny in 2002. In addition to the cellar door, the property has 2 restaurants, a retail shop and an expansive natural amphitheatre and observation tower – a showpiece in the region.

95 **la Gauche Yarra Valley Cabernet Sauvignon 2019** The colour is good, the bouquet full of promise that is duly delivered by the medium-bodied palate, cassis riding high, superfine tannins sealing deal. Great value. Screw cap | 13.3% alc. | To 2034 | $29 | JH

Rouleur

80 Laurens Street, North Melbourne, Vic 3051 **T** 0419 100 929 **www**.rouleurwine.com **OPEN** By app **WINEMAKER** Matthew East **EST.** 2015 **DOZENS** 2500

Between February 1999 and December 2015 Owner Matt East's day job was in sales and marketing, culminating in his appointment in '11 as national sales manager for Wirra Wirra (which he had joined in '08). Following his retirement from that position, he set in motion the wheels of Rouleur. He lives in Melbourne, and has transformed a dilapidated milk bar in North Melbourne into his inner-city cellar door.

96 **Yarra Valley Pinot Gris et al 2020** A wonderful white. Aromatic, texturally bold, flamboyant and da easy to drink, especially with food. Mandarin, cumquat, musk, rosewater and Moroccan souk. Pith detailed and tannic, with a saline and pumice-like finish. But poised and measured, with nothing excessive in fruit or structure. Delicious! Screw cap | 12.2% alc. | To 2024 | $34 | NG | ♥

95 **McLaren Vale Shiraz 2019** A sumptuous shiraz made in a restrained style. This dichotomy alone infers intrigue and complexity. 20% whole bunch, wild ferment (as is standard at this address) and largely neutral wood. Sensible. Blueberry, lilac florals, iodine, salumi, tapenade and a skein of peppery acidity punctuate a plush finish. Delicious drinking. Screw cap | 14.4% alc. | To 2028 | $32 | NG

McLaren Vale Grenache 2019 Superlative grenache. Mid weight, with that febrile friskiness more reminiscent of elevated Gredos than, say, the Southern Rhône. Briary pithy tannins, tactile and fir corral an almost ethereal veil of bright red fruits, from raspberry and cranberry to pomegranate, orange zest and bergamot. Pliant, expansive, savoury and long. Great value. Screw cap | 14.3% alc. | To 2023 | $32 | NG

antolin Wines ★★★★☆

· 21-23 Delaneys Road, South Warrandyte, Vic 3134 **T** 0402 278 464 **www**.santolinwines.com.au
IEMAKER Adrian Santolin **EST.** 2012 **DOZENS** 1000

rian Santolin grew up in Griffith, NSW, and has worked in the wine industry since he was He moved to the Yarra Valley in 2007 with wife Rebecca, who has worked in marketing es at various wineries. Adrian has a love of pinot noir; in '12 his dream came true when he s able to buy 2t of pinot noir from the Syme-on-Yarra Vineyard, increasing production in to 4t, split between chardonnay and pinot noir. The Boy Meets Girl wines are sold through vw.nakedwines.com.au.

Cosa Nostra Yarra Valley Arneis 2020 Reminiscent of a spring garden full of white flowers and oregano. The palate has a delicacy and joy with soft acidity and a hint of lemon. A lovely rendition. Screw cap | 12.3% alc. | To 2023 | $25 | JF

errat ★★★★★

5 Simpsons Lane, Yarra Glen, Vic 3775 **T** (03) 9730 1439 **www**.serrat.com.au
IEMAKER Tom Carson, Kate Thurgood **EST.** 2001 **DOZENS** 1000 **VYDS** 3.5ha

rrat is the family business of Tom Carson and wife Nadège. As well as being a consummate nemaker, Tom has one of the best palates in Australia and a deep understanding of the e wines of the world, which he and Nadège drink at every opportunity (when they aren't inking Serrat). Viticulture and winemaking hit new heights with the 2014 Yarra Valley Shiraz ognier named *Wine Companion 2016* Wine of the Year (from a field of 8863 wines).

Yarra Valley Shiraz Viognier 2020 It's little wonder these wines sell out. They're priced so well for the quality offered. This wine a case in point. Firstly there's a vibrancy and freshness. It is awash with intense flavours, with black pepper, cinnamon and sarsaparilla infusing the sweetest cherries. It's hedonistic. It's full bodied, with plush and expansive tannins. Rather majestic. Screw cap | 14% alc. | To 2035 | $45 | JF

Yarra Valley Grenache Noir 2020 This is gorgeous. It's really, really hard to put down. The aromas are intoxicating, with their musk and red fruits, the dash of sarsaparilla, red licorice and cinnamon. The medium-bodied palate has intense, sweet fruit swooshing across it, with sandy tannins and neat acidity dutifully following. Another glass, please. Screw cap | 14% alc. | To 2028 | $45 | JF

eville Estate ★★★★★

Linwood Road, Seville, Vic 3139 **T** (03) 5964 2622 **www**.sevilleestate.com.au **OPEN** 7 days 10-5
NEMAKER Dylan McMahon **EST.** 1972 **DOZENS** 8000 **VYDS** 12ha

ville Estate was founded by Dr Peter and Margaret McMahon in 1972. After several changes ownership, Yiping Wang purchased the property in early 2017. Yiping is a wine retailer the Guangxi province of China. Yiping's supportive yet hands-off approach has allowed nemaker and general manager Dylan McMahon (grandson of founder Peter McMahon) to eer the ship. Seville Estate also has luxury accommodation with the original homestead and self-contained apartments.

Yarra Valley Pinot Noir 2020 A beautiful wine that pleases from the moment it is poured, with its bright hue, heady aromas and very fine palate. Expect wild strawberries and cherries, a flutter of dried herbs and woodsy spices, with exceptional tannins appearing light yet smooth. The palate is sheer elegance. Screw cap | 13.2% alc. | To 2032 | $45 | JF

tefani Estate 

5 Old Healesville Road, Healesville, Vic 3777 **T** 0492 993 446 **www**.stefaniwines.com.au
EN Thurs-Fri by appt, Sat-Sun 11-5 **WINEMAKER** Peter Mackey **EST.** 1998 **DOZENS** 5730 **VYDS** 18ha

efano Stefani came to Australia in 1985. Business success has allowed him and wife Rina to llow in the footsteps of his grandfather, who had a vineyard and was an avid wine collector. nong plantings across various vineyards, 1.6ha of sangiovese have been established, using ion material from the original Stefani Vineyard in Tuscany.

The View Yarra Valley Pinot Blanc 2019 What a delightful drink that flutters with compelling flavours of pear drops and essence, citrus, basil and other cool herbs. It's a touch estery, but there's a gentleness across the palate, an interesting texture, a quinine/lemon/saline thing going on, aside from mouth-watering lemon sorbet acidity. Screw cap | 13% alc. | To 2023 | $30 | JF

TarraWarra Estate ★★★★

311 Healesville-Yarra Glen Road, Yarra Glen, Vic 3775 **T** (03) 5957 3510 **www**.tarrawarra.com.au
OPEN Tues-Sun 11-5 **WINEMAKER** Clare Halloran, Adam McCallum **EST.** 1983 **DOZENS** 9000 **VYDS** 28ha

TarraWarra is, and always has been, one of the top-tier wineries in the Yarra Valley. Founded Marc Besen AC and wife Eva Besen AO, it has operated on the basis that quality is paramoun cost a secondary concern. The creation of the TarraWarra Museum of Art (twma.com.au) in a purpose-built building provides another reason to visit; indeed, many visitors come specifically to look at the ever-changing displays in the Museum.

95 **Yarra Valley Barbera 2019** I love the way some varieties can inveigle their way into the landscape, such as barbera in the Yarra, and rise to the occasion. Among all those French grapes, this is the li wine that could. It's fragrant, different, really spicy with juniper and bitter herbs dousing the dark cherries within. Medium bodied with neat acidity, just so, light tannins and savoury stamp. Juicy a delicious. Saluté. Screw cap | 14% alc. | To 2026 | $30 | JF

94 **Yarra Valley Chardonnay 2019** This estate chardonnay seems to be finer, a tad more complex and almost tighter than previous incarnations. It certainly has an amalgam of flavours, but is more citru toned and spiced with ginger. There's really fine, tangy acidity throughout and nothing is out of place. Screw cap | 13.2% alc. | To 2028 | $30 | JF

The Wanderer

2850 Launching Place Road, Gembrook, Vic 3783 **T** 0415 529 639 **www**.wandererwines.com
OPEN By appt **WINEMAKER** Andrew Marks **EST.** 2005 **DOZENS** 500

The Wanderer wines are a series of single-vineyard wines made by Andrew Marks, winemaker and viticulturalist at Gembrook Hill Vineyard. He has worked numerous vintages in France an Spain including Etienne Sauzet in Puligny Montrachet in '06 and more recently over 10 vintag in the Costa Brava, Spain. Andrew seeks to achieve the best expression of his vineyards through minimal handling in the winery. In '12 he founded The Melbourne Gin Company.

96 **Upper Yarra Valley Chardonnay 2019** Only a puncheon and hogshead (800L) made. This is a class wine. It has pristine fruit, a touch of lemon and white nectarine, a light dusting of spice, a lemon verbena and curd flavour adding some richness, yet this is very fine and long. The palate just flows beautifully and it's effortless to drink. I mean taste. Nah, drink. Diam | 12% alc. | To 2030 | $35 | JF

Tillie J

305 68B Gadd Street, Northcote, Vic 3070 (postal) **T** 0428 554 311 **www**.tilliejwines.com.au
WINEMAKER Natillie Johnston **EST.** 2019 **DOZENS** 200

Mark my (James') words. Tillie Johnston is going to become a great winemaker. She began her career in 2012, one of the vintage crew at Coldstream Hills, and says her love for pinot n began there. She then spent 4 of the next 8 years drifting between the Northern and Southe hemispheres unerringly picking the eyes out of an all-star cast of wineries. Since then, she's been assistant winemaker at Giant Steps to Steve Flamsteed and Jess Clark. In '19 she was offered the opportunity to buy 2t of grapes from Helen's Hill of whatever variety she chose which was, of course, pinot noir.

95 **Yarra Valley Pinot Noir 2020** Bright, clear crimson/purple. The perfumed bouquet straddles red berry and plum; the relatively light-bodied palate brings substance to the purity promised by the bouquet. It does so with panache, surprising with the length and savoury finish/aftertaste. A dab c French oak also adds to the equation. Screw cap | 13% alc. | To 2030 | $35 | JH

Toolangi

At il Vigneto Pizzeria **T** (03) 5947 3388 **www**.toolangi.com **OPEN** Sat 11.30-8.30, Sun 11.30-5.30
WINEMAKER Kaspar Hermann, Kelly Healey **EST.** 1995 **DOZENS** 7500 **VYDS** 14ha

Helmut Konecsny, owner of Rochford Wines, purchased Toolangi in 2018 and immediately started ringing in the changes. Apart from new-look packaging, Konecsny and his winemaki and vineyard team also set about rejuvenating and upgrading the vineyard and introducing new winemaking practices.

Yarra Valley Shiraz 2019 This is still in a youthful, primary phase, but that won't stop anyone drinking it today. Super-bright fruit, laced with spices, well-handled smoky/meaty reduction, more of the prosciutto variety. A grind of pepper, juniper and mint add to the savoury flavours. The palate is taut, tannins giving, and bright acidity to match. Well played. Screw cap | 13% alc. | To 2030 | $27 | JF

arra Yering

Winery of the Year 2022 ★★★★★

iarty Road, Coldstream, Vic 3770 **T** (03) 5964 9267 **www.yarrayering.com** **OPEN** 7 days 10-5
NEMAKER Sarah Crowe **EST.** 1969 **DOZENS** 5000 **VYDS** 112ha

September 2008, founder Bailey Carrodus died and in April '09 Yarra Yering was on the arket. It was Bailey Carrodus' clear wish and expectation that any purchaser would continue manage the vineyard and winery, and hence the wine style, in much the same way as he d done for the previous 40 years. Its acquisition in June '09 by a small group of investment nkers has fulfilled that wish. The low-yielding, unirrigated vineyards have always produced nes of extraordinary depth and intensity. Sarah Crowe was appointed winemaker after the)13 vintage. She has made red wines of the highest imaginable quality right from her first ntage in '14 and, to the delight of many, myself (James) included, has offered all the wines th screw caps. For good measure, she introduced the '14 Light Dry Red Pinot Shiraz as a retaste of that vintage and an affirmation of the exceptional talent recognised by her being med Winemaker of the Year in the *Wine Companion 2017*.

3 **Dry Red No. 2 2019** Shiraz, mataro, viognier. It's easy to be bowled over by this wine's beauty, from its bright colour to its heady fragrance of violets, Middle Eastern spices, fresh currants and blue fruits. Then magic happens. It is superfine, graced with perfectly formed silky tannins. The oak is seamlessly integrated, then flavour builds across the barely medium-bodied palate. While there's a lightness of touch, it's layered and complex. A complete wine full of style, elegance and substance. Screw cap | 13.5% alc. | To 2034 | $120 | JF | ♥

Dry Red No. 1 2019 Winner of 3 awards in the *Wine Companion 2022*: Wine of the Year, Red Wine of the Year and Cabernet & Family of the Year. This is mesmerising. Do take time to bask in its fragrance – all floral and spicy with some aniseed and fresh herbs. Enjoy the poised fruit flavours of blackberries, mulberries and a hint of blueberries coated in spicy oak and tethered to the body of the wine. Pulsing acidity and beautiful tannin structure shape this and offer a promise of more to come in time. Wow – what a wine. Screw cap | 13.5% alc. | To 2039 | $120 | JF | ♥

'eringberg

★★★★★

.roondah Highway, Coldstream, Vic 3770 **T** (03) 9739 0240 **www.yeringberg.com.au** **OPEN** By appt
NEMAKER Sandra de Pury **EST.** 1863 **DOZENS** 1500 **VYDS** 3.66ha

uill de Pury and daughter Sandra, with Guill's wife Katherine in the background, make wines r the new millennium from the low-yielding vines re-established in the heart of what was ne of the most famous (and infinitely larger) vineyards of the 19th century. In the riper years, e red wines have a velvety generosity of flavour rarely encountered, while never losing arietal character.

7 **Yarra Valley Cabernet Sauvignon 2019** While this has the exuberance of youth, it is also a composed and classy cabernet. A harmonious blend of mulberries and plums, cedary oak, cigar box and a touch of iodine. The palate is detailed from the ultrafine tannins, the brightness of the acidity to its impressive length. Elegance in a glass. Screw cap | 13.5% alc. | To 2042 | $95 | JF

Yeringberg 2019 This was tasted less than a month after it was bottled and while it's a very fine Yeringberg with its beauty on show, it's reserved and needs time to adjust and settle. Everything is in sync. Lovely aromas of violets, autumn leaves, mulberries and more. The medium-bodied palate is layered with fine, textural tannins, dazzled with fresh acidity and exceptional length. Screw cap | 13% alc. | To 2044 | $95 | JF

5 **Yarra Valley Viognier 2019** Few producers can match Yeringberg's viognier. Harmony is the aspiration, achieved by picking fruit over 8 days, so there's acidity, freshness and ripeness. There's also wild fermentation in barrel, no mlf and maturation in large-format, used oak. Ripe stone fruit, apricot and kernel, with ginger cream drizzled in honey. All tempered by lemon zest acidity and lime marmalade tang. There's richness here, without heaviness. A lovely viognier. Screw cap | 13.5% alc. | To 2027 | $35 | JF

Zonzo Estate ★★★

957 Healesville-Yarra Glen Road, Yarra Glen, Vic 3775 **T** (03) 9730 2500 **www**.zonzo.com.au
OPEN Wed-Sun 12-4 **WINEMAKER** Caroline Mooney **EST.** 1998 **VYDS** 18.21ha

This is an iteration of Train Trak, best known by Yarra Valley locals for the quality of its wood-fired oven pizzas. The vineyard was planted in 1995, the first wines made from the 1998 vintage. The business was acquired by Rod Micallef in 2016. The restaurant is open Wed–Su for lunch and Fri–Sun for dinner.

93 **Yarra Valley Pinot Noir 2020** This is good, actually very good, given the price. It delivers big time. A complete package of dark cherries, chinotto and blood-orange zest with smoky, meaty, savoury inputs and the oak neatly in place. It's fuller bodied but not big. The palate is actually very smooth with light and fine tannins and a juiciness throughout. It's a terrific drink right now. Screw cap | 13.5% alc. | To 2026 | $27 | JF

ZONE

Western Victoria

REGION

Ballarat

Nintingbool 

56 Wongerer Lane, Smythes Creek, Vic 3351 (postal) **T** 0429 424 399 **www**.nintingbool.com.au
WINEMAKER Peter Bothe **EST.** 1998 **DOZENS** 600 **VYDS** 2ha

Peter and Jill Bothe purchased the Nintingbool property in 1982 and built their home in '84, using bluestone dating back to the gold rush. They established an extensive Australian nativ garden and home orchard but in '98 diversified by planting pinot noir, with a further plantin the following year lifting the total to 2ha.

95 **Pinot Noir 2018** In the style of previous releases with its distinctive firm, linear structure and cool, leafy herbals, but showing more depth of flavour and intensity. The 2018 year seems to have been very kind. Brambly, dark berry fruits, wood smoke, earth notes, deep spice, with a spray of fine tannins from edge to edge. A work of some complexity. Screw cap | 13.8% alc. | To 2027 | $35 | JP

Sinclair of Scotsburn 

256 Wiggins Road, Scotsburn, Vic 3352 **T** 0419 885 717 **www**.sinclairofscotsburn.com.au
OPEN W'ends by appt **WINEMAKER** Scott Ireland **EST.** 1997 **DOZENS** 150 **VYDS** 2ha

The late David and Barbara Sinclair purchased their property in 2001, an acquisition that 'wasn't even on the horizon of plan B'. Winemaker Scott Ireland (Provenance Wines) was the winemaker from the beginning, making wine under the Sinclair of Scotsburn label and his own Provenance wines. With the passing of David Sinclair in December 2020, the future of the Sinclair of Scotsburn vineyard and brand remains unclear.

95 **Wallijak Chardonnay 2018** Juicy and complex with layers of flavours and interest from white peac grapefruit and quince to lemon curd and almond meal. Nicely measured vanillan oak caresses. Elegance and freshness live here. Screw cap | 13.3% alc. | To 2028 | $25 | JP

REGION

Grampians

ATR Wines 

103 Hard Hill Road, Armstrong, Vic 3377 **T** 0457 922 400 **www**.atrwines.com.au **OPEN** Thurs-Sun & public hols 1-5 **WINEMAKER** Adam Richardson **EST.** 2005 **DOZENS** 4000 **VYDS** 7.6ha

Perth-born Adam Richardson began his winemaking career in 1995; in '05 he put down roots in the Grampians region, establishing a vineyard with old shiraz clones from the 19th century and riesling, extending the plantings with tannat, nebbiolo, durif and viognier. The wines are exceptionally good, no surprise given his experience and the quality of the vineyard. He has so set up a wine consultancy business, drawing on experience that is matched by few nsultants in Australia.

Hard Hill Road Writer's Block Great Western Riesling 2019 This is why we get excited by Grampians riesling! An enduring classic in the making, with impressive intensity from the start. A rich vein of lime cordial, lemon curd, citrus blossom, fresh-cut green apple and wet stone runs deep. Smooth, dry (that tweak of sugar melts into the richness), mouth-watering acidity and a sleek restraint. Quite an accomplishment. Screw cap | 12% alc. | To 2032 | $38 | JP | ♥

Chockstone Grampians Riesling 2020 Another good reason to look to the Grampians as a serious premium producer of riesling. The grape is so beautifully and expressively in charge, with just a bare minimum of winemaking input. The quality of the fruit is the key. Fragrant aromas of apple blossom, honeysuckle. lemon drop, nashi pear and green apple. Even in its youth it has great powers of persuasion with additional flinty, stony notes on the palate and lip-smacking acidity. Screw cap | 12.5% alc. | To 2027 | $25 | JP

Chockstone Grampians Shiraz 2019 Fully ripe grapes picked for pepper/spice overtones to the fruit, matured in used American and French oak. A full-bodied shiraz, full of character and spice; texture, structure and balance all good. Thirty years won't tire it, and it needs 5+ more to open all the secrets lurking in the forest. Screw cap | 14.5% alc. | To 2044 | $28 | JH

Chockstone Grampians Rosé 2020 Pretty tea rose in hue, with light, dusty florals, dried raspberry and a wild strawberry bouquet. It's a complex flavour profile, to be sure; textural too, but it also slips down very easily as well. Screw cap | 13.5% alc. | To 2024 | $25 | JP

est's Wines

1 Best's Road, Great Western, Vic 3377 **T** (03) 5356 2250 **www**.bestswines.com
EN Mon-Sat 10-5, Sun 11-4 **WINEMAKER** Justin Purser **EST.** 1866 **DOZENS** 25000 **VYDS** 147ha

est's winery and vineyards are among Australia's best kept secrets. Indeed the vineyards, ith vines dating back to 1866, have secrets that may never be revealed: for example, ne of the vines planted in the Nursery Block has defied identification and is thought to kist nowhere else in the world. Best's consistently produces elegant, supple wines; the n No. 0 is a classic, the Thomson Family Shiraz (largely from vines planted in 1867) is agnificent. In the *Wine Companion 2017* Best's was awarded the mantle of Wine of the Year om a field of almost 9000 wines; in 2021 they were Best Value Winery.

Great Western Riesling 2020 The vines are direct descendants of the 1866 plantings in the nursery block. A core of sweet lime-juice essence and spine-tingling acidity makes a wine that follows in the footsteps of its multi-gold-medal-winning predecessors. An indefinite lifespan. Screw cap | 12% alc. | To 2040 | $25 | JH

Foudre Ferment Great Western Riesling 2020 One of those pure genius moments where the winemaker decides to break in a new foudre intended for red winemaking, with a riesling. The rest is history. Fermentation and maturation on lees in large-format oak broadens the reach of riesling. It's not oaky – it's textural, and fruit characters become way more concentrated: lime cordial, green apple, orange peel. You may never look at riesling in the same way again. Screw cap | 12% alc. | To 2030 | $35 | JP

LSV Great Western Shiraz 2019 Co-fermented with a small amount of viognier, elevating this wine into deliberate Rhône-like territory, the maker admitting to be inspired by the wines of the Old World. This is one decadent, spiced-up, juicy, red-hearted shiraz, pulsing in energy. Bush mint, pepper, anise, red and black cherry, dried raspberry aromas. A light savouriness enhances what is one impressive wine. Screw cap | 14% alc. | To 2032 | $35 | JP

Great Western Cabernet Sauvignon 2019 Comes fully formed into the world in every respect, and ready to go. So composed and nicely poised with cassis, black olive, plum, well-measured oak and ripe, supple tannins. Hosts a serious density, too, which adds up to one stunning wine for the price. Screw cap | 14.5% alc. | To 2034 | $25 | JP | ♥

larnette & Ludvigsen Wines

'0 Westgate Road, Armstrong, Vic 3377 **T** 0409 083 833 **www**.clarnette-ludvigsen.com.au
EN By appt **WINEMAKER** Leigh Clarnette **EST.** 2003 **DOZENS** 400 **VYDS** 15.5ha

inemaker Leigh Clarnette and viticulturist Kym Ludvigsen's career paths crossed in late 1993 hen both were working for Seppelt. They met again in 2005 when both were employed by altarni. The premature death of Kym in '13 was widely reported, in no small measure due to is (unpaid) service on wine industry bodies. With next generations on both sides, the plans re to continue the business.

5 **Grampians Riesling 2020** The C&L style, so zesty and lively, remains on top form, as ever. Billson's lime cordial, lemon drop, talc and pear sorbet aromas. Fruit tingle brightness, zingy and citrus-infused, moves across the palate aided by rapier-like acidity. Another reason not to ignore Grampians riesling. Screw cap | 12% alc. | To 2027 | $28 | JP | ♥

Kimbarra Wines ★★★★

422 Barkly Street, Ararat, Vic 3377 **T** 0428 519 195 **www**.kimbarrawines.com.au **OPEN** By appt
WINEMAKER Peter Leeke, Justin Purser, Adam Richardson **EST**. 1990 **DOZENS** 180 **VYDS** 11ha

Peter Leeke has 8.5ha of shiraz, 1.5ha of riesling and 1ha of cabernet sauvignon – varieties th have proven best suited to the Grampians region. The particularly well-made, estate-grown wines deserve a wider audience.

95 **Great Western Shiraz 2019** Once again a challenging vintage has seen well-grown fruit shine, boasting highish alcohols that nevertheless present a pretty harmonious whole. Deep colour, trace of bush mint and sage, black cherry, ripe plum, dark chocolate. A fleshy, smooth middle palate finishes taut. Screw cap | 14.6% alc. | To 2029 | $30 | JP

94 **Great Western Riesling 2020** This is one serious riesling, with a penetrating steeliness common to the rieslings of Great Western. A solid core of lemon zest, lime cordial, kaffir lime leaf – tight and coiled – is at the heart of this wines. A good sign for a bright future. It hasn't finished showing us what it's got, not by a long shot. Screw cap | 12% alc. | To 2030 | $30 | JP

Miners Ridge  

135 Westgate Rd, Armstrong, Vic 3377 **T** 0438 039 727 **www**.minersridge.com.au **OPEN** By appt
WINEMAKER Adam Richardson **EST**. 2000 **DOZENS** 450

Andrew and Katrina Toomey established Miners Ridge Wines in 2000 after many years growing grapes in the Great Western region for other wineries. They decided to take small parcels of their finest fruit and craft a range of wines to reflect their 17ha vineyard site at Armstrong, enlisting experienced local winemaker Adam Richardson (ATR Wines) as their contract winemaker. (JP)

95 **A.T. Grampians Shiraz 2018** Comes with an impressive wine show record at the 2020 Western Victorian Wine Challenge picking up trophy for Best Shiraz, Best Single Vineyard Wine of Show and Best Wine of Show. Ripe loganberry, black cherry, bakery spices, chocolate, dusty oak with an almost quiet restraint and finesse. Carries its 14.5% alcohol very well. Integrated tannins, velvety in texture and with a long finish. Wine of the show indeed! Screw cap | To 2031 | $35 | JP

Mount Langi Ghiran Vineyards  

80 Vine Road, Bayindeen, Vic 3375 **T** (03) 5354 3207 **www**.langi.com.au **OPEN** 7 days 10-5
WINEMAKER Adam Louder, Darren Rathbone **EST**. 1969 **DOZENS** 45000 **VYDS** 65ha

A maker of outstanding cool-climate peppery shiraz, crammed with flavour and vinosity, and very good cabernet sauvignon. The shiraz has long pointed the way for cool-climate example of the variety. Wine quality is exemplary.

95 **Cliff Edge Grampians Shiraz 2019** A range of clones lend character to the delicious complexity in this wine. You have to wonder about their powerful role. Deep, dense purple. A beautifully elegant expression of concentrated spice, pepper and black-hearted shiraz. Revels in lifted aromatics of violet and woodsy spice, anise and chocolate, with a surge of fine tannins and vanillan oak through to the finish. Screw cap | 14.5% alc. | To 2032 | $35 | JP

Cliff Edge Grampians Cabernet Sauvignon Merlot 2019 The cabernet comes off old vines planted in 1974 in Great Western and, wow, what a contribution they make! Brilliant, deep-hued purple. A powerfully good aroma of concentrated fruit and spice: blackberry, boysenberry, musky sweet aromatics, pepper and violets. It resonates across the tongue, the 2 grapes in complete unison. Tannins run deep but fine, through to the finish. Screw cap | 14.5% alc. | To 2032 | $35 | JP

Norton Estate 

758 Plush Hannans Road, Lower Norton, Vic 3401 **T** (03) 5384 8235 **www**.nortonestate.com.au
OPEN Fri-Sun & public hols 11-4 **WINEMAKER** Best's Wines **EST**. 1997 **DOZENS** 1200 **VYDS** 5.66ha

In 1996 the Spence family purchased a rundown farm at Lower Norton and, rather than looking to the traditional wool, meat and wheat markets, trusted their instincts and planted vines on the elevated, frost-free, buckshot rises. The vineyard is halfway between the Grampians and Mt Arapiles, 6km northwest of the Grampians region, and has to be content with Western Victoria, but the wines show regional Grampians character and style.

94 **Arapiles Run Shiraz 2019** Wears its Grampians regional identity proudly with prominent spice – cinnamon, nutmeg, bay leaf and pepper – which is well suited to the ripe, sweet-berried fruit. The palate is lively, brisk in tannin and juicy. Should age a treat. Screw cap | 14% alc. | To 2029 | $30 | JP

he Story Wines ★★★★★

0 Riverend Road, Bangholme, Vic 3175 **T** 0411 697 912 **www.thestory.com.au** **WINEMAKER** Rory Lane
r. 2004 **DOZENS** 2500

ver the years I have come across winemakers with degrees in atomic science, doctors with
ecialties spanning every human condition, town planners, sculptors and painters; Rory Lane
lds yet another to the list: a degree in ancient Greek literature. He says that after completing
s degree and 'desperately wanting to delay an entry into the real world, I stumbled across
d enrolled in a postgraduate wine technology and marketing course at Monash University,
here I soon became hooked on ... the wondrous connection between land, human
d liquid'.

R. Lane Vintners Westgate Vineyard Grampians Syrah 2019 The winemaker says this wine represents 'the best that I can do.' In 2019 the season was warm and yields were lower than usual. There are many layers of sometimes-intricate winemaking involved here and it shows. This is a most complex tale of syrah. Enjoy the unravelling that is ahead of you; dark and brooding fruit, tastes of the earth, fields of wildflowers, with savoury touches and rich in Grampians super-spice. It's all here. Screw cap | 13.5% alc. | To 2034 | $75 | JP

Grampians Marsanne Roussanne Viognier 2018 This is a beauty. Pretty, aromatic marsanne leads the way (a nice change from viognier) and sets the tone of spring blossom, jasmine, white musk, peach and pear. The palate is concentrated and textural, yet dances in bright acidity. Sensitive winemaking on display right here. Screw cap | 12.5% alc. | To 2026 | $30 | JP

Hyrdra Grampians Syrah 2019 This is another strong Grampians example of the breed (shiraz) with the addition of 10% grenache. Bursts out of the blocks, so fresh and arresting in tantalising spice and bright red/black berries. Keeps the pulse racing on the palate with a vibrancy and density of fruit, with restrained oak. Can imagine it settling down for a long time in bottle. Screw cap | 13.5% alc. | To 2029 | $30 | JP

Grampians Grenache 2019 As winemaker Rory Lane comments, late-ripening grenache is a recent arrival in the Grampians, warmer vintages opening the door. This has a perfumed bouquet of rose petals, violets and powder puff, the palate rapier-like with its savoury clothing of wild strawberry fruits. Screw cap | 13.5% alc. | To 2029 | $30 | JH

Super G Grampians Grenache Syrah Mourvèdre 2020 45/40/15% grenache/syrah/mourvèdre. A nod to the future stars of the Grampians, in addition to syrah. Complex, with the 3 varieties complementing each other beautifully here. In keeping with the vibrancy of fruit and lifted, aromatic style of the maker. Plush red cherry, dark plum cake and violets combine forces with an earthy, dried herb and spicy intensity. It's a powerful mix, but understated. This wine is still in building mode. Screw cap | 13.5% alc. | To 2030 | $30 | JP | ♥

4 **Whitlands Close Planted Riesling 2019** Some (bright) colour pickup suggests good fruit flavours, and so it has. Acidity, the result of the vineyard's 800m elevation, is balanced by RS. It's an easy wine to enjoy. Screw cap | 12.5% alc. | To 2027 | $30 | JH

GION

Henty

rawford River Wines

41 Hotspur Upper Road, Condah, Vic 3303 **T** (03) 5578 2267 **www.crawfordriverwines.com**
PEN By appt **WINEMAKER** John and Belinda Thomson **EST.** 1975 **DOZENS** 3000 **VYDS** 11ha

nce a tiny outpost in a little-known wine region, Crawford River is now a foremost producer
f riesling (and other excellent wines), originally thanks to the unremitting attention to detail
nd skill of its founder and winemaker, John Thomson. His eldest daughter Belinda has worked
longside her father part-time from '04–11 (full-time between June '05–08) and has been chief
inemaker since '12. Younger daughter Fiona is in charge of sales and marketing.

6 **Riesling 2020** Hard to believe this complex, astounding riesling is so, so, very young. It comes fully formed, in balance, bursting with freshness, purity of varietal expression and beautiful fruit. And, yes, by usual standards it is riper, with stone fruits joining lemon drop, grapefruit and baked apple. But it brings added complexity and texture, which joins with a tingly acidity to produce something memorable. Screw cap | 13.5% alc. | To 2030 | $48 | JP

5 **Young Vines Riesling 2020** So youthful, so fresh in a squeezed juice kind of way. Lemon jelly crystals, lemon drop, grapefruit pith, orange peel, lime blossom, in scent and on the palate. Nice texture in building phase. But, as usual, the co-star with equal billing in this production is the crunchy, tangy acidity. Screw cap | 13.5% alc. | To 2031 | $35 | JP

Henty Estate

657 Hensley Park Road, Hamilton, Vic 3300 (postal) **T** 0458 055 860 **www**.henty-estate.com.au
WINEMAKER Michael Hilsdon **EST.** 1991 **DOZENS** 1400 **VYDS** 7ha

Peter and Glenys Dixon hastened slowly with Henty Estate. In 1991 they began the planting of shiraz, cabernet sauvignon, chardonnay and riesling. In their words, 'we avoided the temptation to make wine until the vineyard was mature', establishing the winery in 2003. Michael Hilsdon and Matilda McGoon purchased Henty Estate in 2018, their first vintage in '1

95 **Hamilton Chardonnay 2020** Henty Estate is establishing a name for its chardonnay, such is its elegance and Chablis-like presence. Looking smart just months after vintage, with energy in the glass and the arresting aromas of nougat, white flowers, lemon zest and straw. Firm acidity across the palate, grapefruit pith, citrus skin, apple, but a growing, warming spice, too. Mineral tang to close. A natural beauty. Screw cap | 12.4% alc. | To 2028 | $30 | JP

Jackson Brooke

126 Beaconsfield Parade, Northcote, Vic 3070 (postal) **T** 0466 652 485 **www**.jacksonbrookewine.com.a
WINEMAKER Jackson Brooke **EST.** 2013 **DOZENS** 500

Jackson Brooke studied oenology at Lincoln University in NZ. A vintage at Wedgetail Estate in the Yarra Valley was followed by stints in Japan, Southern California and then 3 years as assistant winemaker to Ben Portet. With his accumulated knowledge of boutique winemakin he has abandoned any idea of building a winery for the foreseeable future, currently renting space at Witchmount Estate.

95 **Henty Chardonnay 2019** Cool-climate Henty presents a petite, fine-boned body upon which to bui a chardonnay. The maker shows a deft hand with oak, not overpowering the subtlety but working alongside it. Impressive fruit purity of citrus, green plum, spiced apple, almond-meal aromas. Smooth and supple across the palate with creamy fruit flavours, pear and crunchy acidity. Of the less-is-more school of chardonnay. Screw cap | 12.5% alc. | To 2027 | $28 | JP

REGION

Pyrenees

DogRock Winery

114 Degraves Road, Crowlands, Vic 3377 **T** 0409 280 317 **www**.dogrock.com.au **OPEN** By appt
WINEMAKER Allen Hart **EST.** 1998 **DOZENS** 1000 **VYDS** 6.2ha

This is the venture of Allen (now full-time winemaker) and Andrea (viticulturist) Hart. Given Allen's former post as research scientist/winemaker with Foster's, the attitude taken to winemaking is unexpected. The estate-grown wines are made in a low-tech fashion, without gas cover or filtration; the Harts say, 'All wine will be sealed with a screw cap and no DogRock wine will ever be released under natural cork bark'. DogRock installed the first solar-powered irrigation system in Australia, capable of supplying water 365 days a year, even at night or in cloudy conditions.

95 **Pyrenees Shiraz 2019** Makes an immediate impact with deep inky hues and intensity of aromas and flavour. Resolutely a Pyrenees shiraz with trademark notes of pepper, Aussie bush and menthol. A very warm growing season has brought out a glorious array of ripe black fruits, heady spice and a relative richness matched with toasty, chocolatey oak and supple tannins. For now or later. Screw cap | 13.5% alc. | To 2032 | $30 | JP

Pyrenees Cabernet Sauvignon Shiraz 2019 A 60/40% blend matured for 10 months in French oak (40% new). A brightly coloured, medium-bodied wine with a mix of red and black fruits, spices and fine tannins that have almost casually absorbed the contribution of new oak. The low alcohol is all good. Screw cap | 12.5% alc. | To 2030 | $30 | JH

altarni  ★★★★★

9 Taltarni Road, Moonambel, Vic 3478 **T** (03) 5459 7900 **WWW**.taltarni.com.au **OPEN** 7 days 11-5
NEMAKER Robert Heywood, Peter Warr, Ben Howell **EST.** 1969 **DOZENS** 80000 **VYDS** 78.5ha

ltarni is the largest of the Australian Goelet Wine Estates ventures, its estate vineyards of eat value and underpinning the substantial annual production. Insectariums are established permanent vegetation corridors, each containing around 2000 native plants that provide ollen and nectar source for the beneficial insects, reducing the need for chemicals and ner controls of the vineyards.

Old Vine Estate Pyrenees Cabernet Sauvignon 2018 Harks back to some of the glorious cabernets of the 80s, with strong regional and varietal clarity, complexity and structure. Shows just how exciting the grape can be in a region dominated by shiraz. Densely coloured, with a roaming bouquet of dark plums, cassis, black cherries and subtle, spicy oak. Intense and concentrated, fine and long in tannic energy. Wow! Screw cap | 14% alc. | To 2032 | $45 | JP | ♥

Western Australia

10784ha | 5 zones | 9 regions

Technically Western Australia has five zones, but only two have vineyards: Greater Perth and South West Australia.

The Greater Perth zone has three regions. **Peel** has shiraz as the leader, cabernet sauvignon next, then verdelho and chardonnay, all wines that are medium-bodied and immediately approachable. The **Swan District** has a very unusual split between red and white varieties. Instead of the usual more than 65% reds, less than 35% whites, here the varieties that made Houghton Blue Stripe White Burgundy the largest-selling white wine in the early 1980s see chenin blanc in pole position, followed by verdelho, chardonnay and semillon.

The South West Australia zone accounts for the remainder of Western Australia's output. It has six regions, with one, **Great Southern**, having five subregions: Albany, Denmark, Frankland River, Mount Barker and Porongurup. Tony Smith, founder of Plantagenet and for long a leading figure in WA's fine-wine scene, makes no secret in regretting that these subregions are responsible for more fine wine than the other five regions.

Great Southern has shiraz way out in front, reflecting its nigh-on magical blend of intense varietal fruit expression, tannin-derived texture and structure, balance and length, all within medium-bodied freshness. What is bewildering is riesling, equal fifth with semillon, both representing just a small proportion of plantings. Porongurup, Frankland River and Mount Barker make lissom riesling of world class. Cabernet sauvignon shares the purity that is also part of riesling's character. Albany and Denmark complete the mosaic.

Margaret River produced just under two-thirds of the state's 2021 crush, thanks first to majestic cabernet sauvignon, then sauvignon blanc, semillon, sumptuous chardonnay and shiraz, merlot and chenin blanc. **Geographe** has as its neighbours Peel to the northeast, **Blackwood Valley** to the southeast, the northern tip of Margaret River on its southeastern corner, and the Indian Ocean, its entire eastern boundary. Diminutive **Manjimup** is dominated by pinot gris/grigio (making up more than half of plantings), the remainder split between pinot noir and chardonnay. Nearby **Pemberton** is a two-horse race with sauvignon blanc and chardonnay.

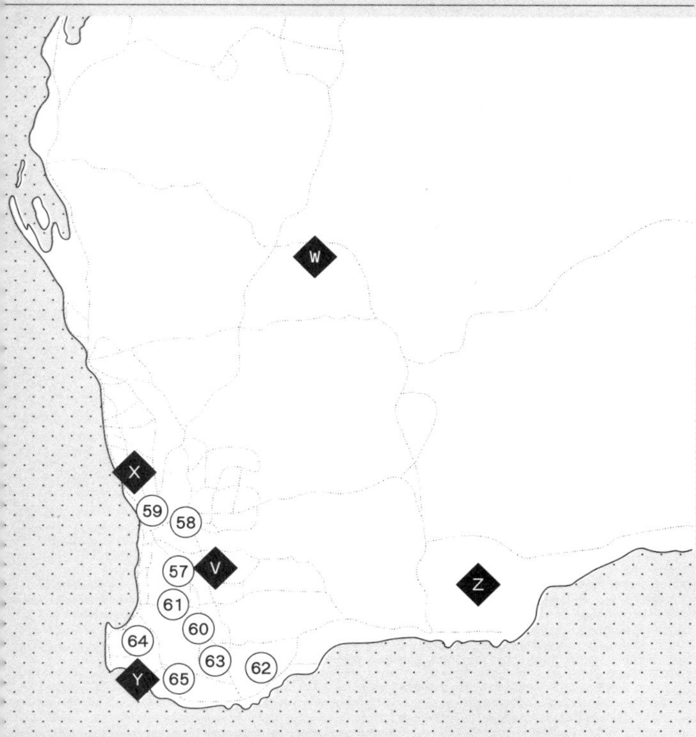

ZONE	REGION
V Central Western Australia	
W Eastern Plains, Inland and North of Western Australia	
X Greater Perth	57 Peel
	58 Perth Hills
	59 Swan District
Y South West Australia	60 Blackwood Valley
	61 Geographe
	62 Great Southern
	63 Manjimup
	64 Margaret River
	65 Pemberton
Z West Australian South East Coastal	

Battles Wine

★★★★

77 Aitken Drive, Winthrop, WA 6150 (postal) **T** 0434 399 964 **www**.battleswine.com.au
WINEMAKER Lance Parkin **EST.** 2018 **DOZENS** 850

Battles Wine was started by friends Lance Parkin (winemaker) and Kris Ambrozkiewicz (sommelier, sales) in 2019. Battles focuses on a small collection of tiny-quantity wines from a variety of regions (at this stage, Margaret River, the Great Southern and Geographe) made with great attention to detail, and vineyard provenance top of mind. (EL)

96 **Frankland River Shiraz 2020** Spiced mulberry, pomegranate, raspberry, red licorice and pink peppercorn. Szechuan spice, star anise and bucketloads of berries. This is a fete. A party. It's epic It could do with another year in bottle to help things settle down, but the pedigree of tannin and structure inherent in this wine, along with fruit weight and density, shows it will go the distance ar then some. Welcome to WA's new-breed shiraz. It's happening. Screw cap | 14.2% alc. | To 204 $50 | EL

Risky Business Wines

PO Box 6015, East Perth, WA 6892 **T** 0457 482 957 **www**.riskybusinesswines.com.au
WINEMAKER Andrew Vesey **EST.** 2013 **DOZENS** 8900

The name Risky Business is decidedly tongue-in-cheek because the partnership headed by Rob Quenby has neatly side-stepped any semblance of risk. The grapes come from vineyar in Great Southern and Margaret River that are managed by Quenby Viticultural Services. Since the batches of wine are small, the partnership is able to select grapes specifically suit to the wine style and price. So there is no capital tied up in vineyards, nor in a winery – the wines are contract-made.

95 **King Valley Prosecco NV** So easy to get to love. Simple enjoyment assured with delicious lemon sorbet, citrus, fresh cut apple and harmonious slurpy, bright acidity. Does the grape proud. Crown seal | 10.5% alc. | To 2023 | $25 | JP

94 **Margaret River Cabernet Sauvignon 2019** The 2019 vintage will forever fall in the shadow of the exceptional 2018, however many of the cabernets that have presented themselves over the past 6–12 months of releases have shown an energy, a structure and a distinct blackness that speaks volumes about their inherent quality. This is no exception. It possesses all the beauty and intrigue that the '19 cabernets exhibit, and it finishes with a long tendril of luscious, ripe, pure cassis fruit. Quite beautiful, and certainly impressive for the price. Screw cap | 14.5% alc. | To 2031 | $25 |

Frankland River Shiraz Tempranillo Grenache 2019 Quite delicious – juicy, almost slurpy, and with an abundance of red berries. Chalky tannins shape the back palate, and guide it through the finish Better-than-average pizza wine. Find it. Screw cap | 14.5% alc. | To 2027 | $25 | EL

ZONE

Greater Perth

REGION

Perth Hills

MyattsField Vineyards

Union Road, Carmel Valley, WA 6076 **T** (08) 9293 5567 **www**.myattsfield.com.au **OPEN** Fri–Sun & public hols 11–5 **WINEMAKER** Josh Davenport, Rachael Davenport, Josh Uren **EST.** 1997 **DOZENS** 4000 **VYDS** 4.5ha

MyattsField Vineyards is owned by Josh and Rachael Davenport. Both have oenology degree and domestic and Flying Winemaker experience, especially Rachael. In 2006 they decided they would prefer to work for themselves. They left their employment, building a winery in time for the '07 vintage.

95 **Durif 2019** A flamboyantly full-bodied wine, with a consistent drive and evolution of flavour over the palate; morphing from black cherries laced with bitter chocolate, through to blood plum, salte licorice and a host of other flavours. The tannins are plump and chewy and while very present, they provide structure and direction. The alcohol is fully entrenched and as such, imperceptible. Screw cap | 15% alc. | To 2036 | $30 | EL

94 **Vermentino 2020** Crunchy, crisp and frisky, with plenty of go. Nashi pear, saline acid and a cleansi finish come together to create this decidedly Euro-style vermentino. You know when a wine takes you places in your mind that it's doing its job well. Screw cap | 13.4% alc. | To 2023 | $22 | EL

wan District

orymbia

Nolan Avenue, Upper Swan, WA 6069 **T** 0439 973 195 **www**.corymbiawine.com.au **OPEN** By appt
EMAKER Robert Mann, Genevieve Mann **EST.** 2013 **DOZENS** 900 **VYDS** 3.5ha

ɔ Mann is a 6th-generation winemaker from the second-oldest wine region in stralia. He was chief winemaker at Cape Mentelle in Margaret River, where he and wife nevieve lived. Between them they now have 2 children and 3.5ha in Margaret River d the Swan Valley, planted to 1.6ha chenin blanc, 0.4ha tempranillo, 0.2ha malbec and ha cabernet sauvignon.

Margaret River Cabernet Sauvignon 2019 Luminescent ruby with glints of purple and black. It shines as if with its own dense internal light. The telltale ripe and chewy tannin profile handled masterfully by Rob Mann, with pristine fruit and great length of flavour. An exceptionally elegant, powder-fine cabernet, part of the new Margaret River breed. A massive, resounding YES. Screw cap | 13.3% alc. | To 2035 | $64 | EL

Swan Valley Chenin Blanc 2020 Fruit from Rocket's vineyard. This is pure, pristine, texturally edgy, and layered with all the good things: sheepy lanolin, beeswax, apricots at the height of summer, green apple, crushed limestone and saline acidity. It has rivulets of flavour that course over the tongue ... it's brilliant. Finesse and poise from such a warm part of town, very impressive. Screw cap | 12.5% alc. | To 2036 | $30 | EL

ber Vineyard

Haddrill Road, Baskerville, WA 6056 **T** (08) 9296 0209 **www**.fabervineyard.com.au
N Fri-Sun 11-4 **WINEMAKER** John Griffiths **EST.** 1997 **DOZENS** 4000 **VYDS** 4.5ha

n Griffiths, former Houghton winemaker, teamed with wife Jane Micallef to found Faber eyard. John says, 'It may be somewhat quixotic, but I'm a great fan of traditional warm-area stralian wine styles, wines made in a relatively simple manner that reflect the concentrated e flavours one expects in these regions. And when one searches, some of these gems can found from the Swan Valley.'

Swan Valley Liqueur Muscat NV What a glorious wine this is. Extraordinarily opulent. It has a core of salted dried fig, bitter orange and quince that together showcase the heat of the Swan Valley sunshine. After all of that ... the finish is cleansing. Layer upon layer of flavour and texture. Cork | 18% alc. | $60 | EL

Swan Valley Grenache 2020 Swan Valley grenache is a beautiful thing. Raspberry humbugs, red licorice and apple skins form the foundation of this wine. On the palate it is sinewy and muscular (not a tautology in this instance); the tannins have a shapely finesse through the finish. Excellent grenache from a warm climate – where it belongs. Screw cap | 14.5% alc. | To 2030 | $27 | EL

Riche Swan Valley Shiraz 2020 The fruit is vibrant and lifted and layered with red fruits and licorice root. The oak has a surprisingly restrained impact on the wine at this time, however it will likely settle in and spread out its sweet wings with further time in the bottle. Quite delicious, with a distinct clove, red licorice, and aniseed character woven through the finish. Screw cap | 13.5% alc. | To 2031 | $27 | EL

hn Kosovich Wines

Memorial Avenue/Great Northern Highway, Baskerville, WA 6056 **T** (08) 9296 4356
w.johnkosovichwines.com.au **OPEN** Wed-Mon 10-4.30 **WINEMAKER** Anthony Kosovich **EST.** 1922
ENS 2000 **VYDS** 10.9ha

Kosovich family, headed by Jack Kosovich and his brothers, immigrated from Croatia rtly before the outbreak of World War I. After cutting railway sleepers in the southwest of and thereafter in the goldmines of Kalgoorlie, Jack purchased the property in 1922; the t vines planted in that year still grace the entrance to the winery. In 1995, Jack's son John came a member of the Order of Australia for his long contribution to the wine industry l in '04 won the prestigious Jack Mann Medal for services to the WA wine industry; in the ne year the winery won the trophy for Best WA Small Producer at the Perth Royal Wine ow. Son Anthony (Arch) took over the winemaking and is looking forward to the 100-year iversary in '22.

97 **Bottle Aged Reserve Swan Valley Chenin Blanc 2015** Toasty and complex, with cheesecloth, savo preserved lemon, toasted/crushed nuts, apricot, sheepy lanolin and jasmine tea. This is an ever-evolving wine of depth and intensity. I can write long after the wine has been swallowed. For min it seems ... Screw cap | 13% alc. | To 2036 | $48 | EL | ♥

Mandoon Estate ★★★★

10 Harris Road, Caversham, WA 6055 **T** (08) 6279 0500 **www**.mandoonestate.com.au **OPEN** 7 days 10
WINEMAKER Ryan Sudano, Lauren Pileggi **EST.** 2009 **DOZENS** 10000 **VYDS** 50ha

Mandoon Estate, headed by Allan Erceg, made a considerable impression with its wines in a very short time. In 2008 the family purchased a site in Caversham in the Swan Valley. Construction of the winery was completed in time for the first vintage in '10. Winemaker Ry Sudano has metaphorically laid waste to Australian wine shows with the quality of the wines he has made from the Swan Valley, Frankland River and Margaret River.

96 **Reserve Margaret River Chardonnay 2019** Salty, saline, fine and yet rich, all the beauty of Margar River chardonnay in a sentence (and a glass). Really good length of flavour, the acidity giving a ta jolt of excitement that pierces the heart of the ripe orchard fruit. The cooler '19 vintage has birthe a wine of nuance and restraint, both of which look good here. Screw cap | 13% alc. | To 2036 | $59 | EL

95 **Old Vine Shiraz 2018** At below $30 this is an unassailable proposition. Justifies Swan Valley's reputation for old-vine shiraz. Great depth and intensity of flavour, which in the hands of Ryan Sudano is also coupled with restraint. A core of berry fruits is ensconced in spice, cooling acid ar clever oak handling. Don't miss it. Screw cap | 14.5% alc. | To 2030 | $30 | EL

Old Vine Grenache 2019 If you don't get excited by the prospect of Swan Valley grenache, we ne to talk. In the hands of winemaker Ryan Sudano, this is possessed of both supple, bouncy raspbe fruit, and muscular, structuring tannins. The wine in the mouth is frankly delicious, and wears its alcohol with ease. On reflection, there is a jasmine tea note on the palate that is very attractive, to Likely a long life ahead of it. Gold medal Swan Valley Wine Show '20. Screw cap | 14.5% alc. | To 2032 | $30 | EL

94 **Margaret River Sauvignon Blanc 2020** Pungent aromas of Cape gooseberry, cassis, juniper and sprinklings of exotic spice to boot. The fine phenolics create interest and direction, steering the wine through the long finish. Screw cap | 12.5% alc. | To 2025 | $23 | EL

Block 1895 Verdelho 2020 From the oldest verdelho block in WA, planted in 1895 by the Roe fami A touch of sweat and funk on the nose, but the palate is tight as a drum. Lean and savoury citrus characters underpinned by white pepper and spice. Passionfruit. The finish draws out into a linge a curl and a waft. Lovely stuff. Lyrical, almost. Screw cap | 13% alc. | To 2031 | $28 | EL

Old Vine Grenache 2018 Fruit from the Sita vineyard planted 1955. Matured in seasoned French oak. Savoury and structured, this has redcurrants, raspberry and mulberry, with licorice and fenn through the finish. More muscular and gnarly than it is juicy and sweet, this is an altogether more serious grenache than many. Screw cap | 14.5% alc. | To 2028 | $30 | EL

Surveyors Red 2018 Grenache, syrah, mataro. Sweet berry fruits and satsuma plum on the nose lead the way for the flavours in the mouth, which obediently follow suit. Supple tannins create shape on the palate. This is a spicy, delicious and satisfying rendition of the blend. Definitely wort crossing the road for. Screw cap | 14.5% alc. | To 2030 | $28 | EL

Nikola Estate ★★★

148 Dale Road, Middle Swan, WA 6056 **T** (08) 9374 8050 **www**.nikolaestate.com.au
OPEN Thurs-Mon 10-5 **WINEMAKER** Damien Hutton, Daniel Charter **EST.** 2019 **VYDS** 56ha

While the Nikola brand may be new to the Swan Valley, the Yukich family behind it is anythin but. In 2019, Houghton Estate in the Swan Valley (vineyards, historic cellar door, est. 1836, a the winemaking facility) was purchased by brothers Graeme and Kim Yukich (3rd generatio from the private equity Carlyle Group, forming what is now the Nikola Estate. Winemaker Damian Hutton has moved from a long history at Millbrook (Fogarty Group) to assume the mantle at Nikola. (EL)

94 **Verdelho 2020** Fruit from the Swan Valley (as the oldest wine region in WA, and the first place tha verdelho was planted, this should proudly be on the front label!). Fresh and pure, this has lashings of nashi pear, exotic white spice, cooling saline acid and an irrepressibly silky texture. A lot to love here. Screw cap | 12% alc. | To 2027 | $25 | EL

Tempranillo 2020 Succulent yet tannic, this has brilliant length of flavour, confirming the multilayered approach of the palate. Raspberry, cassis, tobacco leaf, sage, pepper, jasmine tea and blueberries. Very impressive. Screw cap | 14.5% alc. | To 2031 | $30 | EL

akover Wines  ★★★★

'ukich Close, Middle Swan, WA 6056 **T** (08) 9374 8000 **www**.oakoverwines.com.au
Wed-Sun 11-4 **WINEMAKER** Daniel Charter **EST.** 1929 **DOZENS** 15000 **VYDS** 27ha

minent Perth funds manager Graeme Yukich and his family have been involved in the Swan ey region since Nicholas Yukich purchased his first block of land in 1929. In 2002 Oakover ate became Oakover Wines and is now the 3rd-largest winery in the Swan Valley. Oakover's ite Label brand is currently sold in over 500 independent liquor outlets in WA and Vic, with ansion into NSW and Qld planned.

Shiraz 2019 70/30% Perth Hills/Swan Valley. As expected, this is juicy, vibrant and energetic with a smooth core of purple fruits wrapped in spicy tannin. There is a lot of pleasure here for the price. Screw cap | 14% alc. | To 2026 | $16 | EL

ul Conti Wines 

Wanneroo Road, Woodvale, WA 6026 **T** (08) 9409 9160 **www**.paulcontiwines.com.au
Tues-Sat 11-5 **WINEMAKER** Jason Conti **EST.** 1948 **DOZENS** 4000 **VYDS** 11ha

rd-generation winemaker Jason Conti has assumed control of winemaking, although ner Paul (who succeeded his own father in 1968) remains involved in the business. Over the rs Paul challenged and redefined industry perceptions and standards. The challenge for on is to achieve the same degree of success in a relentlessly and increasingly competitive rket environment, and he is doing just that.

Lorenza Sparkling Chenin Blanc NV Pretty and floral – all the lovely chenin-y things are there; lanolin, citrus fruits, summer apricots and waxy texture. The phenolics are fine and serve to cradle the fruit, contributing to the already plump mouthfeel. Fabulous aperitif-style chenin. Cork | 12.5% alc. | $25 | EL

Tuart Block Chenin Blanc 2020 Pure and fine, the palate has a satisfying textural complexity before extending into the long finish. Overall, this is almost simple in its expression of chenin, but absolutely true to the variety. White pepper through the finish. Trophy Swan Valley Wine Show 2020. Screw cap | 13.5% alc. | To 2030 | $18 | EL

verBank Estate  

Hamersley Road, Caversham, WA 6055 **T** (08) 9377 1805 **www**.riverbankestate.com.au **OPEN** 7 days
5 **WINEMAKER** Digby Leddin **EST.** 1988 **DOZENS** 4500 **VYDS** 12ha

erBank Estate was first planted on the fertile banks of the Swan River in 1988 and has own to encompass 12ha of mature, low-yielding vines (18 varieties), the wines made onsite. e property was purchased by the Lembo family in 2017 and has been rebranded into 3 wine ges: On The Run, Rebellious and Eric Anthony. RiverBank was named Winery of the Year 19 by Ray Jordan and Best Small Cellar Door in the Swan Valley 2019 by Peter Forrestal *Gourmet Traveller*.

Eric Anthony Swan Valley Shiraz 2018 Highly aromatic forest fruits, blood plum and star anise. The palate is medium bodied, fleshy and supple, with fine tannins and great length. Not strictly classical in style, but not exactly modern, either. A lovely wine. Gold medal Blackwood Valley and WA Boutique wine shows '20. Screw cap | 14.7% alc. | To 2030 | $35 | EL

ttella Wines  

Barrett Street, Herne Hill, WA 6056 **T** (08) 9296 2600 **www**.sittella.com.au **OPEN** Tues-Sun &
lic hols 11-5 **WINEMAKER** Colby Quirk, Yuri Berns **EST.** 1998 **DOZENS** 15000 **VYDS** 25ha

non and Maaike Berns acquired a 7ha block (with 5ha of vines) at Herne Hill, making the first ne in 1998 and opening a most attractive cellar door facility. They also own the Wildberry ate Vineyard in Margaret River. Consistent and significant wine show success has brought ll deserved recognition for the wines.

A-G Rare Series Golden Mile Swan Valley Grenache 2020 Boiled raspberry lolly on the nose; both muscular and fine on the palate, with layers of salted blackberry, rosewater, strawberry pastille and red licorice. The Swan Valley GI gives a real tannic grunt to the finish, saving it from 'pretty' and elevating it to serious. Screw cap | 13.5% alc. | To 2036 | $50 | EL

Pedro Ximénez NV Rich and dense this is mini (tiny bottle) yet mighty. Luscious quince and dried fig are slathered upon nutmeg, date, toffee and crushed coffee grounds. The rancio characters that provide bitter foil to the sweetness on the palate serve only to engage and draw you back in for more. An astoundingly delicious wine of poise and stature. Length, too. 350ml. Screw cap | 18.5% alc. | $50 | EL

95 **Cuvée Rosé Brut NV** Disgorged 21 Mar '20. Rose petals, strawberry, red apple skins and pink peppercorn are overlaid by very fine market spice and curls of saffron. The fine acidity weaves th chalky phenolics and the fruit together. All in all, extremely classy, and clearly one of, if not the, greatest sparkling rosé in Western Australia released to date. Cork | 12.5% alc. | $34 | EL | ♥

Upper Reach

77 Memorial Avenue, Baskerville, WA 6056 **T** (08) 9296 0078 **WWW**.upperreach.com.au **OPEN** 7 days 11-5 **WINEMAKER** Derek Pearse **EST.** 1996 **DOZENS** 4000 **VYDS** 8.45ha

This 10ha property on the banks of the upper reaches of the Swan River was purchased by Laura Rowe and Derek Pearse in 1996. The RiverBrook Restaurant serves share plates and t cellar door received a string of *Gourmet Traveller WINE* awards between 2013 and 2018.

94 **Swan Valley Verdelho 2020** Concentrated and intense, this has loads of flavour packed in arounc the significant acidity that is coiled on the mid palate. The phenolics create a spicy and textural framework, from which the flavours of nashi pear, Granny Smith apples and white pepper can ha Impressive. Some verdelhos from the Valley are showing well in their older age and this has those hallmarks. Screw cap | 13% alc. | To 2031 | $26 | EL

Vino Volta

184 Anzac Road, Mount Hawthorn, WA 6016 **T** (08) 9374 8050 **WWW**.vinovolta.com.au/ **OPEN** By appt **WINEMAKER** Garth Cliff **EST.** 2018 **DOZENS** 1800

Garth Cliff was winemaker at Houghtons in the Swan Valley for 10 years prior to starting Vino Volta with his partner Kristen McGann in January 2019. Vino Volta largely (although no exclusively) focuses on chenin blanc (they make 4, pushing the grape in 4 different directio and grenache from the Valley. Chenin blanc is in a revival phase currently, much of it thanks to Cliff, culminating in the inaugural nationwide Chenin Blanc Challenge in 2020, held in th Swan Valley. (EL)

95 **Funky And Fearless Swan Valley Chenin Blanc 2019** This has that stern, textural edge that chenin have, plumped out by crushed cashew, native bush blossoms and oyster shell. It's still sheepy, it's layered, and the acidity that weaves in and out of the fruit is salty and very fine. A lot going on he and a beautiful expression of one of the many directions in which chenin will be amiably pushed. Screw cap | 13.5% alc. | To 2031 | $35 | EL

La Chingadera Tempranillo Grenache Touriga 2019 Dense, layered and delicious – this packs pur red fruits in with exotic market spice. The salty and refreshing acidity laces it all together. The tannins are pervasive, but that's OK given the mix of varieties. Long, modern and exciting – anoth win for Vino Volta. Screw cap | 14% alc. | To 2031 | $35 | EL

94 **Nothing Wrong With Old Skool Swan District Chenin Blanc 2020** Super-pretty; Geraldton wax, shaved macadamia, Pink Lady apple, cheesecloth, lanolin, fennel flower and beeswax. The palate follows in exactly this manner, leaving a trail of nashi pear on the tongue. Gorgeous. Screw cap | 12.5% alc. | To 2036 | $30 | EL

Post Modern Seriousism Swan Valley Grenache 2020 This is crunchy and juicy with fine, furry, pervasive tannins that shape the raspberry fruit. The mid palate has an edgy bramble laced throu it, and to top it all off, the Peters Raspberry Freeza finish (best ice cream of all time) is laced with salty, earthy minerality that elevates it from delicious to serious. Ripping example of modern Swan Valley grenache. Screw cap | 13.5% alc. | To 2031 | $30 | EL

ZONE

South West Australia

REGION

Geographe

Aylesbury Estate

72 Ratcliffe Road, Ferguson, WA 6236 **T** 0427 922 755 **WWW**.aylesburyestate.com.au **WINEMAKER** Luke Eckersley, Damian Hutton **EST.** 2015 **DOZENS** 6500 **VYDS** 9ha

Ryan and Narelle Gibbs (and family) are the 6th generation of the pioneering Gibbs family in the Ferguson Valley. When the family first arrived in 1883, they named the farm Aylesbury, r the town in England whence they came. For generations the family ran cattle on the ha property, but in 1998 it was decided to plant grape vines as a diversification of business.

Q05 Ferguson Valley Gamay 2020 Strawberry, red licorice, fennel flower, camphor, ash and red frog lollies. There is enough spicy nuance to make this more interesting than the bright nose suggests, the tannins almost subliminally wedged into the fine structure. The acidity has a real edge and refreshing lift on the palate. This is firmly in the nouveau style, delivering pleasure and smiles all round. Everything about this is well put together: the packaging, the wine and the price. Screw cap | 14% alc. | To 2025 | $30 | EL | ♥

kkheia

Ferguson Road, Lowden, WA 6240 **T** (08) 9732 1394 **www**.bakkheia.com.au **OPEN** By appt
MAKER Michael Edwards **EST.** 2006 **DOZENS** 1000 **VYDS** 3ha

is the retirement venture of Michael and Ilonka Edwards. They have an unusual approach arketing, starting with the winery name, which is linked to the Roman words for Bacchus bacchanalian frenzies induced by wine, lots of wine. When the time came to make and wine, rather than sell through liquor stores, they set up a membership system.

Cojones Muy Grandes Preston Valley Rosé 2020 Organic grenache, cabernet sauvignon and mourvèdre from the Preston Valley. The rosé is both fine and juicy, with plenty of berry fruit and great length of flavour. Cheesecloth, pomegranate, Turkish delight and raspberry humbug. A lot to like. Screw cap | 12.4% alc. | To 2022 | $20 | EL

pel Vale

Mallokup Road, Capel, WA 6271 **T** (08) 9727 1986 **www**.capelvale.com.au **OPEN** 7 days 10-4
MAKER Daniel Hetherington **EST.** 1974 **DOZENS** 21000 **VYDS** 52ha

blished by Perth-based medical practitioner Dr Peter Pratten and wife Elizabeth in 1974. first vineyard adjacent to the winery was planted on the banks of the quiet waters of Capel r. The viticultural empire has since expanded, spreading across Geographe (9ha), Mount er (15ha) and Margaret River (28ha).

Single Vineyard Series Whispering Hill Mount Barker Riesling 2020 With all of the citrus blossom and finesse of the Mount Barker Regional Series Riesling, the game is upped significantly here in the Whispering Hill. The coil of saline acid that is the heart of this wine is surrounded by cushy, plush citrus fruit. The whole package is ripe, structured, long and lean – what a wine! Screw cap | 12% alc. | To 2041 | $33 | EL

een Door Wines

Henty Road, Henty, WA 6236 **T** 0439 511 652 **www**.greendoorwines.com.au **OPEN** Thurs–Sun 11–4.30
MAKER Ashley Keeffe, Vanessa Carson **EST.** 2007 **DOZENS** 1200 **VYDS** 4ha

ey and Kathryn Keeffe purchased what was then a rundown vineyard in '06. With a bination of new and pre-existing vines, the vineyard includes fiano, mourvèdre, grenache, lelho, tempranillo and shiraz. The wines are made in a small onsite winery using a range of emaking methods, including the use of amphora pots.

Amphora Geographe Tempranillo 2019 Characters of beeswax, Geraldton wax florals, Mariposa plum and red licorice all rise to the fore here. This is a pleasure to drink, as previous vintages have been: layered and complex, fine tannins wrap a core of pure fruit, which lingers through the long finish. Screw cap | 14% alc. | To 2030 | $35 | EL

rvey River Estate

d Street, Harvey, WA 6220 **T** (08) 9729 2085 **www**.harveyriverestate.com.au **OPEN** 7 days 10-4
MAKER Stuart Pierce **EST.** 1999 **DOZENS** 20000 **VYDS** 18.5ha

vey River Estate has a long and significant tradition of winemaking in WA's southwest. Its l was established in 1999, the range of popular varietals designed to be enjoyed in the t to medium term including Sauvignon Blanc, Chardonnay, Sauvignon Blanc Semillon, e, Merlot, Shiraz, Cabernet Sauvignon. The fruit for these wines is predominantly from the ly-owned vineyards in Geographe.

95 **Geographe Barbera 2020** With 5% dolcetto. This is delicious. Vibrant red berries, licorice, raspb anise and pomegranate. A faint undercurrent of charcuterie makes it all the more interesting. Fin natural acid takes it from slurpy to crunchy; the phenolics structuring, chalky and imperceptible. A brilliant first release. Screw cap | 14.8% alc. | To 2025 | $30 | EL

Iron Cloud Wines

Suite 16, 18 Stirling Highway, Nedlands, WA 6009 (postal) **T** 0401 860 891
www.ironcloudwines.com.au **WINEMAKER** Michael Ng **EST.** 1999 **DOZENS** 2500 **VYDS** 11ha

In 2003 owners Warwick Lavis and Geoff and Karyn Cross purchased the then-named Pepperilly Estate, which had been planted in 1999 on red gravelly loam soils. Peppermint t line the Henty Brook, the natural water source for the vineyard. In 2017 Michael Ng, former chief winemaker for Rockcliffe, succeeded Coby Ladwig.

95 **Rock of Solitude Ferguson Valley Touriga 2019** As is usual for Iron Cloud Wines, this shows brillia purity of fruit, combined with succulent, chewy tannins that mean the bottle has the propensity evaporate. Good length of favour rounds it all out. Another cracker here; the earthy finish (arnica aniseed, clove, freshly turned earth and satsuma plum) elevates it beyond a delicious, gluggable drink and catapults it into the realm of serious. Screw cap | 14.5% alc. | To 2031 | $32 | EL

94 **Rock of Solitude Ferguson Valley Chardonnay 2020** Majority Dijon clones (95, 96, 277, 76). Hand picked, wild ferment, matured 9 months in French oak (30% new). Impressive winemaking for the price. The clones explain the shape and feel; Dijon acidity is on the citrus spectrum and runs a linear course straight over the palate – often put through some mlf to assist with the acid, which contributes the crushed nut character here. Nectarine, white peach and cashew. Classy. Screw cap | 13.8% alc. | To 2029 | $25 | EL

Pepperilly Ferguson Valley Cabernet Shiraz 2019 This is supple, alive and packed to the rafters with bright, summer raspberry, strawberry, mulberry and red licorice. The tannins are very fine, almost willowy, and gently shape the fruit through the finish. Not complex, but utterly delicious in a nouveau way. Screw cap | 14.5% alc. | To 2025 | $25 | EL

Mandalay Road

254 Mandalay Road, Glen Mervyn via Donnybrook, WA 6239 **T** (08) 9732 2006 www.mandalayroad.com
OPEN 7 days 11-5 **WINEMAKER** Peter Stanlake, John Griffiths **EST.** 1997 **DOZENS** 600 **VYDS** 4.2ha

Tony and Bernice O'Connell left careers in science and education to establish plantings of shiraz, chardonnay, zinfandel and cabernet sauvignon on their property in 1997 (followed b durif). A hands-on approach and low yields have brought out the best characteristics of th grape varieties and the region.

94 **Geographe Durif 2019** Very pretty, floral and saturated in dark forest fruits. The tannins on the pa are soft and shapely, giving the whole thing an air of opulence. The quibble is that it's over soone than is desired, but it is delicious while it lasts. A truly lovely example of the variety. Screw cap | 13.4% alc. | To 2031 | $30 | EL

Mazza Wines

PO Box 480, Donnybrook, WA 6239 **T** (08) 9201 1114 www.mazza.com.au **WINEMAKER** Contract **EST.** 20
DOZENS 1000 **VYDS** 4ha

David and Anne Mazza were inspired by the great wines of Rioja and the Douro Valley, and continue a long-standing family tradition of making wine. They have planted the key varieti of those 2 regions: tempranillo, graciano, bastardo, sousão, tinta cão and touriga nacional. They believe they were the first Australian vineyard to present this collection of varieties or single site and I am reasonably certain they are correct.

96 **Geographe Touriga Nacional 2018** Delicious. Exciting. Savoury, layered and complex, this has oodles of mulberry, blackberry, raspberry and red licorice. It's both salty and sweet, with juicy ac firmly entrenched between the two, providing balance, finesse and depth. Not enough can be sa in favour of this wine. It has great length of flavour, and evolution across the palate, too. A super from a brilliant vintage. Screw cap | 14.5% alc. | To 2031 | $32 | EL

akway Estate ★★★★☆

Farley Road, Donnybrook, WA 6239 **T** (08) 9731 7141 **WWW**.oakwayestate.com.au **OPEN** W'ends 11-5
EMAKER Tony Davis **EST.** 1997 **DOZENS** 1500 **VYDS** 2ha

and Wayne Hammond run a vineyard, beef cattle and sustainable blue-gum plantation in dulating country on the Capel River in the southwest of WA. The grapes are grown on light vel and loam soils that provide good drainage, giving even sun exposure to the fruit and imising the effects of frost. The vineyard is planted to shiraz, merlot, cabernet sauvignon, o d'Avola, malbec, muscat, sauvignon blanc, vermentino and chardonnay, and the wines 'e won a number of medals.

Los Ninos Single Vineyard Geographe Malbec 2018 Wildly aromatic nose: Mariposa plum, raspberry and licorice. The palate follows exactly, making this a succulent, delicious little number which for the price (especially for the price) should not be missed. Should you have the patience to wait, layers of flavour and texture will unfurl themselves in the glass. Screw cap | 13.5% alc. | To 2030 | $28 | EL

Il Sardo Single Vineyard Vermentino 2020 Pretty! White melon, spring florals and green apple and pear. The palate is vibrant and energetic with a line of citric acid that courses over the middle of the palate. Plugs you in and zaps you (in a good way). Energising and delicious. Screw cap | 12.3% alc. | To 2021 | $25 | EL

Il Vino Rosato 2020 100% Nero d'Avola. Now we're talking ... flavour: this is intense and moving to full concentration. Pretty salmon onion-skin colour. Red berry, szechuan peppercorn, red licorice and spice. The palate is plump and plush, with plenty of succulence and bounce. Well crafted, with some creamy characters on the mid palate for interest, bolstered by fine phenolics through the finish. Great effort. Super-saline tang. Screw cap | 12.2% alc. | To 2021 | $25 | EL

Il Siciliano Single Vineyard Nero d'Avola 2019 A juicy and vibrant nose reminiscent of purple wine gums, black licorice and red snakes – all appealing things. The palate delivers all the plush comfort promised by the nose. A sobering flick of acid and tannins through the finish brings it into a more balanced space. Lovely wine, full of pleasure. Another example of Geographe bringing home the (alternative red) bacon. Screw cap | 14.6% alc. | To 2025 | $28 | EL

Aidan

Ferguson Road, Dardanup, WA 6236 **T** (08) 9728 3007 **WWW**.saintaidan.com.au **OPEN** Mon–Tues
urs–Fri 11–4, w'ends & public hols 11–5 **WINEMAKER** Mark Messenger (Contract) **EST.** 1996
ENS 1500 **VYDS** 2.6ha

and Mary Smith purchased their property at Dardanup in 1991, a 20-min drive from the bury hospital where Phil works. They first ventured into Red Globe table grapes, planting in 1994–2005, followed by 1ha of mandarins and oranges. With this experience, and with y completing a TAFE viticulture course, they extended their horizons by planting 1ha h of cabernet sauvignon and chardonnay in '97, 0.5ha of muscat in '01, and semillon and vignon blanc thereafter.

Geographe Tempranillo 2019 Pure red berries and juicy succulence for days. The fine, chalky and shapely tannins hold this off being slurpy ... that guilt-ridden, delicious space that reds can sometimes move towards. This makes a fabulous case for modern tempranillo. Screw cap | 14% alc. | To 2025 | $25 | EL

Geographe Sauvignon Blanc Semillon 2020 Pale straw in colour, aromas of lemon citrus mingle with white florals, green guava and nashi pear. The palate has a juicy, chewy acid backbone, partnered with a gently plump viscosity. There is chalky phenolic finesse that elevates this wine into excellence. Purity, with brilliant intensity and concentration of flavour. Yes! Screw cap | 13.9% alc. | To 2023 | $20 | EL

nallwater Estate

Tramline Rd, Newlands WA 6251 **T** (08) 9731 6036 **WWW**.smallwaterestate.com **OPEN** Sat–Sun 10–4
EMAKER Bruce Dukes, Remi Guise **EST.** 1993 **DOZENS** 2500 **VYDS** 7.2ha

allwater Estate was planted in 1993 by John Small and his late wife Robyn, with the ntion of developing a marron farm and a vineyard to grow contract grapes. After selling pes to other wineries for over a decade, in 2005 John decided to make wine under the allwater Estate label. The 2006 release was small (zinfandel, 250 dozens), however since n, production has grown tenfold. (EL)

Geographe Shiraz 2019 Pomegranate, blackberry, mulberry and raspberry are the first to jostle out of the glass, followed closely by red licorice, vanilla pod and anise. The palate is inky, layered and spicy, weaving its way across the tongue in a most hypnotic fashion. Good length of flavour finishes this off. Shiraz is another of Geographe's weapons, for this reason. One gold and 3 trophies Geographe Wine Show '20. Screw cap | 15.2% alc. | To 2031 | $35 | EL

Talisman Wines ⓘ

Wheelman Road, Wellington Mill, WA 6236 **T** 0401 559 266 **www**.talismanwines.com.au **OPEN** By app' **WINEMAKER** Peter Stanlake **EST.** 2009 **DOZENS** 3000 **VYDS** 9ha

Kim Robinson (and wife Jenny) began the development of their vineyard in 2000. Kim says that 'after 8 frustrating years of selling grapes to Evans & Tate and Wolf Blass, we decided tc optimise the vineyard and attempt to make quality wines'. The measure of their success has been consistent gold-medal performance (and some trophies) at the Geographe Wine Shov They say this could not have been achieved without the assistance of vineyard manager Victor Bertola and winemaker Peter Stanlake.

96 **Gabrielle Ferguson Valley Chardonnay 2019** This label leaves a trail of gold medals and trophies i its wake, and the cooler vintage 2019 is no exception. Gunflint, curry leaf, brine, white peach and red apple skins define the aromatics, and more than clearly replicate themselves on the palate. Th texture is fine and slippery. A lot to love and discover if you haven't tried it before. Screw cap | 13.6% alc. | To 2031 | $40 | EL

95 **Ferguson Valley Malbec 2019** This is aromatically on the midnight end of the spectrum: blackberry, raspberry bramble, black pepper, star anise and szechuan peppercorns. Awesome. The palate delivers just what the nose promised, layering it with fine and grippy tannins. The acid energises this to unfurl both in the glass and the mouth. Savoury and plush at once. What a wine! Screw cap | 15% alc. | To 2030 | $35 | EL

94 **Ferguson Valley Cabernet Malbec 2019** The Talisman vineyard is one of the highest points in the Ferguson Valley, elevation giving the wines a poise and freshness. The fruit on the palate here is dense and yet restrained; it holds back, conserving its power, which it meters out over the long finish. This has all the hallmarks of good cellaring (fruit, acid, tannin, length), but it is also deliciou now. And the price! Screw cap | 14.4% alc. | To 2036 | $30 | EL

Willow Bridge Estate ⓘ

178 Gardin Court Drive, Dardanup, WA 6236 **T** (08) 9728 0055 **www**.willowbridge.com.au **OPEN** 7 da 11–5 **WINEMAKER** Kim Horton **EST.** 1997 **DOZENS** 25000 **VYDS** 59ha

Jeff and Vicky Dewar have followed a fast track in developing Willow Bridge Estate since acquiring the spectacular 180ha hillside property in the Ferguson Valley. Many of its wines offer exceptional value for money. Kim Horton, with 25 years of winemaking in WA, believes that wines are made in the vineyard; the better the understanding of the vineyard and its unique characteristics, the better they reflect the soil and the climate.

95 **Bookends Fumé Geographe Sauvignon Blanc Semillon 2020** An outstanding example of the style at a reasonable price. The fruit is ripe, almost tropical (guava, green pineapple, with hints of gree mango, Granny Smith apples and sugar snap peas). Oak is seamlessly integrated into the fruit (in fact, it is almost invisible, save for the complexity and softening effect it has had on the texture). Classy to the end. Screw cap | 13.7% alc. | To 2027 | $25 | EL

Rosa de Solana Geographe 2020 87/13% tempranillo/grenache. A Turkish delight vibe on the nos The fruit on the mid palate plumes generously, showing pomegranate, redcurrant, raspberry pip a rosewater. There's a suggestion of pistachio, joined by cumin and a whiff of cinnamon. The acid th binds the fruit together is tense and nervy, bringing this home as a balanced, structured, pure anc layered rosé, worthy of any stage of a meal. Yes. Screw cap | 13% alc. | To 2022 | $25 | EL

Gravel Pit Geographe Shiraz 2019 An unbelievably vibrant colour – somewhere between magenta fuschia and midnight. The Geographe region excels in shiraz and winemaker Kim Horton is a mast at protecting fruit purity in his wines. This is layered, with rippling intensity of flavour, imperceptib oak, and exotic spices that net szechuan, star anise, aniseed and much more. A gorgeous wine ar a flag-bearer for the region. Screw cap | 14.2% alc. | To 2035 | $30 | EL

Geographe GSM 2020 A bouncy, pure, and delicious wine. Raspberry lolly, salami, blackberry, licorice and satsuma plum mingle on the palate, within the confines of fine, chalky tannins. With length of flavour that punches well above its price, this is a very compelling little wine. Screw cap | 14.5% alc. | To 2028 | $25 | EL

Solana Geographe Tempranillo 2019 100% barrel matured in new and old oak puncheons and hogsheads. The new oak component is evident on the nose, but once this wine is in your mouth the fruit intensity is on high: it can wear the oak gracefully. Purity and texture are the calling cards here. Crunchy acidity keeps this refreshing and taut; the length of flavour is very good. Screw cap | 14% alc. | To 2035 | $30 | EL

94 **G1-10 Geographe Chardonnay 2020** Glassy texture and bright, briny acidity pave the way for an avalanche of ripe stone fruits to tumble across the palate. Once the dust settles (so to speak), the pockets of flavour unfurl through the finish. Impressive and affordable. Screw cap | 13.8% alc. | To 2027 | $30 | EL

;reat Southern

obey Creek Vineyard

8 Porongurup Road, Porongurup, WA 6324 **T** (08) 9853 1044 **www**.abbeycreek.com.au **OPEN** By appt
EMAKER Castle Rock Estate (Robert Diletti) **EST.** 1990 **DOZENS** 1000 **VYDS** 1.6ha

s is the family business of Mike and Mary Dilworth. The name comes from a winter creek t runs alongside the vineyard and a view of The Abbey in the Stirling Range. The rieslings /e had significant show success for a number of years.

Porongurup Sauvignon Blanc 2019 This delicate and fresh little sauvignon blanc is one of only 3 varieties planted here and the 2019 vintage was sadly the last for owners Mary and Mike. This is their curtain call. Screw cap | 12% alc. | To 2025 | $23 | EL

koomi

1 Wingebellup Road, Frankland River, WA 6396 **T** (08) 9855 2229 **www**.alkoomiwines.com.au
N 7 days 10-4.30 Frankland River Mon-Sat 11-5 Albany **WINEMAKER** Andrew Cherry **EST.** 1971
ENS 80000 **VYDS** 164ha

ablished in 1971 by Merv and Judy Lange, Alkoomi is now owned by daughter Sandy Hallett I her husband Rod. They are continuing the tradition of producing high-quality wines ich showcase the Frankland River region. Alkoomi is actively reducing its environmental tprint; future plans will see the introduction of new varietals.

Black Label Frankland River Shiraz 2019 Viognier is well enveloped by powerful shiraz, but it still manages to contribute a slinkiness to the tannins - a slip on the tongue. This is both concentrated and floral, with tannins that create form and structure on the palate and provide framework from which the fruit hangs. A very smart wine indeed, especially at this price. Screw cap | 14.5% alc. | To 2031 | $35 | EL

White Label Frankland River Riesling 2020 If ever there was a segment of wines that represented great value it would have to be riesling. The wines have potential in the cellar, they offer deliciousness early and with change from $20, what more could you possibly ask for? This vintage holds true to the success of all of the others that came before. It is taut, powerful, pretty and plump. Cracking value, and a cracking wine. Screw cap | 12% alc. | To 2035 | $18 | EL

Black Label Frankland River Cabernet Sauvignon 2019 This is frequently one of the 'if you know, you know' cabernets in the sub-$30 bracket. It's got it all: supple, succulent and spicy fruit, fine yet firm, structuring tannins and great length of flavour. The characteristic ferrous, gravel, petrichor flavours endemic to Frankland cabernet are all there. Through the lens of the 2019 vintage, this is elegant and long, packing punch within the confines of its restraint. Screw cap | 14% alc. | To 2030 | $28 | EL

›ricus Hill

McLeod Road, Denmark, WA 6333 **T** 0427 409 078 **www**.apricushill.com.au **WINEMAKER** James Kellie
1995 **DOZENS** 800 **VYDS** 8ha

ıes and Careena Kellie (of Harewood Estate) purchased Somerset Hill Vineyard with urposes: first, to secure a critical fruit source for Harewood, and second, to make and rket a small range of single-vineyard, single-varietal wines for sale exclusively through the ctacular cellar door, with its sweeping vista. Thus Somerset Hill is now Apricus Hill.

Single Vineyard Denmark Pinot Noir 2019 Wildly aromatic – black cherry, chinotto, strawberry and olive tapenade. The palate follows suit; layered and distinctly Western Australian in its savoury, tannin-led approach to the palate. The phenolic structure carries the succulent fruit over the tongue and leads it through into a long finish. Really impressive. Screw cap | 14% alc. | To 2028 | $35 | EL

astelli Estate

Mount Shadforth Road, Denmark, WA 6333 **T** (08) 9364 0400 **www**.castelliestate.com.au
N By appt **WINEMAKER** Mike Garland **EST.** 2007 **DOZENS** 20000

en Sam Castelli purchased the property in late 2004, he was intending simply to use it as mily holiday destination. But because there was a partly constructed winery he decided to complete the building work and simply lock the doors. However, wine was in his blood courtesy of his father, who owned a small vineyard in Italy's south. The temptation was too much and in '07 the winery was commissioned.

97 **Il Liris Rouge 2018** 66/27/7% cabernet sauvignon/shiraz/malbec. Matured in French oak (70% new Ferrous, gravel, ironstone, graphite, satsuma plum, raspberry, blood and red licorice. The oak is there, but requires effort to find it among the cavalcade of flavours. The tannins are omnipresent. This is a beast, but a friendly one. A lifetime awaits it, if you have the patience. Otherwise drink it now, it's ready. Vino-Lok | 14.8% alc. | To 2051 | $80 | EL

96 **Il Liris Chardonnay 2019** The Il Liris Chardonnay is one of the shining chardonnay lights in the regi Freshly picked and crushed curry leaf, toasted, crushed macadamia and ripe, dripping yellow pea The acidity on the palate is bright and salty, the texture is shaped by fine phenolics. This is luxurio but not in a sweet, opulent way. Rather, in a pared-back, 6-star hotel's 'every detail considered' ki of way. Very long. Awesome. Vino-Lok | 12.5% alc. | To 2036 | $70 | EL

Frankland River Cabernet Sauvignon 2018 This is a harmonious, powerful and exciting rendition, only of cabernet sauvignon, but of the Frankland River regional characteristics of the grape. Grave ferrous, salted cassis. Licorice. It's a cracker. Supple and dense at once. This will age, too. Buy it a drink it now or when your newborn turns 15. Screw cap | 14.7% alc. | To 2035 | $38 | EL

95 **Pemberton Chardonnay 2019** Toasty, spicy oak on the nose and interwoven throughout the palate Abundant ripe stone fruit in the mouth plays into the hands of salty acid and the cushioning catch oak. Home run. Screw cap | 13.6% alc. | To 2030 | $34 | EL

94 **The Sum Cabernet Sauvignon 2019** This kind of quality for under $20? Bring it on. This is the younger, sweeter, juicier and plumper sibling to the estate cabernet. It has all the regional greatne from Frankland: ferrous, gravel, petrichor and firm tannin structure. But in this context, all of it gently sidles up to bouncy blackcurrant fruit and leaves us with a glass of straight-up pleasure. Cheap doesn't mean 'cheap' – if you want to learn this lesson, start here. Screw cap | 14.7% alc. To 2028 | $18 | EL

Castle Rock Estate 

2660 Porongurup Road, Porongurup, WA 6324 **T** (08) 9853 1035 **WWW**.castlerockestate.com.au
OPEN 7 days 10–4.30 **WINEMAKER** Robert Diletti **EST.** 1983 **DOZENS** 4500 **VYDS** 11.2ha

An exceptionally beautifully sited vineyard, winery and cellar door on a 55ha property with sweeping vistas of the Porongurup Range, operated by the Diletti family. The standard of viticulture is very high, and the vineyard itself is ideally situated. The 2-level winery, set on a natural slope, maximises gravity flow. Rob Diletti's excellent palate and sensitive winemakin mark Castle Rock as one of the superstars of WA.

97 **A&W Porongurup Riesling 2020** It's like the oak has taken all the top notes off the fruit, but left a rumbling undercurrent of power and depth. The oak has gifted this with a thunderous baritone, ye the delicacy of Porongurup fruit keeps it understated and textural. A deeply quiet, almost introver riesling yet with an enduring and composed voice. Screw cap | 12.1% alc. | To 2040 | $35 | EL

96 **Porongurup Riesling 2020** Simple vinification has produced a far-from-simple wine. This is a superfine, delicate, layered riesling with lacy acidity that courses its way through the fruit. Citrus blossom, ripe citrus, jasmine tea, white pepper, hints of fennel flower and a drop of star anise. Routinely a ridiculous wine for the money. Rob Diletti has a reputation for riesling and this, my friends, is why. Screw cap | 12.4% alc. | To 2035 | $25 | EL

95 **Skywalk Porongurup Riesling 2020** The highest RS of Castle Rock's rieslings, at 1.3g/L (hardly sweet!). Textbook white spring blossom aromatics that so define the rieslings from the Porongurup region, rising out of the glass alongside sweet citrus pith and crushed limestone. White pepper, fleshy citrus and saline acid is the story in the mouth, while the unassailable length of flavour is th conclusion. A ridiculously good wine for the money. Screw cap | 12.8% alc. | To 2035 | $20 | E

Porongurup Pinot Noir 2019 A recent vertical tasting of Castle Rock pinots back to 2006 showed two things: that they age gracefully, picking up typical earth and mushroom notes along the way; and that there seemed to be more complexity in the younger wines, indicating that they would perform even more favourably in the cellar. This is case in point; vibrant fruit and acid tension on palate, unfurling to a long and lingering finish. Nuance and finesse here. Screw cap | 13.8% alc. To 2040 | $34 | EL

Great Southern Shiraz 2018 At $30, this is the 2nd-most expensive wine that Rob Diletti makes: his wines represent extreme value for money. This is muscular, as we know Mount Barker shiraz can be, yet within those firm tannins lies layers of delicate flavour, like the fine folds underneath a mushroom. The length of flavour further confirms the quality of the fruit. Despite all of these grea things, the balance is the ultimate winner here. Screw cap | 13.8% alc. | To 2031 | $30 | EL

Porongurup Cabernet Sauvignon 2018 Refined, fine-boned, pretty cabernet, shaped by chalky tannins that linger and whip around the palate. The impact of oak is minimal, leaving ample room cassis to fully unfurl and eddy about. Something utterly satisfying on the palate here. Power witho weight. From talented hands comes this quietly elegant wine, grown in a tiny, beautiful little regio And the price: don't start. Screw cap | 13% alc. | To 2030 | $25 | EL

Diletti Chardonnay 2018 If I had to describe this wine in only a handful of words (imagine that), they would be: classy, glassy, restrained and fine. Gold medal Mount Barker Wine Show '20. Screw cap | 12% alc. | To 2025 | $25 | EL

uke's Vineyard

★★★★★

'ongurup Road, Porongurup, WA 6324 **T** (08) 9853 1107 **www**.dukesvineyard.com **OPEN** 7 days 4.30 **WINEMAKER** Robert Diletti **EST**. 1998 **DOZENS** 3500 **VYDS** 10ha

ıen Hilde and Ian (Duke) Ranson sold their clothing manufacturing business in 1998, they 're able to fulfil a long-held dream of establishing a vineyard in the Porongurup Range. de, a successful artist, designed the beautiful, scalloped, glass-walled cellar door sales ıa, with its mountain blue cladding. Great wines at great prices.

Magpie Hill Reserve Riesling 2020 Its power, length and layer upon layer of kaffir lime is wrapped in a pure silver cloak of acidity running through – but never challenging – the fruit. Duke Ranson has every reason to suggest this is one of the best rieslings to come from this jewelled vineyard at the heart of the estate plantings. Screw cap | 13.2% alc. | To 2040 | $42 | JH | ♥

The First Cab 2019 This is the first vintage, its history dating back to '74 when Duke Ranson tasted a wine made with a clone of cabernet sauvignon he chased for over 40 years to plant. With an entrancing bouquet and a beautifully structured, supremely elegant palate, it is liquid, heart-stopping cassis, handled with great skill. Screw cap | 13.5% alc. | To 2039 | $60 | JH

Magpie Hill Reserve Shiraz 2019 The colour here is as vibrantly hued as the aromas that waft out of the glass – evident from a foot away. As with the cabernet – this is all things from the Single Vineyard but all things dialled up. Oak. Intensity and voluminous fruit. Gorgeous stuff. Spice and structure. Screw cap | 14% alc. | To 2040 | $42 | EL

Magpie Hill Reserve Cabernet Sauvignon 2019 As with previous years, this is super-concentrated: amazing that so much flavour can be packed into a glass. Astoundingly powerful fruit, matched by the seamless integration of oak and structure. The tannins are fine, almost subliminal, and hold the fruit in check from start to finish. The natural acidity from both the cooler growing area and vintage is impressively juicy, wrapping up a sensational package. Supple, generous, layered and lingering. What a wine. Screw cap | 13.9% alc. | To 2050 | $42 | EL

Single Vineyard Riesling 2020 And what a single-vineyard it is. The scented bouquet of apple blossom and crushed lime leaves is faithfully replayed on the light-as-air palate that throws passionfruit and ethereal fruit (not RS) on the unsuspecting taster's mouth. Screw cap | 13.1% alc. | To 2030 | $26 | JH

Single Vineyard Shiraz 2019 Cool-climate shiraz, people: get around it! White pepper, exotic spice and red fruit. Abundance and opulence with restraint. A core of intense fruit and fine-structured tannins. This is a banger. A beautiful wine that whistles a tune of purity – what expression! Red licorice to boot. Absolutely yes. Screw cap | 13.5% alc. | To 2035 | $30 | EL

Single Vineyard Cabernet Sauvignon 2019 The cooler 2019 vintage has given rise to this gloriously elegant and layered cabernet. Unbelievably vibrant and saturated in colour; almost luminescent fuchsia. Pomegranate and raspberry on the nose – the palate is concentrated and elegant with abundant dark berries and spice, chalky tannins and a core of pastille fruit. Gorgeous stuff. Screw cap | 13.5% alc. | To 2040 | $30 | EL

ɜrngrove

Ferngrove Road, Frankland River, WA 6396 **T** (08) 9363 1300 **www**.ferngrove.com.au **N** By appt **WINEMAKER** Craig Grafton, Adrian Foot **EST**. 1998 **VYDS** 220ha

' over 20 years, Ferngrove has been producing consistent examples of cool-climate wines 'oss multiple price brackets. The Ferngrove stable includes the flagship Orchid wines, Black bel, White Label and Independence ranges. Ferngrove Vineyards Pty Ltd enjoys the benefits majority international ownership.

Dragon Shiraz 2019 Ruby red with glints of pink, this is a veritable fete of flavour and (like the Dragon Cabernet Shiraz) it is comfort and pleasure in a bottle. Perhaps not as complex as some of the very best, but utterly, undeniably beautiful, charming and balanced. Cork | 14% alc. | To 2036 | $70 | EL

Independence Great Southern Cabernet Sauvignon 2019 All the body, flesh and structure of cabernet here, while 6% nebbiolo is responsible for the distinctive tannins and the lick of rose petal aromatics. All in all, a juicy, bouncy and joyful execution of 2 unlikely bedfellows. Screw cap | 14% alc. | To 2028 | $26 | EL

Frankland River Malbec 2019 With 2% cabernet sauvignon. Brilliant intensity of flavour, with retention of elegance besides; quite a cool achievement for malbec (which can often stray towards rambunctious flavour intensity with little restraint). Crunchy acid rounds this out into a thoroughly modern New World interpretation of the style; glossy and spicy and mighty fine. Ridiculous price. Screw cap | 13% alc. | To 2030 | $22 | EL

Forest Hill Vineyard

Cnr South Coast Highway/Myers Road, Denmark, WA 6333 **T** (08) 9848 2399 **www**.foresthillwines.com. **OPEN** 7 days 10.30-5 **WINEMAKER** Liam Carmody, Guy Lyons **EST.** 1965 **DOZENS** 12000 **VYDS** 36ha

This family-owned business is one of the oldest 'new' winemaking operations in WA and was the site of the first grape plantings in Great Southern in 1965. The Forest Hill brand became well known, aided by the fact that a '75 Riesling made by Sandalford from Forest Hill grapes won 9 trophies. The quality of the wines made from the oldest vines (dry-grown) on the property is awesome.

98 **Block 1 Mount Barker Riesling 2020** There's only one thing to do while in the presence of a wine such as this: stand aside and allow it to pass. This is statuesque power and grace, with an army of following flavours that trail in its very long wake. Fifty-seven cases. Screw cap | 12.8% alc. | To 2045 | $55 | EL | ♥

96 **Block 8 Mount Barker Chardonnay 2020** Yields were so low in 2019 that this wine wasn't even mad Then 2020 came around – another low-yielding year, producing a tiny quantity. Crushed curry leaf peach, brine and apple on the nose. On the palate, this is incredibly concentrated and powerful, and although closed right now, it will continue to evolve and unfurl over time. Very impressive. Screw cap | 13% alc. | To 2031 | $45 | EL

95 **Highbury Fields Riesling 2020** Savoury exotic nose of sesame, soy, citrus pith, creamed honey on buttered toast and graphite. The palate is taut and powerful, the oak coming through on the finish. This is a wine of layering, power, poise and adaptability. Quite astounding for the price. Screw cap | 13% alc. | To 2031 | $24 | EL

Mount Barker Shiraz 2019 Spicy, lifted and savoury, this is all about berry bramble. The fruit on the palate moves from black cherry to pomegranate, blackberry and raspberry, all embossed with finely inlaid tannins and saline acid. These elements create a tension across the fruit, pulling it all together in a very classy way. Cracking wine and a must-buy for the money. Screw cap | 14% alc. | To 2028 | $30 | EL

Frankland Estate

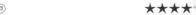

Frankland Road, Frankland, WA 6396 **T** (08) 9855 1544 **www**.franklandestate.com.au **OPEN** Mon-Fri 10-4, public hols & w'ends by appt **WINEMAKER** Hunter Smith, Brian Kent **EST.** 1988 **DOZENS** 20000 **VYDS** 34.5ha

A significant operation, situated on a large sheep property owned by Barrie Smith and Judi Cullam. The introduction of an array of single-vineyard rieslings has been a highlight, driven by Judi's conviction that terroir is of utmost importance, and the soils are indeed different; the Isolation Ridge Vineyard is organically grown. Frankland Estate has held important International Riesling tastings and seminars for more than a decade.

94 **Riesling 2020** Totally captivating from the outset. Lime juice, kaffir leaf and the suggestion of something a tad sweeter – palm sugar, even. But this doesn't translate to the palate, which is deliciously zingy and flavourful, those exotic notes echoed. Screw cap | 12.5% alc. | To 2026 | $30 | TL

Galafrey

Quangellup Road, Mount Barker, WA 6324 **T** (08) 9851 2022 **www**.galafreywines.com.au **OPEN** 7 days 10-5 **WINEMAKER** Kim Tyrer **EST.** 1977 **DOZENS** 3500 **VYDS** 13.1ha

The Galafrey story began when Ian and Linda Tyrer gave up high-profile jobs in the emerginc computer industry and arrived in Mount Barker to start growing grapes and making wine, the vine-change partially prompted by their desire to bring up their children in a country environment. Daughter Kim Tyrer is now CEO of the business, with Linda still very much involved in the day-to-day of Galafrey.

96 **Dry Grown Reserve Mount Barker Riesling 2020** Talcy and floral nose, perhaps more so than previous vintages. The palate is intense and focused, searing acidity – an austerity that makes it almost hard, but gosh it's good. Phenolic structure provides a framework from which the fruit clinc There is a saline flick through the finish – crushed oyster shell, creamy, green-apple skin and taut lime pith. Really smart. Screw cap | 12.5% alc. | To 2040 | $25 | EL

95 **Dry Grown Mount Barker Merlot 2017** This is concentrated and dense with classy layering of flavou and lingering length of flavour. It was a cool vintage in '17 and this is a good representation: fine, elegant and lingering. The nose is redolent of cacao nibs and mulberry ... it has intensity and line. A structured and lingering wine, lovely stuff. Screw cap | To 2025 | $30 | EL

4 **Dry Grown Mount Barker Müller Thurgau 2020** The 2020 rendition is fermented dry in tank, the vintage giving awesome intensity and purity. Orange peel and turmeric, with saffron and essence of mandarin. It's viscous and rich, and the tannins are powder-fine and grippy. Screw cap | 12% alc. | To 2025 | $28 | EL

arewood Estate

70 Scotsdale Road, Denmark, WA 6333 **T** (08) 9840 9078 **www**.harewood.com.au **OPEN** Fri-Mon 11-5 chool hols 7 days) **WINEMAKER** James Kellie **EST.** 1988 **DOZENS** 15000 **VYDS** 19.2ha

2003 James Kellie, responsible for the contract making of Harewood's wines since 1998, urchased the estate with his wife Careena. A 300t winery was constructed, offering both ontract winemaking services and the ability to expand the Harewood range to include ıbregional wines from across the Great Southern region.

5 **Mount Barker Riesling 2020** This is pretty cool; flavour base of cheesecloth, salty saline acid, citrus pith and green apple skin. The fine, chalky phenolics on the palate elevate this into a very interesting space; softer and rounder than many Mount Barker rieslings, but that regional stamp of coiled acid remains entrenched in the fruit on the mid palate. Screw cap | 12.5% alc. | To 2041 | $30 | EL

Reserve Denmark Semillon Sauvignon Blanc 2019 Pungently grassy, with a quenching core of gooseberry and passionfruit. This is moreish. The oak is seamlessly countersunk into the concentrated fruit. A very impressive wine, especially for the price. Screw cap | 13% alc. | To 2028 | $28 | EL

Flux-II Great Southern Pinot Gris 2020 Fruit from Frankland River. Nashi pear, summer florals and a lick of winter stewed apple through the finish. Saline acid and dried apple rings are coupled with orange zest and sherbet. A lot to like here. Not your average pinot gris. Screw cap | 13% alc. | To 2028 | $30 | EL

Flux-VII Great Southern White Blend 2020 The classic sauvignon blanc/semillon is bookended by gewürz and riesling – this is a proper white blend. All the varieties are like passengers on a carousel, gently bobbing up and down, taking it in turns to go in and out of view. Lovely, lyrical, spicy and refreshing. The gewürztraminer is the last to leave the palate, leaving a wisp of lychee, rosewater and crushed pistachio in its wake. Screw cap | 12.5% alc. | To 2020 | $30 | EL

4 **Porongurup Riesling 2020** Fleshy, creamy and rounded, this is a beautiful curvy riesling that speaks clearly of place. Some RS is in perfect concert with the fruit and acid, all things coming together in a most pleasurable way. Screw cap | 12.5% alc. | To 2035 | $30 | EL

Denmark Riesling 2020 Very different from Harewood's Mount Barker Riesling, and rightly so. This Denmark iteration is grassy, herbaceous and more floral; the acid sits outside the fruit on the palate, it's not countersunk into it. There is a tingly, sherbet vivacity about this wine. It is more obvious than some of the others in this range, but a brilliant example of why Great Southern rieslings are so great. Screw cap | 12% alc. | To 2036 | $30 | EL

Flux-V Great Southern Pinot Noir 2019 Coffee oak leads the charge on the nose, closely followed by cherry and strawberry. This has spunk and lift on the palate, with a distinct stemmy crunch that gives it an extra layer of crushed green ant interest. Length of flavour is a plus. Screw cap | 14% alc. | To 2025 | $30 | EL

.ange Estate

33 Frankland-Cranbrook Road, Frankland River, WA 6396 **T** 0438 511 828 **www**.langestate.com.au **PEN** By appt **WINEMAKER** Liam Carmody, Guy Lyons **EST.** 1997 **DOZENS** 7000 **VYDS** 20ha

he eponymous Lange Estate is owned and run by the family: Kim and Chelsea, their children ack, Ella and Dylan, together with parents Don and Maxine. The vineyard is situated in ne picturesque Frankland River, tucked away in the far northwestern corner of the Great outhern. The vineyard, with an elevation of almost 300m and red jarrah gravel loam soils, roduces wines of great intensity.

6 **Fifth Generation Frankland River Cabernet Sauvignon 2019** People talk about 'wine being made in the vineyard', and to a certain extent this is true. But when you put good fruit in the hands of talented craftspeople, you get this. Exotic spices imbue the nose with a density and seriousness, the fruit on the palate lives up to that expectation too. Serious, structural, concentrated and long – bitter chocolate laces the finish. This is a beautiful, long-lived wine. Screw cap | 14.5% alc. | To 2040 | $50 | EL

5 **Providence Road Frankland River Cabernet Sauvignon 2019** This is the middle child between the big Fifth Generation cabernet, and the little TSR cabernet. The fruit here is verging on opulent and luxurious, the tannins and acidity keeping everything in check. Harmony and balance are the key words – not at all what we know of middle children. Lovely wine, a lot to like. Screw cap | 14% alc. | To 2030 | $32 | EL

4 **TSR Frankland River Cabernet Sauvignon 2019** This is the juicy, supple and vibrant younger sibling to the Fifth Generation cabernet sauvignon. Bouncy fruit and chewy tannins pave the way for pleasure here. Brilliant drinking for the price. Screw cap | 14% alc. | To 2028 | $23 | EL

Lonely Shore

18 Bavin Street, Denmark, WA 6333 (postal) **T** 0418 907 594 **www**.lonelyshore.com.au
WINEMAKER Liam Carmody **EST.** 2014 **DOZENS** 200 **VYDS** 2ha

Liam Carmody's grandmother (Freda Vines) was the author of a historical novel published in 1958, telling the story of early settlement on the south coast of WA. Liam graduated from Curtin University in 2003, since working in Sonoma, California, NZ, France, South Africa and the Mornington Peninsula before settling in Denmark and taking up a full-time winemaking role at Forest Hill. Thus Lonely Shore is very much a busman's holiday.

95 **DeiTos Vineyard Pinot Noir 2020** As is usual for this vineyard, the fruit is on the darker end of the spectrum: mulberry, black licorice, black cherry and exotic spice. The palate is structured, tannic and a wee bit grungy, propped up by a stemmy, bunchy character mid palate that lifts it way up. The acidity is cooling and woven through the finish. Another very smart release from Lonely Shore. Screw cap | 13.5% alc. | To 2031 | $35 | EL

Lowboi

PO Box 40, Denmark, WA 6333 **T** 0438 849 592 **www**.lowboiwines.com.au **WINEMAKER** Guy Lyons **EST.** 201
DOZENS 400 **VYDS** 3.5ha

In 2017 winemaker Guy Lyons (Forest Hill) and his wife bought the Springviews vineyard on the south side of the dramatically beautiful Porongurup range in Great Southern and created their brand, Lowboi. Planted on the south-facing slope is riesling and Gingin clone chardonnay. Their grüner veltliner comes from the Lyons family farm in Mount Barker. The 'Lowboi' name originates from the farm Lyons' mother grew up on in the Great Southern shir of Tambellup. (EL)

96 **Porongurup Riesling 2020** The year 2020 was a warm, generous vintage, but thanks to the cool aspect of the site this is exploding with spring florals, citrus blossom and green apple. The palate is laced with fine, talcy phenolics. All coiled power and grace. Epic length. What a wine. Screw cap | 12.5% alc. | To 2040 | $36 | EL

Porongurup Chardonnay 2018 There is something very special about the Springviews vineyard site and this wine. Flinty, fine, cool-climate chardonnay here, with layers of curry leaf, brine, citrus pith, white peach, nectarine, cap gun and fennel flower. The phenolics have a jasmine tea character to them, and cradle the fruit in the cups of their hands, all the way across the palate and into a long finish. Screw cap | 13% alc. | To 2036 | $40 | EL

95 **Mount Barker Grüner Veltliner 2020** Densely packed with flavour and showing the Mount Barker muscle, this is concentrated, dense and long, with a swathe of exotic spice and grilled citrus fruit. Another firm statement of talent for winemaker Guy Lyons. Screw cap | 12.5% alc. | To 2031 | $32 | EL

Monty's Leap

45821 South Coast Highway, Kalgan, WA 6330 **T** 0407 424 455 **www**.montysleap.com.au
OPEN Tues–Thurs 10–5, Fri–Sat 10–10, Sun 10–7 **WINEMAKER** Castle Rock (Robert Diletti) **EST.** 1996
DOZENS 3000

Hospitality and IT professionals Phil Shilcock and Michelle Gray had long shared the dream o owning a vineyard and restaurant; they purchased the former Montgomery's Hill in October 2017 and launched the Monty's Leap brand. The mature vineyard (planted in 1996–97 by founders Pamela and Murray Montgomery) is planted on the banks of the Kalgan River, 16km northeast of Albany.

91 **Great Southern Appleshed Red 2019** Cabernet franc, cabernet sauvignon, merlot and a small dash of shiraz. Matured for 10 months in French oak (10% new). This is a vibrant and juicy blend with lip-smacking red berries (raspberry and mulberry), lashings of licorice, aniseed and freshly ground ba pepper. Plenty to like, especially at the price. Screw cap | 14.2% alc. | To 2027 | $20 | EL

Mount Trio Vineyard

2534 Porongurup Road, Mount Barker WA 6324 **T** (08) 9853 1136 **www**.mounttriowines.com.au
OPEN By appt **WINEMAKER** Gavin Berry, Andrew Vesey, Caitlin Gazey **EST.** 1989 **DOZENS** 3500 **VYDS** 8.5ha

Mount Trio was established by Gavin Berry and wife Gill Graham (plus business partners) shortly after they moved to the Mount Barker area in late 1988, Gavin to take up the position o chief winemaker at Plantagenet, which he held until 2004, when he and partners acquired th now very successful and much larger West Cape Howe.

Porongurup Riesling 2020 A piercingly pretty and plump riesling with layers of sweet citrus fruit, gentle exotic spice and citrus florals. The 6g/l RS is tucked so neatly away into the folds of flavour that it simply amplifies the deliciousness, rather than presenting in an obvious way. Hard to imagine a more quenching wine in the heat of summer. Screw cap | 12.5% alc. | To 2031 | $23 | EL

Great Southern Shiraz 2019 Fresh and peppery cool-climate syrah. Layers of black fruit flavours are shaped by fine tannins and a distinct licorice character that cools everything down. Remarkably elegant drinking for $23. Bravo. Screw cap | 13.5% alc. | To 2028 | $23 | EL

aul Nelson Wines

Roberts Road, Denmark, WA 6333 (postal) **T** 0406 495 066 **www**.paulnelsonwines.com.au
EN School hols 11-5 **WINEMAKER** Paul Nelson **EST.** 2009 **DOZENS** 1500 **VYDS** 2ha

ul Nelson started making wine with one foot in the Swan Valley, the other in the Great outhern, while completing a bachelor's degree in viticulture and oenology at Curtin iversity. He then worked at a range of wineries across both hemispheres, before returning work for Houghton. He has since moved on from Houghton and (in partnership with wife anca) makes small quantities of table wines.

Karriview Vineyard Denmark Chardonnay 2018 Curry leaf, grilled yellow peach, brine, red apple skin, salted stone-fruit succulence. This is viscous and rich with a cool-climate saline line of acid straight down the centre of the palate. Really impressive length of flavour. Minerality and crushed shell alongside thundering depth of flavour and juicy acid. Screw cap | 13.5% alc. | To 2035 | $65 | EL | ♥

Loam Frankland River Syrah 2019 Elegant, fine, restrained and frothing with red fruits and exotic spice. The persistent length of flavour ultimately defines this wine, although it is the most supple and delicate syrah made in the region. Interesting, often the most expensive wines have the most oak thrown at them ... this has been made with a light hand, the oak seamlessly and imperceptibly countersunk into the fruit. Cork | 13.5% alc. | To 2041 | $95 | EL

Karriview Vineyard Denmark Pinot Noir 2018 Sour red cherry and field strawberry at the height of summer meander out of the glass, backed by spicy, freshly ground nutmeg. On the palate, pomegranate underpins a tight line of acid that courses over the tongue, and the tannins prop up the fine fruit, keeping it all in line. This is restrained and exciting. Shapely tannins ultimately define this savoury pinot noir, capable of gracefully evolving for decades. Screw cap | 13.5% alc. | To 2041 | $65 | EL

lantagenet

Albany Highway, Mount Barker, WA 6324 **T** (08) 9851 3111 **www**.plantagenetwines.com **OPEN** 7 days -4.30 **WINEMAKER** Luke Eckerseley, Chris Murtha **EST.** 1968 **DOZENS** 30000 **VYDS** 126ha

antagenet was established by Tony Smith, who continues to be involved in its management ver 45 years later, notwithstanding that it has been owned by Lionel Samson & Son for many ears. He established 5 vineyards; they are the cornerstones of the substantial production the consistently high-quality wines that have always been the mark of Plantagenet: highly omatic Riesling, tangy citrus-tinged Chardonnay, glorious Rhône-style Shiraz and ultra-ylish Cabernet Sauvignon.

Tony Smith Mount Barker Shiraz 2018 Only made in exceptional years. Densely packed with concentrated, reverberating fruit that ripples across the tongue and through to the long finish. There is oak here, but it is swamped by the fruit which allows nothing to stand in its way. An exceptional wine of muscular definition and streamlined length of flavour. A very impressive first release: bravo. Screw cap | 14.5% alc. | To 2046 | $150 | EL

Lionel Samson Mount Barker Cabernet Sauvignon 2018 Salted cassis and blackberry pie on the nose and palate. This is supple and elegant and although concentrated, it doesn't have the palate weight of the shiraz. This is not a bad thing, just interesting. Elegance and longevity live here side by side. A masterful first release, and quite delicious now or in decades to come. Screw cap | 14% alc. | To 2056 | $150 | EL

5 **Angevin Great Southern Riesling 2020** Fruit from Mount Barker. This is powder fine and racy with concentrated fruit power. Quite an astoundingly beautiful and pure wine of poise, line and length. Screw cap | 11% alc. | To 2036 | $32 | EL

oacher's Ridge Vineyard

30 Spencer Road, Narrikup, WA 6326 **T** (08) 9857 6066 **www**.poachersridge.com.au **OPEN** Fri-Sun -4 **WINEMAKER** Robert Diletti **EST.** 2000 **DOZENS** 1000 **VYDS** 6.9ha

ne Poacher's Ridge property had previously been used for cattle grazing. The vineyard cludes shiraz, cabernet sauvignon, merlot, riesling, marsanne, viognier and malbec.

Winning the Tri Nations 2007 merlot class against the might of Australia, NZ and South Africa with its '05 Louis' Block Great Southern Merlot was a dream come true. And it wasn't a one-time success – Poacher's Ridge Merlot is always at, or near, the top of the tree.

94 **Great Southern Riesling 2020** The fruit here has that intense muscularity that riesling from the region can have; it speaks of lychee, red apple, sea salt, nutmeg, citrus pith and white nectarine, al backed by fine, chalky phenolics. A lot going on, good length of flavour and a satisfying eucalyptus spritz through the finish, making it savoury as well as concentrated. Brilliant. Screw cap | 12.8% alc. | To 2036 | $28 | EL

Great Southern Marsanne 2020 A shining example of marsanne in WA. It's fine, with a pluming bac palate that seems to expand with volumes of flavour as time goes by. It is richly layered and builds upon itself. Ultimately dry and built around a core of acid and phenolics. For lovers of this grape, you must try this. It has a proven track record for ageing gracefully, too. Screw cap | 13.5% alc. | To 2031 | $26 | EL

Rockcliffe

18 Hamilton Road, Denmark, WA 6333 **T** (08) 9848 1951 **www**.rockcliffe.com.au **OPEN** 7 days 11-5 or by appt **WINEMAKER** Elysia Harrison, Mike Garland, Neil Miles **EST**. 1990 **DOZENS** 30000 **VYDS** 11ha

The Rockcliffe winery and vineyard business, formerly known as Matilda's Estate, is owned by citizen of the world Steve Hall. The wine ranges echo local surf place names, headed by Rockcliffe itself but extending to Third Reef and Quarram Rocks. Over the years, Rockcliffe ha won more than its fair share of trophies and gold and silver medals in wine shows.

95 **Third Reef Great Southern Shiraz 2019** Powerfully structured and intensely flavoured – this is why we love Frankland River shiraz! Here, it expresses with cooling, mineral acidity, gravelly tannins and a lush red fruit opulence at its heart. Impressive. Screw cap | 14.5% alc. | To 2031 | $35 | EL

Shepherd's Hut

PO Box 194, Darlington, WA 6070 **T** (08) 9299 6700 **www**.shepherdshutwines.com **WINEMAKER** Rob Diletti **EST**. 1996 **DOZENS** 2000 **VYDS** 15.5ha

The shepherd's hut that appears on the wine label was one of four stone huts used in the 1850s to house shepherds tending large flocks of sheep. When WA pathologist Dr Michael Wishart (and family) purchased the property in 1996, the hut was in a state of extreme disrepair. It has since been restored, still featuring the honey-coloured Mount Barker stone. Most of the grapes are sold to other makers in the region, but those retained make high-quality wine at mouth-watering prices thanks to the skill of winemaker Rob Diletti.

94 **Porongurup Pinot Noir 2019** This wine has made a local name for itself for its low price, high quality and small quantity – it sells out each vintage. In the glass it is vibrantly pink tinged. The palate is silk and fine with spice to spare. Pretty red and pink berry, raspberry lolly aromatics and an appealing creamy texture that is one and the same with the fruit. Good length of flavour. Screw cap | 13.2% alc. | To 2023 | $27 | EL

Silverstream Wines

241 Scotsdale Road, Denmark, WA 6333 **T** (08) 9848 2767 **www**.silverstreamwines.com **OPEN** Summer Tues-Sun 11-5, winter by appt **WINEMAKER** Michael Garland **EST**. 1997 **DOZENS** 2500 **VYDS** 9ha

Tony and Felicity Ruse have 9ha of chardonnay, merlot, cabernet franc, pinot noir, riesling and viognier in their vineyard 23km from Denmark. The wines are contract-made and, after some hesitation, the Ruses decided their very pretty garden and orchard more than justified opening a cellar door, a decision supported by the quality of the wines on offer at very reasonable prices.

97 **Limited Release Denmark Riesling 2018** In the hands of winemaker Andrew Hoadley, who crafted the Limited Release range in 2018, this unexpected riesling makes perfect sense; zippy, texturally complex, layered and long. Hoadley has a way with wines that defies one's ability/desire to write down tech specifics ... you learn to just put down the pen, pick up a glass and listen. It's an undefinable energy that he injects into his wines. This has a plush cheesecloth character on the palate that begs another sip. And another. And, it's gone. Screw cap | 12.4% alc. | To 2041 | $32 | EL

95 **Single Vineyard Denmark Cabernet Franc 2018** Pretty and fine, both aromatically and flavour-wise. The tannins are the standout feature of this wine; they are fine, chalky and cleverly woven through the fruit. Present at every stage of the mouthful – they never overstay their welcome. A very elegar wine. Screw cap | 14.5% alc. | To 2027 | $30 | EL

inglefile Wines ⓘ ★★★★★

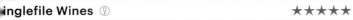

Walter Road, Denmark, WA 6333 **T** 1300 885 807 **www**.singlefilewines.com **OPEN** 7 days 11-5
NEMAKER Mike Garland, Coby Ladwig, Patrick Corbett **EST.** 2007 **DOZENS** 10000 **VYDS** 3.75ha

2007 Phil Snowden and wife Viv bought an established vineyard (planted in '89) in e beautiful Denmark subregion. They pulled out the old shiraz and merlot vines, kept d planted more chardonnay and retained Larry Cherubino to set up partnerships with tablished vineyards in Frankland River, Porongurup, Denmark, Pemberton and Margaret ver. The cellar door, tasting room and restaurant are strongly recommended. The nsistency of the quality of the Singlefile wines is outstanding, as is their value for money.

The Vivienne Denmark Chardonnay 2018 This is a wine of great provenance, with singular intensity. The fruit flavours hinge on grapefruit zest and juice alike, tightly framed acidity is also centrally involved. French oak is present, but in no way threatens the fruit. This will outlive the patience of many of those who purchase it. Screw cap | 13% alc. | To 2035 | $100 | JH

5 **Single Vineyard Mount Barker Riesling 2020** All class, as befits its Blue Lake Vineyard birthplace. The blossom and talc bouquet is shadowed by the intense, crisp palate where Granny Smith apple, crisp lemon-and-lime infusion, and detailed acidity carry the wine to a vibrantly fresh finish. Screw cap | 11.9% alc. | To 2035 | $35 | JH

Family Reserve Single Vineyard Denmark Chardonnay 2019 Chilled overnight and whole-bunch pressed direct to French barriques (40% new) for fermentation and 10% mlf, stirred weekly for 6 months. Opens with touches of smoky oak/grilled cashew on the bouquet. White peach, citrus and nashi pear follow on the long palate, which has layers of texture. Screw cap | 13.2% alc. | To 2033 | $60 | JH

Great Southern Chardonnay 2019 Chilled, whole-bunch pressed into French barriques (28% new). Lees stirred for 5 months, total time in oak 10 months. The oak is obvious on the bouquet, but fruit takes command on the rich and intense palate – grapefruit wrapped around white peach. Screw cap | 13.3% alc. | To 2033 | $30 | JH

Single Vineyard Frankland River Shiraz 2019 Frankland River is arguably the epicentre of Great Southern shiraz, the Riversdale Vineyard always in the frame. There is a combination of blackberry, pepper, spice and red licorice, classy tannins underwriting the longevity of a very good wine. Screw cap | 14.5% alc. | To 2044 | $39 | JH

4 **Run Free by Singlefile Riesling 2020** Great Southern fruit. The bright, crisp, mineral edge to the fruit is derived from the high acidity (8.7g/L) and nigh-on zero RS. Bursting with tingling lime sherbet flavours and aftertaste. Screw cap | 11.1% alc. | To 2032 | $25 | JH

Run Free by Singlefile Chardonnay 2019 Pressed direct to French barriques for a slow ferment and 8 months maturation, no mlf. White peach/nectarine/grapefruit sing together, oak spice a whisper. Overall intensity and length are impressive. Bargain. Screw cap | 13.4% alc. | To 2029 | $25 | JH

winney

25 Frankland-Kojonup Road, Frankland River, WA 6396 **T** (08) 9200 4483 **www**.swinney.com.au
NEMAKER Robert Mann **EST.** 1998 **DOZENS** 2500 **VYDS** 160ha

he Swinney family (currently parents Graham and Kaye, and son and daughter Matt and nelle) has been resident on their 2500ha property since it was settled by George Swinney 1922. In the '90s they decided to diversify and now have 160ha of vines across 4 vineyards, cluding the Powderbark Ridge Vineyard in Frankland River (planted in '98, purchased in artnership with former Hardys winemaker Peter Dawson).

8 **Farvie Frankland River Syrah 2019** Bacon fat, maple, salted pomegranate, raspberry, graphite, red dirt, mulberry and pink peppercorn. Like the Hokusai wave, this crashes and courses with flavours and textures, ebbing and flowing on the palate. This is balanced, restrained, long, powerful and most importantly, shaped and structured by supple, chewy tannins. They hold the fruit in the cups of their hands and usher it through a very long finish. A weightlessly poetic wine. Screw cap | 14% alc. | To 2031 | $150 | EL | ♥

Farvie Frankland River Grenache 2019 What sets hearts on fire the world over for Châteauneuf-du-Pape is the muscular, ferrous, salty raspberry humbug and minerally hutzpah. It sets the high-tide mark for grenache. We grenache drinkers yearn for it. And here it is. The strength of Frankland River is its ability to marry sweet (glossy) red fruit to savoury, gravelly earth. The 2018 was a staggering showpiece, this is more restrained, cooler and finer, yet equally long. Choose your weapon. Screw cap | 14% alc. | To 2041 | $150 | EL | ♥

6 **Frankland River Grenache 2019** In a nutshell, this wine is supple, slinky, crunchy and very long; packed to the rafters with raspberry, exotic spice, and defined by fine, silty tannins. What a wine. Screw cap | 14% alc. | To 2035 | $42 | EL

5 **Frankland River Riesling 2020** This has all the austere acidity that makes Frankland River riesling what it is, but it comes with a plump fruit profile that gives it a richness and almost an opulence. Lychee, lime, green apple and talc. The acidity has a zing and a pop and finishes with a crunch of sea salt. Screw cap | 12.5% alc. | To 2031 | $33 | EL

CENTRAL WA

EASTERN PLAINS/ INLAND/NORTH

GREATER PERTH

SOUTH WEST AUSTRALIA

SOUTH EAST COASTAL

3 Drops

PO Box 1828, Applecross, WA 6953 **T** (08) 9315 4721 **www**.3drops.com **WINEMAKER** Robert Diletti (Contract) **EST.** 1998 **DOZENS** 3500 **VYDS** 21.5ha

3 Drops is the name given to the Bradbury family vineyard at Mount Barker. The name reflects 3 elements: wine, olive oil and water – all of which come from the substantial property. The vineyard is planted to riesling, sauvignon blanc, semillon, chardonnay, cabern sauvignon, merlot, shiraz and cabernet franc, and irrigated by a large wetland on the propert

96 **Great Southern Chardonnay 2019** A deliberately understated wine directing all traffic to its varietal fruit, white stone fruit/grapefruit/apple flavours driving the immensely long palate. Purity in a sip. Screw cap | 13% alc. | To 2034 | $28 | JH

95 **Great Southern Pinot Noir 2019** Rob Diletti's touch is evident from start to finish. Good colour and clarity. The red berry fruits of the bouquet flow directly onto the palate, there joined by notes of spice and the impression of whole berry and/or whole bunch. Superfine tannins give support to both the texture and length of a classy pinot. Screw cap | 13.5% alc. | To 2034 | $32 | JH

West Cape Howe Wines

Lot 14923 Muir Highway, Mount Barker, WA 6324 **T** (08) 9892 1444 **www**.westcapehowewines.com.au **OPEN** 7 days (various hours) **WINEMAKER** Gavin Berry, Caitlin Gazey **EST.** 1997 **DOZENS** 60000 **VYDS** 310ha

West Cape Howe is owned by a partnership of 4 WA families, including winemaker/managing partner Gavin Berry and viticulturist/partner Rob Quenby. Grapes are sourced from estate vineyards in Mount Barker and Frankland River. West Cape Howe also sources select parcels of fruit from valued contract growers. Best Value Winery in the *Wine Companion 2016*.

95 **Mount Barker Riesling 2020** Pure and beautiful. This has it all – lean austerity, ripe citrus fruit, taut acid and long length of flavour. It's a little ripper, and the price is well below the pleasure it delivers. Don't miss it. Screw cap | 11.5% alc. | To 2036 | $22 | EL

Two Steps Mount Barker Shiraz 2018 Intense and full bodied, with a red-fruited core that nestles into the mid palate – raspberry, mulberry, and pink peppercorn. The oak is quite robust (but tight) at the front of the palate, and thanks to that succulent reserve of fruit, this is balanced and serious. Good length of flavour means this is a very good wine indeed. Screw cap | 14.5% alc. | To 2035 | $30 | EL

94 **Porongurup Riesling 2020** The irrepressible purity of Porongurup permeates every corner of this wine. The palate is plush and plump, with characters of mandarin blossom, lemon pith and green apple; the acid a mineral-laden river coursing below it all. 5g/L of RS plumps out the texture, giving it a slip and slide that is most attractive. Not quite sweet, but not quite dry either. A thoroughly quenching and lovely riesling. Screw cap | 12.5% alc. | To 2031 | $30 | EL

Styx Gully Mount Barker Chardonnay 2019 Toasted nuts and grilled yellow peach on both nose and palate. Plenty to touch and feel here, the texture courtesy of oak fermentation. A creamy wine with electrifying acidity that props up the orchard fruit. Lovely stuff. Screw cap | 13% alc. | To 2028 | $30 | EL

Book Ends Mount Barker Cabernet Sauvignon 2018 Brilliant intensity of flavour and tannins, and brilliant value for money. Good length of flavour indicates some potential joy in the cellar going forward. It's got that attractive Mount Barker muscle about it ... Screw cap | 14.5% alc. | To 2031 | $30 | EL

Frankland River Tempranillo 2019 Violets, raspberries and fresh mulberries off the bush, with black pepper, licorice and anise sprinkled around the edges. The fruit on the palate has a sweet core – this is juicy and pleasurable and great. A modern, glossy rendition of temp – it basically begs for a barbecue. Screw cap | 14.5% alc. | To 2027 | $22 | EL

Zarephath Wines

424 Moorialup Road, East Porongurup, WA 6324 **T** (08) 9853 1152 **www**.zarephathwines.com.au **OPEN** Mon-Sat 10-5, Sun 10-4 **WINEMAKER** Robert Diletti **EST.** 1994 **DOZENS** 1500 **VYDS** 8.9ha

The Zarephath vineyard was owned and operated by Brothers and Sisters of The Christ Circle a Benedictine community. In 2014 they sold the property to Rosie Singer and her partner Ian Barrett-Lennard, who live on the spot full-time and undertake all the vineyard work, supplemented by the local Afghani community during vintage and pruning.

95 **Porongurup Syrah 2018** Graphite and mineral. Blackberry and mulberry. This is luscious – and that' the vintage. The 2018 season yields wines like this: power with inky ripeness. The cool-climate acid is the key to giving an extra dimension of pedigree. Concentrated and intense – a beautiful wine. Screw cap | 13.5% alc. | To 2035 | $30 | EL

ION

ɅIanjimup

raphite Road  ★★★★

ʒ3 Graphite Road, Manjimup, WA 6258 **T** 0408 914 836 **www**.graphiteroad.com.au **OPEN** By appt
IEMAKER Kim Horton **EST.** 2017 **DOZENS** 4250 **VYDS** 9ha

aphite Road is the name of the thoroughfare in South Western Australia leading to the wnship of Manjimup. The road winds through state forests filled with towering Karri trees, ɔssing the Gairdner River and passing the historic 'One Tree Bridge' on the journey through ɘ scenic natural landscape.

Cross Sections Sauvignon Blanc 2020 Straw green aromas of passionfruit, Granny Smith and kiwi mesh on the palate with bright acidity. Refreshing and lifted. Lovely. Screw cap | 13.3% alc. | To 2023 | $22 | EL

eos Estate 

ʔ4 Graphite Road, Manjimup, WA 6258 **T** (08) 9772 1378 **www**.peosestate.com.au **OPEN** By appt
IEMAKER Willow Bridge (Kim Horton) **EST.** 1996 **DOZENS** 13000 **VYDS** 37.5ha

e Peos family has farmed in the west Manjimup district for almost a century, the 3rd ıneration of 4 brothers developing the vineyard from 1996. There are over 37ha of vines ɔluding shiraz, merlot, chardonnay, cabernet sauvignon, sauvignon blanc, pinot noir d verdelho.

Four Kings Single Vineyard Manjimup Shiraz 2019 Smelling this elicited a smile, such is the vibrancy and potent intensity of the aromatics: blackberry, violets, fennel flower, licorice. The palate is juicy, fleshy and almost bouncy – the tannins have a jolly chew about them that trampolines the flavours around the mouth. Once gone, the wine leaves a satisfying, cleansing aftertaste. Screw cap | 14.5% alc. | To 2027 | $32 | EL

ƷION

ɅIargaret River

bbey Vale 

71 Wildwood Road, Yallingup Hills, WA 6282 **T** (08) 9755 2121 **www**.abbeyvalewines.com.au
EN Wed–Sun 10–5 **WINEMAKER** Ben Roodhouse, Julian Langworthy **EST.** 2016 **DOZENS** 2000 **VYDS** 17ha

tuated in the north of the Margaret River region, the Abbey Vale vineyards were established 1985 by the McKay family. The picturesque cellar door offers a range of local produce and tisan cheeses to accompany the wines, and overlooks a large dam that provides visitors ith one of the most sublime views in the region.

Premium RSV Margaret River Chenin Blanc 2020 Flinty, funky and delicious, this has concentrated flavour for days, and (like all the Abbey Vale wines) it offers extreme value for money. Unthinkable that you should buy anything else for the same amount. Saline acid courses and weaves through the lanolin, apricot and beeswax characters. Ultimately the oak cradles and supports the finish, rather than coercing it. What a wine. Screw cap | 12.5% alc. | To 2031 | $25 | EL

Premium RSV Margaret River Shiraz 2020 Ridiculous value for money here. Balanced, savoury/sweet, rich/fine, dense/layered – all the good things we want to see in shiraz. At $25 – run, don't walk. Screw cap | 14.5% alc. | To 2031 | $25 | EL

Premium RSV Margaret River Cabernet Sauvignon 2019 Now we're talking – this is serious cabernet at a ridiculous price. The tannins form a streamlined shape that cup the fruit and urge it along the palate. Cassis and raspberry fall over themselves to beat licorice and star anise to the fore. The acidity keeps everything fresh and relevant. Lovely wine, great price. Screw cap | 14% alc. | To 2030 | $25 | EL

ʌmelia Park Wines 

57 Caves Road, Wilyabrup, WA 6280 **T** (08) 9755 6747 **www**.ameliaparkwines.com.au **OPEN** 7 days
–5 **WINEMAKER** Jeremy Gordon **EST.** 2009 **DOZENS** 25000 **VYDS** 9.6ha

Jeremy Gordon and wife Daniela founded Amelia Park Wines with business partner Peter Walsh. Amelia Park initially relied on contract-grown grapes, but in 2013 purchased the Moss Brothers site in Wilyabrup, allowing the construction of a new winery and cellar door.

97 **Reserve Margaret River Cabernet Sauvignon 2018** Cabernet can be so exciting when it walks the tightrope between ripe/succulent/supple and herbaceous (fresh garden herbs, with sprinklings of Margaret River salt bush). This is everything we expect from the perfect 2018 vintage: concentrate ripe cassis, raspberry, pomegranate and red licorice. The acidity is bright and salty and punched deep into the fruit. The oak, wherever that is, is completely, seamlessly integrated. A triumphant wine. Bravo. Screw cap | 14.5% alc. | To 2041 | $65 | EL

96 **Reserve Frankland River Shiraz 2018** From the exceptional 2018 vintage springs this aromatic, brooding, concentrated and complex shiraz from one of WA's great shiraz regions. Salted mulberry raspberry, blackberry and licorice, layered with red licorice, bitter cocoa, star anise and that regional stamp of ferrous/red dirt/earth. Ripe acidity weaves in and out of the long finish. This will bring pleasure now, and well into the future. Screw cap | 14.5% alc. | To 2036 | $65 | EL

Aravina Estate

61 Thornton Road, Yallingup, WA 6282 **T** (08) 9750 1111 **www**.aravinaestate.com **OPEN** 7 days 10–5 **WINEMAKER** Ryan Aggiss **EST.** 2010 **DOZENS** 10 000 **VYDS** 28ha

In 2010 Steve Tobin and family acquired the winery and vineyard of Amberley Estate from Accolade, but not the Amberley brand. Steve has turned the property into a multifaceted business with a host of attractions including a sports car collection, restaurant and wedding venue.

94 **The 'A' Collection Margaret River Cabernet Merlot Malbec 2020** Every year it seems there are mor wineries in Margaret River producing cabernet malbec blends – and thank goodness. This blend is a match made in southwest heaven. Vibrant, juicy fruit bounces out of the glass: pomegranate, pink peppercorn, raspberry and licorice. This is brilliantly delicious, and the value for money is superb. Drink it while you wait for other such blends to come of age. It's a beauty. Screw cap | 13.5% alc. | To 2031 | $23 | EL

Arlewood Estate

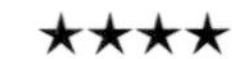

679 Calgardup Road West, Forest Grove, WA 6286 **T** (08) 9757 6676 **www**.arlewood.com.au **OPEN** Fri–Sun 11–5 or by appt **WINEMAKER** Cath Oates **EST.** 1988 **DOZENS** 3000 **VYDS** 6.08ha

Garry Gossatti purchased the run-down, close-planted Arlewood vineyard in 2008, and livec in the onsite house from '08–12, driving to Perth 1 day per week for his extensive hospitality/ hotel business (which paid Arlewood's bills). His involvement in the resurrection of the vineyard was hands-on, and the cool site in the south of Margaret River was, and remains, his obsession.

92 **Villaggio The Fumé Blanc Margaret River 2020** Intense passionfruit, gooseberry and kiwifruit on the nose and palate. The oak is surprisingly well integrated at this stage, perhaps owing to the very concentrated fruit. A well-executed partnership. Screw cap | 12% alc. | To 2027 | $22 | EL

Ashbrook Estate 

379 Tom Cullity Drive, Wilyabrup, WA 6280 **T** (08) 9755 6262 **www**.ashbrookwines.com.au **OPEN** 7 days 10–5 **WINEMAKER** Catherine Edwards, Brian Devitt **EST.** 1975 **DOZENS** 12 500 **VYDS** 17.4ha

This fastidious producer of consistently excellent estate-grown table wines shuns publicity and is less known than is deserved, selling much of its wine through the cellar door and to a loyal mailing list clientele.

94 **Margaret River Verdelho 2020** Crunchy acidity and a salivating plump mid palate which is cramme to bursting with nashi pear, green apple, soft talcy florals and gentle suggestions of citrus pith. Incredibly pretty, almost dusty, very satisfying and has great length of flavour. Screw cap | 13.5% alc. | To 2027 | $27 | EL

Brash Road Vineyard 

PO Box 455, Yallingup, WA 6282 **T** 0448 448 840 **www**.brashvineyard.com.au **WINEMAKER** Bruce Dukes (Contract) **EST.** 2000 **DOZENS** 1500 **VYDS** 18ha

Brash Vineyard was established in 1998 as Woodside Valley Estate. While most of the grapes were sold to other Margaret River producers, cabernet sauvignon, shiraz, chardonnay and merlot were made, and in '09 the Cabernet Sauvignon and the Shiraz earned the winery a star rating. It is now owned by Chris and Anne Carter (managing partners, who live and work site), Brian and Anne McGuinness, and Rik and Jenny Nitert. The vineyard is now mature d produces high-quality fruit.

Single Vineyard Margaret River Sauvignon Blanc 2020 This wine leaves a trail of medals and trophies in its wake, and it is clear to see why: punchy sauvignon aromatics of gooseberry, cassis, green apple and sugar snap peas fold seamlessly into a textural and layered palate. The resounding impression is one of concentration – this vineyard is known for it. Screw cap | 13.4% alc. | To 2025 | $28 | EL

:lairault Streicker Wines  

77 Caves Road, Wilyabrup, WA 6280 **T** (08) 9755 6225 **www**.clairaultstreicker.com.au
EN 7 days 10-5 **WINEMAKER** Bruce Dukes **EST.** 1976 **DOZENS** 12000 **VYDS** 113ha

is multifaceted business is owned by New York resident John Streicker. It began in 2002 nen he purchased the Yallingup Protea Farm and vineyards. This was followed by the rchase of a number of other notable vineyards, and in April '12 Streicker acquired Clairault, inging a further 40ha of estate vines, including 12ha now over 40 years old. The two brands e effectively run as one venture.

Streicker Ironstone Block Old Vine Margaret River Chardonnay 2019 Perhaps unsurprisingly oak-driven at this very early stage, but the underlying fruit has persistence and quiet concentration that lingers on the palate, determined to outlast the oak. Which it does. Eminently classy and layered, by the time this is released it will be a superstar. Screw cap | 14% alc. | To 2035 | $50 | EL

Clairault Estate Margaret River Cabernet Sauvignon 2017 Elegant, balanced and fine cabernet from a cool year. The supple fruit is wrapped up in a package of finely gripping tannins, cooling acidity and exotic spice, hinting at both a long future in the cellar and pleasure on the table tonight. Wonderful stuff. Screw cap | 14% alc. | To 2035 | $60 | EL

Streicker Bridgeland Block Margaret River Fumé Blanc 2019 Cracked coconut, coriander seed, fennel flower, sugar snap peas and graphite against a backdrop of turmeric, saffron, lemon pith and brine. On the palate, this shows just as much of the vineyard as it does the winemaker's hand – the oak and fruit are at constant war with each other for dominance. This needs a year in bottle for the peace treaties to be signed, but life post-signing promises harmony, interest and deliciousness. It has the potential to polarise, but on my page, this is impressive. Screw cap | 13% alc. | To 2032 | $30 | EL

Clairault Margaret River Cabernet Sauvignon 2019 An interesting wine – the flavour is not intensely concentrated, but it is exceedingly long. When you think it has finished, it continues. Cassis, raspberry, bay leaf and violets. There is pepper and saline acid in there, too. Elegant, understated and restrained; a cabernet for the ages. Screw cap | 14.5% alc. | To 2035 | $30 | EL

:owaramup Wines  

Tassel Road, Cowaramup, WA 6284 **T** (08) 9755 5195 **www**.cowaramupwines.com.au **OPEN** By appt
NEMAKER Naturaliste Vintners (Bruce Dukes) **EST.** 1996 **DOZENS** 3000 **VYDS** 11ha

ussell and Marilyn Reynolds run a biodynamic vineyard with the aid of sons Cameron iticulturist) and Anthony (assistant winemaker). Notwithstanding low yields and the scipline that biodynamic grapegrowing entails, wine prices are modest. Wines are released nder the Cowaramup and Clown Fish labels.

3 **Clown Fish Margaret River Sauvignon Blanc Semillon 2020** Gooseberry, sugar snap, jasmine florals and fine chalky phenolics. This is pretty, zesty and energetic – perfect summertime drinking. Screw cap | 13.5% alc. | To 2024 | $20 | EL

Clown Fish Margaret River Sauvignon Blanc 2020 Stainless-steel ferment has created a light, bright, juicy and concentrated sauvignon blanc. Pretty, if uncomplicated summer drinking. Screw cap | 13.5% alc. | To 2023 | $20 | EL

:ullen Wines  

323 Caves Road, Wilyabrup, WA 6280 **T** (08) 9755 5277 **www**.cullenwines.com.au **OPEN** 7 days
)-4.30 **WINEMAKER** Vanya Cullen, Andy Barrett-Lennard **EST.** 1971 **DOZENS** 20000 **VYDS** 49ha

pioneer of Margaret River, Cullen Wines has always produced long-lived wines of highly dividual style from the mature estate vineyard. Margaret Cullen has been named Viticulturist f the Year in the *Wine Companion 2022*. The vineyard has progressed beyond organic to iodynamic certification and, subsequently, has become the first vineyard and winery in ustralia to be certified carbon neutral. Winemaking is in the hands of Vanya Cullen, daughter f founders Kevin and Diana Cullen; she is possessed of an extraordinarily good palate and enerosity to the cause of fine wine.

98 **Kevin John 2019** As usual, the Kevin John arrives with an aura about it ... it undulates in the mouth, whipping and changing like Melbourne weather, 4 seasons in one day. It has exotic market spice, ripe orchard fruit, orange blossom, turmeric, saffron curls and saline acid. It's extraordinarily long, incredibly exciting and with phenolic texture that elevates it beyond the excitement that it delivers. Through it all meanders a coastal breeze, keeping it light and airy; the thundering power of Gingin fruit is concealed under many folds of flavour. Screw cap | 13% alc. | To 2041 | $127 | EL

Diana Madeline 2019 Cassis and red licorice on the nose, bay and salt bush, too. The palate is salty and fine with layers upon layers of spice and texture. The tannins are like finely textured gills, stacked as delicately as the folds in a mushroom. The length of flavour unfurls and extends across the palate, taking so long to fade that this entire tasting note is possible off one sip. The rest are just for pleasure. Drink it now, or in 40+ years from now ... both will be possible. Screw cap | 13.5% alc. | To 2061 | $140 | EL

Diana Madeline 2018 An icon wine from a watershed vintage. This is Margaret River pedigree of the highest order; powdery-fine tannins that shape and caress the perfectly ripe red fruits. The acidity the driver over the tongue, the layers of flavour and texture seem never-ending. Show stopping. Pu fruit concentration. Blimey. Screw cap | 13% alc. | To 2061 | $135 | EL

97 **Legacy Margaret River Sauvignon Blanc 2019** It was a cool year for the 2019 vintage, producing mineral, aromatic and very fine wines. This is no exception. Salted edamame, sugar snap, jasmine tea, white currant, green apple skin, juniper berry and salt bush eddy around on the palate, swirling in and out of exotically spiced oak, crushed limestone/talc/basalt/petrichor. Evokes cicadas on a hot afternoon sea breeze, somehow. This is the most profound sauvignon blanc in Australia. Screw cap | 12.2% alc. | To 2035 | $100 | EL | ♥

96 **Amber 2019** This is easily one of the most exciting Amber releases to date. Bitter orange, citrus zest, saffron and brine, the phenolics are very fine, curling their way in and out of the ever moving fruits on the palate. Balanced, fine and thrilling to drink. Skin contact, amphora ferment, oak-matured sauvignon blanc ... who'd have thought it could steal the heart so thoroughly ... but it does. Screw cap | 12.5% alc. | To 2031 | $39 | EL

94 **Dancing in the Sun Wilyabrup 2018** 54/43/3% semillon/sauvignon blanc/verdelho. Salted pineappl jalapeño, chamomile flower, sugar snap pea, gooseberry, jasmine tea and white currants form the core of this wine. It is salty, savoury and spiced; driven by a strong undercurrent of phenolic structure. It stands to reason that verdelho is a potent if negligible inclusion here, such is the shape of the wine, while the regional marriage of semillon and sauvignon blanc lead the charge. Brilliant length of flavour to finish. Screw cap | 13.5% alc. | To 2031 | $25 | EL

Deep Woods Estate

889 Commonage Road, Yallingup, WA 6282 **T** (08) 9756 6066 **www**.deepwoods.wine **OPEN** Wed-Sun 11-5, 7 days during hols **WINEMAKER** Julian Langworthy, Emma Gillespie, Andrew Bretherton **EST.** 1987 **DOZENS** 30000 **VYDS** 14ha

Deep Woods Estate is a key part of the dynamic wine business of Peter Fogarty that includes Millbrook in the Perth Hills, Evans & Tate (70% owned), Margaret River Vintners and extensive vineyard holdings in Wilyabrup and elsewhere in Margaret River, plus in Smithbrook in Pemberton. The business is the largest producer in WA with 600000 dozen.

97 **Single Vineyard G5 Margaret River Cabernet Sauvignon 2019** Elegant, fragrant, medium bodied ar silky. This is riddled with cassis, raspberry, licorice, fennel flower, supple fruit and salivating balanc Will require a decant – the tannins call 'present' on the roll call. Cellar it with total confidence, but drink it whenever you want, because it is absolutely beautiful. Screw cap | 14% alc. | To 2051 | $50 | EL

Reserve Margaret River Cabernet Sauvignon 2018 From the original vineyard planted in '87, the wine matured in new and used French oak for 18 months. This is high-quality, autocratic cabernet, with blackcurrant, earth and bay leaf on the bouquet and palate alike. Minimalist winemaking allows the fruit maximum room to speak. Screw cap | 14% alc. | To 2038 | $75 | JH | ♥

Single Vineyard Margaret River Cabernet Malbec 2019 This is unbelievably delicious – the malbec adds a backdrop of salty pomegranate, raspberry and rhubarb to the chorus of cassis and exotic spice. This has a long cellaring potential, perhaps a touch behind the G5 cabernet from the same vintage, but boy oh boy ... this is going to give you pleasure, right now. Wow. Screw cap | 14% alc. | To 2041 | $50 | EL

96 **Reserve Margaret River Chardonnay 2019** While the 2018 was all about latent fruit power and ripe concentration, this vintage is defined by intricate layers of flinty stone fruit and taut minerally acidit It sings with poise and line, and doesn't stop for breath. Another astoundingly delicious chardonnay from an unbroken run. If this isn't on your annual purchase list, it should be. Screw cap | 13% alc. To 2036 | $55 | EL

Margaret River Rosé 2020 For the first time, 100% tempranillo from Yallingup Hills. Handled oxidatively and clearly the product of a warmer, richer year, this has admirable phenolic structure and shape on the palate, which contains ripe red berry fruit. Fermented to dry and yet astoundingly generous, this is straight-up delicious, and far longer and more thought provoking than a rosé has any business to be. Screw cap | 13% alc. | To 2025 | $35 | EL | ♥

94 **Harmony Margaret River Rosé 2020** Shiraz, merlot and tempranillo. Juicy, flavoursome, rollicking red berries and briny acid – this is a little superstar. Routinely reliable rosé for a really reasonable price. A go-to. Screw cap | 13% alc. | To 2023 | $15 | EL

evil's Lair ★★★★★

ky Road, Forest Grove via Margaret River, WA 6286 **T** (08) 9759 2000 **www**.devils-lair.com
EMAKER Ben Miller, Matt Godfrey **EST.** 1990

ving rapidly carved out a high reputation for itself through a combination of clever ckaging and impressive wine quality, Devil's Lair was acquired by Southcorp in 1996. e estate vineyards have been substantially increased since; production has increased m 40000 dozen to many times greater, largely due to its Fifth Leg and Dance with the vil wines.

Dance with the Devil Margaret River Chardonnay 2019 The bouquet has pronounced barrel-fermentation aromas benefiting from a hint of smoky oak, and the palate takes the baton in a smooth movement. It's easy to take this level of chardonnay for granted, but that's the gift of a climate that is so reliable for crystal-clear varietal expression. Screw cap | 13% alc. | To 2025 | $25 | JH

omaine Naturaliste  

) Johnson Road, Wilyabrup, WA 6280 **T** (08) 9755 6776 **www**.domainenaturaliste.com.au
N 7 days 10-5 **WINEMAKER** Bruce Dukes **EST.** 2012 **DOZENS** 12000 **VYDS** 21ha

uce Dukes' career dates back over 30 years, its foundations built around a degree agronomy from the University of WA, followed by a master's degree in viticulture and ronomy from the University of California (Davis). A 4-year stint at Francis Ford Coppola's onic Niebaum-Coppola winery in the Napa Valley followed. Back in WA, his winery was set to handle small and large amounts of fruit, but it was not until '12 that he made his own ne under the Domaine Naturaliste label. The quality of all the wines is excellent.

Artus Margaret River Chardonnay 2019 Whole-bunch pressed, wild-yeast fermented in new (40%) and used French oak. The bouquet is complex with funky (good) aromas, the palate briefly nodding to the bouquet before moving on to a pure stream of fresh citrus and white peach. The balance and aftertaste are special. Screw cap | 13% alc. | To 2034 | $49 | JH

Rachis Margaret River Syrah 2019 Stemmy/sappy/spicy nose that basically jumps out of the glass. While the fruit occupies the midnight end of the spectrum, the pink-peppercorn spice brings it back closer to the middle. This is succulent, fleshy, crunchy ... quite gorgeous. A resounding YES, and thoroughly of the 'modern Margaret River way' for shiraz. Bravo. Screw cap | 14% alc. | To 2030 | $32 | EL

Sauvage Margaret River Sauvignon Blanc 2018 Spicy white pepper and nectarine play alongside red apple skins and star anise. This is modern, glossy, seamless winemaking. Nothing but good things to say here, brilliant stuff. Screw cap | 13% alc. | To 2030 | $32 | EL

Floris Margaret River Chardonnay 2019 Spicy yellow peach, flakes of sea salt and sprinklings of crushed cashew and star anise make for a complex, rich (yet somehow delicate) and precise chardonnay. Glassy texture and very fine phenolic structure places this in top-shelf company. Unbelievable value for money. Screw cap | 13% alc. | To 2031 | $30 | EL

Discovery Margaret River Cabernet Sauvignon 2018 Perfect weather and yields in '18, the resulting wines standing on the shoulders of their predecessors. The nose here is tempting to say the least – cassis, raspberry and fields of violets and sage. The palate follows obediently, the acidity being the last thing that swoops in and cleans everything up ... what a gorgeous wine. Testament to the year, the hands and the vineyards. Ridiculous price. Screw cap | 14% alc. | To 2030 | $24 | EL

Discovery Margaret River Sauvignon Blanc Semillon 2020 Salivating gooseberry, sugar snap pea, jasmine florals and white spice define the nose, the palate follows suit. This is bouncy and delicious, with brilliant expression of flavour. The barrel work is almost imperceptible, save for the chalky phenolics and plush texture on the palate. Lovely. Screw cap | 13% alc. | To 2024 | $24 | EL

riftwood Estate  

14 Caves Road, Wilyabrup, WA 6282 **T** (08) 9755 6323 **www**.driftwoodwines.com.au
EN 7 days 10.30-5 **WINEMAKER** Kane Grove **EST.** 1989 **DOZENS** 18000 **VYDS** 22ha

iftwood Estate is a well-established landmark on the Margaret River scene. Quite apart from fering a casual dining restaurant capable of seating 200 people (open 7 days for lunch and nner) and a mock Greek open-air theatre, its wines feature striking and stylish packaging d opulent flavours.

Single Site Margaret River Chardonnay 2019 This is one of 'those' wines. The blindsiding wines that take you by surprise and imprint big on your memory. While the oak is playing a significant role right now, it pales in comparison to the concentrated fruit that lingers behind it. Yellow peach, curry leaf, red apple skins and salty acidity that courses through the very heart of the wine. 2019 was a cooler year, and is one to watch. Wines like this show why. Screw cap | 13% alc. | To 2036 | $70 | EL

94 **Artifacts Margaret River Sauvignon Blanc Semillon 2020** 63/33/3/1% sauvignon blanc/semillon/ viognier/chardonnay. Matured for 7 months in French oak (33% new). As expected, a dash of viognier has a disproportionate impact on this wine, introducing slippery texture, apricots, juniper, elderflower and hints of star anise. The palate is textural and layered; the oak is evident, ye supportive rather than dominant. Saline acid ties it all together, cleaning up the finish and refreshi the palate. Screw cap | 12.5% alc. | To 2027 | $30 | EL

Eddie McDougall Wines

801 Glenferrie Road, Hawthorn, Vic 3122 (postal) **T** 0413 960 102 **www.eddiemcdougallwines.com.**
WINEMAKER Eddie McDougall, Lilian Carter **EST.** 2007 **DOZENS** 1000

Eddie McDougall is an award-winning winemaker, wine judge, columnist and TV personality. Eddie's winemaking credentials extend over a decade of experience with some of the world most influential wineries. In '13 he was one of 12 elite wine professionals selected for the annual Len Evans Tutorial, regarded as the world's most esteemed wine education program.

90 **The Flying Winemaker Margaret River Cabernet Sauvignon 2019** Aromatic, ripe and juicy. Intense saturated red fruit on the palate – a crowd-pleasing, fleshy wine. Screw cap | 15% alc. | To 2027 $20 | EL

Evans & Tate

Cnr Metricup Road/Caves Road, Wilyabrup, WA 6280 **T** (08) 9755 6244 **www.evansandtate.wine**
OPEN 7 days 10.30-5 **WINEMAKER** Matthew Byrne **EST.** 1970 **VYDS** 12.3ha

The history of Evans & Tate has a distinct wild-west feel to its ownership changes since 1970, when it started life as a small 2-family-owned business centred on the Swan District. Suffice it to say, it was part of a corporate chess game between McWilliam's Wines and the Fogarty Wine Group. It is now 100% owned by Fogarty, who previously held 70%. This doubles Fogarty's production to 600000 dozen, cementing its place as the largest producer of WA wine.

96 **Single Vineyard Margaret River Chardonnay 2018** This wine is a statement of excellence for Margaret River chardonnay: spicy, rich, saline and very long. Classy wine and detailed winemaking Yes please. Screw cap | 13.5% alc. | To 2030 | $35 | EL

Redbrook Reserve Margaret River Cabernet Sauvignon 2017 The cooler year has birthed yet anot cabernet of delicacy, length and finesse. Matt Byrne's Redbrook Reserve cabernet is worthy of the same praise heaped upon prior vintages. Succulent red fruits and densely packed flavour, held together with fine-knit tannins. Ready to drink now, but with a determined future in the cellar, too – this is what defines the wonder of great Margaret River cabernet. Screw cap | 14% alc. | To 2041 $65 | EL

Fermoy Estate

838 Metricup Road, Wilyabrup, WA 6280 **T** (08) 9755 6285 **www.fermoy.com.au** **OPEN** 7 days 10-5
WINEMAKER Jeremy Hodgson **EST.** 1985 **DOZENS** 25000 **VYDS** 27.28ha

A long-established winery with plantings of semillon, sauvignon blanc, chardonnay, caberne sauvignon and merlot. The Young family acquired Fermoy Estate in 2010 and built a larger cellar door which opened in '13, signalling the drive to increase domestic sales. They are happy to keep a relatively low profile, however difficult that may be given the quality of the wines.

96 **Reserve Margaret River Chardonnay 2019** As with the Reserve cabernet, the fruit quality in this wi stands up and speaks for itself. Yellow peach, salted cashews and warm roasted spices are at the forefront. Long-lingering flavours are defined once again by the fruit. The winemaking is subtle an has shaped the wine rather than coerced it in any way. Chalky phenolics with a slight bitter edge create some real interest and saliva through the finish. Utterly lovely. Three trophies at the Wine Show of WA '20. Screw cap | 13% alc. | To 2036 | $60 | EL

94 **Margaret River Chardonnay 2019** In the context of chardonnay, 2019 was a vintage of delicacy, spice, minerality and restraint. In another word, excellent. Grilled stone fruit, salty acid and layers of curry leaf and exotic market spices come together in this sophisticated and expressive wine. There's a sparkly core of purity that is very attractive. Delicious, in a word. Screw cap | 13% alc. | To 2027 | $30 | EL

ametree 

★★★★★

Caves Road/Chain Avenue, Dunsborough, WA 6281 **T** (08) 9756 8577 **www**.flametreewines.com
N 7 days 10-5 **WINEMAKER** Cliff Royle, Julian Scott **EST**. 2007 **DOZENS** 20000

metree, owned by the Towner family (John, Liz, Rob and Annie), has had extraordinary
:cess since its first vintage in 2007. The usual practice of planting a vineyard and then
ding someone to make the wine was turned on its head: a state-of-the-art winery was
lt, and grape purchase agreements signed with growers in the region. Show success was
ped by the winning of the Jimmy Watson Trophy with its '07 Cabernet Merlot.

S.R.S. Wallcliffe Margaret River Chardonnay 2019 From a single site, wild-yeast fermented and matured for 10 months in French puncheons (40% new). Intense white peach and pink grapefruit dance a pas de deux on the long palate, creamy cashew oak nuances beating a rhythm in a perfectly judged support role. Screw cap | 13% alc. | To 2032 | $65 | JH

Margaret River Chardonnay 2019 Compelling struck-match nose. Silky, viscose palate - rounded almost, shaped by phenolic edge and grip. Flinty and mineral, but with hallmark yellow peach, pink grapefruit and curry leaf. Rounding out in a tight back palate and defined by saline acid. Tremendous value at the price! Screw cap | 13.2% alc. | To 2030 | $29 | EL

Margaret River Chardonnay 2020 Salted preserved lemon, yellow peach and brine on the nose. Even at first glance, this has all the concentration and complexity that we have become accustomed to from this label. On the palate, it is both graceful and heady, with flavour packed into every corner of the glass. Screw cap | 13% alc. | To 2028 | $30 | EL

owstone Wines 

98 Bussell Highway, Forest Grove, WA 6286 **T** 0487 010 275 **www**.flowstonewines.com
N By appt **WINEMAKER** Stuart Pym **EST**. 2013 **DOZENS** 1500 **VYDS** 3ha

teran Margaret River winemaker Stuart Pym's career constituted long-term successive
es: '13 was the year he and Perth-based wine tragic Phil Giglia established Flowstone
nes. In '03 Stuart had purchased a small property on the edge of the Margaret River
teau, and from '17, Flowstone leased a vineyard at Karridale, planted to long-established
uvignon blanc and chardonnay, having previously purchased part of the crop for its
gional wines. The lease puts the vineyard on par with the estate plantings; the best fruit is
ained, the balance sold.

Queen of the Earth Margaret River Sauvignon Blanc 2019 This is sensational. Serious layers of flavour and texture on the palate show a reverence for the variety by Stuart Pym. Long, lean and lithe; this shares guava, lychee, red apple skins, white stone fruit, exotic spice and a distinct oriental leaning of anise and pink peppercorn. Serious stuff. Screw cap | 12.9% alc. | To 2030 | $55 | EL

Margaret River Sauvignon Blanc 2019 The palate has a fine textural creaminess that massages the flavour into the mouth rather than asserting it. The characters of salted jalapeño, snow pea and cassis fold seamlessly into the saline acid line. An incredibly elegant and seamless wine - the attention to detail is evident. Very long. Screw cap | 12.5% alc. | To 2027 | $32 | EL

Queen of the Earth Margaret River Cabernet Sauvignon 2017 Stuart Pym is not afraid of pushing boundaries: 3 years in oak! Well ... it's nowhere near as evident in the glass as it should be, thanks to the pedigree of the fruit. Savoury, dense, flavourful and very long, this is built to last. Buy it now, but don't look at it until 2027. Screw cap | 14% alc. | To 2047 | $74 | EL

Margaret River Gewürztraminer 2019 Intoxicatingly aromatic, spicy and opulent. All the hallmarks of a brilliant Asian food match (lychee, cumin, lemon pith, strawberry, nashi pear and lemongrass) - but the infinitesimal production says it better be great food, too! It's refreshing like a cold pool on a hot day. Screw cap | 13.5% alc. | To 2030 | $32 | EL

Moonmilk White Margaret River 2020 59/29/8/4% savagnin/viognier/gewürztraminer/sauvignon blanc. Hard to imagine how the low price could repay the work that goes into this tiny quantity of wine (226 cases). Textural, salty, taut and exciting. The floral gewürz and oily viognier make a statement, but it is the edgy savagnin that reins it all in. Chalky phenolics through the finish elevate this into the 'delicious and compelling' category. Screw cap | 13% alc. | To 2024 | $22 | EL

Moonmilk Margaret River Shiraz Grenache 2019 70/25/5% shiraz/grenache/viognier, vinified separately. Matured 10 months in a combination of old barriques and Cognac barrels (older than 20 years). This wine is brilliant. The complex vinification effort was worth it. Buy it if you can find it. Screw cap | 14% alc. | To 2030 | $25 | EL

Forester Estate ⚲

1064 Wildwood Road, Yallingup, WA 6282 **T** (08) 9755 2000 **www**.foresterestate.com.au **OPEN** By ap
WINEMAKER Kevin McKay, Todd Payne **EST.** 2001 **DOZENS** 52000 **VYDS** 33.5ha

Forester Estate is owned by Kevin and Jenny McKay. Winemaker Todd Payne has had a distinguished career, starting in the Great Southern, thereafter the Napa Valley, back to Plantagenet, then Esk Valley in Hawke's Bay, plus 2 vintages in the Northern Rhône Valley, or with esteemed producer Yves Cuilleron in 2008. His move back to WA completed the circle

94 **Margaret River Sauvignon Blanc 2020** Sweaty complexity on the nose – saffron, curry leaf, sugar snap peas and ripe summer-green capsicum. The palate is texturally layered, with a spicy green jalapeño character that bursts onto the mid-palate scene. Interesting and delicious, complex drinking for the price. Screw cap | 12.5% alc. | To 2030 | $25 | EL

Fraser Gallop Estate ⚲

493 Metricup Road, Wilyabrup, WA 6280 **T** (08) 9755 7553 **www**.frasergallopestate.com.au
OPEN 7 days 11–4 **WINEMAKER** Clive Otto, Ellin Tritt **EST.** 1999 **DOZENS** 10000 **VYDS** 20ha

Nigel Gallop began the development of the vineyard in 1999, planting cabernet sauvignon, semillon, petit verdot, cabernet franc, malbec, merlot, sauvignon blanc and multi-clone chardonnay. The dry-grown vines have modest yields, followed by kid-glove treatment in th winery. The wines have had richly deserved success in wine shows and journalists' reviews.

96 **Parterre Wilyabrup Margaret River Cabernet Sauvignon 2018** Reaching heights of near perfectio '18 was a vintage responsible for wines just like this. Supple intensity, concentration of flavour without a gram of weight, the length of flavour possessed only by very healthy, perfectly ripe and balanced grapes. What a gloriously seamless wine, continuing the proud legacy of Parterre. Screw cap | 14% alc. | To 2041 | $50 | EL

95 **Parterre Wilyabrup Margaret River Semillon Sauvignon Blanc 2019** From the cool '19 vintage, this wine presents salivating graphite and wet-slate characters both on the nose and palate, interming with white stone fruit, sweet green sugar snap pea and pink grapefruit. Co-fermented in a combination of older French oak barriques, puncheons and long skinny cigar barrels (these enabl better extraction of the thiols from the sauvignon lees), this is a texturally rich yet restrained wine. A recent tasting of the 2013 Parterre shows its ageing potential. Screw cap | 12% alc. | To 2030 | $35 | EL

Margaret River Chardonnay 2020 This is the very definition of crystalline purity. The oak and fruit interplay is seamless – it is impossible to detangle one from the other. The acidity laces it up with a fine saline thread, and together it courses over the tongue through to a very (very) long finish. Qu remarkable for the price! Extremely classy effort. Screw cap | 13% alc. | To 2029 | $26 | EL

94 **Margaret River Semillon Sauvignon Blanc 2020** 69/31% Wilyabrup semillon/Karridale sauvignon blanc. A small portion of the semillon was barrel fermented. Pretty, juicy, vibrant and alive. Classy execution has yielded a distinguished, taut and mineral rendition of the classic SSB blend for whic Margaret River is so famous. Beautiful. Screw cap | 11.7% alc. | To 2022 | $24 | EL

Grace Farm ⚲

741 Cowaramup Bay Road, Gracetown, WA 6285 **T** (08) 9384 4995 **www**.gracefarm.com.au **OPEN** By app
WINEMAKER Jonathan Mettam **EST.** 2006 **DOZENS** 3000 **VYDS** 8.19ha

Situated in the Wilyabrup district, Grace Farm is the small, family-owned vineyard of Elizabeth and John Mair. It takes its name from the nearby coastal hamlet of Gracetown, and is situated beside picturesque natural forest. Viticulturist Tim Quinlan conducts tastings (by appointment), explaining Grace Farm's sustainable viticultural practices.

94 **Margaret River Sauvignon Blanc Semillon 2020** Oak is very evident on the nose and palate at this stage, but in time the fruit swells up and overtakes it, a sure sign of a well-executed match. The br acid that further secures the union is interwoven throughout, making this a very classy propositio indeed. Screw cap | 12.5% alc. | To 2028 | $23 | EL

Happs

575 Commonage Road, Dunsborough, WA 6281 **T** (08) 9755 3300 **www**.happs.com.au **OPEN** 7 days 10–5
WINEMAKER Erl Happ, Mark Warren **EST.** 1978 **DOZENS** 15000 **VYDS** 35.2ha

One-time schoolteacher, potter and winemaker Erl Happ is the patriarch of a 3-generation family. More than anything, Erl has been a creator and experimenter: building the self-designed winery from mudbrick, concrete form and timber; and making the first crusher. In

4 he planted a new 30ha vineyard at Karridale to no less than 28 varieties, including some he earliest plantings of tempranillo in Australia.

Margaret River Viognier 2020 On skins for 4 days, tank fermented with lees stirring. Crystalline fruit on the nose and palate; nashi pear, glacé ginger, green apple, summer apricot and white currant. The palate is viscose and rich, but with line and poise also. A lovely viognier with fine chalky phenolics laced through the mid palate and finish. Really long. Screw cap | 13% alc. | To 2027 | $30 | EL

ay Shed Hill Wines 

Harmans Mill Road, Wilyabrup, WA 6280 **T** (08) 9755 6046 **www**.hayshedhill.com.au
N 7 days 10-5 **WINEMAKER** Michael Kerrigan **EST**. 1987 **DOZENS** 24000 **VYDS** 18.55ha

ke Kerrigan, former winemaker at Howard Park, acquired Hay Shed Hill in late 2006 th co-ownership by the West Cape Howe syndicate) and is now the full-time winemaker. had every confidence that he could dramatically lift the quality of the wines and has done cisely that.

Margaret River Sauvignon Blanc Semillon 2020 Aromas of fresh green sugar snap pea, nashi pear and white currant. The palate follows in this vein, with a plush buoyancy to the texture. Showing both restraint and generosity, there is a lot to like. It induces thoughts of dappled shade and warm breezes. The subtle tartness through the finish (no doubt due to earlier picking for that taut acid line) is holding it off an even higher score. Screw cap | 12.5% alc. | To 2023 | $22 | EL

igher Plane

Tom Cullity Drive, Cowaramup, WA 6284 **T** (08) 9755 9000 **www**.higherplanewines.com.au
N At Juniper Estate, 7 days 10-5 **WINEMAKER** Mark Messenger, Luc Fitzgerald **EST**. 1996
ENS 3000 **VYDS** 14.52ha

gher Plane was purchased by Roger Hill and Gillian Anderson, owners of Juniper Estate, 2006. The brand was retained with the intention of maintaining the unique and special pects of the site in the south of Margaret River distinct from those of Wilyabrup in the north. e close-planted vineyard is sustainably farmed using organic principles.

Margaret River Cabernet Malbec 2018 Ripeness, power and balance, all in equal measure. This is a vibrant beauty, with enough subdued tannins and supple fruit to keep one entertained for some time. Elegant, too. Awesome. Screw cap | 14.1% alc. | To 2041 | $28 | EL

ouse of Cards 

'3220 Caves Road, Yallingup, WA 6282 **T** (08) 9755 2583 **www**.houseofcardswine.com.au
N 7 days 10-5 **WINEMAKER** Travis Wray **EST**. 2011 **DOZENS** 5000 **VYDS** 12ha

e name of the winery is a reflection of the gamble that all viticulturists and winemakers ce every vintage: 'You have to play the hand you are dealt by Mother Nature'. They only use rtified organic estate-grown grapes, open-top fermentation, hand plunging and manual sket pressing. It's certainly doing it the hard way, but it must seem all worthwhile when they oduce wines of such quality.

Dead Man's Hand Margaret River Shiraz 2019 Margaret River saw a cool year in 2019, and so far, the reds that have been released onto the market are showing high spice aromas and detail/nuance on the palate. As does this wine, bolstered by a juicy succulence and bounce from 60% whole bunches. Very attractive. Screw cap | 13.9% alc. | To 2028 | $26 | EL

oward Park

amup Road, Cowaramup, WA 6284 **T** (08) 9756 5200 **www**.burchfamilywines.com.au **OPEN** 7 days 10-5
NEMAKER Janice McDonald, Mark Bailey **EST**. 1986 **VYDS** 183ha

ver the last 30 or so years the Burch family has slowly acquired vineyards in Margaret River d Great Southern. The feng shui–designed cellar door is a must-see. A founding member of stralian First Families of Wines.

Howard Park Mount Barker Riesling 2020 Wow. What a ripper this is. Powerful and intensely concentrated. Scintillating. Titillating. Rippling layers of flavour – I often describe Mount Barker as capable of producing rieslings of muscularity, strength and prowess: this is the very definition. The warmer year is seductive in this context, with the ripe, plush fruit propped up by vertical tent poles of acid. Awesome. Screw cap | 12.5% alc. | To 2041 | $34 | EL

Jilyara 

2 Heath Road, Wilyabrup, WA 6280 **T** (08) 9755 6575 www.jilyara.com.au **OPEN** By appt
WINEMAKER Kate Morgan, Laura Bowler **EST.** 2017 **DOZENS** 4000 **VYDS** 10ha

Craig Cotterell and partner Maria Bergstrom planted the 9.7ha Jilyara Vineyard in 1995, finishing the task the following year. The packaging is very smart, a design-house dream, visually bringing together the local Noongar word of 'Djilyaro' for bee (there is a beehive at each corner of the block).

96 **The Williams' Block Margaret River Chardonnay 2019** I love this wine. It is intensely salty, rich, worked, complex and layered. Salted peach, sun-dried kelp (the crispy kind), Dragon Pearl tea, cu leaf, walnuts and pecans. Endlessly interesting, highly worked, intense. It's not for everyone. If yo a fan of gateway Jura, then you might like to give this a burl. Screw cap | 12.5% alc. | To 2031 | $75 | EL

Juniper

98 Tom Cullity Drive, Cowaramup, WA 6284 **T** (08) 9755 9000 www.juniperestate.com.au **OPEN** 7 da 10-5 **WINEMAKER** Mark Messenger, Luc Fitzgerald **EST.** 1973 **DOZENS** 12000 **VYDS** 19.5ha

Roger Hill and Gillian Anderson purchased the Wrights' Wilyabrup property in 1998, driven by the 25yo vineyard with dry-grown cabernet as the jewel in the crown. They also purchase complementary vineyards in Forest Grove (Higher Plane) and Wilyabrup; the vineyards are sustainably farmed using organic principles.

96 **Cornerstone Karridale Chardonnay 2019** In general, 2019 was a cool and wet year in Margaret Riv The resulting wines are highly aromatic, finely detailed and nuanced. This wine is the product of the powerful Gingin clone, grown in a cool area in a cool year. This, in combination with blocked mlf, lends a fierceness to the acidity, however the fruit stands up to it: guava, white peach, toaste almonds, brine and pink grapefruit. Outstanding. Screw cap | 13% alc. | To 2036 | $70 | EL

Estate Margaret River Aquitaine Rouge 2018 The 2018 vintage was the greatest on record in Margaret River, and was responsible for wines of ripe power, grace, longevity and balance. This w is no exception. Supple, lithe fruit is framed by fine oak, both of which see it pull away into a long and graceful finish. The saline acidity that courses over the palate keeps things fresh and bright. There is pleasure here. Screw cap | 13.8% alc. | To 2041 | $40 | EL

Crossing Margaret River Cabernet Sauvignon Merlot 2018 Bright, clear crimson-purple; this punches way above its weight from the outset. Supple cassis and persistent – but silky – tannins sketch the outline of a wine with freshness and a balance that will sustain its shape for however lo you elect to cellar it. Exceptional value. Screw cap | 14% alc. | To 2030 | $20 | JH

94 **Small Batch Margaret River Fiano 2020** Yellow peach fuzz, red apple, nashi pear, strawberry, cust powder and white pepper. The oak is nowhere to be seen, but contributes a supportive structure from which the fruit can hang. A lot to like here! Very smart. Screw cap | 12.5% alc. | To 2025 | $27 | EL

Small Batch Margaret River Cabernet Sauvignon 2018 It's unfair on other Australian regions that Margaret River can so effortlessly produce cabernet sauvignon with pure varietal definition, coupl with mouthfeel that reassures, not challenges, as cabernet is wont to do. This covers all the bases with blackcurrant and soft tannins, leaving little else to be said. Screw cap | 14% alc. | To 2028 $27 | JH

KarriBindi

111 Scott Road, Karridale, WA 6288 (postal) **T** (08) 9758 5570 www.karribindi.com.au
WINEMAKER Kris Wealand **EST.** 1997 **DOZENS** 1500 **VYDS** 32.05ha

KarriBindi is owned by Kevin, Yvonne and Kris Wealand. The name comes from Karridale and the surrounding karri forests, and from Bindi, the home town of one of the members of the Wealand family. In Noongar, 'karri' means strong, special, spiritual, tall tree; 'bindi' means butterfly.

94 **Margaret River Sauvignon Blanc 2020** Tank-fermented sauvignon blanc can get a bad rap. But wi like this display all of the pungent virtues of the variety: gooseberry, jalapeño, sugar snap pea, pin grapefruit and ripe (but a little bit sweaty, too) citrus. It's all backed by saline acid, which so often pops its head up in Margaret River. Simple, but pure, this is a brilliant example of sauvignon blanc Screw cap | 12.5% alc. | To 2025 | $20 | EL

ɪrrigan + Berry

ꞩox 221, Cowaramup, WA 6284 **T** (08) 9755 6046 **www**.kerriganandberry.com.au **OPEN** At Hay Shed
l and West Cape Howe **WINEMAKER** Michael Kerrigan, Gavin Berry **EST.** 2007 **DOZENS** 1500

ners Michael Kerrigan and Gavin Berry have been making wine in WA for a combined iod of over 50 years and say they have been most closely associated with the 2 varieties t in their opinion define WA: riesling and cabernet sauvignon. They have focused on what nportant, and explain, 'We have spent a total of zero hours on marketing research, and no sultants have been injured in the making of these wines'.

Mount Barker Margaret River Cabernet Sauvignon 2018 Mount Barker fruit brings the structure and the density, Margaret River the red-fruit succulence and latent power. All things as one here, the perfect example of greatness exceeding the sum of its parts. Muscular in its own way and built for long-term gratification. Screw cap | 14% alc. | To 2045 | $60 | EL

Mount Barker Great Southern Riesling 2020 Produced from the near-50yo vines on the Langton Vineyard. A wine with intensity and outright power from low yields reflecting the dry season. The mineral framework of lime zest, pith and juice flavours does its job in this classic regional wine. Screw cap | 11.5% alc. | To 2032 | $30 | JH

A.S. Vino

Box 361 Cowaramup, WA 6284 **www**.lasvino.com **WINEMAKER** Nic Peterkin **EST.** 2013 **DOZENS** 800

ner Nic Peterkin is the grandson of the late Diana Cullen (Cullen Wines) and the son of Mike erkin (Pierro). After graduating from the University of Adelaide with a master's degree in ology and travelling the world as a Flying Winemaker, he came back to roost in Margaret er with the ambition of making wines that are a little bit different, but also within the unds of conventional oenological science.

CBDB Margaret River Chenin Blanc Dynamic Blend 2019 From the cooler 2019 vintage, this brings cheesecloth, rind and preserved lemon on the nose, all of which pave the way for nashi pear and saline acid. This is a texturally complex and layered wine of poise and personality. Length of flavour is long and bang on point. Some wines have a charm and an intrigue that compel a 2nd (and 3rd) glass. This is one. Cork | 13.5% alc. | To 2030 | $50 | EL

a Kooki Wines

Settlers Retreat, Margaret River, WA 6285 **T** 0447 587 15 **www**.lakookiwines.com.au
EMAKER Eloise Jarvis, Glenn Goodall **EST.** 2017 **DOZENS** 335

cept for the fact that the proprietors of La Kooki have accumulated 42 years of winemaking tween them, there would be little or nothing to say about a winery that has a small wine rtfolio. Two detailed A4 sheets cover the conception and birth of La Kooki's Rosé, one ting the quantity made as 114 dozen, the other 250 dozen. Either way, you'd better be ick, because it's an unusual wine.

Boya Margaret River Chardonnay 2020 Sit – there is a story here. Karridale fruit is fermented wild in barrel (20% new), with stones collected from the local coast. 'Boya' means 'stones' in the local Wadandi language. The barrels are periodically rolled, agitating the stones within, stirring the lees and creating layers of phenolic complexity. White peach, fennel flower, white pepper, brine, crushed macadamia and suggestions of curry leaf. On the palate, the pristine and formidable saline acid infuses a staunch backbone, which spools out through a long finish. Screw cap | 12.6% alc. | To 2036 | $65 | EL

arry Cherubino Wines

★★★★★

32 Caves Road, Wilyabrup, WA 6280 **T** (08) 9382 2379 **www**.larrycherubino.com **OPEN** 7 days 10-5
IEMAKER Larry Cherubino, Andrew Siddell, Matt Buchan **EST.** 2005 **DOZENS** 8000 **VYDS** 120ha

rry Cherubino has had a particularly distinguished winemaking career, first at Hardys ntara, then Houghton and thereafter as consultant/Flying Winemaker in Australia, NZ, uth Africa, the US and Italy. The range and quality of his wines is extraordinary, the ices irresistible.

Cherubino Budworth Riversdale Vineyard Frankland River Cabernet Sauvignon 2018 Great colour, deep but vivid crimson/purple. Cedary French oak and blackcurrant fruit are joined at the hip by superb tannins that reflect the day-by-day assessment of the must during the latter weeks of maceration. The mouth-watering savoury aftertaste is the coup de grace for this great cabernet. Screw cap | 14% alc. | To 2043 | $175 | JH | ♥

97 **Cherubino Dijon Karridale Chardonnay 2019** Fermented and matured for 10 months in new and 1 French oak. The elegance and detail of the perfectly balanced mix of white peach, pink grapefrui and quality oak reflects the marriage of the Dijon clones and quality oak. The length and balance immaculate. `Screw cap | 13% alc. | To 2030 | $45 | JH`

Cherubino Margaret River Chardonnay 2019 Rich and layered on the nose, with crushed nuts, sa peach and preserved lemon. Marzipan, nougat, nashi pear, brine and loads of creamy softness o the palate, no doubt thanks to partial mlf. Delicious. 'Oh yum' was muttered aloud while tasting th not a common occurrence. Length of flavour shows this will continue to evolve gracefully for yea `Screw cap | 13.5% alc. | To 2036 | $65 | EL`

Cherubino Frankland River Cabernet Sauvignon 2018 An iridescent ruby in the glass. Saturated in flavour and packed with fine, chalky tannins that provide substance and structure for the swee fruit. There is so much going on here that 2nd and 3rd sips are needed. The tannins and the fruit a generous, chewy and expansive. This bottle could evaporate in a moment. A ruminating wine and showpiece for Frankland River pedigree. `Screw cap | 13.5% alc. | To 2041 | $75 | EL`

96 **Cherubino Great Southern Riesling 2020** Piercing intensity on the palate which spears the tongu with acid, citrus fruit and blossom. It then glides over the rest of the mouth leaving bursts of flavo in its wake. Stopping short of fearsome (only just) this has latent power and structure to spare. It w evolve for decades in your cellar. `Screw cap | 12.5% alc. | To 2041 | $35 | EL`

Cherubino Frankland River Shiraz 2019 The fruit has a plush succulence that crouches on the co of the palate. Savoury tannins shape and guide the fruit through a long finish. It has thundering intensity and a jet stream of length behind it. All things in place for a very long life ahead, but it's tight and closed right now. Perhaps, for all its layers, this is how it should be. `Screw cap | 14% alc. | To 2041 | $55 | EL`

Pedestal Margaret River Cabernet Sauvignon 2018 From vineyards in Wilyabrup, matured in Fren oak for 12 months. It ticks all the boxes with its cassis fruit on the one hand, firm cabernet tannins the other, providing all-up balance. Exceptional value for a wine with an extended drinking windo of opportunity. `Screw cap | 14% alc. | To 2033 | $25 | JH`

95 **The Yard Riversdale Frankland River Riesling 2020** Hand picked from the Riversdale Vineyard. It takes the first sip for the treasure cave of intense lime juice to unroll in waves of flavour that keep coming on each retaste. A classic each-way bet: now, and in 7 or so years as the depth of the wav grows and changes both in flavour (toast) and feel. `Screw cap | 12% alc. | To 2033 | $25 | JH`

Laissez Faire Riesling 2020 Porongurup can express a very particular character in its rieslings; they are talcy and chalky (both in texture and flavour), with a distinct floral nose (jasmine and stephanotis are the most oft observed) and the acidity is intricately woven in and out of the fruit. This has all of those characteristics, which steer it in a most regal and beautiful direction. Very, ve long length of flavour. `Screw cap | 12.4% alc. | To 2041 | $29 | EL`

Laissez Faire IV 2019 72/13/12/3% shiraz/grenache/mataro/counoise. Delicious balance of red varieties here. It's muscular and supple at once, focused only on delivering pleasure. Which it doe Big glass, please. `Screw cap | 13.9% alc. | To 2030 | $29 | EL`

Pedestal Vineyard Elevation Margaret River Cabernet Sauvignon 2018 With 18/9% cabernet franc/malbec. 12 months in oak, further 12 months in bottle prior to release. Cassis, blackberry and mulberry laced with arnica and black licorice. There is a resinous midnight backdrop to all of this, which pushes concentration and power. Pretty remarkable for the price. `Screw cap | 13.9% alc. | To 2030 | $32 | EL`

Ad Hoc Avant Gardening Frankland River Cabernet Sauvignon Malbec 2018 Frankly, this is stunni Texturally like velvet, the fruit is concentrated and pure, reaching into every corner of the mouth. Satsuma plum, raspberry, pink peppercorn, pomegranate and beetroot. Really, really brilliant drinking, at a preposterous price. `Screw cap | 14.5% alc. | To 2031 | $22 | EL`

Leeuwin Estate

`Stevens Road, Margaret River, WA 6285` **T** `(08) 9759 0000` **WWW**`.leeuwinestate.com.au` **OPEN** `7 days 10-5` **WINEMAKER** `Tim Lovett, Phil Hutchison, Breac Wheatley` **EST.** `1974` **DOZENS** `50000` **VYDS** `160ha`

The Art Series Chardonnay is, in my (James') opinion, Australia's finest example based on th wines of the last 30 vintages. The move to screw cap brought a large smile to the faces of those who understand just how superbly the wine ages. The large estate plantings, coupled with strategic purchases of grapes from other growers, provide the base for high-quality Art Series Cabernet Sauvignon and Shiraz; the hugely successful, quick-selling Art Series Riesli and Sauvignon Blanc; and lower priced Prelude and Siblings wines.

98 **Art Series Margaret River Chardonnay 2018** One of three joint winners for Chardonnay of the Year 2022. Benchmark pedigree Margaret River chardonnay from the perfect 2018 vintage. Kaffir leaf, ocean spray, nectarine, yellow peach, custard apple and white peach are the start. Saffron curls, vanilla pod and freshly grated nutmeg frame saline acidity, crouched and coiled. Length of flavour extends across the palate in an endless procession of texture and complexity. All of the power, grace and excellence of previous years is here, amplified. `Screw cap | 13.5% alc. | To 2051 | $126 | EL | ♥`

Art Series Margaret River Cabernet Sauvignon 2017 Wow. Silky smooth aromas of red berries, grey minerality (granite, graphite, etc) and breaths of ocean air whispered about. The palate is exactly as the nose promises, elegant and refined. Length of flavour is where this really kicks into gear, extending seamlessly across the palate, lingering and swirling in its profile. Beautiful, classical cabernet from a cool vintage. What a pleasure this is. Screw cap | 13.5% alc. | To 2041 | $70 | EL

Art Series Margaret River Shiraz 2018 The same layers of complexity and spice as the 2017, with all the ripe fruit and power hallmarks of the 2018 vintage. Bouncy and chewy, the tannins are woven into the fruit. Fruit, oak, acid and tannins are integrated and elegant, showing cohesion and harmony from the get-go. Cool-climate elegance is the lasting impression of this wine, as is the fine, chalky tannin profile that ultimately carries the fruit over the course of the palate. Very detailed. Margaret River can be responsible for seriously beautiful shiraz – this is one. Screw cap | 14% alc. | To 2031 | $42 | EL

Prelude Vineyards Margaret River Cabernet Sauvignon 2018 In case you missed it, '18 may be the greatest cabernet and chardonnay vintage in living memory in Margaret River. So goes it for the Prelude: sheer density of fruit and rippling length of flavour are the calling cards. Bargain at the price. Screw cap | 13.5% alc. | To 2035 | $35 | EL

enton Brae Wines 

37 Caves Road, Margaret River, WA 6285 **T** (08) 9755 6255 **www**.lentonbrae.com **OPEN** 7 days 10-5
IEMAKER Edward Tomlinson **EST.** 1982 **VYDS** 7.3ha

e late architect Bruce Tomlinson built a strikingly beautiful winery (heritage-listed by the ire of Busselton) that is now in the hands of winemaker son Edward (Ed), who consistently akes elegant wines in classic Margaret River style. A midwinter (French time) trip to Pomerol Bordeaux to research merlot is an indication of his commitment.

Wilyabrup Margaret River Semillon Sauvignon Blanc 2020 A distinctly cassis-driven nose and palate, with wisps of juniper, jasmine tea and red apple skin. The palate morphs into layers of vanilla pod, lychee and brine. A really restrained expression of the blend. Screw cap | 13.5% alc. | To 2024 | $22 | EL

S Merchants 

3 Treeton Road North, Cowaramup, WA 6284 **T** 0492 962 348 **www**.lsmerchants.com.au
EN Mon-Sat 10.30-4.30, Sun 10.30-6 **WINEMAKER** Dylan Arvidson **EST.** 2017 **DOZENS** 7000

Merchants is focused on making wine from many different regions in Western Australia argaret River, their base, the Great Southern and Geographe). While founder Dylan vidson adheres to a minimalist winemaking approach he does not identify as a 'natural nemaker', rather allowing wild fermentation to occur where possible and pushing wine apes and styles in many different directions. There is plenty of variety in the LS Merchants rtfolio, but they are bound together by his clean, bright and expressive winemaking yle. (EL)

Margaret River Chenin Blanc 2019 Initially this drinks more like a flinty, funky chardonnay than a chenin, until the waxy mid palate kicks in – then it's all chenin sailing. Hints of summer florals and sheepy tufts pop up here and there, but it's the briny acid that really calls out the variety. Screw cap | 13.6% alc. | To 2031 | $30 | EL

Margaret River Vermentino 2020 OK, this is delicious. All the components are playing harmoniously here – the acidity is ripe and salty and the oak is seamlessly punched into the fruit, which speaks of nashi pear, crunchy green apples, summer florals and Asian spice ... there's a lot to like here. The phenolics are the final box ticked – chalky, fine and shapely. What a cracker. Screw cap | 12.9% alc. | To 2026 | $30 | EL

IcHenry Hohnen Vintners

62 Caves Road, Margaret River, WA 6285 **T** (08) 9757 7600 **www**.mchenryhohnen.com.au **OPEN** 7 days .30-4.30 **WINEMAKER** Jacopo Dalli Cani **EST.** 2004 **DOZENS** 7500 **VYDS** 50ha

e McHenry and Hohnen families have a long history of grapegrowing and winemaking Margaret River. They joined forces in 2004 to create McHenry Hohnen with the aim of oducing wines honest to region, site and variety. Vines have been established on the cHenry, Calgardup Brook and Rocky Road properties, all farmed biodynamically.

Hazel's Vineyard Margaret River GSM 2019 Hazel's vineyard was only planted in 1999 and already this smacks of pedigree. Let's start at the finish: this is a ripping wine. It has both radiant and pretty fruit on nose and palate. Firm, structuring tannins pervade every aspect of the experience and the oak serves to hold it altogether in an unseen way. This is delicious and serious. Brilliant winemaking and craftsmanship. What a pleasure. Screw cap | 14.5% alc. | To 2035 | $40 | EL

Rolling Stone Margaret River 2017 85/5/5/5% cabernet sauvignon/malbec/merlot/petit verdot from the biodynamically farmed Hazel's Vineyard (certified from 2021 vintage). 16 months in Frenc oak (40% new). Savoury, oak-driven and structured tannins are the standout feature here; shapely, finely knit and supple. They provide a frame from which the red berries and exotic spice can hang Long and rippling, this is a wine of savoury succulence and longevity. Screw cap | 14.1% alc. | To 2046 | $135 | EL

96 **Calgardup Brook Vineyard Margaret River Chardonnay 2019** This is perhaps my favourite (by a whisker) of these 2 single-vineyard chardonnays. It has a bitter phenolic kick through the finish that adds a layer of sparkle, interest and excitement to the wine and creates a salty undulation through the finish. It moves in a dappled way, this wine. I like it. Screw cap | 13.3% alc. | To 2036 | $65 | EL

Hazel's Vineyard Margaret River Cabernet Sauvignon 2018 Savoury, textured and very long, this is not the succulent red-fruited explosion of Margaret River cabernets (neither a good nor bad thing, just an observation). It has the layered complexity we often find in Bordeaux, with a plumply satisfying core of cassis and redcurrant. Not overt, but restrained, with willowy tannins. Cellar or drink – both will bring immense pleasure. Screw cap | 14% alc. | To 2041 | $70 | EL

Marq Wines

860 Commonage Road, Dunsborough, WA 6281 **T** (08) 9756 6227 **www**.marqwines.com.au **OPEN** Fri–Sun public hols 10–5 **WINEMAKER** Mark Warren **EST.** 2011 **DOZENS** 2500 **VYDS** 1.5ha

Mark Warren lectures in wine science and wine sensory processes at Curtin University, Margaret River. He also produces the extensive Happs range as well as wines under contrac for several other Margaret River brands, making him responsible for 60 to 70 individual wine each year, now including wines under his own Marq Wines label. The underlying philosophy an exploration of the potential of alternative varieties and unusual winemaking methods by someone with an undoubted technical understanding of the processes involved.

96 **DNA Margaret River Cabernet Sauvignon 2018** In a truly great vintage like '18, it is right to expect excellence. This is concentrated, layered and bursting at the seams with flavour. The palate is a bounty of seamlessly countersunk oak, succulent fruit, exotic spice and slinky tannins. Major yes, here. Screw cap | 14.3% alc. | To 2035 | $35 | EL

95 **Wild Ferment Margaret River Chardonnay 2019** Winemaker (and owner) Mark Warren has got a reputation for making interesting, affordable and high-quality wines – a lusty combination. This wine is no exception. Here, cap gun/flint/funk exist alongside yellow peach, red apple skins and th telltale curry leaf – all of it stitched up by briny acidity and fine phenolics. A lot to like, especially a the price. Screw cap | 12.9% alc. | To 2031 | $30 | EL

Margaret River Fiano 2019 Whole-bunch pressed, 3 months in 4yo oak with regular bâtonnage. White pepper, white peach, nectarine and honeydew melon. This has the benefit of being both ric and refreshing at once, thanks to the taut acid that curls its way through the fruit. Phenolics provic shape and structure in the mouth. This is a cracker. Screw cap | 13.2% alc. | To 2025 | $25 | EL

Margaret River Vermentino 2020 The alcohol indicates an early pick, so the expectation is a crunchy, crispy vermentino. We are well met. Zingy, sherbety acid and orchard fruit so pretty and light that it is almost lyrical. One could consume quite a bit of this without noticing. Quite deliciou An excellent match for a seafood barbecue in summer. Screw cap | 12.1% alc. | To 2023 | $25 | EL

Margaret River Tempranillo 2019 Lifted violets and raspberry on the nose; lashings of sweet fruit and salted pomegranate on the palate. Lovely balance between oak, fruit and acid. A graceful and attractive medium-bodied tempranillo with a bounty of exotic spice, sprinkled over chalky tannins Screw cap | 14.2% alc. | To 2028 | $30 | EL

94 **Margaret River Semillon Sauvignon Blanc Verdelho 2020** 75/15/10% semillon/sauvignon blanc/ verdelho. Wild ferment in tank. Tropical, ripe and laden with graphite phenolics, this is an atypical spin on the trad SSB blend. A lot to touch and feel here, with bucket loads of concentrated flavour that rolls over the tongue in waves. Impressive. Screw cap | 13.3% alc. | To 2027 | $22 | EL

Margaret River Malbec 2019 Raspberry leaf tea, red licorice, anise and pink peppercorn. The pala has tannins that are fine, soft, plump – they create a boudoir vibe – like freshly fluffed pillows. The acidity runs counter to this, keeping the wine balanced and taut. The length of flavour beyond tha draws out into an elongated close. Brilliant stuff. Restraint and interest at once. Bravo. Screw cap 14.1% alc. | To 2030 | $30 | EL

Miles from Nowhere

PO Box 128, Burswood, WA 6100 **T** (08) 9264 7800 **www**.milesfromnowhere.com.au **WINEMAKER** Frederique Perrin, Gary Stokes **EST.** 2007 **DOZENS** 20000 **VYDS** 46.9ha

Miles from Nowhere is one of the 2 wineries owned by Franklin and Heather Tate. Franklin returned to Margaret River in 2007 after working with his parents establishing Evans & Tate from 1987 to 2005. The Miles from Nowhere name comes from the journey Franklin's cestors made over 100 years ago from Eastern Europe to Australia: upon their arrival, they t they had travelled 'miles from nowhere'.

Margaret River Sauvignon Blanc 2020 Grassy and pure on the nose, the palate follows suit with a complexing chalky phenolic structure that engages and creates interest in the mouth. The acid leaves a lingering saline impression through to the finish, with some crushed shell and lemon pith for good measure. Screw cap | 12.6% alc. | To 2024 | $18 | EL

Margaret River Sauvignon Blanc Semillon 2020 Typically grassy on the nose with a floral, talcy, ashy perimeter. The sauvignon blanc (60%) packs a tidy little punch, and the balance of semillon elevates the texture to almost chewy. With no oak or lees to speak of, this is pure and taught with a fine, salty acid line defining the finish. Pretty brilliant value for money here. Screw cap | 13.2% alc. | To 2024 | $18 | EL

r Barval Fine Wines  

87 Caves Road, Margaret River, WA 6285 **T** 0481 453 038 **www**.mrbarval.com **OPEN** 7 days 11-5
NEMAKER Robert Gherardi **EST.** 2015 **DOZENS** 1300

bert Gherardi was born with wine in his blood. As a small boy he'd go to Margaret River pick grapes with 3 generations of his extended Italian family. The grapes were taken to s grandmother's suburban backyard to begin the fermentation, followed by a big lunch or nner to celebrate the arrival of the new vintage to be. He returns to Italy each year for his utique travel business, with customised tours of Barolo, Valtellina and further north. And so arrived at the name for his winery: Margaret River, Barolo and Valtellina.

Vino Rosso 2019 Merlot, petit verdot and malbec. Whole berries, wild-yeast fermented, basket pressed to 3yo oak and matured for 21 months. Smells like red snakes, jubes, red licorice and other delicious lollies. The palate is made far more serious by finely structuring, chalky tannins and a swathe of subtle, spicy oak. The briny acid cleans it all up. So much to love, most of all the bouncy texture, which demands another sip. Screw cap | 14.5% alc. | To 2028 | $29 | EL

oss Brothers 

Wattle Place, Margaret River, WA 6285 **T** 0402 010 352 **www**.mossbrotherswines.com.au
NEMAKER Rory Parks **EST.** 1984 **DOZENS** 7000 **VYDS** 16.03ha

is is the reincarnation of the Moss Brothers brand, though not its vineyards, which were quired by Amelia Park in 2015. It is a parallel business to Trove Estate. Paul Byron and alph Dunning are the major forces in both ventures, both with extensive whole-of-business pertise across Australia.

6 **Fidium Margaret River Cabernet Sauvignon 2019** Highly aromatic and very pretty, laden with cassis, raspberry and pomegranate. Totally supple and elegant. The oak is there in a supportive and structuring manner, but is almost imperceptible. Delicious. Screw cap | 14% alc. | To 2041 | $55 | EL

oss Wood  

6 Metricup Road, Wilyabrup, WA 6284 **T** (08) 9755 6266 **www**.mosswood.com.au **OPEN** By appt
NEMAKER Clare Mugford, Keith Mugford **EST.** 1969 **DOZENS** 11000 **VYDS** 18.14ha

idely regarded as one of the best wineries in the region, producing glorious chardonnay, ower-laden semillon and elegant cabernet sauvignon that lives for decades. Moss Wood so owns RibbonVale Estate, the wines treated as vineyard-designated within the Moss ood umbrella.

8 **Wilyabrup Margaret River Cabernet Sauvignon 2018** Rippling layers of flavour and texture here. So long that it carries itself over the palate and through into the finish ... what a finish! Pedigree and happenstance have collided to create a legend. The 2018 will go down as one of the greatest Moss Wood cabernets ever made, alongside the 2001. Screw cap | 14.5% alc. | To 2061 | $160 | EL

7 **Ribbon Vale Margaret River Cabernet Sauvignon 2018** We live in hallowed times: the '18 cabernets from Margaret River are being released into the wild ... there's never been a better time to be alive. Concentrated, fine, pedigree cabernet with explosive, low-down torque that drags the flavours over the palate into the interminably long finish. Epic. Will live as long as you do. Screw cap | 14.5% alc. | To 2050 | $77 | EL

6 **Wilyabrup Margaret River Semillon 2020** Although vinified à la Hunter Valley – clear juice with multiple yeasts, bottled straight after cold fermentation – the result is a universe away from young Hunter semillon. It has striking depth to its supple lemongrass and white peach fruit flavours, lengthened and balanced by demure acidity. Screw cap | 14.2% alc. | To 2035 | $44 | JH

Nocturne Wines

PO Box 111, Yallingup, WA 6282 **T** 0477 829 844 **www**.nocturnewines.com.au
WINEMAKER Alana Langworthy, Julian Langworthy **EST.** 2007 **DOZENS** 1300 **VYDS** 8ha

Alana and Julian Langworthy were newly minted winemakers when they met in SA over 15 years ago and set up a small winery project called Nocturne Wines. The intention was to make small quantities of project wines as an adjunct to their day jobs as employed winemakers. The SR range explores Margaret River's subregions; the 2019 SR Rosé was awarded Best Rosé in the 2021 *Wine Companion*.

97 **Sheoak Vineyard Margaret River Cabernet Sauvignon 2019** In a line-up of wines that were often double and triple the price (and more), the Sheoak single-vineyard cabernet stood out. No wonder this sells out in a nanosecond each year. Ridiculous price for the quality. Supple, pristine and densely packed with sweet fruit from every angle, this is long and dark and layered and awesome. The oak is almost imperceptible, but the wine's structure and tannins ensure a long future. We'll all be old by the time this fades. Screw cap | 14% alc. | To 2051 | $53 | EL

96 **Tassell Park Vineyard Margaret River Chardonnay 2019** We're starting to know what to expect from the Langworthy duo and this wine: flinty curry leaf, yellow peach, brine, crunchy acid and good length of flavour. This vintage is no exception, although perhaps a slightly leaner iteration due to the cooler year. Crushed macadamia and cashew are laced through the finish ... awesome. Yes. (Try decanting it for extra pleasure). Screw cap | 13% alc. | To 2036 | $53 | EL

95 **Treeton SR Chardonnay 2019** Creamy cashew and ripe citrus nose, the palate has a searing line of shaley, minerally acid that courses over the very centre of the tongue. The mid palate onwards plumes into a concentrated and rich cloud of flavour. The fruit spectrum is very much in the yellow peach, white nectarine and pink grapefruit space. Engaging, chalky phenolics through the finish. Textbook brilliance. Screw cap | 13% alc. | To 2027 | $30 | EL

Carbunup SR Sangiovese Nebbiolo Rosé 2020 The previous vintage was awarded Best Rosé at the *Halliday Wine Companion* Awards Australia in August, and deservedly so. Aromatically, this is all about laid-back red-berry spice. Pomegranate, shale, mineral and graphite characters and white pepper. The palate has full and generous flavour, full texture and full concentration. The grip it exhibits is an extra layer of sass and charm. Really good length of flavour, which moves through to creamy in the lingering and morphing finish. Pleasure here. Also bottled in magnum. Screw cap | 13% alc. | To 2022 | $30 | EL

Oates Ends

22 Carpenter Road, Wilyabrup, WA 6280 **T** 0401 303 144 **www**.oatesends.com.au **OPEN** By appt
WINEMAKER Cath Oates **EST.** 1999 **DOZENS** 2000 **VYDS** 11ha

Cath Oates returned home to Margaret River after an international winemaking career spanning 15 years. The wines are made from the family Wilagri Vineyard, planted in 1999 and now owned and managed by viticulturist brother Russ Oates. Oates Ends is the culmination of both of their respective experience and wine philosophies: sustainable farming principles, family farming traditions and sheep for winter mowing and leaf plucking during the growing season.

96 **Margaret River Cabernet Sauvignon 2018** Cath Oates' vineyard is in Wilyabrup, oft regarded as the heartland of Margaret River. The nose is savoury and spiced, laden with raspberry, Cherry Ripe, cassis and violets. The acidity exerts a taut mineral presence over the mouth: it swoops in and captures the soul. Fine, elegant cabernet; the perfect example of what sensitive winemaking, good vineyards and a brilliant vintage can do. Screw cap | 14% alc. | To 2036 | $50 | EL

95 **Margaret River Tempranillo 2020** Amaro, Italian mountain herbs, garden mint, and freshly diced fennel are the backdrop to purple violets and sweet cherry fruit on the nose. The fruit sweeps across the palate, leaving a trail of fresh summer raspberries in its wake. Pure, cleansing and quite alluring, the small component of seasoned American oak fleshes out the finish. Beautiful. Modern. Slinky. Fresh. Yes. Screw cap | 13.5% alc. | To 2025 | $30 | EL

Passel Estate

655 Ellen Brook Road, Cowaramup, WA 6284 **T** (08) 9717 6241 **www**.passelestate.com
OPEN 7 days 10.30-5 **WINEMAKER** Bruce Dukes **EST.** 1994 **DOZENS** 1500 **VYDS** 6.7ha

Wendy and Barry Stimpson made Margaret River home in 2005 and in '11 purchased and expanded the vineyard, which is planted to shiraz, cabernet sauvignon and chardonnay. Viticulturist Andy Ferreira manages the vineyard with sustainable practices, keeping yields restricted to 6.5–7t/ha. The very talented and highly experienced contract winemaker Bruce Dukes is responsible for the wines.

Margaret River Sauvignon Blanc 2019 20% barrel fermented in new French oak, 80% in stainlesss steel, blended post-fermentation, then left on lees and stirred fortnightly for 5 months until bottling. The nose has a really attractive corporeal funk to it - reminiscent of skin after an ocean swim. The palate is delicate and fine, the oaked component providing a plush bed of texture on which the delicate fruit lingers. Complex layers of texture elevate this to serious. Screw cap | 13% alc. | To 2030 | $30 | EL

eccavi Wines

21 Wildwood Road, Yallingup Siding, WA 6282 **T** 0404 619 861 **www**.peccavi-wines.com
EN By appt **WINEMAKER** Bruce Dukes, Remi Guise **EST.** 1996 **DOZENS** 6000 **VYDS** 16.5ha

remy Muller was introduced to the great wines of the world by his father when he was ung and says he spent years searching New and Old World wine regions (even looking at e sites of ancient Roman vineyards in England), but did not find what he was looking for til one holiday in Margaret River. There he found a vineyard in Yallingup that was available r sale and he did not hesitate. The quality of the wines is very good, reflecting the skills and perience of Bruce Dukes.

Estate Margaret River Merlot 2018 We're taught to seek bitter cocoa and mulberry in merlot, but outside of Bordeaux, those characters rarely assert themselves with any conviction. Until now. There is a new clone in Margaret River from Bordeaux - Clone 181. The first thing that hits you is the structure. The tannins serve not only to shape the powerful (textbook) fruit, but they assert themselves so obviously that they become the hallmark of the wine. There is no doubt this is the greatest merlot in Australia. Prove me wrong. Screw cap | 14% alc. | To 2051 | $150 | EL | ♥

ierro

ves Road, Wilyabrup via Cowaramup, WA 6284 **T** (08) 9755 6220 **www**.pierro.com.au **OPEN** 7 days -5 **WINEMAKER** Dr Michael Peterkin **EST.** 1979 **DOZENS** 10000 **VYDS** 7.85ha

Michael Peterkin is another of the legion of Margaret River medical practitioner-vignerons; r good measure, he married into the Cullen family. Pierro is renowned for its stylish white ines, which often exhibit tremendous complexity; the Chardonnay can be monumental in its eight and texture. That said, its red wines from good vintages can be every bit as good.

Margaret River Chardonnay VR 2017 A staggeringly complex wine with layer upon layer of flavour and texture, all working in concert with each other to achieve one goal: excellence. The waves of flavour ripple across the mouth and seep into the soul. Exceptional. Screw cap | 14% alc. | To 2041 | $120 | EL

6 **L.T.C. Semillon Sauvignon Blanc 2020** 50/41/9% sauvignon blanc/semillon/chardonnay. Although '20 has been rough in many ways. in WA vineyards it was warm, early and brilliant quality - a silver lining to what was otherwise a blindside year. This is concentrated and focused; completely balanced and refreshing. A stunning rendition of the LTC, the acidity is juicy and chewy. With the ability to age gracefully in the cellar, this is a cracker. Screw cap | 13.5% alc. | To 2030 | $35 | EL

5 **Nunc Tempus Est Margaret River Chenin Blanc 2018** From a tiny plot of chenin, this is the first varietal bottling. Hand picked and sorted, whole-bunch pressed, fermented in stainless steel and left on ferment lees for 6 months. Dry. Spicy, fine, and bang-on classical chenin. The palate has apricot and pear, littered with Geraldton wax florals and white pepper. There is an extraordinarily exciting interplay of acid and fruit, which comes together to leave an impression of clove/star anise at the end. Screw cap | 14% alc. | To 2035 | $35 | EL

edgate

59 Boodjidup Road, Margaret River, WA 6285 **T** (08) 9757 6488 **www**.redgatewines.com.au
EN 7 days 10-4.30 **WINEMAKER** David Dowden **EST.** 1977 **DOZENS** 5500 **VYDS** 18ha

ounder and owner of Redgate, the late Bill Ullinger, chose the name not simply because f the nearby eponymous beach, but also because - so it is said - a local farmer (with a rominent red gate at his property) had run an illegal spirit still 100 or so years ago, and its atrons would come to the property and ask whether there was any 'red gate' available. True r not, Redgate was one of the early movers in the region, and now has close to 20ha of ature estate plantings.

5 **Ullinger Reserve Margaret River Sauvignon Blanc 2020** From one angle, the aromatics are dominated by asparagus, sugar snap pea and cassis. From another, this is riddled with spicy green jalapeño, white pepper and coriander. The palate is juicy and plush, the oak serving to boost textural complexity rather than leave flavour artefact. Screw cap | 13% alc. | To 2030 | $25 | EL

Margaret River Sauvignon Blanc Semillon 2020 Once you've identified the scent in this wine as being green jalapeño, it is challenging to see much else. Despite how that may sound, it is a positiv trait, and serves to distinguish this vineyard from its regional neighbours. Taut, spicy drinking here with seriously concentrated fruit. Hard to know what food to match it with ... perhaps drink it solo? Screw cap | 13.5% alc. | To 2028 | $23 | EL

94 **Margaret River Semillon 2020** The nose here could be described in a number of ways, but once you smell green jalapeño, it is impossible to unsmell it. It's all the better for it. Spicy salsa verde, coriander and green apple aromas introduce the flavours on the palate. All things fall into place. This is a cracking wine; pungent, concentrated and salivatingly saline. Yes. Screw cap | 13% alc. | To 2027 | $25 | EL

Robert Oatley Margaret River

3518 Caves Road, Wilyabrup, WA 6280 **T** (08) 9750 4000 **www**.robertoatley.com.au **OPEN** 7 days 10.30-4.30 **WINEMAKER** Larry Cherubino **EST.** 2006 **VYDS** 155ha

Robert Oatley Wines, founded by the late Robert (Bob) Oatley AO BEM in 2006, is a family-owned winery led by his eldest son Sandy Oatley who, with his father, brother and sister, planted the first Oatley vineyards in the late 1960s. Focusing on wines from Margaret River (and Great Southern) and McLaren Vale, the business now bases itself in the Margaret River, with a vineyard and cellar door on Caves Road in the heart of the region.

95 **Signature Series Margaret River Cabernet Sauvignon 2018** This is first-class Margaret River cabernet at an economy price. It has elegance and poise, the cassis and black-olive flavours fresh and detailed, the crisp tannins likewise. The colour, too, is bright and clear. Screw cap | 13.5% alc. | To 2033 | $24 | JH

Rosabrook Margaret River Wine

1390 Rosa Brook Road, Rosabrook, WA 6285 **T** (08) 9368 4555 **www**.rosabrook.com.au **WINEMAKER** Severine Logan, Brian Fletcher **EST.** 1980 **DOZENS** 12000 **VYDS** 25ha

The original Rosabrook estate vineyards were established between 1984 and '96. In 2007 Rosabrook relocated its vineyard to the northwestern end of the Margaret River wine region, overlooking Geographe Bay and the Indian Ocean. Warm days and cool nights, influenced by the ocean, result in slow, mild-ripening conditions.

94 **Tempranillo 2018** Silky and juicy aromatics of raspberry, mulberry, hints of violet and vanilla pod. Quite delicious. Perfect ripeness is marbled throughout this wine, the tail speaking of succulent forest fruits and red berries. The flavour complexity stops short of cascading, but in terms of satisfaction and beauty – this is spot on. Screw cap | 14% alc. | To 2027 | $26 | EL

Sandalford

3210 West Swan Road, Caversham, WA 6055 **T** (08) 9374 9374 **www**.sandalford.com **OPEN** 7 days 10-5 **WINEMAKER** Hope Metcalf **EST.** 1840 **DOZENS** 60000 **VYDS** 106.5ha

Sandalford is one of Australia's oldest and largest privately owned wineries. In 1970 it moved beyond its original Swan Valley base, purchasing a substantial property in Margaret River that is now the main source of its premium grapes. Wines are released under the 1840 (Swan Valley), Element, Winemakers, Margaret River and Estate Reserve ranges with Prendiville Reserve at the top.

95 **Estate Reserve Wilyabrup Vineyard Margaret River Shiraz 2018** Gorgeous nose – all raspberry, blackberry, clove, peppercorn and licorice. The palate follows in exactly this manner; lively, succulent and statuesque. A beautiful wine. Screw cap | 14.5% alc. | To 2030 | $35 | EL

Snake + Herring

3763 Caves Road, Wilyabrup, WA 6284 **T** 0427 881 871 **www**.snakeandherring.com.au **OPEN** 7 days 11- summer, 11-4 winter **WINEMAKER** Tony Davis **EST.** 2010 **DOZENS** 12000

Tony (Snake) Davis and Redmond (Herring) Sweeny both started university degrees before finding that they were utterly unsuited to their respective courses. Having stumbled across Margaret River, Tony's life changed forever; he enrolled at the University of Adelaide, thereafter doing vintages in various regions, then roles at Yalumba, Millbrook Winery in the Perth Hills and Howard Park in Margaret River. Redmond's circuitous course included chartered accountancy degree and employment with an international accounting firm in usselton, and the subsequent establishment of Forester Estate in 2001. Back on home turf e is the marketing and financial controller of Snake + Herring.

4 **Perfect Day Margaret River Sauvignon Blanc Semillon 2020** There's a distinct cassis note on the nose here, accompanied by green apple, lemon pith, brine and a really succulent delicious 'something' on the back of the palate. The effect is totally moreish and refreshing. The texture is standout – fine chalky phenolics elevate it from 'uncomplicated' to great. Screw cap | 12% alc. | To 2027 | $25 | EL

Redemption Great Southern Syrah 2019 This is juicy and redolent with red snakes and a stemmy crunch woven through the very heart of it. Spices like star anise and aniseed embroider the edges of the jubilant fruit. Quite delicious, more delicate than the ripper 2018. Screw cap | 13.5% alc. | To 2031 | $25 | EL

At First Sight Great Southern Grenache 2020 Definitely stemmy and definitely crunchy, possessed of brilliant flavour and colour intensity. A slight little wine, defined in part by very fine, chalky tannins. The fruit has a way of permeating the palate from front to back and hooking in another sip. Yes. Screw cap | 13.5% alc. | To 2027 | $25 | EL

outh by South West

Coronation Street, Margaret River, WA 6285 (postal) **T** 0438 001 181 ww.southbysouthwest.com.au **WINEMAKER** Livia Maiorana **EST.** 2016 **DOZENS** 4000 **VYDS** 2ha

via (Liv) Maiorana and Mijan (Mij) Patterson, engineer and graphic designer, share a love of avel. They embarked on a 'wine odyssey' to study the cycle of winemaking in different wine egions around the world. 'We learned from masters of the craft at some of the biggest and nallest players in California, Italy, France and British Columbia. We learned about terroirs nd varietals, viticultural practices, cultural winemaking tricks and techniques. We drank a lot f wine.'

4 **Fieldie Margaret River Semillon Sauvignon Blanc 2020** It is difficult to draw the line between varieties once this aromatic and layered skin-contact wine is in the mouth, but it ceases to matter when the fruits cascade over one another creating a tidal wave of flavour. Kept in check by chalky phenolics and salty acid, this seems like a pretty perfect summer seafood wine. Screw cap | 12.7% alc. | To 2031 | $30 | EL

tella Bella Wines ⑦

)5 Rosabrook Road, Margaret River, WA 6285 **T** (08) 9758 8611 **www.stellabella.com.au** **PEN** 7 days 10–5 **WINEMAKER** Luke Jolliffe, Jarrad Olsen **EST.** 1997 **DOZENS** 40000 **VYDS** 55.7ha

his enormously successful winemaking business produces wines of true regional expression vith fruit sourced from the central and southern parts of Margaret River. The company owns nd operates 6 vineyards, and also purchases fruit from small contract growers. Substantial uantities of wine covering all styles and price points make this an important producer for largaret River.

7 **Luminosa Margaret River Chardonnay 2019** Pink grapefruit, salted yellow peach, curry leaf and crushed nuts. It's worked, but it's got it all, including a core of pure fruit on the palate. Like a Tardis, this wine contains more flavour than it lets on. Ripples of flavour slowly radiate out from its centre, keeping the drinker engaged for quite some time. Gorgeous, salivating stuff. Screw cap | 13.3% alc. | To 2036 | $70 | EL

Luminosa Margaret River Cabernet Sauvignon 2018 Luminous is right ... what a beautiful wine this is. Succulent raspberry, pomegranate, redcurrant and satsuma plum are sprinkled with pink peppercorn and sea salt and harnessed by supple, almost chewy tannins. The flavour undulates in waves. This is an incredible wine – do your future self a favour and seek this out. It's just pure pleasure. Screw cap | 14.1% alc. | To 2041 | $90 | EL

6 **Suckfizzle Margaret River Chardonnay 2019** More restrained and less obviously worked than the Luminosa, the power here comes from the undertow of fruit. It carries on far past the expected limit of endurance. If the key to quality is length of flavour, then this must be very good indeed. A spectacular wine. Screw cap | 13.6% alc. | To 2036 | $70 | EL

4 **Skuttlebutt Margaret River Sauvignon Blanc Semillon 2020** Margaret River does this style so well it would be hard to deny at any price, let alone this. It's made in the vineyard, vinification without any embellishment – except perhaps a hint of sweetness. No matter; the blend of kaffir lime, white peach and passionfruit is balanced and freshened by crisp acidity. Screw cap | 12.9% alc. | To 2025 | $19 | JH

tripe.Iscariot

20 McDowell Road, Witchcliffe, WA 6286 **T** 0414 817 808 **www**.tripeiscariot.com
WINEMAKER Remi Guise **EST.** 2013 **DOZENS** 800

This has to be the most way-out winery name of the century. Remi Guise courteously responded to my (James') query about it with a reference to Judas as 'the greatest black shee of all time', and a non-specific explanation of 'tripe' as 'challenging in style'. He added, 'I hope this sheds some light, or dark, on the brand'. The wines provide a better answer, managing to successfully harness highly unusual techniques at various points of their elevage.

96 **Brawn Margaret River Chardonnay 2019** Wild ferment in barrel (40% new), matured for 10 months. Blocking mlf here has created a staunch line of acidity that spears through the very heart of the ripe orchard fruit. Concentrated, saline and very classy. This is for the acid freaks and the lovers of mineral Chablis; there is finesse, complexity, length and line here in spades. Screw cap | 12.8% alc. | To 2036 | $42 | EL

95 **Absolution Karridale Margaret River Chenin Blanc 2019** Cheesecloth, green apple, saline and that sheepy little suggestion of unripe pear/lanolin. Karridale is cooler than Wilyabrup, which gives this wine a tension and poise. Classic chenin has that edgy phenolic drift on the palate – it is here, too. Screw cap | 12.5% alc. | To 2036 | $32 | EL

Absolution Wilyabrup Margaret River Chenin Blanc 2019 Being further north, Wilyabrup is slightly warmer than Karridale, lending this wine a plushness through the back palate. This is the fleshy, pristine and spicy one (the Karridale the lean, staunch and edgy one). Awesome to see. Very classy, totally delicious. Screw cap | 12.5% alc. | To 2036 | $32 | EL

Cock's Foot Madrigal 2019 An unbelievably pretty nose! Lychee and exotic spice, white spring flora and a host of delicate fruit. The balancing acidity is tight and tingly, giving the palate a real saline edge. This is lovely, almost chewy. It dances through the finish with an on-point, lyrical rhythm. The lighter, finer alternative to gewürz when pairing with spicy Thai cuisine. Screw cap | 12.4% alc. | To 2020 | $32 | EL

Twinwoods Estate

Brockman Road, Cowaramup, WA 6284 **T** 0419 833 122 **www**.twinwoodsestate.com **WINEMAKER** Deep Woods Estate (Julian Langworthy), Aldo Bratovic **EST.** 2005 **DOZENS** 2500 **VYDS** 8.5ha

This is a winery that was bound to succeed. It is owned by the Jebsen family, for many years a major player in the importation and distribution of fine wine in Hong Kong, more recently expanded into China. Jebsen invested in a NZ winery, following that with the acquisition of this vineyard in Margaret River in 2005. Its widespread distribution is interesting, not all the eggs being put in the Hong Kong/China markets. The quality of the wines I (James) have tasted fully lives up to what one would expect. (I tasted the wines without any knowledge of the background of Twinwoods.)

94 **Margaret River Chardonnay 2018** Flinty, funky and concentrated, this has a salivating seam of sea salt and curry powder on a bed of crushed nuts. What a cracking wine for the price! It has it all: fruit power, complex texture and good length of flavour. Yes. Screw cap | 13% alc. | To 2028 | $25 |

Vasse Felix

Cnr Tom Cullity Drive/Caves Road, Cowaramup, WA 6284 **T** (08) 9756 5000 **www**.vassefelix.com.au
OPEN 7 days 10-5 **WINEMAKER** Virginia Willcock **EST.** 1967 **DOZENS** 150000 **VYDS** 330ha

Vasse Felix is Margaret River's founding wine estate, established in 1967 by regional pioneer Dr Tom Cullity. Owned and operated by the Holmes à Court family since 1987, Paul Holmes à Court has brought the focus to Margaret River's key varieties of cabernet sauvignon and chardonnay. Chief Winemaker Virginia Willcock has energised the winemaking and viticultur team with her no-nonsense approach and fierce commitment to quality.

97 **Heytesbury Margaret River Chardonnay 2019** Everyone has their favourites. The Heytesbury chardonnay style is typically the wine that my heart reaches for. I love it. The 2019 iteration is minerally; laden with graphite and crushed rocks, brine, white currant, white peach and curry leaf. Heavily worked and wild, with an attractive rawness to it. Where 2018 was about fruit power, 2019 is about complex winemaking input. This still has my heart, but for different reasons to its predecesso Screw cap | 13% alc. | To 2036 | $92 | EL

96 **Margaret River Cabernet Sauvignon 2018** Powerfully ripe and dense, with epic length of flavour. This is a structural and concentrated cabernet capable of decades of graceful evolution in the cella Wild raspberry, salted licorice, aniseed, pomegranate, ferrous and kelp. Saline acid. It comes in at

under $50, and long may that continue, for it is one of the great-value premium wines of the region. Agglomerate | 14.5% alc. | To 2041 | $47 | EL

5 **Margaret River Sauvignon Blanc 2019** Creamy, rounded and supremely textural, this moves away from the spiny sauvignon blanc we are accustomed to and moves into a New World European space. Heady Margaret River florals and leafy greens (coriander, broad beans and sugar snap peas) linger in the background, making this a brilliant excuse for lunch. From the land and into the glass – what a beauty. Screw cap | 13% alc. | To 2030 | $28 | EL

4 **Filius Margaret River Cabernet Sauvignon 2018** This is the youngest brother in the family of cabernets at Vasse and has built a loyal following for its supple deliciousness and accessibility (both in price and quality). So: wild raspberry, red licorice, pomegranate, kelp, iodine, crushed pepper, spicy oak and the all important saline acid. The vintage has contributed a fruit power that gives the wine great length of flavour. Screw cap | 14.5% alc. | To 2031 | $29 | EL

ʼictory Point Wines

2 Holben Road, Cowaramup, WA 6284 **T** 0417 954 655 **www.victorypointwines.com** **OPEN** Wed-Sun 11-4 **ʼINEMAKER** Mark Messenger (Contract) **EST.** 1997 **DOZENS** 2500 **VYDS** 13.7ha

udith and Gary Berson have set their sights high. They established their vineyard without ʼrigation, emulating those of the Margaret River pioneers (including Moss Wood). The fully nature plantings comprise of chardonnay and pinot noir; the remainder Bordeaux varieties vith cabernet sauvignon, cabernet franc, malbec and petit verdot. The cellar door overlooks he 20+yo vineyard.

6 **Margaret River Pinot Noir 2019** This is beautiful. Layered and spicy, with folds of delicate red berry flavours, marbled with exotic spice like pink peppercorn, cardamom and succulent, ripe acidity. There is a lot of pleasure here, all of which can be experienced at any time over the long, lingering finish. The cool year has helped craft a wine of finesse and balance, making this one of the smartest pinots in the state. Screw cap | 13.5% alc. | To 2036 | $55 | EL

Margaret River Cabernet Sauvignon 2018 Rich, ripe and with a meaty undertow, this cabernet makes a serious statement on both the nose and palate. Powerful fruit and dense weight shows a wine capable of immense pleasure in the short term, but with all the generous stuffing that will ensure it a long and graceful future in the cellar, too. This has grunt and Euro structuring, aniseed and clove through the long finish. Screw cap | 14% alc. | To 2041 | $45 | EL

5 **The Mallee Root Margaret River Cabernet Sauvignon Malbec Petit Verdot 2018** Some wines demand that you smell them over and over ... this is one. Elegant, savoury and aromatic, it's all about salted cassis, pomegranate, whiffs of pink peppercorn and loads of exotic spice. The palate is shaped by curvy tannins. Demanding though it may be, you get more than you pay for. Impressive. Screw cap | 14% alc. | To 2035 | $29 | EL

ʼintners Ridge Estate

.ot 18 Veraison Place, Yallingup, Margaret River, WA 6285 **T** 0417 956 943 **www.vintnersridge.** **ːom.au** **OPEN** By appt **WINEMAKER** Flying Fish Cove (Simon Ding) **EST.** 2001 **DOZENS** 250 **VYDS** 2.1ha

When Maree and Robin Adair purchased the Vintners Ridge Vineyard in 2006 (cabernet ːauvignon), it had already produced 3 crops, having been planted in November '01. The ʼineyard overlooks the picturesque Geographe Bay.

92 **Margaret River Cabernet Sauvignon 2019** Energetic cabernet laden with cassis and spice. The tannins serve to bolster the fruit, and while firm and structuring, are perfectly in balance. Good length of flavour rounds it all out. Screw cap | 14.4% alc. | To 2031 | $25 | EL

Voyager Estate

.ot 1 Stevens Road, Margaret River, WA 6285 **T** (08) 9757 6354 **www.voyagerestate.com.au** **OPEN** 7 days 10-5 **WINEMAKER** Steve James, Travis Lemm **EST.** 1978 **DOZENS** 40000 **VYDS** 112ha

The late mining magnate Michael Wright bought what was then called Freycinet Estate from ʼounder and leading viticulturist Peter Gherardi in 1991. Apart from the Cape Dutch-style ːasting room and vast rose garden, the signpost for the estate is the massive Australian ʼlagpole – after Parliament House in Canberra, it's the largest flagpole in Australia. Michael's daughter, Alexandra Burt, has been at the helm of Voyager Estate for many years, supported by general manager Chris Furtado and a long-serving and committed staff. Michael is ʼemembered as a larger-than-life character, more at home in his favourite work pants and boots than a suit, and never happier than when trundling around the estate on a four-wheeler or fixing a piece of machinery.

NSW SA VIC WA TAS

98 **MJW Margaret River Chardonnay 2018** The pinnacle. A culmination of different clones, parcels and processes. The Gingin clone brings explosive power and density, Clone 95 provides linearity, line, focus and acidity. Partial mlf (50%) softens the 95 on the palate, and 10 months maturation knits the whole piece together. Sophisticated winemaking and top-notch fruit selection come together in thi perfect vintage. Screw cap | 13% alc. | To 2041 | $110 | EL

95 **Margaret River Chenin Blanc 2020** White pear, summer apricot, jasmine tea and white spice. The palate has a waxy Vouvray vibe going on, which really builds on itself through the evolution over the palate. Desperately pleasurable, jolly good drinking. Screw cap | 13.5% alc. | To 2030 | $20 | EL

Walsh & Sons

4/5962 Caves Road, Margaret River, WA 6285 **T** (08) 9758 8023 **www**.walshandsons.com.au
WINEMAKER Ryan Walsh, Freya Hohnen **EST.** 2014 **DOZENS** 1500 **VYDS** 20ha

Ryan Walsh and Freya Hohnen have had a Burgundian family association, having made wine for McHenry Hohnen from 2004 to '12, and over that time visiting/working for wineries in France, Spain, Switzerland and the US. At present, part of the crop from their 11ha Burnside Vineyard (where they base themselves) and the Walsh 7ha Osmington Vineyard is sold to McHenry Hohnen, Yalumba and Domain & Vineyards. The Burnside Vineyard is in biodynamic conversion.

95 **Felix Margaret River Syrah 2019** A gorgeous midnight ruby colour. The nose has crunchy black fruits, licorice and exotic spice, but most of all, it is interesting. Engaging, with brilliant density and intensity. A core of berry fruits huddle in the centre of the palate, the surrounding characters dominated by pepper, anise and toasty oak. Good length of flavour. A lot to love here. Modern rusticity and charm. Cork | 13.5% alc. | To 2030 | $30 | EL

94 **Little Poppet White 2019** Semillon/chardonnay blend. Mineral and spiced, this is saline with fresh garden herbs and bags of warm citrus (think along the lines of pink grapefruit, salted/preserved lemon and tangerine). The palate is zingy, textural and exciting – both lean and fleshy at once. Engaging phenolic grip through the mid palate and finish. Esoteric style owing to the distinctive fine ash character on the nose. Screw cap | 12.2% alc. | To 2025 | $26 | EL

Wills Domain

Cnr Abbeys Farm Road/Brash Road, Yallingup, WA 6281 **T** (08) 9755 2327 **www**.willsdomain.com.au
OPEN 7 days 10-5 **WINEMAKER** Richard Rowe **EST.** 1985 **DOZENS** 20000 **VYDS** 20ha

When the Haunold family purchased the original Wills Domain Vineyard in 2000, they were adding another chapter to a family history of winemaking stretching back to 1383 in what is now Austria. Their Yallingup vineyard is planted to shiraz, semillon, cabernet sauvignon, sauvignon blanc, chardonnay, merlot, petit verdot, malbec, cabernet franc and viognier. The onsite restaurant has won numerous accolades.

97 **Paladin Hill Margaret River Matrix 2019** Brambly cassis pastille, pomegranate and ripe summer raspberry. This is supple, bouncy, beautiful and long, with elegance and harmony to spare. Glorious expression of cabernet from a cool and aromatic year. Screw cap | 14% alc. | To 2046 | $110 | EL

Windance Wines

2764 Caves Road, Yallingup, WA 6282 **T** (08) 9755 2293 **www**.windance.com.au **OPEN** 7 days 10-5
WINEMAKER Tyke Wheatley **EST.** 1998 **DOZENS** 4500 **VYDS** 8.65ha

Drew and Rosemary Brent-White founded this family business, situated 5km south of Yallingup. The estate wines are all certified organic. Daughter Billie and husband Tyke Wheatley now own the business: Billie, a qualified accountant, was raised at Windance and manages the business and the cellar door; and Tyke has taken over the winemaking and manages the vineyard.

96 **Margaret River Shiraz 2019** An elegant, medium-bodied wine with red and black cherry fruit on the smooth and supple palate. Exemplary handling of extract and the use of oak puts this in the class of its '18 predecessor, even if the show record of that wine was momentous. Great balance and mouthfeel. Screw cap | 14% alc. | To 2034 | $28 | JH

94 **Margaret River Cabernet Merlot 2019** Organic. 71/15/14% cabernet sauvignon/merlot/malbec. Vibrant, soft, layered and leafy with oodles of cassis, raspberry, and spice. This is a masterstroke in easy-drinking and clever construction. Gold at Perth Royal Show 2020. Screw cap | 14% alc. | To 2028 | $26 | EL

Windows Estate ★★★★★

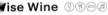

Quininup Road, Yallingup, WA 6282 **T** (08) 9756 6655 **www**.windowsestate.com **OPEN** 7 days 10-5
WINEMAKER Chris Davies **EST.** 1999 **DOZENS** 2000 **VYDS** 7ha

Chris Davies planted the Windows Estate vineyard in 1996, at the tender age of 19. He has tended the vines ever since, gaining organic certifcation in 2019. Initially selling the grapes, Chris moved into winemaking in 2006 and has had considerable show success for the consistently outstanding wines.

La Fenetre Margaret River Chardonnay 2017 PSA: There is a new kid on the block (in case you didn't already know). Chris Davies performs sensitive and detailed winemaking, which sees every clone and parcel treated differently in bâtonnage, oak and skin contact. Scintillating acidity lays the track for the taut citric fruit to glide along. In every respect this oozes elegance, restraint and pure beauty. If it isn't obvious already, I love it. Heartily. Screw cap | To 2036 | $85 | EL

Petit Lot Chardonnay 2019 A scintillating wine. The acidity is like a jolt right through the centre of the tongue, getting the saliva coursing through the mouth. Citrus pith, white peach, red apple skins, brine, fennel flower and crushed cashews are at the heart of this very pure chardonnay. Quite simply outstanding. Trophy Best Single Vineyard White, Margaret River Wine Show '20. Screw cap | 13% alc. | To 2036 | $48 | EL

Petit Lot Chenin Blanc 2019 There's a lot to love about this family-owned and -operated estate. Nectarine, green apple, nashi pear and apricot. The palate is where the beauty lies: intense fruit concentration, briny acid, built on very fine, waxy phenolics. The length of flavour is brilliant – it courses with no sign of slowing down. Manages restraint, as well. Screw cap | 11.5% alc. | To 2030 | $37 | EL | ♥

Petit Lot Semillon Sauvignon Blanc 2019 68/27/5% semillon/sauvignon blanc/chardonnay. Hand-picked fruit. Each variety was wild-yeast fermented separately in barrel. Nine months in oak (500L barriques, 25% new). Incredibly exciting and energetic. The oak contributes a sweaty, corporeal funk to the crystalline fruit, the combination of which creates a salty party in the mouth. This is happening. Screw cap | 12% alc. | To 2030 | $30 | EL

Wise Wine  

7 Eagle Bay Road, Eagle Bay, WA 6281 **T** (08) 9750 3100 **www**.wisewine.com.au **OPEN** 7 days 11-5
WINEMAKER Andrew Siddell, Matt Buchan, Larry Cherubino (Consultant) **EST.** 1986 **DOZENS** 10 000
VYDS 2.5ha

Wise Wine, headed by Perth entrepreneur Ron Wise, has been a remarkably consistent producer of high-quality wine. The vineyard adjacent to the winery in the Margaret River is supplemented by contract-grown grapes from Pemberton, Manjimup and Frankland River. The value for money of many of the wines is extraordinarily good.

4 **Leaf Series Porongurup Riesling 2020** Eminently pure, fermented in stainless steel and bottled early. This speaks wholeheartedly of the Porongurups; that is to say, jasmine florals, citrus pith, chalky phenolics and subtle, yet coiled acidity. Glorious. Screw cap | 12% alc. | To 2036 | $30 | EL

Woodlands 

3948 Caves Road, Wilyabrup, WA 6284 **T** (08) 9755 6226 **www**.woodlandswines.com **OPEN** 7 days 10-5
WINEMAKER Stuart Watson **EST.** 1973 **DOZENS** 16 000 **VYDS** 26.58ha

Founders David Watson and wife Heather had spectacular success with the cabernets he made in 1979 and the early '80s. Commuting from Perth on weekends and holidays, as well as raising a family, became all too much and for some years the grapes from Woodlands were sold to other Margaret River producers. With the advent of sons Stuart and Andrew (Stuart primarily responsible for winemaking), the estate has bounced back to pre-eminence.

6 **Emily Margaret River 2019** A cabernet franc-led Bordeaux blend, with merlot, malbec, cabernet sauvignon and petit verdot in support. A supple and chewy style that oozes restraint, pedigree and charm. Redcurrant, pink peppercorn, clove, star anise, fennel, red licorice, pomegranate and raspberry all mingle within the constraints of judiciously handled oak, laced up by saline acidity. The length is awesome, telling us we can either drink it now or cellar it with confidence. Screw cap | 13.5% alc. | To 2041 | $45 | EL

4 **Wilyabrup Valley Margaret River Chardonnay 2020** This wine is routinely one of the great-value chardonnays from Margaret River. It exemplifies intensity of stone-fruit flavour, creamy crushed nuts on the palate and taut salty acidity. Through the lens of the warmer, lower-yielding but brilliant 2020 vintage, this is concentrated, punchy and, above all, very classy. Screw cap | 13% alc. | To 2028 | $28 | EL

Xanadu Wines ★★★★

316 Boodjidup Road, Margaret River, WA 6285 **T** (08) 9758 9500 **WWW**.xanaduwines.com **OPEN** 7 days 10-5 **WINEMAKER** Glenn Goodall, Brendan Carr, Steve Kyme, Darren Rathbone **EST.** 1977 **DOZENS** 45000 **VYDS** 82.8ha

Xanadu Wines was established in 1977 by Dr John Lagan. In 2005 it was purchased by the Rathbone family and together with Glenn Goodall's winemaking team they have significantly improved the quality of the wines. The vineyard has been revamped via soil profiling, improved drainage, precision viticulture and reduced yields.

98 **Reserve Margaret River Cabernet Sauvignon 2018** It should be said from the outset – this is quite likely the best wine, white or red, ever made at Xanadu. The intersection between a perfect vintage pedigree fruit and sensitive winemaking look just like this: cassis, blackberry pastille, marri blossom raspberry, pomegranate, black pepper and star anise. Hints of fennel flower and salty licorice are t lingering impressions. What a wine. Screw cap | 14% alc. | To 2051 | $110 | EL

97 **Reserve Margaret River Chardonnay 2019** As ever, sophisticated, lithe, glassy and svelte. Through the lens of the cool 2019 vintage, this wine has a scintillating energy, the acid jolts a burst onto the tongue, stinging it into life. The length of flavour goes on and on. Xanadu chardonnays have a prov track record of graceful ageing in the cellar, often not truly coming into their own until 3+ years aft release. Pedigree, in a word. Screw cap | 13% alc. | To 2041 | $110 | EL

Stevens Road Margaret River Chardonnay 2019 This 2019 Stevens Road provided a moment of unadulterated joy when I drank it on Christmas Day. The salty acid and taut citrus fruit cut through the conversation and the heat of the day, injecting pleasure and calm. This is svelte, with salty lime Briny and delicious. Buy both the 2019 Reserve and Stevens Road chardonnays: cellar the Reserve, drink this. Screw cap | 13% alc. | To 2036 | $80 | EL

Stevens Road Margaret River Cabernet Sauvignon 2018 Dutch licorice on the nose and shining on the palate. The tannins really steal the attention from the pristine fruit. Such finely knit tannins, cleverly inlaid into the fruit without being hidden, are one of the standouts of this beautiful wine. They shape and structure the pure cassis fruit, ushering it through to a long and lingering finish. Screw cap | 14% alc. | To 2051 | $80 | EL

96 **Margaret River Cabernet Sauvignon 2019** Scintillatingly pure and taut, this is elegant, supple cabernet at its finest. Garden mint and purple fruit dominates; the length of flavour an enduring ripple on a still lake. Brilliant stuff, even more so given the price and its ability to age gracefully. Screw cap | 14% alc. | To 2035 | $40 | EL

94 **DJL Margaret River Sauvignon Blanc Semillon 2020** A very classy wine, especially at this price: clean and layered, with crystalline purity and good length of flavour. Some barrel influence enhances the beauty of the fruit, lending elegance to the passionfruit, snow pea and Geraldton wax. The texture is a highlight – slippery and fine. Screw cap | 12.5% alc. | To 2027 | $26 | EL

DJL Margaret River Shiraz 2019 This is pristine; crunchy, juicy and pure, with layers of cassis, blueberry, mulberry, red licorice and raspberry. There's a supple bounce on the palate that might lend it to a slight chill in warmer weather. A delight for the price. Screw cap | 14% alc. | To 2026 | $26 | EL

Exmoor Margaret River Shiraz 2018 With 0.5% viognier. All cool-area fruit (Wallcliffe and Karridale), matured 14 months in French oak (25% new). Pure, slippery, juicy, bouncy, delicious shiraz. What more could you possibly want for $20? This has structure, length, line and succulent fruit. The oak is countersunk into the salty, juicy fruit. Cracking little wine. Screw cap | 14.5% alc. | To 2027 | $20 | EL

DJL Margaret River Cabernet Sauvignon 2019 Super-pretty raspberry, raspberry lolly and red licorice aromas give an indication of what to expect ... the palate does not disappoint. Supple, verging on slinky; fine tannins provide seamless structure and shape. Modern, lithe and darn delicious. Screw cap | 14% alc. | To 2028 | $26 | EL

'emberton

ellarmine Wines

Balyan Retreat, Pemberton, WA 6260 **T** 0409 687 772 **www**.bellarmine.com.au **OPEN** By appt
NEMAKER Dr Diane Miller **EST.** 2000 **DOZENS** 5000 **VYDS** 20.2ha

is vineyard is owned by German residents Dr Willi and Gudrun Schumacher. Long-term wine vers, the Schumachers decided to establish a vineyard and winery of their own, choosing ıstralia partly because of its stable political climate. The flagship wines are 3 styles of esling – dry, off-dry and sweet.

Pemberton Riesling Dry 2020 Single-vineyard from 20+yo vines, fermented in stainless steel to dryness in the pursuit of purity. And pure it surely is. Mandarin pith, citrus frosting, orange blossom and a chalky, sherbet minerality that laces in and out of the fruit. This is beautiful. Light on its feet yet plush, chalky and very long, it is a riesling of understated power and restraint. Di Miller is known for her riesling. This is why. Screw cap | 13.5% alc. | To 2036 | $27 | EL

Pemberton Riesling Half-dry 2020 The sweetness is undeniable, but the acid has a savoury saline crunch to it. The aromatics are an abundant feast of orange blossom (a character I normally reserve for grüner veltliner), lemon flesh, green apple and white pepper. Curls of garden mint and white pepper colour the edges of the fruit. Screw cap | 12% alc. | To 2036 | $27 | EL

ilkwood Estate

80 Channybearup Road, Pemberton, WA 6260 **T** (08) 9776 1584 **www**.silkwoodestate.com.au
EN Fri-Mon & public hols 10-4 **WINEMAKER** Michael Ng **EST.** 1998 **DOZENS** 20000 **VYDS** 25ha

lkwood Wines has been owned by the Bowman family since 2004. The vineyard is patrolled y a large flock of guinea fowl, eliminating most insect pests and reducing the use of ıemicals. In '05 the adjoining vineyard was purchased, lifting the estate plantings to 23.5ha. ıe cellar door, restaurant and 4 luxury chalets overlook the large lake on the property.

The Walcott Pemberton Chardonnay 2020 Crushed cashew, white peach and layers of brine, rockmelon, pear and nectarine. More complex and layered than the Bowers chardonnay of the same vintage. This is very classy. Screw cap | 13% alc. | To 2028 | $30 | EL

The Walcott Pemberton Shiraz 2019 Supple and chewy, this bursts with ripe red berries and lush spice that speaks of juniper berries, Bengal pepper and star anise. Very pretty, lithe, syrah-styled shiraz. A lot going on, a lot to like. Screw cap | 13.5% alc. | To 2028 | $30 | EL

mithbrook

ithbrook Road, Pemberton, WA 6260 **T** (08) 9750 2150 **www**.smithbrook.wine **OPEN** By appt
NEMAKER Ben Rector **EST.** 1988 **DOZENS** 10000 **VYDS** 57ha

ıe picturesque Smithbrook property is owned by Perth businessman Peter Fogarty and mily, who also own Lake's Folly in the Hunter Valley, Deep Woods Estate in Margaret River ıd Millbrook in the Perth Hills. Originally planted in the 1980s and one of the first in the emberton region, the Smithbrook Vineyard covers over 57ha of the 110ha property and ocuses on sauvignon blanc, chardonnay and merlot.

2 **Single Vineyard Pemberton Pinot Noir 2020** The Pemberton character comes through on the finish, in the form of cherry bramble, strawberry, black-olive tapenade and white spice. Working backwards, the palate is fine, spicy and laden with cherries and strawberries. This is pretty, delicate and quite delicious. Screw cap | 13.5% alc. | To 2025 | $25 | EL

Single Vineyard Pemberton Merlot 2019 Quite frankly, this is delicious. It has jubilant fruit and bright acid that is countersunk into the flavours. It doesn't have the tannin structure required for ageing, but the length of flavour is good and there is an appealing purity about it. Screw cap | 14.5% alc. | To 2028 | $25 | EL

Estate Pemberton Red Blend 2019 The varietal mix changes each year: 2019 sees a predominance of cabernet sauvignon, complemented by merlot, cabernet franc and petit verdot. This is astoundingly good value for money. Eyewatering. It is straightforward/simple – but who cares about that at this price? It is delicious, bouncy, elegant, supple, fresh and straight-out yum. Screw cap | 14% alc. | To 2026 | $15 | EL

1702ha | 1 zone | 3 regions

TAS

Whether your standpoint is grapegrower, winemaker or wine consumer, Tasmania is an enchanted island. The 2021 harvest displayed spectacular quality, even without the bountiful yields that makers were hoping for to satiate an ever-increasing taste for their elegant and refreshing wines.

Pinot noir is Tasmania's pig's back, comprising the lion's share of the harvest. Chardonnay is its handmaiden, followed by sauvignon blanc, pinot gris, riesling and pinot meunier. An incredible 36% of all wine coming from the '21 vintage is sparkling. Moreover, the average price per tonne of grapes dedicated to this use rose to $3116, while table wine grape prices inflated to $3207 per tonne. The average of $3146 per tonne dwarfs the $701 per tonne for the overall Australian crop.

The Tamar Valley again took the lead in the size of its harvest, followed by the Coal River Valley, the East Coast, Pipers River, Derwent Valley, Cradle Coast and Huon Valley, the latter the southernmost part of the island, with but tiny yet exciting plantings.

All of the above raises the question whether Tasmania should seek official recognition of at least some areas by the Geographic Indications Committee. Since the island is a self-comprised zone, the relevant demarcations are regions and subregions.

The language used is vague and bureaucratic, and until the last years of the 20th century, it was of academic interest, as most potential regions lacked the basic size requirements. That has now changed, but the formal position of Wine Tasmania is to maintain the single GI for now, while continuing to 'explore, promote and discuss individual winegrowing areas and – perhaps more importantly in Tasmania given the incredible diversity over small distances – individual vineyard sites'.

For this chapter, we have divided the island into three 'regions': **East Coast**, **Northern** and **Southern Tasmania.**

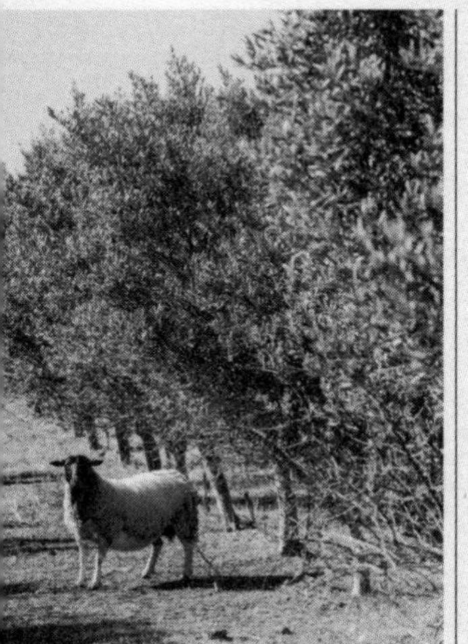

ZONE	REGION
Tasmania	66 East Coast Tasmania
	67 Northern Tasmania
	68 Southern Tasmania

ZONE

Tasmania

REGION

East Coast Tasmania

Devil's Corner

★★★★

The Hazards Vineyard, Sherbourne Road, Apslawn, Tas 7190 **T** (03) 6257 8881
WWW.devilscorner.com.au **OPEN** 7 days 10-5 **WINEMAKER** Tom Wallace, Anthony de Amicis **EST**. 1999
DOZENS 70000 **VYDS** 175ha

This is one of the separately managed operations of Brown Brothers' Tasmanian interests, taking The Hazards Vineyard on the east coast as its chief source. The avant-garde labels ma a decided change from the past and also distinguish Devil's Corner from the other Tasmania activities of Brown Brothers.

95 **Resolution Tasmania Chardonnay 2018** Devil's Corner has grown up, and this is a very serious Tasmanian chardonnay of larger-than-life proportions. Grand fruit concentration brims with grapefruit, juicy white peach, spicy fig and wild lemon. The delicate white blossom fragrance of th bouquet changes up a gear on the palate, spicy, rich and powerful, rumbling with wild honey, ging even toasted sweet corn. Cashew-nut oak unites with high-tensile Tasmanian acidity to charge a finish of incredible presence and disarming stamina. Screw cap | 13% alc. | To 2028 | $32 | TS

Tasmania Pinot Noir Rosé 2020 Tom Wallace has made quite a splash with this new and delicious Tassie rosé, and it deserves to be everyone's house pour this year. The delicacy of pinot noir is captured in a medium, bright salmon hue and pristine rose petals, morello cherries and strawberry hull. Sensitive barrel work amplifies wonderfully fine-grained texture and draws out a long finish, without for a moment interrupting fruit purity or flow. Crystalline Tasmanian acidity illuminates a brilliant finish. This is my shade of pink. Screw cap | 12% alc. | To 2021 | $22 | TS | ♥

Freycinet

15919 Tasman Highway via Bicheno, Tas 7215 **T** (03) 6257 8574 **WWW**.freycinetvineyard.com.au
OPEN 7 days 10-5 (Oct-Apr), 10-4 (May-Sept) **WINEMAKER** Claudio Radenti, Lindy Bull **EST**. 1979
DOZENS 9000 **VYDS** 15.9ha

The Freycinet vineyards are situated on the sloping hillsides of a small valley. The combinatic of aspect, slope, soil and heat summation produces red grapes with unusual depth of colour and ripe flavours. One of the foremost producers of pinot noir, with an enviable track record of consistency – rare in such a temperamental variety. The Radenti (sparkling), Riesling and Chardonnay are also wines of the highest quality.

95 **Riesling 2020** Tasmania showcases riesling's wonderfully exotic side and its high-tensile enduranc but rarely are these united as effortlessly as this. Low yields made for impressive concentration of star fruit, wild lemon and golden kiwifruit. Honed by gloriously crystalline acidity, it glides with consummate control, precision and endurance. One of the greats, it will live forever. Screw cap | 13% alc. | To 2040 | $32 | TS

REGION

Northern Tasmania

Alex Russell Wines

1866 Pipers River Road, Lower Turners Marsh, Tas 7267 **T** 0400 684 614
WWW.alexrussellwines.com.au **WINEMAKER** Alex Russell **EST**. 2014 **DOZENS** 1200 **VYDS** 21ha

Alex Russell studied viticulture at La Trobe Bundoora. After finishing that degree he moved to Mildura to take on a technical role. He then enrolled in wine science at Charles Sturt University, made wine at Zilzie (2008) and then at Angove Family Winemakers, where he was introduced to the Riverland Vine Improvement Committee (RVIC). After establishing RVIC's Cirami Estate brand he moved on in '14 to establish his own winery in a leased shed ir Renmark, making 17 different varietal wines.

92 **Alejandro Riverland Fiano 2020** A neat combo of honeysuckle, creamed honey and lemon zest topping stone fruit, plus some apricot kernel, all of which fleshes out the palate. It's juicy, refreshir yet textural and ready for summer. Or perhaps right now. Screw cap | 12.5% alc. | To 2022 | $24 | JF

NSW SA VIC WA TAS

ɔogee ★★★★☆

3 Golconda Road, Lebrina, Tas 7254 **T** (02) 6395 6358 **www**.apogeetasmania.com **OPEN** By appt
EMAKER Dr Andrew Pirie **EST.** 2007 **DOZENS** 1000 **VYDS** 2ha

ietly spoken and humble Andrew Pirie (or Dr Andrew Pirie AM) has stood tall among those culturists and winemakers who have sought to understand and exploit Tasmania's terroir d climate over the past 40 years. While making some of the best table wines to come from smania in the last quarter of the 20th century, his focus shifted to sparkling wine in '99. ogee's historic farm cottage is now an intimate cellar door where (by appointment) visitors n observe a hand disgorging demonstration.

Deluxe Brut 2016 53.3/39/7.7% chardonnay/pinot noir/meunier, traditional method, with 45 months on lees, disgorged Jan '20. Pale salmon hue; the bouquet is very complex, the palate even more so, with spiced strawberry fruits, brioche and soft acidity on the long finish. Diam | 12.6% alc. | $63 | JH

ellebonne

alfour Place, Launceston, Tas 7250 (postal) **T** 0412 818 348 **www**.bellebonne.wine
EMAKER Natalie Fryar **EST.** 2015 **DOZENS** 600

llebonne is the passion project of Natalie Fryar, who spent 14 years as sparkling winemaker Jansz, establishing herself as one of Australia's top sparkling winemakers and winning e title of 'rosé queen,' while gaining an intimate knowledge of Tasmania's top sparkling es. She crafts her elegant and sublime Bellebonne cuvées in miniscule quantities from y pockets of growers' vines in Tasmania's sparkling epicentre of Piper's River. (TS)

Natalie Fryar Vintage Rosé 2017 Sparkling Rosé of the Year 2022. A true execution of talent, masterfully articulating the concentration, character and energy of a powerful vintage. Piper's River pinot noir (100%) declares a dramatic contrast between great depth and the scaffolded frame of acid, phenolic structure and barrel fermentation (6yo oak). The cold winds of Bass Strait whip up energetic structure that holds its drama through a long finish, never for a moment dipping its determined gaze. Diam | 12% alc. | $75 | TS | ♥

ouse of Arras ★★★★★

of Fires, 40 Baxters Road, Pipers River, Tas 7252 **T** (03) 6362 7622 **www**.houseofarras.com.au
N Thurs–Mon 10–5 by appt **WINEMAKER** Ed Carr **EST.** 1995

e rise and rise of the fortunes of the House of Arras has been due to 2 things: the ceptional skills of winemaker Ed Carr, and its access to high-quality Tasmanian chardonnay d pinot noir. While there have been distinguished sparkling wines made in Tasmania for any years, none has so consistently scaled the heights of Arras.

Grand Vintage 2009 65.9/34.1% chardonnay/pinot noir, aged for 9 years on lees, disgorged Apr '20, the dosage only 2.5g/l. Full straw-yellow hue; layered brioche complexity, powerful drive and length. Australia's answer to Krug. Cork | 12.5% alc. | $109 | JH | ♥

ınsz Tasmania

16b Pipers Brook Road, Pipers Brook, Tas 7254 **T** (03) 6382 7066 **www**.jansz.com
N 7 days 10–4 **WINEMAKER** Teresa Heuzenroeder **EST.** 1985 **DOZENS** 38 000 **VYDS** 30ha

nsz is part of Hill-Smith Family Vineyards and was one of the early sparkling wine labels in smania, stemming from a short-lived relationship between Heemskerk and Louis Roederer. 15ha of chardonnay, 12ha of pinot noir and 3ha of pinot meunier correspond almost exactly the blend composition of the Jansz wines.

Single Vineyard Vintage Chardonnay 2013 The most emphatic evidence yet that Piper's River is an exemplar for more than just pinot noir! A year older than previous releases, yet fresher and more vibrant than ever. This is an exceptional blanc de blancs and one of the finest from Jansz yet. All the energy and tension of this cool site is infused in its lively frame and pinpoint precision of lemon fruit. White peach and pear bring body and intensity, backed magnificently by the subtle brioche and mixed spice of lees age. Tremendous cut and drive promise a very long future, charged by a dynamic acid line that melds seamlessly with the creamy texture of barrel fermentation and long lees age. One of Tasmania's finest this year. Diam | 12% alc. | $65 | TS | ♥

Late Disgorged 2012 55/45% chardonnay/pinot noir, 7.5 years on lees (2741 days), disgorged June '20. The result is a very intense wine that is still fresh, fruit and acidity more obvious than brioche/lees complexity. Remarkable. Diam | 12% alc. | $56 | JH

Lost Farm Wines ★★★

527 Glynburn Road, Hazelwood Park, SA 5063 **T** (08) 8397 7100 **www.lostfarmwines.com.au**
WINEMAKER Richard Angove **EST.** 2018 **DOZENS** 2000

Fifth-generation South Australian winemaker and grape grower Richard Angove fell in love with the Tamar Valley while working vintage in 2008, but it took him a decade to realise his ambition to work with a small group of growers to produce wines in the region. Sparkling, pinot noir and a stunning chardonnay are made from well-established vineyards in the Tamar Valley. (TS)

96 **Tasmania Chardonnay 2019** Sophisticated Tasmanian chardonnay, confidently uniting the struck-flint complexity of fermentation with classy French oak cashew nut notes and the cool tension of lemon and white peach. The creamy texture of barrel work harmonises with crystalline acidity, well-married to fruit concentration and body. It holds every detail through an enduring finish. Screw cap | 13.5% alc. | To 2029 | $42 | TS

Pipers Brook Vineyard ★★★★

1216 Pipers Brook Road, Pipers Brook, Tas 7254 **T** (03) 6382 7555 **www.kreglingerwineestates.c**
OPEN By appt **WINEMAKER** Luke Whittle **EST.** 1974 **DOZENS** 70000 **VYDS** 176.51ha

Fastidious viticulture and a passionate winemaking team along with immaculate packaging and enterprising marketing create a potent and effective blend. Pipers Brook operates a cel door at the winery and is owned by Belgian-owned sheepskin business Kreglinger, which ha also established the large Norfolk Rise Vineyard at Mount Benson in SA.

94 **Ninth Island Sparkling Rosé NV** The smartest bargain sparkling rosé is back on form in '19. There's nothing else within miles of this price with such elegance, character, texture and polish. Pipers Ri pinot takes the lead in signature rose petal, strawberry hull and raspberry, with precise balance of flesh and tension. Acidity, dosage and phenolics marry seamlessly with the texture that only méthode traditionnelle can produce. I love this cuvée. Cork | 12.5% alc. | $25 | TS

Stoney Rise ★★★★

96 Hendersons Lane, Gravelly Beach, Tas 7276 **T** (03) 6394 3678 **www.stoneyrise.com**
OPEN Thurs–Mon 11–5 **WINEMAKER** Joe Holyman **EST.** 2000 **DOZENS** 2000 **VYDS** 7.2ha

The Holyman family had been involved in vineyards in Tasmania for 20 years, but Joe Holyman's career in the wine industry – first as a sales rep, then as a wine buyer and more recently working in wineries in NZ, Portugal, France, Mount Benson and Coonawarra – gave him an exceptionally broad-based understanding of wine. In 2004 Joe and wife Lou purchased the former Rotherhythe Vineyard, which had been established in 1986, and set about restoring it to its former glory.

97 **Tasmania Grüner Veltliner 2020** Grüner veltliner is a late-ripening variety that flourishes in a cool climate, the cooler the better. Its varietal signature of white pepper on the bouquet is present, bu even more is the tightly wound spring of acidity. Its length is prodigious, and it is a wine built for t (very) long haul. Screw cap | 11.5% alc. | To 2040 | $32 | JH | ♥

Tamar Ridge | Pirie ★★★★

1a Waldhorn Drive, Rosevears, Tas 7277 **T** (03) 6330 0300 **www.tamarridge.com.au** **OPEN** 7 days 1
WINEMAKER Tom Wallace, Anthony De Amicis **EST.** 1994 **DOZENS** 14000 **VYDS** 130ha

Tamar Ridge has been owned by Brown Brothers since 2010, its vineyards of inestimable va on an island unable to meet more than a small part of demand from the Australian mainland It is focusing its attention on pinot noir for table wine and – along with chardonnay – sparkli wine. An outstanding suite of sparkling cuvées are branded 'Pirie' in honour of founder Dr Andrew Pirie.

96 **Tamar Ridge Reserve Pinot Noir 2019** The distinguished side of Tamar pinot: sensitive, elegant an sophisticated. A captivating air of rose petal and potpourri. Unashamedly red-fruited, celebrating a vibrant core of morello cherry, spicy raspberry and strawberry hull, nuanced with a hint of white pepper. Whole bunches and barrels played gently and eloquently. Fine-grained tannins grace an outstanding finish. Tom Wallace's delicate side is something to behold, and has yielded my top Tasmanian pinot of the year! Screw cap | 13.1% alc. | To 2034 | $65 | TS | ♥

outhern Tasmania

raigow  

Richmond Road, Cambridge, Tas 7170 **T** 0418 126 027 **WWW**.craigow.com.au **OPEN** W'ends 11-4 by appt **WINEMAKER** Frogmore Creek (Alain Rousseau), Tasmanian Vintners **EST**. 1989 **DOZENS** 800 **S** 8.75ha

bart surgeon Barry Edwards and wife Cathy have moved from being grapegrowers with y 1 wine to a portfolio of impressive wines – with long-lived Riesling of particular quality, sely attended by Pinot Noir – while continuing to sell most of their grapes.

Chardonnay 2019 Terrific Tasmanian chardonnay at a cracking price. Elegant, honed and energetic, with every detail in the right place. Plucked at the perfect instant to define precise lemon, fig and white peach. Top-shelf French oak. Just the right sprinkle of struck-flint complexity. It races to the horizon in a glittering fanfare of crystalline acidity. Screw cap | 13% alc. | To 2034 | $35 | TS

ate Hill Wines  

Dowlings Road, Huonville, Tas 7109 **T** 0448 842 696 **WWW**.katehillwines.com.au **EN** Fri-Mon 11-4 **WINEMAKER** Kate Hill **EST**. 2008 **DOZENS** 2000 **VYDS** 4ha

hen Kate Hill (and husband Charles) came to Tasmania in 2006, Kate had worked as a nemaker in Australia and overseas for 10 years. Kate's wines are made from grapes from umber of vineyards across Southern Tasmania, the aim being to produce approachable, licate wines.

Riesling 2020 A captivating contrast of the tension and cut of Southern Tasmania with the exotic allure of a touch of botrytis. Apricot, frangipani and guava is underlined by a core of lime, lemon and Granny Smith apple. Fruit sweetness unites harmoniously with a line of crystalline acidity on a long finish. Appealing drinking right away, with the stamina to age confidently. Screw cap | 12.2% alc. | To 2030 | $32 | TS

aurel Bank  

Black Snake Lane, Granton, Tas 7030 **T** (03) 6263 5977 **WWW**.laurelbankwines.com.au **EN** By appt **WINEMAKER** Greer Carland **EST**. 1986 **DOZENS** 1700 **VYDS** 3.5ha

urel Bank was established by Kerry Carland in 1986 but deliberately kept a low profile by thholding release of most of its early wines. When the time came, Kerry entered the Hobart ne Show in '95 and won the trophy for Most Successful Tasmanian Exhibitor.

Sauvignon Blanc 2020 A blend of earlier- and later-picked parcels (a week apart) contrasting pretty, sweet passionfruit tropicals with sage and thyme. Pale straw-green hue. A focused core of lemon and Granny Smith apple carries long and true, guided by bright acidity and well-handled phenolic grip. A little barrel fermentation has built texture and length without interrupting purity. Top class and top value. Screw cap | 12.8% alc. | To 2025 | $25 | TS

owestoft  

0 Main Road, Berriedale, Tas 7011 **T** (08) 9282 5450 **WWW**.fogarty.wine **OPEN** By appt **NEMAKER** Liam McElhinney **EST**. 2019 **DOZENS** 1250 **VYDS** 3ha

e premium Tasmanian brand of WA-based Fogarty Wine Group, Lowestoft is Tasmania's ost exciting new label this year. The group purchased the 3ha Lowestoft vineyard and storic house at Berriedale near Mona just north of Hobart in 2019. Lowestoft is a worthy ewcomer to Fogarty's lauded suite of boutique wineries across Western Australia, Lake's lly in the Hunter Valley and Dalwhinnie in the Pyrenees. (TS)

Tasmania Chardonnay 2019 Launching Tasmania's most exciting new premium label, the Fogarty Group sure has hit the ground running. This is pitch-perfect chardonnay that embraces the generosity of a warm season and frames it intricately in crystalline acidity, top-class oak and just the right whiff of struck-flint reduction. Masterfully assembled and a joy to taste for the first time. Screw cap | 13% alc. | To 2027 | $65 | TS

Mewstone Wines ★★★★

11 Flowerpot Jetty Road, Flowerpot, Tas 7163 **T** 0425 253 218 **www**.mewstonewines.com.au
OPEN Thurs–Mon 11–4.30 **WINEMAKER** Jonathan Hughes **EST.** 2011 **DOZENS** 5000 **VYDS** 3.6ha

Brothers Matthew and Jonathan (Jonny) Hughes established Mewstone Vineyard on the banks of the D'Entrecasteaux Channel in the tiny hamlet of Flowerpot in 2011. The vineyard i planted on a former cherry orchard, consisting mainly of pinot noir, with riesling, chardonna and a tiny bit of shiraz. Purchasing quality grapes from other local vineyards, this label uses slightly unconventional winemaking techniques that Jonny encountered on his world travels. Small-batch production means he can put maximum effort in. Best New Winery in th *Wine Companion 2019*.

98 **Hughes & Hughes Lees Aged Chardonnay 2019** From a single vineyard in the Coal River Valley, wi yeast fermented in barrel, 100% mlf, matured on lees for 10 months. The power and intensity of th wine is remarkable, as is its funky complexity. Grapefruit is in the saddle, white stone fruit close by A compelling wine. Screw cap | 13.9% alc. | To 2032 | $45 | JH

96 **Hughes & Hughes 25% Whole Bunch Pinot Noir 2019** As the name suggests, this single-vineyard pinot was fermented with 25% whole bunches, the remainder destemmed whole berries, matured French oak for 10 months. Excellent colour; the bouquet is riddled with exotic spices, the powerfu black cherry palate with forest floor notes and abundant tannins. Longevity is assured. Screw cap 13.2% alc. | To 2034 | $45 | JH

Pooley Wines ★★★★

Butcher's Hill Vineyard, 1431 Richmond Road, Richmond, Tas 7025 **T** (03) 6260 2895
www.pooleywines.com.au **OPEN** 7 days 10–5 **WINEMAKER** Anna Pooley, Justin Bubb **EST.** 1985
DOZENS 8500 **VYDS** 12.48ha

Three generations of the Pooley family have been involved in the development of Pooley Wines, although the winery was previously known as Cooinda Vale. In 2003 the family plant pinot noir and pinot grigio (with more recent plantings of pinot noir and chardonnay) at Belmont Vineyard, a heritage property with an 1830s Georgian home and a (second) cellar door in the old sandstone barn and stables.

97 **Margaret Pooley Tribute Single Vineyard Tasmania Riesling 2020** Riesling of the Year 2022. A monumental Tasmanian riesling in which every detail has been intricately placed to fulfil its manifesto of grand character and profound endurance. A core of impeccable, spicy wild lemon is nuanced by stone-fruit exotics. Epic acidity, skin-contact phenolics, lees texture and RS unite in a crystalline display of glittering energy that promises decades in the cellar. Breathtaking line and length in the presence of profound fruit concentration confirm one of Tasmania's finest rieslings o the vintage. Margaret would be proud indeed. Screw cap | 12% alc. | To 2050 | $75 | TS | ♥

96 **Coal River Valley Riesling 2020** From the estate Butcher's Hill and Cooinda Vale Vineyards, whole-bunch pressed and fermented with a specialised (riesling) yeast. A lovely wine that delicately pain the mouth with its kaffir lime juice flavours, cosseted with layered, harmonious acidity. Great lengt too. Screw cap | 12% alc. | To 2033 | $39 | JH

Stargazer Wine ★★★★

37 Rosewood Lane, Tea Tree, Tas 7017 **T** 0408 173 335 **www**.stargazerwine.com.au **OPEN** By appt
WINEMAKER Samantha Connew **EST.** 2012 **DOZENS** 1800 **VYDS** 3ha

Samantha (Sam) Connew has racked up a series of exceptional achievements: obtaining a postgraduate diploma of oenology and viticulture from Lincoln University, Canterbury, NZ; undertaking the Advanced Wine Assessment course at the Australian Wine Research Institut in 2000; being chosen as a scholar at the '02 Len Evans Tutorial; winning the George Mackey Award for the best wine exported from Australia in '04; and being awarded International Red Winemaker of the Year at the International Wine Challenge, London in '07.

98 **Palisander Vineyard Coal River Valley Pinot Noir 2019** The seductive bouquet exudes dried rose petals, spices and some darker foresty notes underneath. The intense palate is all class, blending purity, precision and power. There's a freshness to the mouthfeel that carries through to the long finish and lingering aftertaste. Screw cap | 13% alc. | To 2032 | $55 | JH | ♥

96 **Single Vineyard Derwent Valley Chardonnay 2018** A distinguished Tasmanian chardonnay, at once pure, yet complex, long, intense, and open for business. The interplay between fruit and barrel-ferment oak derivatives is masterful. Tasmanian chardonnay is not by any means a foregone conclusion. Screw cap | 13.5% alc. | To 2030 | $55 | JH

NSW SA VIC WA TAS

:efano Lubiana  ★★★★★

Rowbottoms Road, Granton, Tas 7030 **T** (03) 6263 7457 **www**.slw.com.au **OPEN** Wed-Sun 11-4
EMAKER Steve Lubiana **EST**. 1990 **VYDS** 25ha

nique and Steve Lubiana moved from the hot inland of a brown Australia to the beautiful ıks of the Derwent River in 1990 to pursue Steve's dream of making high-quality sparkling ıe. The sloping site allowed them to build a gravity-fed winery and his whole winemaking ɔroach since that time has been based on attention to detail within a biodynamic ⁄ironment. The Italian-inspired Osteria restaurant is based on their own biodynamically ›duced vegetables and herbs, the meats (all free-range) are from local farmers and the ıfood is wild-caught.

Tasmania Chardonnay 2019 The refinement that Steve Lubiana has brought to his chardonnay over recent vintages is something to behold. He's achieved the holy grail of elegance without sacrificing definition, concentration, persistence or endurance. Pristine white fruits are ever-so-gently propelled by high-class French oak. Crystalline acidity illuminates a finish of pinpoint accuracy, undeterred line and magnificent persistence. Screw cap | 13% alc. | To 2034 | $58 | TS

›lpuddle Vineyard  

Back Tea Tree Road, Richmond, Tas, 7025 **T** (08) 8155 6003 **www**.tolpuddlevineyard.com
N At Shaw + Smith **WINEMAKER** Martin Shaw, Adam Wadewitz **EST**. 1988 **DOZENS** 1800 **VYDS** 20ha

ver a winery was born with blue blood in its veins, Tolpuddle would have to be it. The eyard was established in 1988 on a continuous downhill slope facing northeast; in '06 it n the inaugural Tasmanian Vineyard of the Year Award. Michael Hill Smith MW and Martin aw are joint managing directors. David LeMire looks after sales and marketing; Adam ıdewitz, one of Australia's brightest winemaking talents, is senior winemaker. Vineyard ınager Carlos Souris loses nothing in comparison, with over 30 years of grapegrowing Tasmania under his belt and an absolutely fearless approach to making a great vineyard en greater.

Chardonnay 2019 A strikingly beautiful chardonnay with its flowery bouquet bearing witness to the sheer purity of the incredibly long palate, the full palette of chardonnay flavours on display. Nectarine, white peach and grapefruit zest are sewn together by an invisible silver thread of acidity. Screw cap | 13% alc. | To 2033 | $84 | JH

Published in 2021 by Hardie Grant Books,
an imprint of Hardie Grant Publishing

Hardie Grant Books (Melbourne)
Wurundjeri Country
Building 1, 658 Church Street
Richmond, Victoria 3121

Hardie Grant Books (London)
5th & 6th Floors
52–54 Southwark Street
London SE1 1UN

hardiegrantbooks.com

The *Halliday Wine Companion* is a joint venture between James Halliday and HGX Pty Ltd.

Halliday Pocket Wine Companion 2022
ISBN 978 1 74379 811 9

Design: Pidgeon Ward
Typesetting: Megan Ellis
Photographs: pp. 7, 12, 13 Andrew Poole; pp. 14, 131, 177 Wine Australia; p. 17 Kimberley Low/Wine Australia
Printed by McPherson's Printing Group, Maryborough, Victoria

Hardie Grant acknowledges the Traditional Owners of the country on which we work, the Wurundjeri people of the Kulin nation and the Gadigal people of the Eora nation, and recognises their continuing connection to the land, waters and culture. We pay our respects to their Elders past, present and emerging.

oak has been an integral part of winemaking for at least 1000 years. It is **viticulture** is practised to a greater or lesser degree in all the major wine-pro not been treated or processed to alter their state can be used, but manufac prohibited, as is any organism that has been genetically modified. **oxidation** o certain chemical changes in its composition. In broad terms, these changes r and palate. **palate** is the third leg of the colour, bouquet, palate trilogy used to (or mouthfeel) of the wine once it is taken into the mouth, and after it is swallo described as the negative logarithm of hydrogen ion activity or concentration wine, in the latter case having much to do with the potential longevity. **phyll** While sprays were ultimately developed to control the mildews, effective and remains the most devastating of all vine diseases. **pinot gris** is a white mutat makes its appearance in European historical records earlier than any other va related varieties (pinot gris, pinot meunier and pinot blanc) is not clear. This t France alone), the choice of which has a profound influence on the quality winemaking texts the link is often discussed as the 'redox' potential of a wine. and fructose that, either accidentally or deliberately, remains unconverted to litre of wine, and can vary between 1 gram per litre and more than 500 grams have been fine-tuned but not fundamentally changed since the 1960s, and er made for centuries. There are five ways to make roses, the most common i macerate for between 12 and 48 hours before all or part of the juice is drawn grape variety, was identified in 1997 as one of the two parents of cabernet sa sauvignon will know it offers a mix of crushed herbs, grass and asparagus, with to seal glass jars, and in the 1930s the University of California, Davis, condu through the first decade of the 21st century repeatedly confirmed the supe importantly, freedom from random oxidation. **semillon**, a white grape variety, w viticulture, during his extraordinary wine odyssey through Europe and back to country has shiraz as old as Australia's, nor plantings as large. As with many c become a major problem in parts of Australia, South Africa and California in t drought and associated extreme heat events have increased the risk of fires a Australian grapegrowers and consultants, the most significant soil attributes between free-draining capacity and waterholding capacity; pH (acid soils inh amount of organic compounds present. **solids** is a non-technical term that is fine particles of skin and pulp in suspension in the juice. Makers of chardonr solids in the juice, thus gaining flavour complexity. **sour** is a term denoting a v itself on the back of the palate and in the aftertaste. **sparkling wine** can be addition of a precise amount of sugar and yeast to a blend of still wines imm contains approximately 10 grams of pure alcohol. Because different drinks c container will depend on the alcohol concentration of the drink. **supple** is a la describe a palate that is round and pliant, with no aggressive tannins. **tannin** amount in the pulp of the grape is insignificant. If, as in the case of red wines, be a greater extract of tannin in the resulting solution. By contrast, the skins, s in tear drops, also called 'legs') are especially obvious in white wines that have adhering to the side of the glass and slowly moving down the side like tiny, sl essentially turn on the difference in evaporation rates of alcohol and water. **te** simply because it covers a multitude of environmental factors such as temper mouthfeel and structure but does not concern itself with flavour elements, and the finish and aftertaste. **total acidity** is one of the four most commonly used descriptive term for a wine named after the dominant grape variety from wh maturation of wine. Oak was the traditional medium, but in the late 19th and ea epoxy resin; mild steel with an enamel coating followed, and, in the seco material. **whole bunch** is, in part, self-explanatory. For white wines, whole bun skins and pips of the grapes; the result is very clear juice with pristine varietal is very different. Here it refers to the practice of fermenting whole bunche without which wine would not exist, nor food staples such as bread. **yield** is